EVEREST PIONEER

——— THE PHOTOGRAPHS OF CAPTAIN JOHN NOEL ———

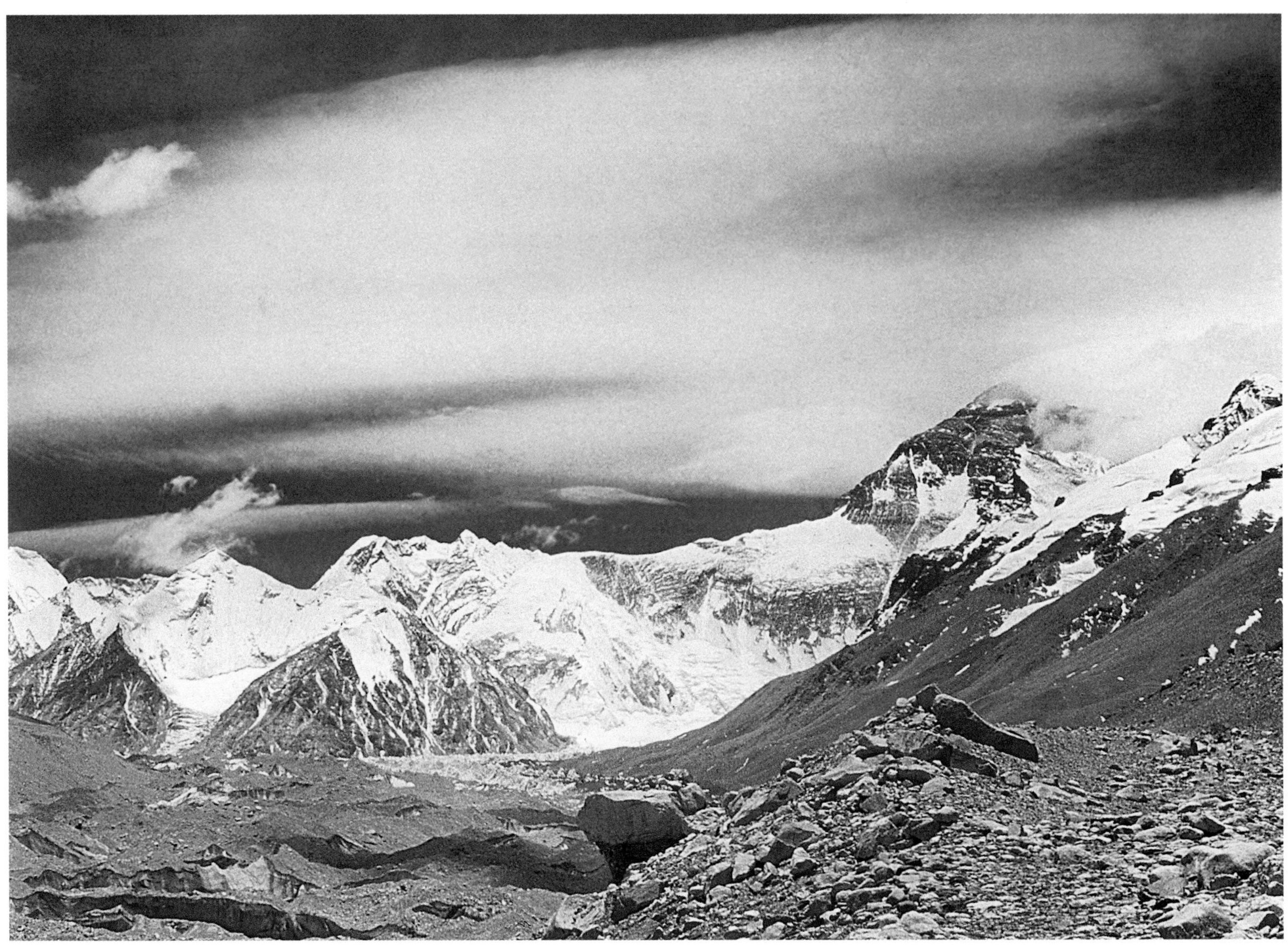

Him-alaya is the name given to the chain of mountains by the people of India; it stretches for 2,000 miles and is 300 miles wide. The discovery of the highest peak in the world was made during the Great Trigonometrical Society of India, which had been started in 1802, a monumental plan to quantify and define India. Since it measured the precise shape of the earth, the secrets of the Himalayas were unravelled incidentally. Such discoveries are usually celebrated by their native name, but, in this case, when it was eventually and formally confirmed as the highest mountain in the world, it was named after the Surveyor-General of India, Sir George Everest. This was probably an apt decision, otherwise, today, since the summit is accessible from both Tibet and Nepal, which name would be chosen?

EVEREST PIONEER

THE PHOTOGRAPHS OF CAPTAIN JOHN NOEL

SANDRA NOEL

Foreword by BRIAN BLESSED

SUTTON PUBLISHING

First published in the United Kingdom in 2003 by
Sutton Publishing Limited · Phoenix Mill
Thrupp · Stroud · Gloucestershire · GL5 2BU

British Library Cataloguing in Publication Data
A catalogue record for this book is available from the British Library.

ISBN 0-7509-3278-3

Typeset in 12/18pt Photina MT.
Typesetting and origination by
Sutton Publishing Limited.
Printed and bound in England by
J.H. Haynes & Co. Ltd, Sparkford.

CONTENTS

To my father, from whom I inherited my love of travel

FOREWORD

From the age of six in 1942 I had dreamed of one day meeting Captain John Baptist Noel. For me, the noble captain represented the total embodiment of the spirit of adventure. In the spring of 1987 I realized that dream and met the great man at his home in Brenzett, Romney Marsh. He was ninety-seven years old. 'They've named a star after me,' he proudly stated, reaching out and showing me the certificate of the British Interplanetary Society. 'They should have named a universe after you,' I laughed. It marked the beginning of a fine friendship. In conjunction with the BBC I had embarked upon a film entitled *Galahad of Everest*, which followed in the footsteps of George Leigh Mallory and his fellow members of the 1922–4 British Everest expeditions. Noel had been the cinematographer on these expeditions. Much to my delight, he agreed to help us with our project.

But how does one appraise such a character? In 1913, with three native porters and disguised as a Muslim, he made an exceptional journey through forbidden Tibet towards Everest. He got to within forty miles of the mountain, the first westerner to do so, and exchanged shots with Tibetan troops before being forced to retreat. What is not commonly known is that he made three attempts before this, over the space of three years.

At a meeting of the Royal Geographical Society on 10 March 1919, he delivered a lecture about his pre-war incursion in Tibet, which aroused intense enthusiasm among his audience. This proved to be the decisive leap forward. In the discussion that followed, the president of the Alpine Club, Captain Percy Farrar, spoke of reaching the summit itself. Having proved a catalyst, Captain Noel was an obvious choice as cinematographer. His achievement of taking a 35mm camera to the top of the north col on Everest, at 23,000 feet, beggars belief. He also developed his film on that col in a makeshift darkroom consisting of a specially designed tent, which was kept warm by burning yak dung! Nothing was too much for him. On one occasion he even sacrificed some of his film by setting it alight at night to show the way for Mallory and his companions.

His fascinating films of the 1922 and 1924 expeditions filled the Scala Theatre in London, and made a huge profit. He followed this with numerous coast-to-coast tours of the USA, where he proved himself to be an outstanding lecturer. His photographic plates, taken on a primitive frame camera and colour-tinted by hand, are miraculous images of the remote, mysterious Tibetan landscape.

After the end of the war, in 1918, Noel had been assigned to the Norpa force, a small army of about 6,000 men in northern Persia. His general ordered him to explore the southern shore of the Caspian Sea, to calculate the chances of the Bolsheviks invading Persia through the Elburz Mountains. Noel set out by horse, and since restrictions on photography had been relaxed, he took with him his Debrie motion picture camera, and made a film about the caviar industry. What a character! My heart shakes when I think of the great man. His zest and energy conveyed to me the great spirit of those early days of exploration in the Himalayas, and left me begging for more!

On a sunny afternoon in 1988 he held me close and said with tears in his old eyes, 'If you had lived as they lived [Mallory and Irvine], and died in the heart of nature, would you, yourself, wish for any better grave than the pure white snow of Everest?'

Brian Blessed
March 2003

PREFACE

My father, John Noel, was truly a product of the nineteenth century. Born in 1890, he lived through many great events – the funeral of Queen Victoria, the demise of some of the most ancient European monarchies and the division of their lands, two world wars, the rise and fall of the Nazi regime and fascism, the rise of communism and the great political changes in the Far East. He witnessed, too, the disintegration of the British Empire, the brutal partition of India, civil war in many corners of the globe, great strides forward in medicine (such as the eradication of smallpox and the first heart transplant), space exploration and other scientific advances, and technological inventions, such as the television set and the computer. Personally, he keenly embraced the growth in car use, bringing one of the first Model A cars off the Ford production line in Detroit and shipping it to England soon after it was launched in 1928. But of all the century's great achievements, probably the most poignant event for him was the first successful climb of Mount Everest in 1953. He never speculated much about earlier expeditions, but he held a mystical belief – a hope perhaps – that George Mallory and Andrew Irvine, in their pioneering expedition of 1924 (of which he, as the group's photographer, was a witness and recorder) had in fact been the first to reach the summit; and he was certainly full of admiration for the brave, tenacious men whose victory was announced to the world on the day of the coronation of Queen Elizabeth in June 1953.

During his lifetime Noel made copious notes on all the things going on around him; unfortunately, thanks to his peripatetic lifestyle, many of these journals have not survived. However, two typewritten accounts of his first venture into Tibet in 1913 remain, and offer a fascinating insight into his thoughts and feelings in that inhospitable land, when, in disguise, he was attempting to enter a forbidden country and reach the great mountain. Later he recorded more impressions in a book, *Through*

*Tibet to Everest,** his account of the British expeditions in 1922 and 1924. Noel was not simply a keen mountaineer and a good photographer. He had an active and enquiring mind, and was a skilled revolver and pistol shot in the First World War, and was later assigned to map-making projects for the British Army. He invented a collapsible boat during the Second World War, but hostilities finished just as it was about to go into production. He was also an accomplished linguist and a fine craftsman. Yet his greatest legacy is the superb collection of still and movie photographic material which tells in pictures the story of the heroic attempts on the mountain. Under extremely difficult conditions, Noel used his specially built cine camera to capture the progress of the climbers as, in pairs, they made attempts to reach the summit, culminating in the tragic loss of his friends and colleagues George Mallory and Andrew Irvine, last seen 600 feet from the top, still going on. Colour photography was relatively new at the time, so Noel made careful notes of the colours of all his photographs, and, using an American colour chart, later hand-painted many of the still images: today, the colours remain as pure and true as they were when they were painted.

It was long an ambition of John Noel to write a book on his adventures in both the First World War and the early Everest expeditions; but he was involved in so many projects that there was never time to complete this epic work, which was to be entitled *Combat*, telling the story of the last great war with hand-to-hand fighting and the battle against the greatest mountain.

With the passage of time, it has become increasingly difficult to collect material on my father's life between 1914 and 1918, and to portray the war as he had experienced it. But, looking through the collection of images he took on the early Everest expeditions – most of which has remained unpublished – recalling the stories he told, and, with some of his lecture notes and his hitherto unpublished accounts to hand, I have been able to give an account of his journeys to the Himalaya, in words and pictures, as he might have done.

* J.B.L. Noel, *Through Tibet to Everest*, Edward Arnold, London 1926; repr. Hodder & Stoughton 1989.

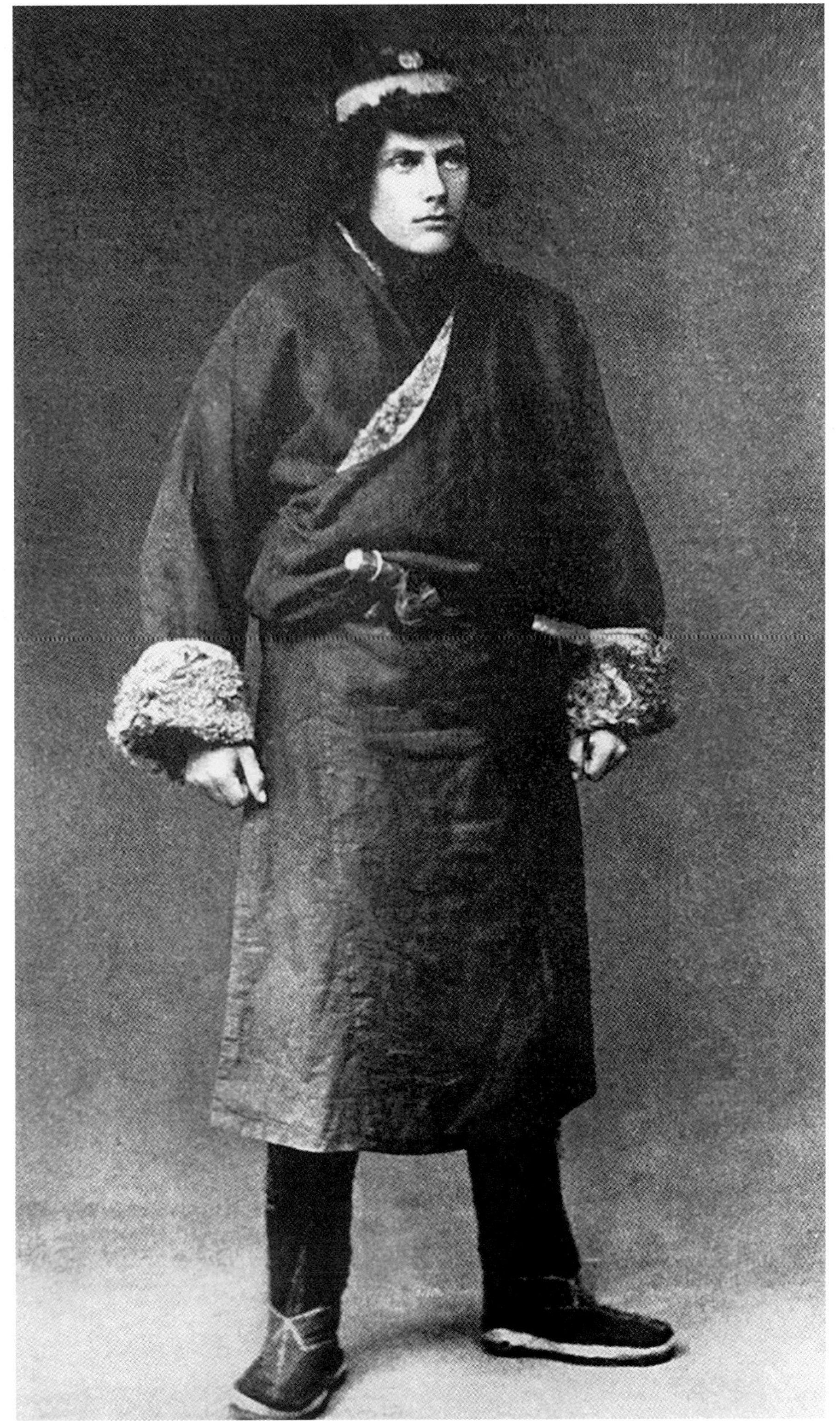

Noel in disguise for his journey into Tibet in 1913. He had dyed his hair black and darkened his skin, hoping to pass as an Indian tea planter looking for a Tibetan worker who had absconded; in fact, he crossed an unguarded pass in an attempt to find Mount Everest.

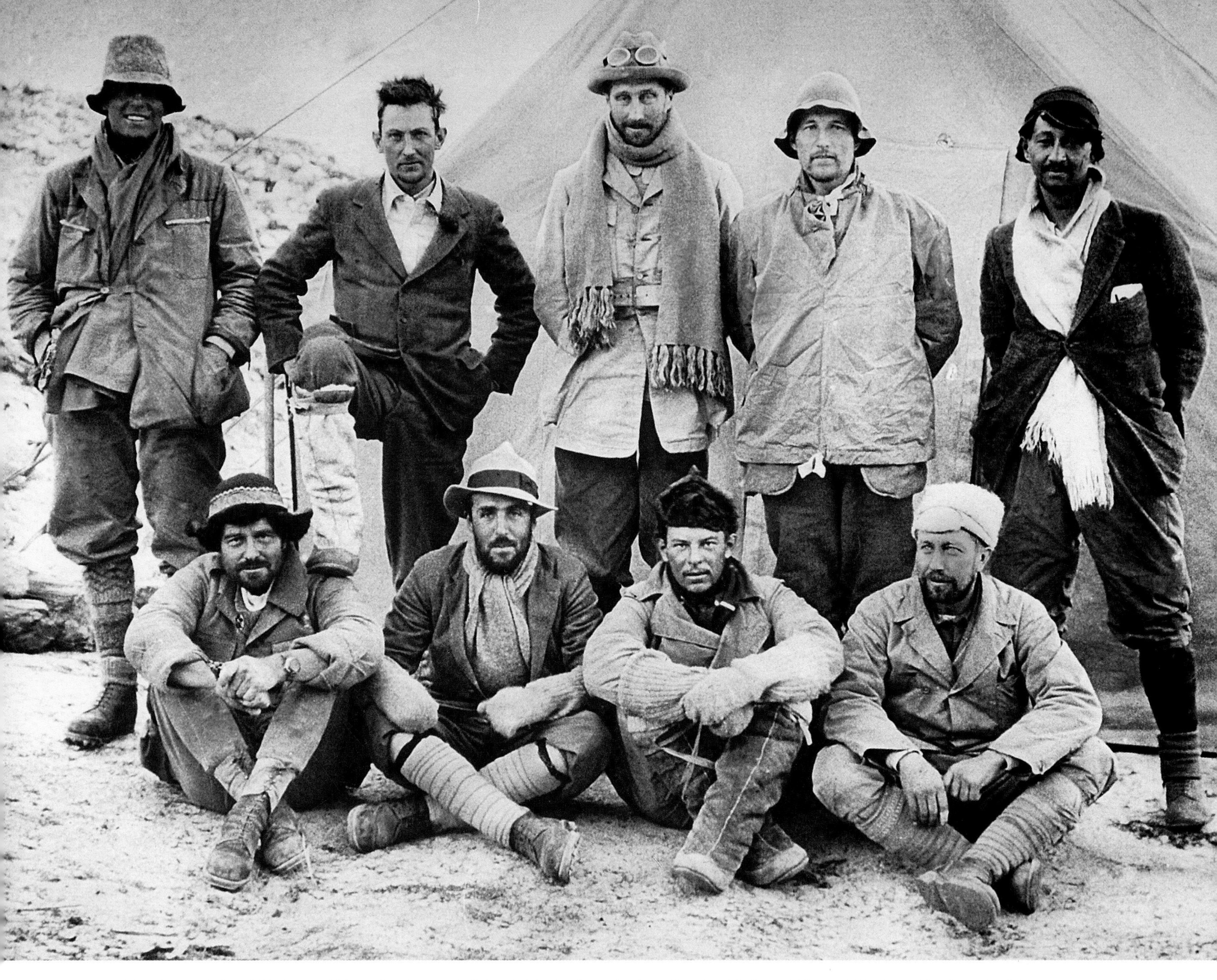

Members of the 1924 expedition. Back row, left to right: Andrew Irvine, George Mallory, Edward Norton, Noel Odell, John Macdonald. Front row: Edward Shebbeare, Geoffrey Bruce, Howard Somervell, Bentley Beetham.

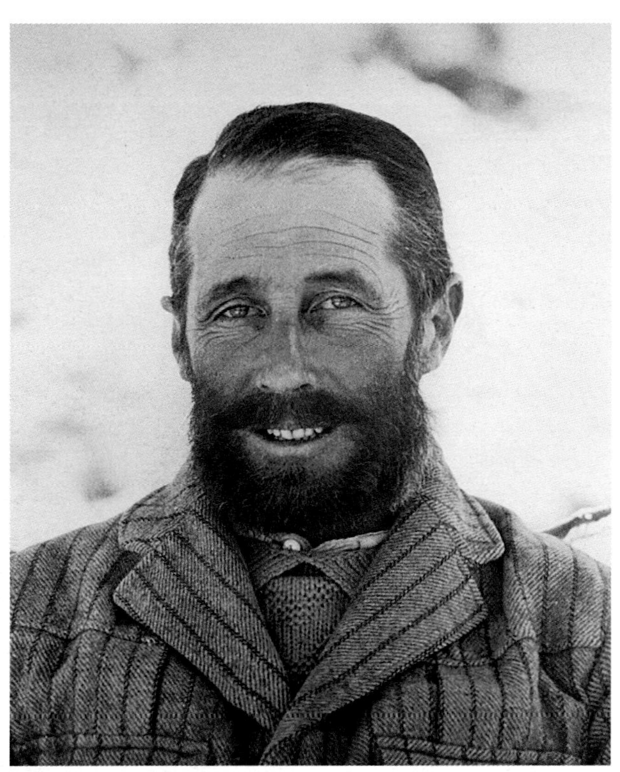

Norton.

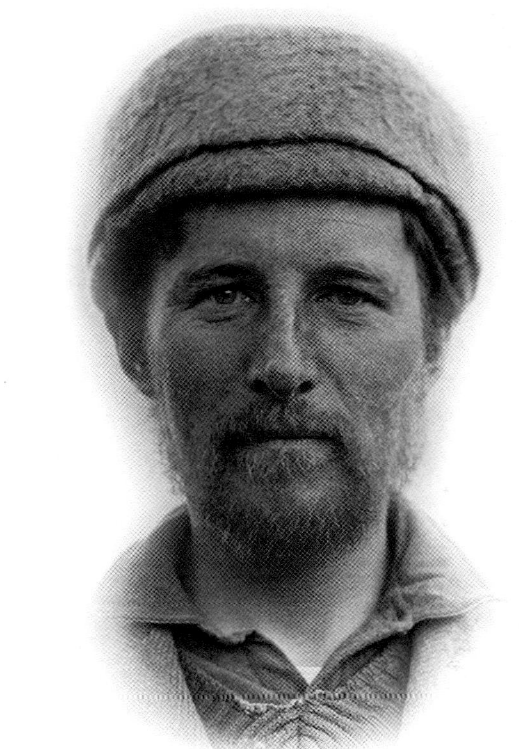

Odell.

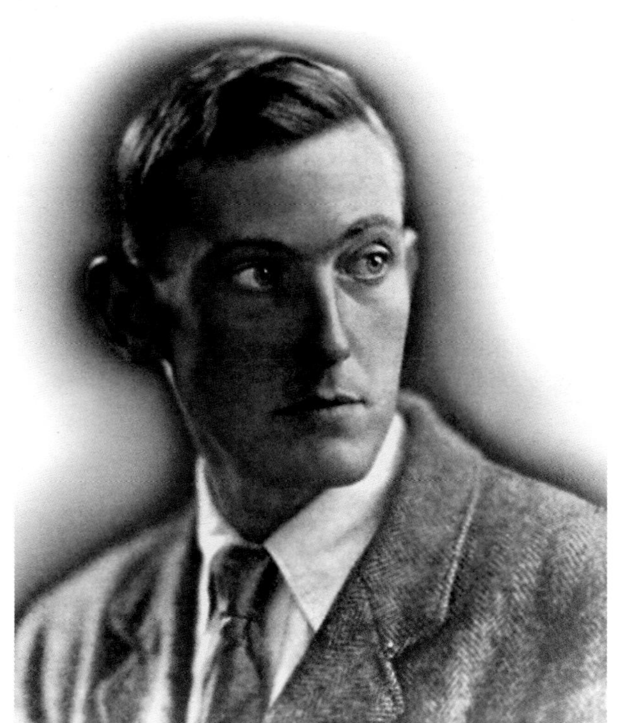

Mallory.

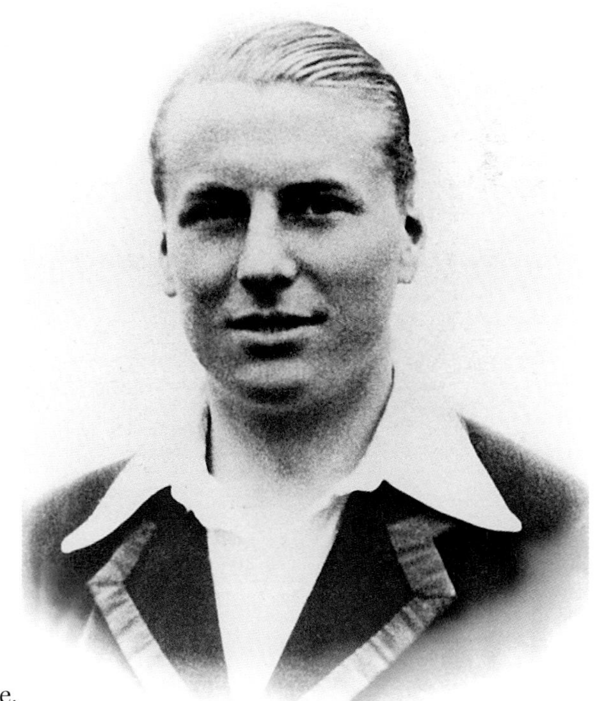

Irvine.

Expedition Members – 1924

Brig Gen Charles G. Bruce
Leader, but indisposed   1866–1939

Lt Col Edward F. Norton
Acting Leader   1884–1954

George H. Leigh-Mallory
Climbing Leader   1886–1924

Bentley Beetham   1886–1963

Capt C. Geoffrey Bruce   1896–1972

John de Vere Hazard   1885–1968

Maj R.W.G. Hingston   1887–1966

Andrew Irvine   1902–1924

Capt John B.L. Noel
Photographer/Filmmaker   1890–1989

Noel E. Odell   1890–1987

E.O. Shebbeare   1884–1964

Dr T. Howard Somervell   1890–1975

ACKNOWLEDGEMENTS

I am grateful to the Royal Geographical Society for their kind permission to reproduce three maps and a photograph of Noel on pages 10, 14, 20–1 and 52.

I believe that all the photographs of the expeditions to Mount Everest in the book form part of the John Noel Photographic Collection, on which I hold copyright. Infringement of any other copyright is unintentional.

All quotations are from John Noel, *Through Tibet to Everest* and unpublished papers from the Noel Archive unless otherwise stated.

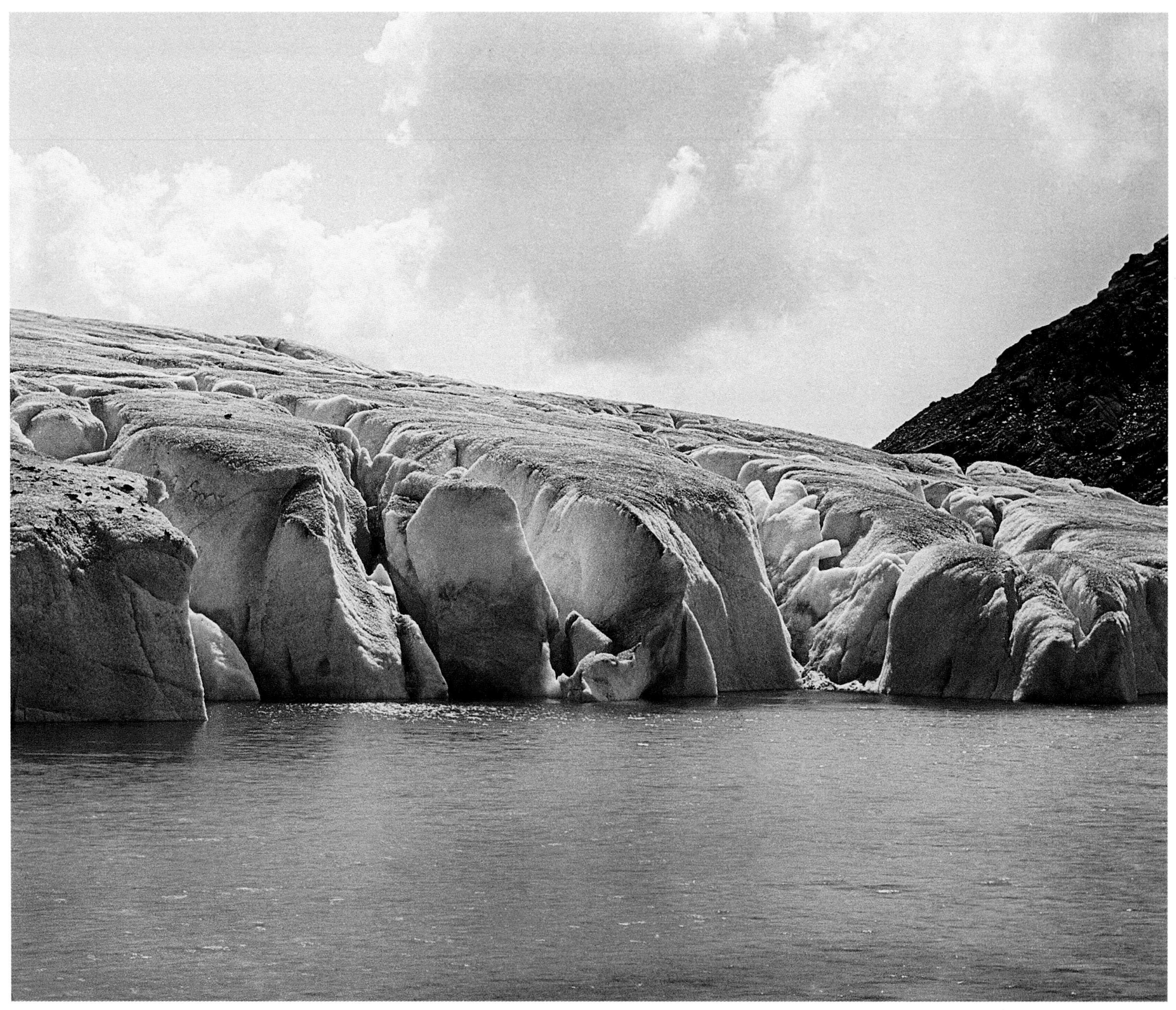

Ice formations.

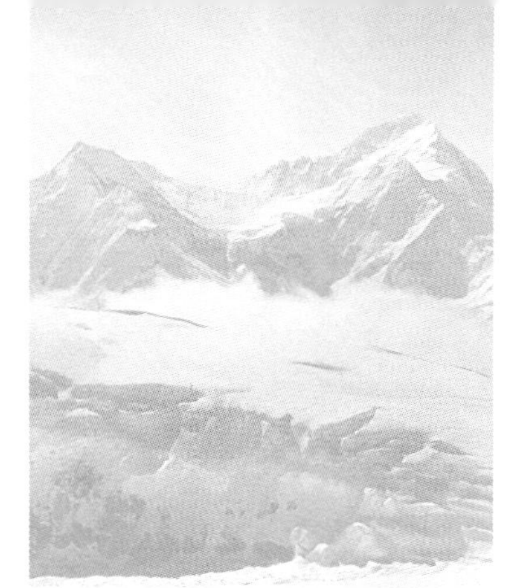

INTRODUCTION

Attention during the last few years has been focused more and more upon the Himalayas; and now that the poles have been reached it is generally felt that the next and equally important task is the exploration and mapping of Mount Everest. It cannot be long before the culminating summit of the world is visited, and its ridges, valleys and glaciers are mapped and photographed. This would perhaps have already been done, as we know, but for the war . . .*

Thus opened a paper, read at the Royal Geographical Society on 10 March 1919, by John Noel, which provided the spur needed to launch a concentrated attempt on Mount Everest. The peak had been named after the Surveyor-General of India, when in 1857 it was established as the highest mountain in the world. It soon became the great goal, but it was not considered appropriate to request permission from either neighbouring country to cross their territory. Lord Curzon, the Viceroy of India at the time, considered approaching Nepal, but then the probability that Tibet might be threatened by Russian imperial expansionism created the political necessity of launching a mission to Lhasa, the capital of Tibet, commanded by Francis

* *RGS Journal*, vol. LIII (5), May 1919.

Younghusband, who had already journeyed to the Karakoram and the Gobi Desert. He easily persuaded the Tibetans to sign a treaty acquiescing to British demands, and thus brought the prospect of an expedition to climb Mount Everest a step closer.

In 1913 a young Army officer, John Noel, had been one of the first Westerners to enter Tibet. Dressed in disguise and with a small band of trusted hillsmen, he reached to within forty miles of the great mountain; but the party ran out of food, and was forced to go to a village for provisions, where their presence was quickly reported to the local governor who swiftly and firmly insisted that the party should leave Tibet. War ended Noel's further hopes of reaching Mount Everest, but he had shown that it was possible; and in 1922 he was part of the team that made so many great strides in mountaineering techniques on the formidable peak. In 1924 he was a member of another expedition, which succeeded in reaching heights thought beyond man's endurance but which was to end in tragedy when George Mallory and Andrew Irvine were last seen, hours behind schedule, but still going on and up. Noel was there to photograph the great endeavours of Man against Nature, and to bring back from those inhospitable regions images, both still and on film, of the people of Tibet; but, above all, his work provides a photographic record of the daring and courage of these pioneers, the first Europeans to attempt to climb Everest, a feat not successfully achieved until 1953 by Hillary and Tenzing.

Young Noel

Baptist Lucius Noel was born on 26 February 1890, in Newton Abbot, Devon, the third son of an Army officer, Edward Noel, and his wife Ruth. The seeds of Noel's thirst for adventure were sown in his childhood: Lieutenant-Colonel the Hon. Edward Noel, the second son of the 2nd Earl of Gainsborough, had spent much of his Army life in India, Gibraltar and the Far East, and the young Noel often accompanied his parents on overseas postings, while his two older brothers, Edward and Hubert, were at school in England. When his father was ADC to the Governor-General of Hong Kong, the family spent much time in the Far East, based in Hong Kong and Japan. But during some of their overseas postings, Noel was left with relations. His aunt, Lady Constance Noel, had married an Irish aristocrat, Sir Henry Bellingham, 4th Baronet of Castle Bellingham in Co. Louth, and Noel enjoyed many happy times with his cousins, particularly Pat(rick), with whom he enjoyed many an ingenious adventure, fishing and hunting on the great estate.

Young Baptist and his brother Edward junior both proved to be excellent linguists, like their father, and enjoyed the thrills of adventure and travel. And there was plenty of opportunity for travel: while Lieutenant-Colonel Edward Noel was researching material for books and articles on military history,* young Baptist Noel was often taken along, in the hope that his interest in soldiering would be fostered; instead, he discovered a love of climbing and was attracted to art and photography. Mrs Noel, an artist of some repute, used these trips to Italy and Switzerland to paint Alpine flowers.

In the end the three brothers took different paths in life. Edward joined the Army, and spent much of his time in the service in the Middle East, while Hubert became a doctor. In his mid-teens Noel was sent to school in Lausanne, which, in those times, was a celebrated international centre of education, especially for languages. He found himself with one other foreigner, Eric Smythe, who was a skilled amateur mountaineer. These two students were not particularly committed to their studies, and often skipped classes to climb some of the peaks in the area – Mont Blanc, the Matterhorn, the Weisshorn and many others, without guides. Smythe, a very accomplished

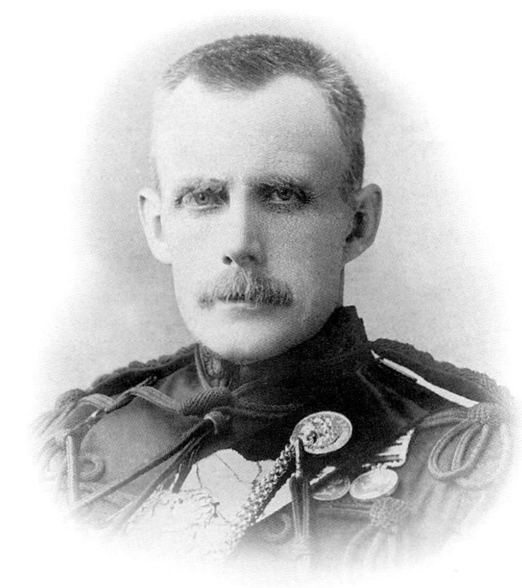

Noel's father, Lieutenant-Colonel the Hon. Edward Noel (1852–1917), an officer in the Rifle Brigade, the second son of the 2nd Earl of Gainsborough.

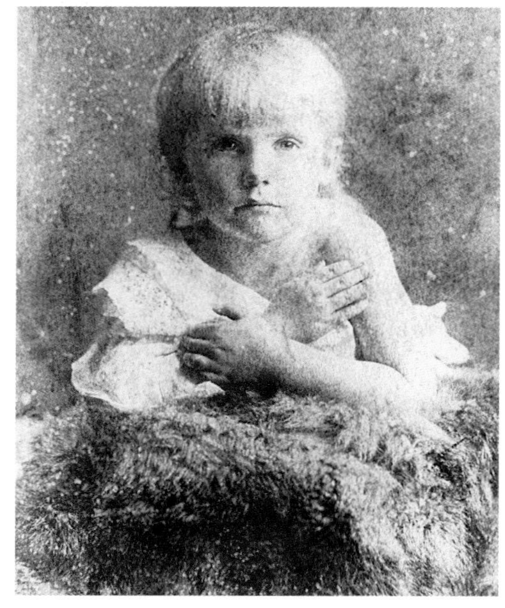

Baptist Lucius Noel as a child.

---

* Including *Gustaf Adolf – The Father of Modern War*, John Bale, Sons and Danielsson Ltd, London 1905.

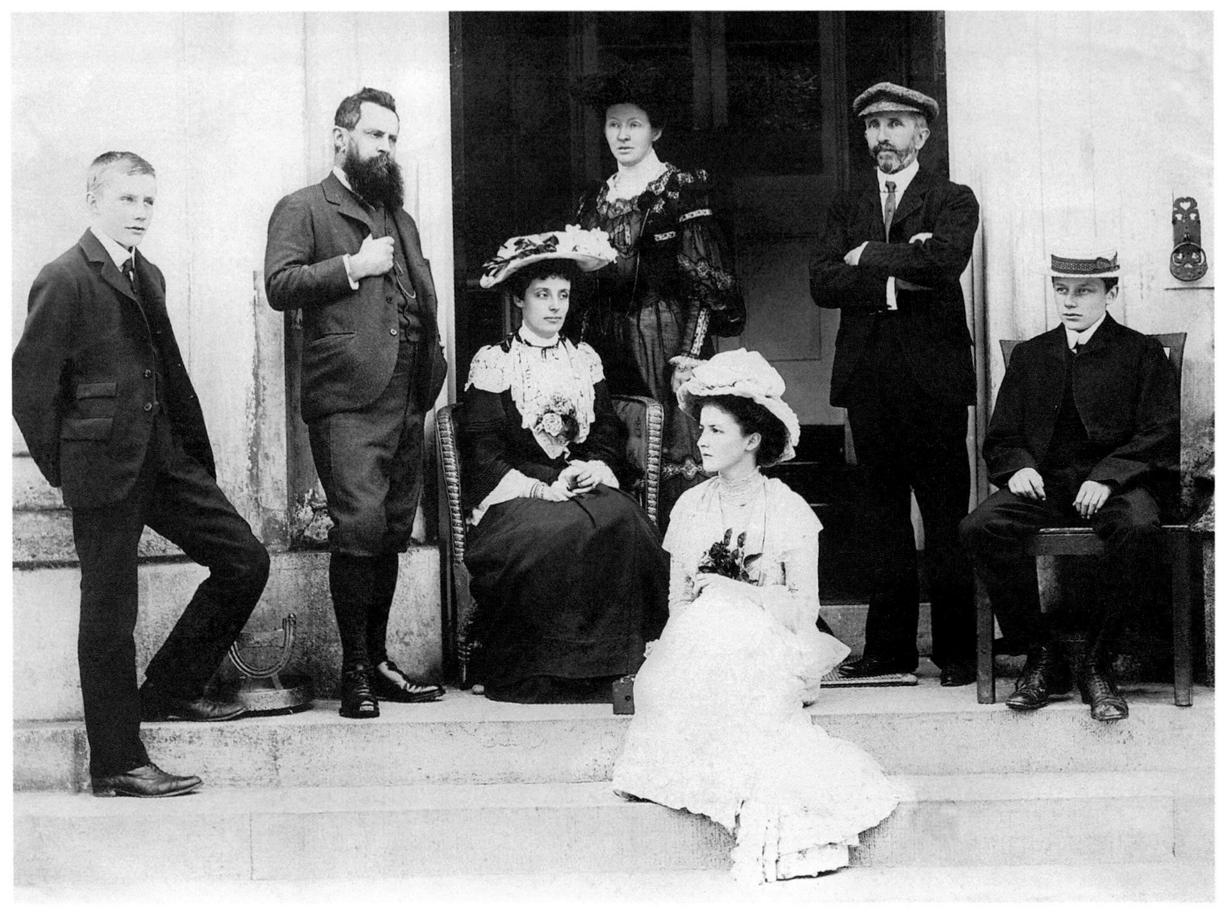

Noel and his brother at Castle Bellingham, Co. Louth, Ireland, with Sir Henry Bellingham, whom their aunt Constance Noel had married in 1874, and their cousins, Pat(rick) and Augusta, who became the Marchioness of Bute on her marriage in 1905. Constance died in 1891, some years before this photograph was taken.

linguist, later became the chief interpreter in German and French at the meeting in a railway carriage in the great forest of Compiègne, near Paris, in November 1918 when the Germans surrendered to the Allies.

The Alps, the so-called playground of Europe, was a fashionable area for climbing, particularly between 1850 and 1900 – the Alpine Club had been formed in 1857. The initial idea of an informal club was soon superseded by a grander notion of a semi-professional association with regular meetings where gentlemen could meet and discuss their exploits, and this, in turn, progressed to a forum where papers relating to climbing were read; ultimately the papers were presented in the form of a journal, detailing the exploits of mountain exploration. Local guides had been considered indispensable on any Alpine climb, and it was even suggested that the best natural guides were born with feet of a different structure and design that made climbing easier. By the time Noel became involved, mountaineering had combined science, art and commercial enterprise. The British were keen participants in this Golden Age of climbing and with the practical advances of better clothing and footwear, combined with knowledge gleaned from previous climbers, it became easier to do without the help and support of guides.

After the brief spell of formal schooling in Switzerland, Noel attended art school in Florence. He was also fascinated by photography, an art form still in relative infancy, and much admired the work of Signor Vittorio Sella (1859–1943), who was reputed to be the finest photographer of mountains. Noel said:

> Sella had accompanied the Duke of the Abruzzi on his famous expedition to the Karakoram Mountains. He was one of the old school, carrying a whole-plate camera, with glass plates, and he thought nothing of taking eight hours over one single picture. He'd sit on the mountain slope until the mist was just right, or the sun sparkled on the ice ridges. I thought that was very wonderful.

But the halcyon days had to come to an end, and, reluctantly following family tradition, Noel applied to join the Army. His total lack of conventional education meant that he failed every subject except French. There followed a hastily arranged stint with a crammer, and his subsequent examination results meant a pass to the Military Academy at Sandhurst, although he did not achieve a high enough score for entry into the crack Indian Army, which was the prize job because it offered a very fine life and double the pay. Before entering Sandhurst he made a move that was, perhaps, to epitomise the eccentric streak which would colour his personality thereafter – while he was staying in Italy, other children had often poured water over the young Baptist, so, by deed poll, he took the additional forename John.

A Subaltern in India

Second Lieutenant J.B.L. Noel passed out from Sandhurst in 1908. When called before a panel to choose a regiment he requested the East Yorkshire Light Infantry, which, as was frequently the case in those days of long journeys to distant overseas postings in the far-flung corners of the empire, was on a long-term posting in northern India, a notoriously hot region. The generals on the panel must have been bemused; for a newly commissioned young officer to select such an undesirable posting must have seemed incredible. But Noel was delighted: he knew that a posting to such a very hot station, Fyzabad, in the fierce heat of India would mean long periods of inactivity, when manoeuvres would be impossible in the searing temperature. All this free time would permit him to find suitable travelling companions with knowledge of the foothills of the Himalayas, and give him the chance to learn enough of the language of the mountain tribes to be able to fulfil an ambition already set in his mind: he intended to find a route to Mount Everest, the highest mountain in the world. In 1856 the summit had been measured from India by long-distance triangulation to be 29,002 feet; 120 miles away the summit could be seen from the mountainous region around Darjeeling, but it lay in forbidden Tibet and was, therefore, out of bounds.

Young Noel arrived in Fyzabad, northern India, knowing that it would probably be his base for the next five years. Army life was exciting and the social life notorious, although it was not possible to live without a private income. Uniform, mess bill, batman and a contribution to the regimental mess bill came from the meagre pay, but Noel's greatest interest was the opportunity for adventure. In those days, owing to the great distances from home, leave was generally taken after five years and lasted twelve months; annual leave was four months. While serving in the East Yorkshire Light Infantry from 1909 to 1913 Noel studied the few incomplete maps of the area, trying to establish a pass unguarded by the Tibetans. Altogether he made three attempts in three years. On the first, he took two trusted servants from India, engaged local guides on the way and used yaks to carry tents and food. But

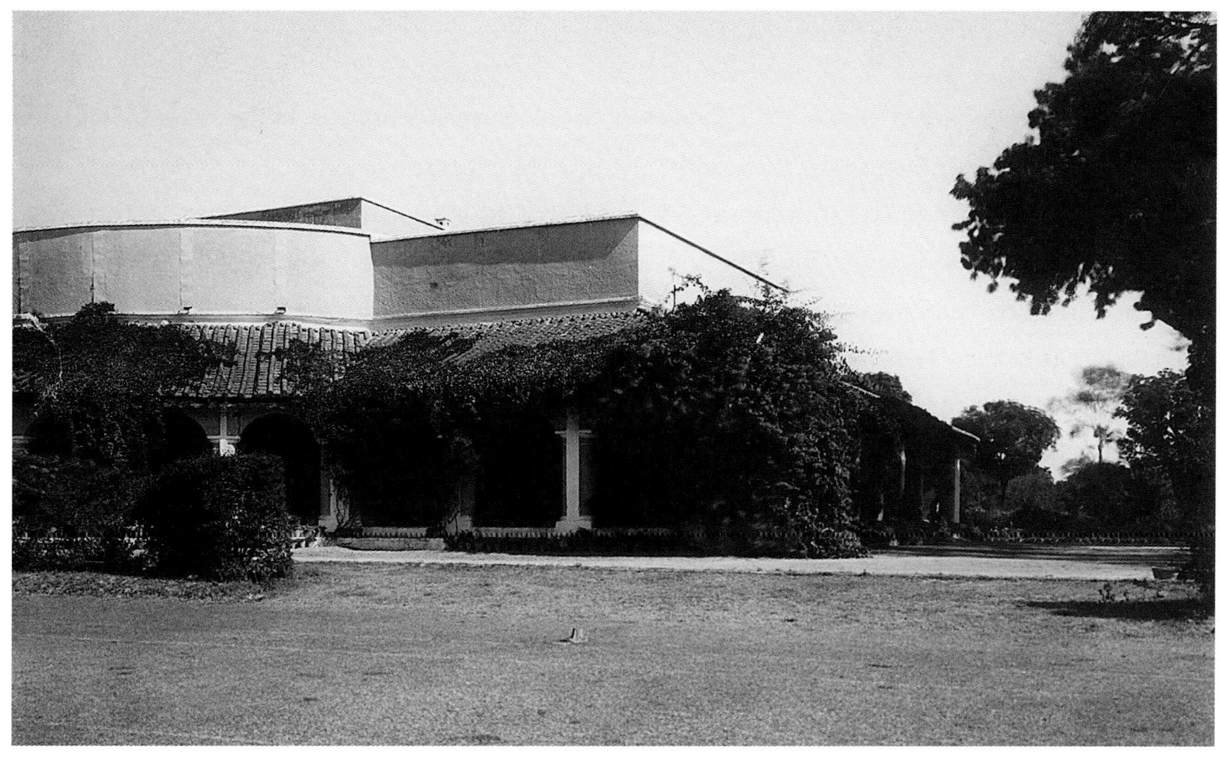

The officers' mess at Fyzabad, northern India, where Noel was stationed from 1909 to 1913.

he learned that it would be better to enlist a band of hillsmen close to the border with Tibet and keep the same group of loyal men with him for the entire journey rather than use pack animals, which meant carrying all the necessary food and equipment for the expected duration of the journey. Finally, having made three attempts, he found the Choten Nyima La, a pass at 18,500 feet, unguarded by the Tibetans – and in 1913 he crossed this pass.

He had studied the language, and made friends with the chosen band of trusted hardy sherpas who would accompany him. In order to avoid attracting attention, he attempted to disguise himself by colouring his skin and dyeing his hair, and also practised a story, which he accepted that he would need, to explain his presence as an unwelcome visitor in a hostile country: he would claim to be a tea planter from India who employed Tibetans on his estate, one of whom had escaped and disappeared back across the mountains.

Endeavouring to avoid villages, the group reached the plateau of Tibet at 15,000 feet, and then travelled west towards Everest. Their plans were thwarted, however, when their food supply ran out; to avoid death by starvation they climbed down a valley into a village, secured food, and continued on their journey. But their presence had been reported to the local Governor of Tin-ki, who rode after the group and surrounded their little camp with his soldiers. The story that the Tibetan worker had absconded was accepted, but the Governor insisted that, as foreigners, Noel and his party were not permitted in Tibet and must leave at once. There was no option but to obey, and Noel was supplied with enough food to last the group back to India. Due to the restrictions on kit, and the need to keep a low profile, Noel did not take many photographs, but he later recorded his impressions in two volumes, *Among the Himalayas* and *Tibet and Nepal*. He had made a prismatic survey route sketch of the journey and estimated a distance of forty miles was all that separated him from the great mountain – he was closer than any white man had ever been. It took six long weeks to get back to India.

Noel had far exceeded his leave entitlement and was prepared for a hard time on his arrival back at his Army base: going 'Absent without Leave' was a serious offence, and an Army officer who knowingly entered a forbidden country could be dealt with by court martial. However, his commanding officer was sympathetic to the young man's adventurous spirit. Noel recounted his reception:

> Noel, you have broken two basic army conditions – AWOL and entering a forbidden country. Why?
> Sir, I lost track of time when we were fording a river and the calendar was washed away.
> Next time, Noel, take two calendars with you!

After five years in the service Noel was now due his first home leave, mindful that a court martial was still a reality on his return to India. He left for England in late 1913, but before his year's leave was up the First World War broke out. Noel was sent to the

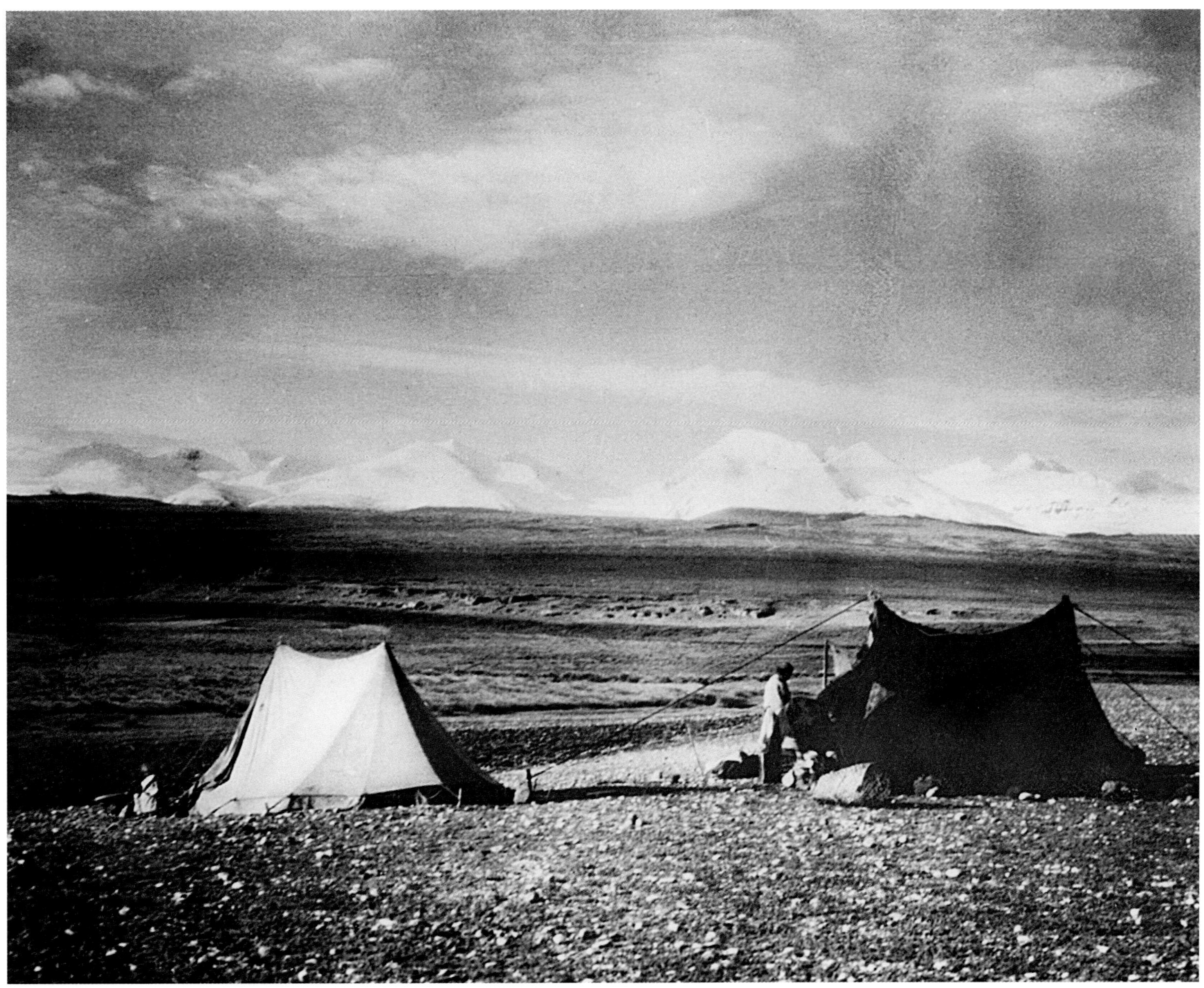

To the pioneers, the magnitude of the mountains must have been awesome. Noel had spent much time climbing in the Alps, but his first views of the Himalaya chain certainly presented a great challenge, although he never doubted that man would succeed in reaching the summit of Everest. This photograph was taken in 1913.

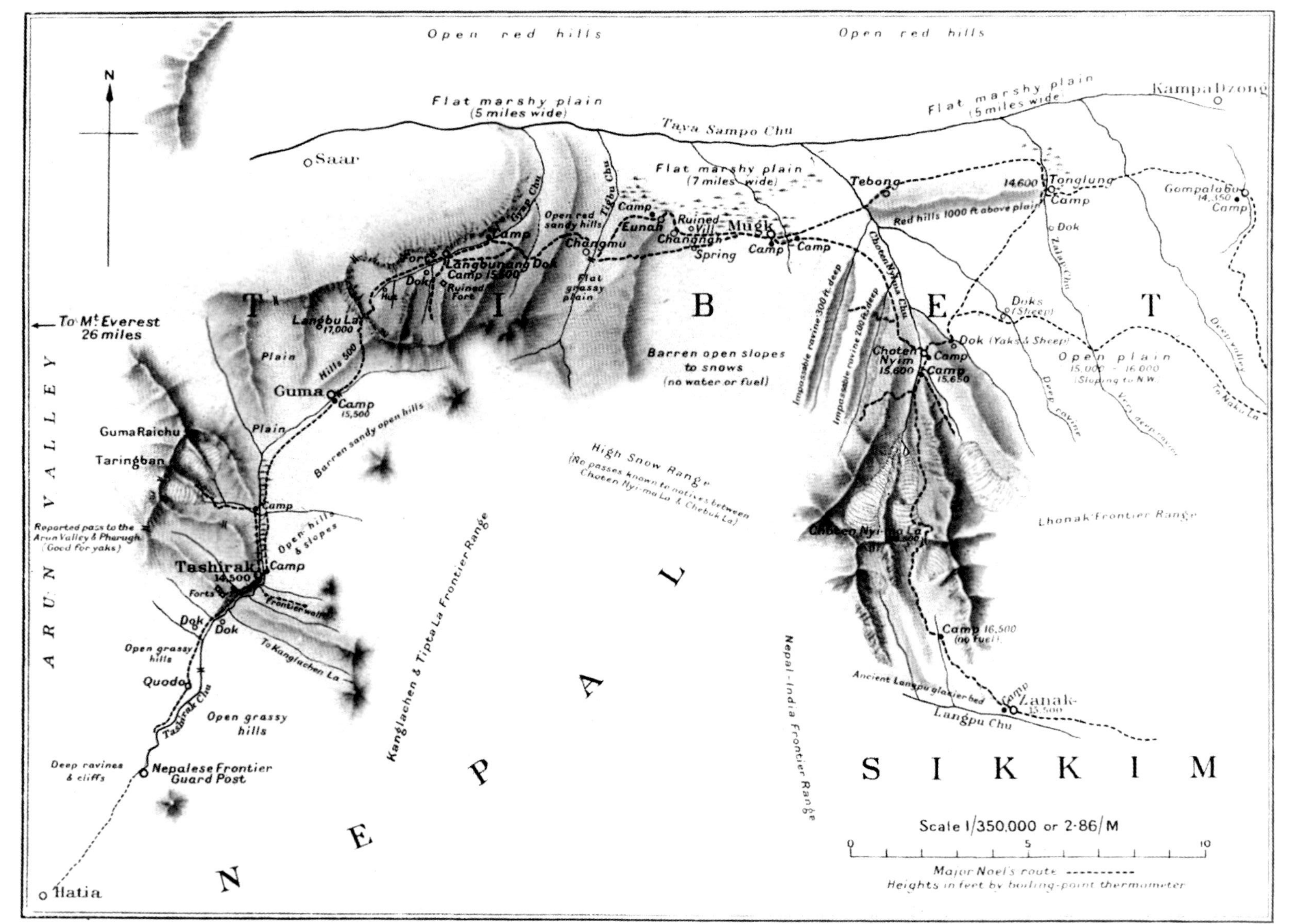

This map was used by Noel to accompany the presentation which he gave to the Royal Geographical Society in 1919, on his illegal journey to Tibet in 1913, and which inspired the members to set up a joint organisation with the Alpine Club – the Mount Everest Committee – to mount an expedition to attempt the highest mountain in the world. 'Some day,' Noel concluded his lecture, 'the political difficulties will be overcome and a fully equipped expedition must explore and map Mount Everest.' (© *Royal Geographical Society*)

front, the court martial forgotten in the chaos. It was to be nine years before he would return to India, to continue his great quest to reach Everest.

The First World War

Initially Noel was ordered to rejoin his regiment in India, but, about to board ship at Tilbury, he received War Office instructions to join the King's Own Yorkshire Light Infantry, already preparing to enter the battle arena. He joined the regiment, stationed in Dublin, as they were ready to embark on a ship bound for France in August 1914. As his luggage had remained on the ship destined for India, he arrived on the quayside without his uniform, which prompted the Colonel to bellow, 'You can't come aboard dressed for grouse-shooting in Scotland – we are going to shoot Germans in Belgium.' Noel was given one hour to dash to a military tailor, where he seized a complete uniform made for another officer, which was a passable fit. With no time to spare, he had to change in a moving horse cab, arriving just before the ship sailed. The British Expeditionary Forces comprised two army corps, No. 1 commanded by General Sir Douglas Haig, and No. 2 by General Sir Horace Smith-Dorrian. Noel wrote at the time:

> The 1st Corps formed up on the left flank of the French Army and the 2nd lined the canal at Mons. The German armies of enormous size, far outnumbering our BEF, were rapidly advancing through Belgium, but their progress and position was little known to us until, on Sunday 23 August, they opened a violent attack on our lines on the South Bank of the Mons Canal. Our Royal Engineers had destroyed all the bridges over the Canal. Very heavy fighting continued all day but our men held the Canal. Then that evening, we suddenly had immediate orders to retire. It transpired that the German Army had broken through the French on our right, and our 1st Corps was threatened by being outflanked. At the same time, German Cavalry divisions in great numbers were sweeping through the open

country between the BEF and the sea coast, so threatening to encircle the BEF. We retired, marching 20 miles all night, to a position at Le Cateau, where General Smith Dorien successfully delayed the German advance long enough to enable Sir John French to retire the BEF, but the battle of Le Cateau cost enormous losses, as we were outnumbered in men and guns. My battalion was practically wiped out [in total, the battalion lost 600 men and 20 officers]. Only a few survivors of my Company, with no ammunition left, were taken prisoners. The official casualty list of the *London Times* reported me: 'MISSING, believed killed'.

Noel was captured with twenty other survivors but the Germans were as exhausted as the British and he managed to escape. Without a map, and with no knowledge of the terrain, it took ten days to reach the British lines, during which time his only source of food was from the pockets of dead men. He was sent back to England as a casualty, and spent two months recovering from the ordeal.

By then (1915) his own regiment, the East Yorkshire, had returned from India, and Noel, now a captain, joined to fight in some of the bloodiest battles of the First World War – the Ypres Salient, followed by a long period of trench warfare. 'I was machine-gun officer,' he later wrote, 'but we only had two Vickers Guns – the Germans had 16 guns to a battalion. Then came the counter-attack against the [chlorine] gas attack [in April 1915] that had broken the front trenches between the Canadians and the French.' With the formation of the Machine Gun Corps, he was appointed revolver instructor at their training centre in Grantham in October 1917, and attained the rank of major. During his time there he wrote three manuals – *The Automatic Pistol, How to Shoot with a Revolver* and *The Map and Compass – A complete guide to Map Reading and the Magnetic Compass*. Highly specialized, these publications were considered to show the highest level of skill in handling small arms at a time when the British Empire was fighting for its life. In addition, Noel wrote two pamphlets – *Hints on Veterinary First Aid*, a useful publication, considering that the Army needed 160,000 horses to send to the front every six months, so high were the casualty figures, and *A Soldier's Simple Cooking Recipes for Cooking in Trenches and Billets*, which must have provided great help and support to the men during those terrible times of deprivation and hardship.

Towards the end of the war Britain was peripherally involved in the fight against the Bolsheviks. In February 1918 Noel was assigned to the command of No. 187 Machine Gun Corps with Norpa Force, a small army of about 6,000 men in north Persia, whose job it was to guard against the possibility of the Bolsheviks seizing the oilfields of Mesopotamia. While at Kazvin in March 1920, with another officer, Captain Fortescue, he received orders to proceed on a reconnaissance tour through Mazandaran to Gilan, to explore and survey the southern shore of the Caspian Sea, to calculate the chances of the Bolsheviks invading Persia through the Elbruz Mountains. This lofty mountain range in North Iran, south of the Caspian Sea, was some 650 miles long, its highest point at 18,571 feet. There were no accurate maps of the area, since, for political reasons, the provinces had intentionally been left with undeveloped communications and were, therefore, among the least-known corners of Persia. It had been considered a dangerous place until the gendarmerie, under Swedish control, disarmed the turbulent, feudal officers of the Shah's army. Noel and Fortescue set out by horse on their two-month journey, and as restrictions on photography had been relaxed he took with him his Debrie motion picture camera. Noel recounted discovering a thriving caviar industry on the Caspian Sea:

I made a very good film on the caviar industry, which I [later] sold to Pathé in London. The sturgeon is six feet long; like the salmon, it swims up the rivers to spawn. There are hundreds of rivers coming down to the sea from the mountains. The Persians laid lines across the rivers, and had no trouble catching the sturgeon. Out of each fish they took twenty pounds of roe. This they boiled in salty water, squeezed out the juice, and put it on a shelf. In three days, it turned from green to black – and it was caviar. They sold it to the Russians. It is one of the most powerful foods in the world for energy; a couple of ounces of caviar is

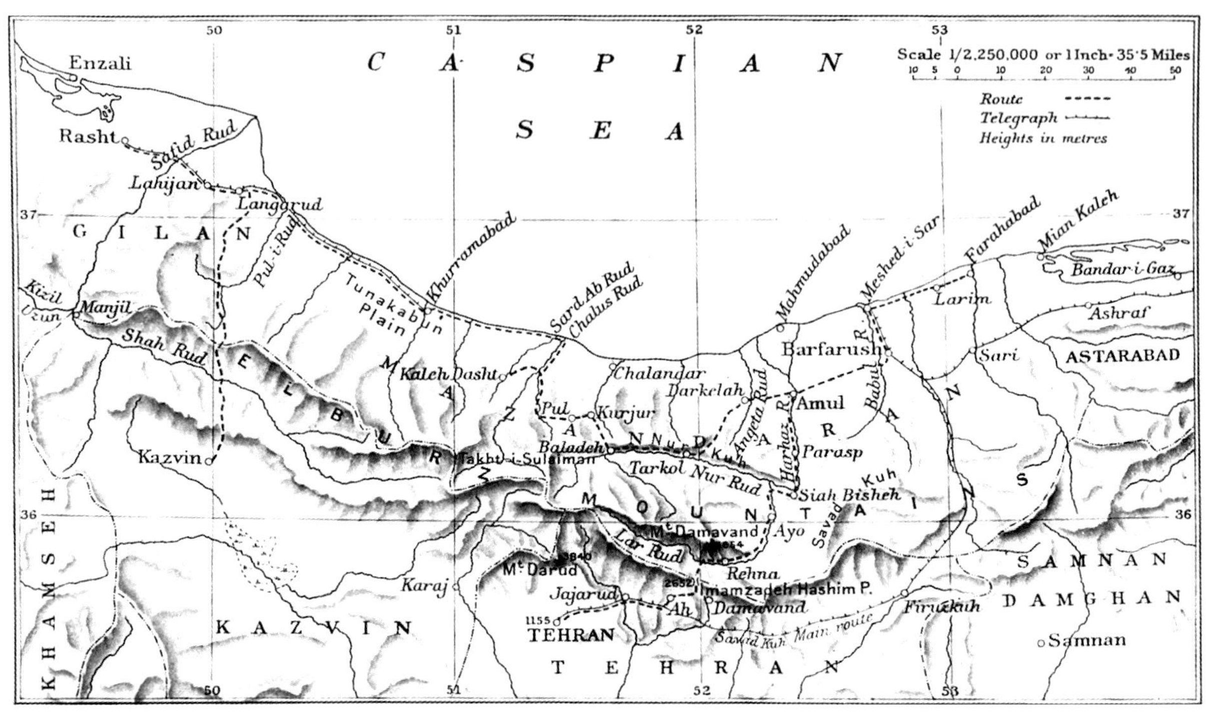

The southern shores of the Caspian Sea; Noel and a fellow officer were sent by the British Government to map out this area in 1919. (© *Royal Geographical Society*)

equivalent to a bottle of brandy for bucking you up! I used to buy it from the Persians at a *toma* (20p) a pound.

Noel described this surveying assignment at the Royal Geographical Society's Meeting on 10 January 1921, in a paper entitled *A Reconnaissance in the Caspian Provinces of Persia*,* and he showed some photographs which he had taken. His conclusion was:

One must hope that peace and order will come again to the Caspian country, for it is well worth development. Russian aggression must be checked, communications

* *RGS Journal*, vol. LVII (6), June 1921.

and roads must be made, the land and sea policed, and the natural riches of the land developed. Then the Caspian provinces will prove their value to Persia by contributing foreign export trade and internal food supply – economic contributions which are both vital for the rebuilding of the country.

Back to Everest

In 1920 Noel was appointed revolver instructor at the newly formed Small Arms School at Hythe, Kent. He had married, in 1915, Sybille Graham, and, while living in Kent, they had fallen in love with the villages of the Weald, and bought two derelict hall houses in Smarden, which Noel later lovingly restored. A year before his appointment, Noel had read the paper on his Tibetan exploits of 1913 at a meeting of the Royal Geographical Society (RGS). It fired an enthusiasm among the climbers and explorers of the day, and Sir Francis Younghusband, the president of the Society, determined that climbing Everest would be the main feature of his three years in office. Great efforts were being made by the RGS to gain permission from the Tibetans for an expedition with the open blessing of the Dalai Lama. Younghusband induced Sir Charles Bell CIE, the Political Officer for Tibetan Affairs and Political Resident of Sikkim, to visit the Dalai Lama, the mysterious ruler of Tibet, at Lhasa, and ask his permission. Bell was the only European who had ever won the confidence of the ruler of Tibet. He spoke the language fluently and was the author of a Tibetan–English dictionary. After Bell's intercession, at the end of 1920 the Tibetan prime minister issued a passport giving an invitation and safe-conduct for an Everest expedition under the *Great Red Seal of the Holy Rulers of Tibet*. The curious parchment, abbreviated, reads:

Be it known to Officers and Headmen of Phari-Dzong, Tin-ki and Shekar that a party of Sahibs will come to the Sacred Mountain Chomolungma. . . . You shall render all help and safe-guard to them. . . . We have requested the Sahibs to keep

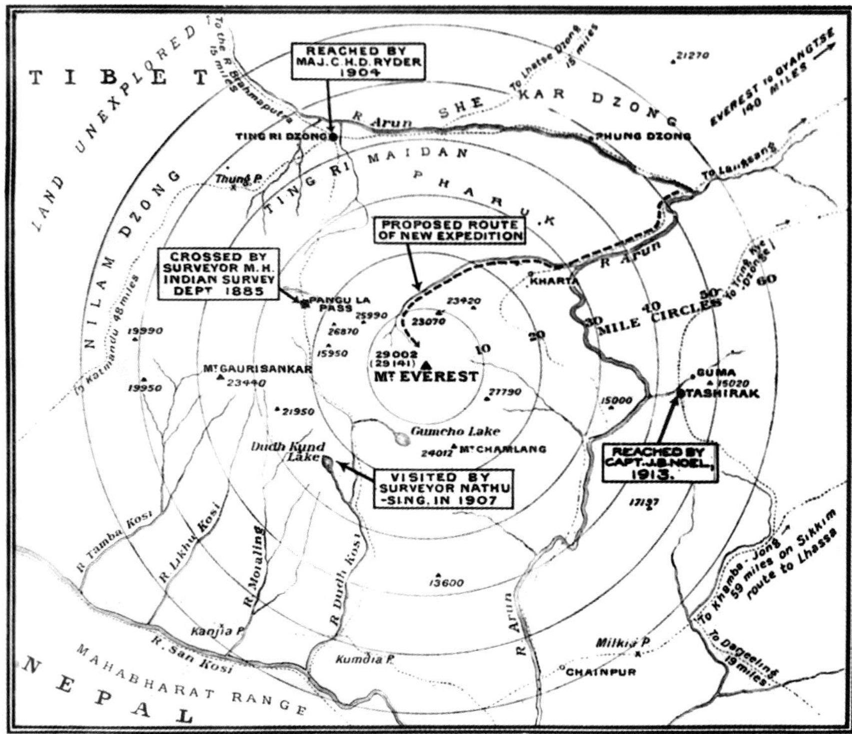

A map of the Everest region, showing the routes of early explorers.

the laws of the country when they visit Chomolungma and not to kill Birds and Animals as the people will feel very sorry for this. . . . His Holiness the Dalai Lama is now on great friendly terms with the Government of India. . . .

Despatched on the seventeenth day of the eleventh month of the Iron Bird Year.

So, plans could begin to map out and prepare for an assault on the highest mountain known to man. The tremendous losses incurred during the war had, however, drained the nation of its pool of fit, able young men with climbing experience, so the first difficult task was to select the men to go. Dr Alexander Kellas (1868–1921), Chemistry Lecturer at Middlesex Hospital, had journeyed many times to the region, and had studied the effect of altitude on humans, so he was an obvious choice for the first attempt. In his book *Through Tibet to Everest*, Noel described their early association:

In the long gap between my own journey of 1913 and the Everest expedition of 1921, I talked with Kellas whenever I had a chance . . . in his chemical laboratory at the hospital. . . . He told me how he had worked out a plan to lay depots of food in uninhabited high valleys west of Kangchenjunga by means of his own trained sherpas, and was confident of reaching Kharta, crossing the river and going up the eastern glaciers of Everest by the Kama Valley, escaping the watching Tibetans. And he asked me to go with him as soon as the War was finished. I said, 'Most certainly I will.' But nothing ever came of this, for the authorized Expeditions took the place of furtive private raids.

Kellas also devised the plan of using the natural resources of the country – yaks and mountain ponies – for transport at the lower heights, as the Tibetans do themselves, and he employed the sherpas, one of the hardiest tribes in the world, dwellers in the highest valleys of the Himalayas, as porters. He had discovered the use of the sherpas on high ascents, and Noel recalls his description:

They are simple shepherd people, as hard as nails. They can run up mountains with immense loads on their backs, and then yodel their songs in pure delight, when the plainsman following them, panting and blue of lips, will fall exhausted to the ground. Kellas found them cheerful under all conditions, willing to undertake risks, and faithful. He made friends with these rough mountaineers, and with their help he conquered virgin peaks one after another with an ease and rapidity that astonished the world.

The officers of the Alpine Club, whose ambition was to climb Mount Everest, and those of the Royal Geographical Society, whose aim was to map and explore the geography of the region, decided to forget their differences and combine forces to mount a joint attempt on the mountain, under the control of the Mount Everest Committee. The main interest of the RGS was map-making, and the exploration of a hitherto unknown area of the globe, while that of the Alpine Club was the climb; the RGS was regarded as having the better facilities for organizing expeditions, while the Alpine Club had better means of choosing the personnel. The pivot of the entire operation was Arthur Hinks (1873–1945), Secretary of the RGS since 1915 and a geographer who would arrange for the Society to add considerably to its aerial photographic map-making at the outbreak of the Second World War: Britain had not been far-seeing enough, and the country was less advanced in both air apparatus and air techniques than most continental countries.

Eventually, in 1921, the team was assembled. It consisted of map-makers, geologists and climbers, a total of nine Europeans on this reconnaissance trip. Sir Francis Younghusband had invited Noel to join, but the Army was unable to grant him the necessary leave. Nor, in 1921, could the Army spare General Bruce, the first choice as leader, so the Mount Everest Committee asked Colonel Charles Howard-Bury to lead. Now aged forty, he had travelled extensively in the region, was a keen plant collector and natural linguist, in addition to being instrumental in gaining permission from the Dalai Lama for a British expedition. The climbing party itself was led by Harold Raeburn, a veteran Alpine climber, although he, like Kellas, was not expected to reach above 25,000 feet. George Mallory immediately resigned his mastership at Charterhouse when he was invited to join the expedition, and persuaded the Committee to take his old schoolfriend and co-mountaineer, Guy Bullock, as climbing partner. Dr A.M. Heron was the geologist, while two officers from the Survey of India, Henry Morshead and Oliver Wheeler, and medical officer and naturalist Sandy Wollaston completed the team. Each was given an allowance of £50 by the Mount Everest Committee, later increased to £100, towards the cost of their kit, which they provided themselves.

Bearing in the mind the lack of accurate maps, the unknown terrain, the problems with the Indian Army transport mules and the fact that most of the Tibetans they met and dealt with had never seen a European, this first expedition was a huge success. By September 1921 they had reached the North Col, above 22,000 feet, on Mount

Everest. Sadly, Kellas died of dysentery en route to Everest in 1921: he is buried in a simple grave on the slopes of the fort at Kampa, looking over the mountain range to the climbing of which he contributed so much.

As soon as the expedition arrived back in England plans began to assemble a larger, more sophisticated team to tackle the mountain again as soon as possible. Noel was determined to be one of the members, and in 1922 resigned his commission to join as official photographer. He later wrote:

> The RGS was a very conservative body . . . it was a scientific climbing expedition; they didn't want any vulgarity in the newspapers; half of them didn't want any pictures at all. So they invited me; I was an amateur photographer and a lover of mountains. The idea was that the film, when it was eventually shown, would produce money for the expedition.

A photographer whom Noel respected and greatly admired was Herbert Ponting (1870–1935). Twenty years Noel's senior, he gained vast experience in picture-making during his globe-trotting, and had accompanied Scott on the great adventure to the South Pole. Noel was greatly impressed by the record of Scott's expedition, as filmed by Ponting, and he haunted the Philharmonic Hall, watching the show again and again. In later years he became a close friend of Ponting, and eventually used the same cine camera designer and maker, Arthur Newman, to supply all the equipment needed for Everest. Ponting's experience in the Antarctic was invaluable to Noel: he learnt that in low temperatures the film would become so brittle it would break; that equipment had to be operated with thick gloves; that Ponting had lost the tip of his tongue while threading a camera, and Noel would have to take every precaution against such an accident. He wrote: 'I asked Mr Newman to make a rubber cover, so, if I had to press my face against the camera, to steady it in the wind, I wouldn't be in contact with the cold metal.'

Noel had decided that, in view of the extremes of temperature which would be endured, and the unknown effects of altitude and wind upon the camera and film, it

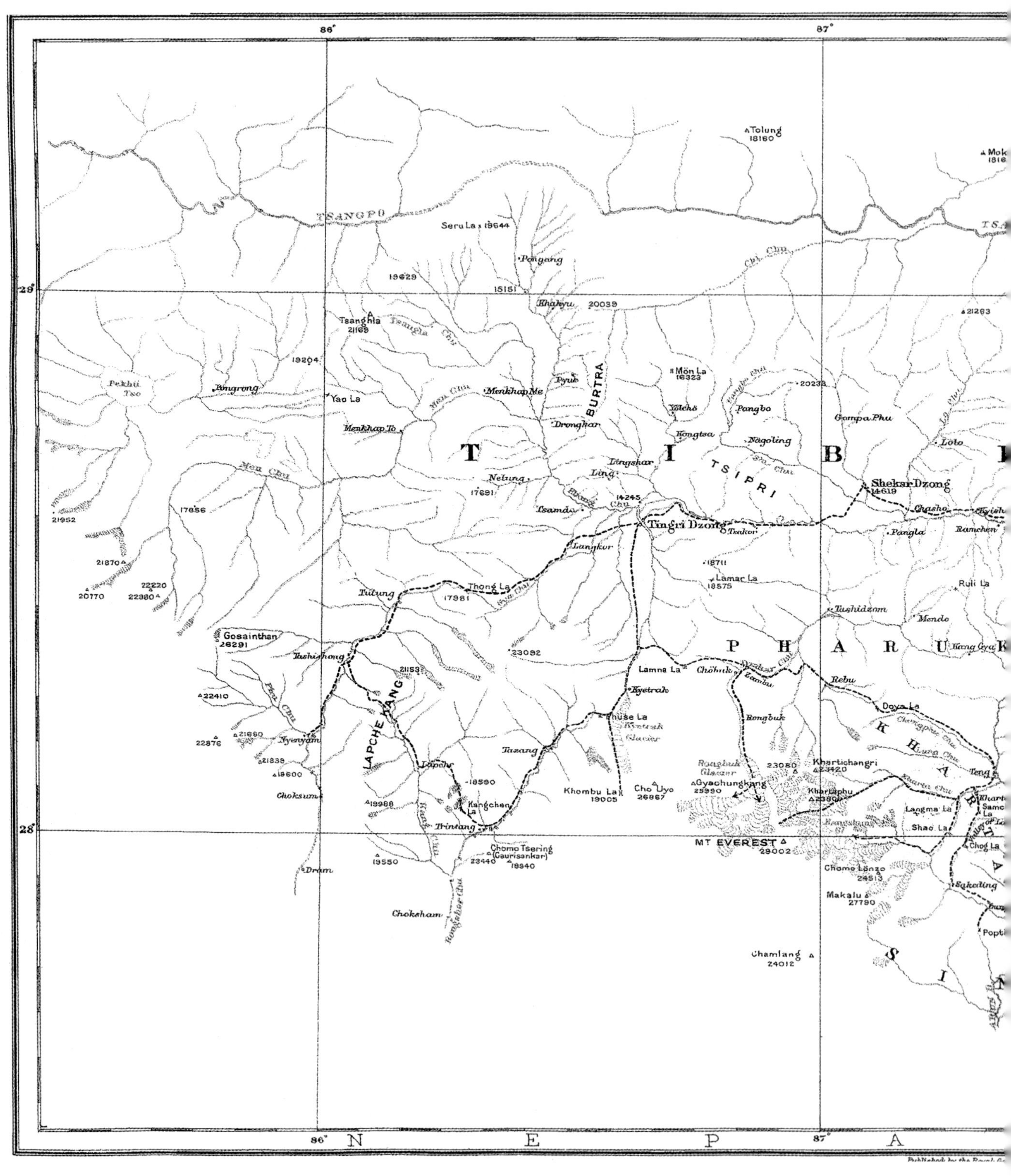

TSANGPO
Tolung
18160
Seru La 18644
Pongang
19629
15151
Khabyu 20039
Tsanghla
2168
Tsaugla Chu
19204
Pekhu Tso
Pongrong
Yao La
Meu Chu
Menkhap Me
Pyuu
BURTRA
Mon La
16323
Pongbo Chu
20233
Yotchö
Pongbo
Gompa Phu
Menkhap To
Drongkar
Kongtsa
Nagoling
Loto
T
TSIPRI
B
Netung
Dingshar
Ling
Shekar Dzong
14619
Chusho
17681
14245
Chu
Tsamda
Meu Chu
Tingri Dzong
Teakor
Pangla
Ramchen
17856
21952
Lanykar
18711
Lamac La
18575
Ruti La
21870
Thong La
17381
Gya Chu
Tutung
Tashidzom
Mendo
Yung Gyu
22220
20170 22380
23082
PHARU
Gosainthan
26291
Lamna La
Chöbük
Rebu
Tashizhong
21153
Eyetrak
Tsamtu
Doya La
22410
Rongbuk
KHA
21660
Nyanyam
Chuse La
Rongbuk Glacier
Rongbuk
Khartichangri
23420
Hlung Chu
Teng
22876
21838
Lapche
Trusang
23080
Khartaphu
23890
18600
LAPCHE KANG
18590
Khombu La
19005
Cho Uyo
26867
Gyachungkang
25990
Langma La
Samo
Choksum
19988
Kangchen La
Shao La
Trintang
Chomo Tsering
(Gaurisankar)
23440
MT EVEREST
29002
Chod La
19550
18840
Chome Lönzo
24513
Dram
Sakeding
Choksham
Rongshar Chu
Makalu
27790
Popti
Chamlang
24012
SI

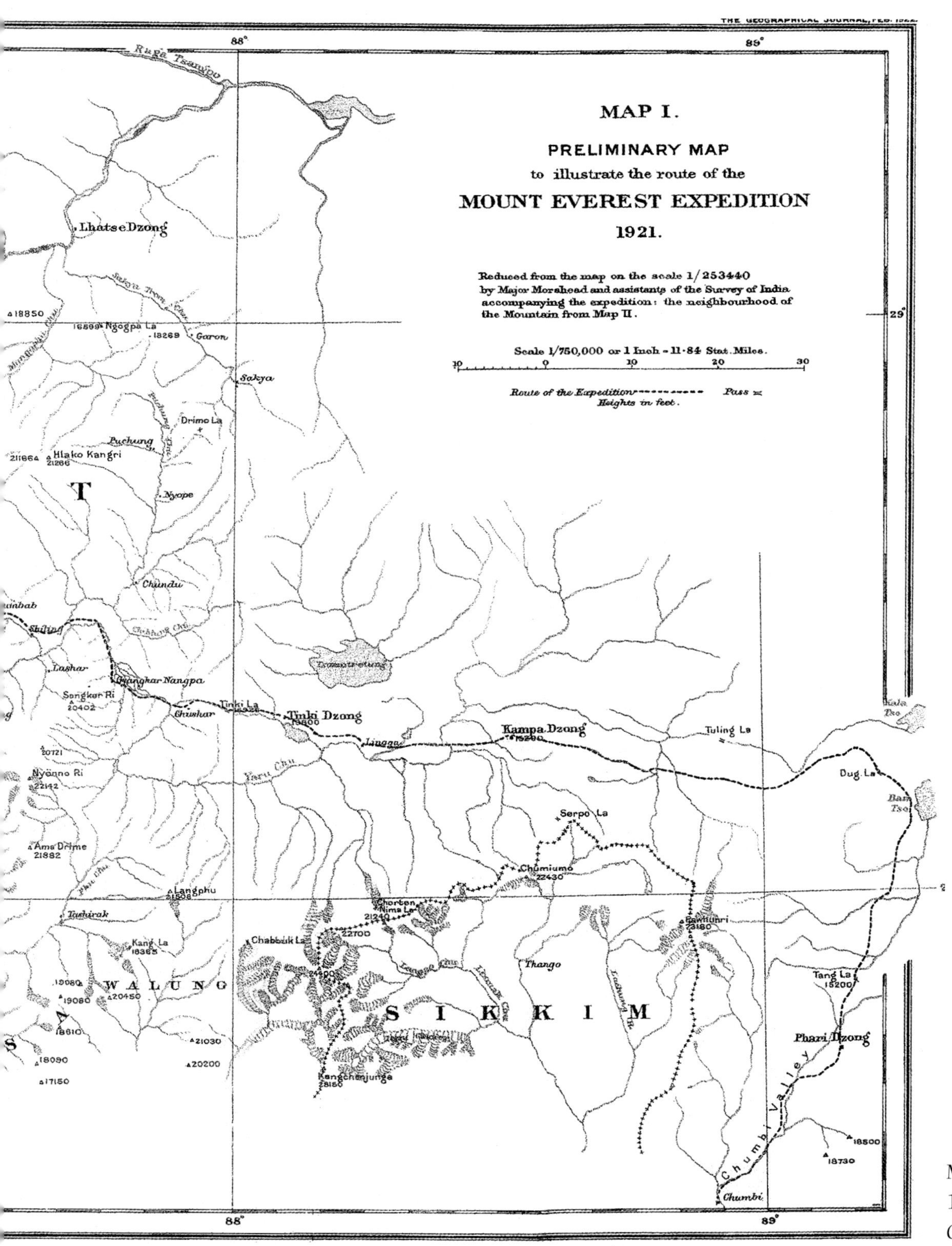

Map showing the routes of the 1921, 1922 and 1924 expeditions. (© *Royal Geographical Society*)

would be better to develop much of the material on the mountain. A special tent was designed and made by Benjamin Edginton, a well-known London firm of camping equipment and tent makers, so that Noel could develop the cine film at Base Camp. He wanted to be sure that all the techniques were as good as possible under the extreme conditions, to have the chance to alter exposure and speed of film and take further frames while still on site. Had the film been sent down to India, then by the time it was recognised that the technique needed changing it would be too late to get a message to him and allow him time to try another shot.

Originally Noel paid for much of the film equipment, but the Mount Everest Committee eventually authorized payment of £600 towards the cost of the cinematograph camera and film. In his specially designed lightproof tent, Noel developed, fixed and washed thousands of feet of 35mm film, hanging it to dry over heated yak-dung, as no other fuel was readily available at Base Camp. Following the departure of the other members at the end of the expedition, Noel still had many reels of film to develop, so he set up a darkroom in the fort at Gyantse to complete the process.

Arthur Hinks made the day-to-day arrangements for the 1922 expedition, and helped Noel to design and commission the necessary equipment for the photographic coverage of the climb. He ordered apparatus and equipment from Kodak, including Vest Pocket cameras for each of the lead climbers, as it was obvious that Noel could not carry heavy photographic equipment high enough to be able to witness the anticipated assaults on the summit.

The aim was to treat the cine film so as to remain faithful to the subject, but, at the same time, win the widest possible commercial interest. Film experts were concerned at the lack of romance as a selling point, and suggested bringing out actors and actresses to create a love scene in the snow. Noel's prime task, however, was to act as photographic historian, to capture the feeling of power and majesty of the mountain; he was to avoid casual, intimate shots, as the climbers were anxious that the public might remark about their antics on the film. At first, Mallory was particularly antagonistic towards the idea of a photographic record, but, while sharing a tent with Noel at Base Camp, he became quite intrigued by the whole process.

Noel – an Expedition Member

Nine years after his journey in disguise across Tibet to approach the great mountain, Noel was now, in 1922, a member of the second expedition. Brigadier-General Charles Bruce had been the obvious choice as leader, and it fell to him and Hinks to select the team. Rank and profession still counted for much in the 1920s, so it was no surprise when Hinks announced with pride:

> Of the eleven members of the expedition six are soldiers: three of the Gurkhas, one of the Royal Scots, one Royal Field Artillery, and one Machine Gun Corps, formerly of the East Yorkshire Regiment. Three members of the party are of Cambridge University; Mr Mallory of Magdalene, Mr Somervell of Caius, and Dr Wakefield of Christ Church. Three are surgeons; two are naturalists; several are expert photographers; one at least is a painter; and all are distinguished mountaineers. It is, in fact, a very strong party, of which much is expected.

Compared with the 1921 expedition, this team had a greater number of climbers, including Mallory and Major Edward Norton, who was well known in the Alpine Club and had served in India, spoke Hindustani and knew how to handle Indian peoples. Dr T. Howard Somervell, a surgeon by profession, was a skilled mountaineer as well as a talented painter and musician, with great energy and stamina. George Finch, a renowned Alpinist, who, while a student at the University of Zurich, had been a prominent member of the Academic Alpine Club of Switzerland, was included in the climbing team, as was Morshead, this time not on surveying duties. Colonel Edward (Frank) Strutt was second-in-command, and would head the team when General Bruce remained at Base Camp. Captain Geoffrey Bruce – younger cousin of the General – was joined by two others familiar with life in India, transport officers Colin Crawford and Captain John Morris. The Medical Officer, Arthur Wakefield, joined the surgeon and naturalist Tom Longstaff. Bruce and Hinks were two very different characters – Bruce was jolly, optimistic, but shrewd, while Hinks was serious, meticulous and exacting, and with a slightly impatient attitude towards the climbing. When he questioned Bruce's need for 500 mules for the start of the expedition, Bruce told him in his boyish manner: 'Captain Noel will be arriving at Darjeeling with a box 40ft-long, and I am currently scouring the country for an adequate mule.'

In 1921 it had been noted that the weather was warm and wet from the first hailstones of April to the last monsoon drizzle in October, so it was decided that an attempt should be planned before the monsoon, and that the group should therefore arrive at Base Camp in April. Furthermore, oxygen was to be used. Dr Kellas had prepared a number of experiments to be conducted during the 1921 climb, but his untimely death had left the matter unfinished. Further systems had been developed at Oxford University for the RAF, and it was generally believed that climbing to the height of 28,000 feet would not be possible without the aid of 'English air'.

The initial plan also allowed for the expedition, if it failed in the spring, to stay on until another attempt could be made in the autumn. It was decided at the outset that the Polar method of depot laying was imperative – men divided into small groups, taking turns in the exhausting preparation work, forging a way for those who would make the last triumphant ascent. Once the highest possible depot is established, then the fittest among the climbers form a party to make the last dash to the summit. Accordingly, three depots were fixed, one at 17,800 feet, the second at 19,800 feet and the third at 21,000 feet. On 20 May Norton, Somervell, Mallory and Morshead broke the previous world's height record, set by the Duke of the Abruzzi, when they reached 25,000 feet. They climbed higher, but did not have the equipment to establish a higher camp, and they were all suffering from exposure in one form or another. They descended, meeting Geoffrey Bruce and Finch preparing to climb, in part with the aid of oxygen. Noel accompanied them to 23,000 feet, and stayed to watch them climbing the north-east ridge; they built a camp at 25,000 feet, and eventually a new altitude record was set with Finch and Geoffrey Bruce reaching 27,250 feet, proving the helpfulness of oxygen. It was hoped to make one more attempt before the monsoon, but seven sherpas were killed in an avalanche and this ghastly accident cast a terrible feeling of gloom over events, as Noel wrote in a letter to Hinks from Base Camp on 12 June 1922:

> I returned a few days ago from the upper camps after the great accident. I was up there at the time and making the ascent of the N[orth] Col with the party.
>
> As I was coming up behind underneath the coolies, photographing them going up and crossing the crevasses, etc., it was lucky that I decided to return owing to the softness of the snow after I had reached 22,500 feet. The work was too heavy for carrying the cameras. My decision to descend and continue photographing the coolies and party from the foot of the Col by means of my big lens, saved my life because the avalanche would have dealt hardest with me being the end of the line.
>
> We were all terribly distressed by the accident – the general [Bruce] most of all as those splendid sherpa coolies have endeared themselves to all the members of the Expedition. Everybody admires them for their splendid pluck and the devotion they have shown to us, their Sahibs. I hope we will be able to recompense their families and relations in a liberal manner.

The impact of the avalanche was widely felt: when General Bruce communicated the news to the Rongbuk Monastery, the great lama was 'intensely sympathetic and kind over the whole matter', and all the porters were later received and blessed by the lama himself. Bruce later received a letter of condolence from the Maharaja of Nepal, which refers to the previous approach by the British government, through Bruce himself, for permission to climb the mountain from the Nepalese side. It states:

. . . it is to the effect that the height is the abode of the god and goddess Shiva and Parvati, and any invasion of the privacy of it would be a sacrilege fraught with disastrous consequences to the Hindu country and its people. And this belief or superstition, as one may choose to call it, is so firm and strong that people attribute the present tragic occurrence to the divine wrath which on no account would they draw on their heads by any action.

Clearly the impact was similarly viewed by the Tibetans on the north and the Nepalese on the south of the great sacred mountain. The disaster put an abrupt end to the expedition plans, but, as Younghusband recorded in his book *The Epic of Mount Everest** in 1926:

It had made a discovery of outstanding importance – and of importance not only for future Everest expeditions but for mankind generally. It had been discovered that man acclimatizes himself to the effects of the highest altitudes. . . . If the spirit of man will drive him on to climbing the highest heights, he will find himself rising to the occasion; he will find both body and mind responding to the call of the spirit.

Much discussion ensued: could men climb to such heights without oxygen, and, if so, would the porters' manpower be better employed in carrying up stores and tents rather than bulky oxygen cylinders? Somervell was firmly of the view that there was no theoretical limit to acclimatization at any level; he believed a successful attempt could be mounted by sending up a party of men to 21,000 feet for about two weeks, making a few higher climbs to 23,000 or 24,000 feet, and that they would then be ready and able to climb the mountain, provided that the weather was fine and the wind not too strong. In Younghusband's words:

* Francis Younghusband, *The Epic of Mount Everest*, Edward Arnold, 1926; repr. Pan, 2000.

We were still oscillating between faith in ourselves and faith in oxygen. We were relying too much on what physics and chemistry could do for us, and too little on what we could do for ourselves. So the next expedition was supplied with oxygen.

Another lesson learned from the experience of 1922 was that the optimum age of the climbers should be around thirty. Older men found it difficult to acclimatize, and most younger men would have neither the necessary experience – since climbing had been impossible anywhere during and immediately after the war – nor the staying power. The ideal climber was deemed to be of the tall, short-bodied, long-limbed type; that is, with not too much weight to carry but with length of leg to lift it. A further clear necessity was the support group. If parties of two were to make an attempt, they would need to know that they had steady, reliable back-up to support them, succour them in distress and have a good meal waiting.

The mountain itself was not an obstacle – in the language of the Alpine Club it was 'an easy rock peak' – but the weather was the main hindrance, with terrific winds, cold and snow. The ceaseless driving wind was a menace, both physically and mentally, and it was obvious that windproof clothing was essential for all climbers and porters. The snow, too, was an ever-present threat: the loss of the porters in the avalanche was a constant reminder to all members of the expedition that it was a challenge which they would have to come to terms with and respect.

The film which Noel took of the expedition, *Climbing Mount Everest*, was a great success technically, and when shown in London and the provinces was highly acclaimed, although it had a shaky start. As Noel wrote:

We booked the Philharmonic Hall for 10 weeks, and lost £400 in the first week! The RGS panicked, but I assured them that, with the good press reviews which it had received, all would be well. In fact, we made an increased profit each week, with over £10,000 taken at the door, and a sign up: NO SEATS by the last week. We couldn't continue, because the hall had been booked by somebody else.

As with Ponting's film, once it had proved a popular success, the film trade was only too delighted to reap the rewards of Noel's efforts and release the film to selected theatres. Much footage is given over to the train journey to Darjeeling, to scenes of the porters, straining through leech-infested forests and hauling reluctant mules across freezing mountain rivers, and the fantastic religious life; the footage of the climb, in the absence of drama, is somewhat anti-climactic. It ends with Finch and Bruce setting out on their oxygen climb, which created a new world record at 27,250 feet. The final title reads, prophetically:

> Though defeated this time, still our climbers will not accept defeat. They will make another expedition soon to complete the conquest of the mountain. They will return to this terrific battle with Nature and, despite the dangers, the storms and the cold, they will win through. They will conquer and they will yet stand on the summit of Everest – the very topmost pinnacle of the world.

There was now a change in the chairmanship of the Mount Everest Committee, which was taken in turns by the president of the RGS and the president of the Alpine Club; in his capacity as president of the latter, General Bruce automatically took over the reins of the Mount Everest Committee. It was time to begin preparing for the next Everest attempt, planned for 1924.

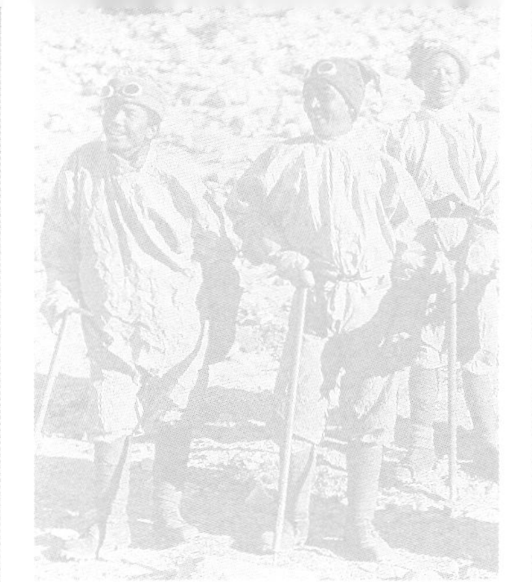

CHAPTER 1

PREPARATIONS

Much had been learned from the 1922 expedition, and the members of the Mount Everest Committee were determined to build on that experience in preparing for the next attempt, in 1924. In the course of 1923, while the tasks of selecting the team members and preparing kit, clothing and provisions were being undertaken, largely by Hinks and Bruce, the unwelcome subject of finance had to be addressed. Both the Royal Geographical Society and the Alpine Club were funded largely by members' subscriptions. There was no history of sponsorship and, in the view of Hinks, any agreement with a newspaper was very undesirable. But the lack of money became an enormous issue. Noel presented a scheme which at a stroke would relieve the Committee of a major financial burden – he proposed buying all the photographic rights, both for film, stills and lecture rights, in return for the vast sum of £8,000. The idea was readily accepted, and Noel agreed to pay the entire sum before the expedition departed, and to pay for all his equipment, film stock, transport to Tibet, assistance and porterage, a contribution which amounted to a further £2,000.

Not himself a wealthy man, he set up a company called Explorers Films and invited friends and businessmen to contribute to the scheme in the expectation that when the film and lecture tours were under way in the autumn of 1924, the company members would soon recoup their initial outlay, and even show a profit. It was an appealing project, and his shareholders included the Aga Khan, with Sir Francis Younghusband as president of the company. The greatest obstacle would be to sustain public interest in the expedition's progress, so that when the film was shown many months later the response would make the entire undertaking worthwhile. Noel's aim was to attract the interest of youngsters in particular, who would persuade their parents to take them to the film or lecture show of the climb, buying a postcard as a souvenir. Noel's design for the postcard used one of the images of Base Camp, and his artist friend Francis Helps designed the commemorative stamp, using the age-old symbol from the Hindu religion in each corner and the names of the three countries around Everest. Noel put an advertisement in one of the daily papers, inviting the public to send in their names and addresses to receive a postcard from Base Camp. Two secretaries were engaged to deal with what he hoped would be a positive response. By 10 a.m. the deluge of mail overwhelmed the girls, who fled in panic. Noel quickly had to engage an agency to handle the sack-loads of mail. Each address was transferred to an Everest postcard, already carrying the commemorative stamp, which was then packed to take to Base Camp, where an Indian stamp would be added and the thousands of cards dispatched by the Indian Postal Service.

By February 1924 initial preparations were complete. Travel to India could only be undertaken by ship, to Bombay or Calcutta. The sea journey to Calcutta was longer, but avoided the train journey across the northern plains of India to Darjeeling, which was the starting point of all early British Everest expeditions. Members did not necessarily travel together, as they came from various corners of the globe – some from Europe, some from southern India, some from Persia. Noel sailed from England on the *City of Simla* on 24 February in the last minutes before the great dock strike of 1924, and he spent the sea voyage to Bombay adjusting and testing equipment. Then came the long train ride across the burning plains to Calcutta, then through Northern Bengal to Siliguri, where he took the Toy Train – the Darjeeling Himalayan Railway – up to Darjeeling, at 7,000 feet the highest point in the 30,000 miles of rail track that, by the end of the nineteenth century, had transformed India economically and socially. Noel wrote:

This miniature railway, quite a curiosity of engineering, runs with its 2-foot gauge, for the most part along the carriage road that winds by long zigzags up this mountain. The powerful little engine, weighing only from ten to fifteen tons, drags the laden carriages of the train up the gradient of about 1 in 28 at a rapid rate; but as the cars are mostly open trollies and there is no plunging into tunnels, this journey is made more like a drive in an open carriage, and you see the scenery to advantage.

As we advance up the gravelly spur, which is clothed with a forest of stately Sal trees, our narrow path seems like an avenue festooned with ferns, pepper-vines and ropes of many-hued climbers, through whose thick foliage the sunbeams filter in broken flocks of dancing light. One of the ferns that encircle these tall trunks crowns them with massive coronets of stiff feathery fronds that stand up like the headdress of a red Indian chief, and many of the trees have six to ten of these coronets, one above the other.

The twisting train curved in and out of shaggy ravines, carrying us through a swift succession of ever-changing scenery. Our thirsty little engine, toiling up the mountain, stopped frequently in the ravines for water, and thus enabled us to get out, as from a coach when changing horses, for a few minutes now and then, to pick a few wild flowers, or ferns, where cascades tumble down cliffs of gneiss with micaschist glistening in the sun. And we got time to study our fellow passengers.

The fresh faces and robust figures of the planters who have joined us by the way attest the healthiness of their exile in these hills, and contrast strikingly with the pale pinched faces of the tired workers whose lot is cast in the plains, and who are now hurrying to the cool hills to restore their lost strength. There are a few soldiers proceeding to their batteries or detachments in the mountains, British and Indian. Then there are several of the perky hill peasantry, the women loaded with jewellery and the men carrying ugly knives stuck in their girdles.

In Darjeeling, you may see representatives of most of the varied native population. There are the timid, plaited Lepchas, the aboriginals of these mountains, numerically very few as they are being swamped by swarms of the sprightly little chattering Nepalese, who have immigrated in enormous numbers to settle in the Darjeeling district, as the well-paid workers on the tea-gardens here. Most picturesque of all are the mounted Tibetans, dashing along on sturdy ponies with jingling harness bells.

Noel prophesied in his book, published in 1927, 'Should they ever become animated by a sporting desire to reach the top of the mountain, the sherpas could undoubtedly do it more easily than any white man.' This in fact, proved to be the case, as they easily carried loads as high as 25,500 feet in 1922, and it was soon realized that there was no reason why they could not carry even higher.

Once in Darjeeling, it remained for General Bruce and the transport officers to select a tough team of 150 local men, from which a porter corps of 50 would be chosen, upon whom so much rested to start the great adventure. The expedition members gathered and began the long overland journey. They headed north through Sikkim to Tibet, then west and finally south towards Everest, in total a march of 300 miles.

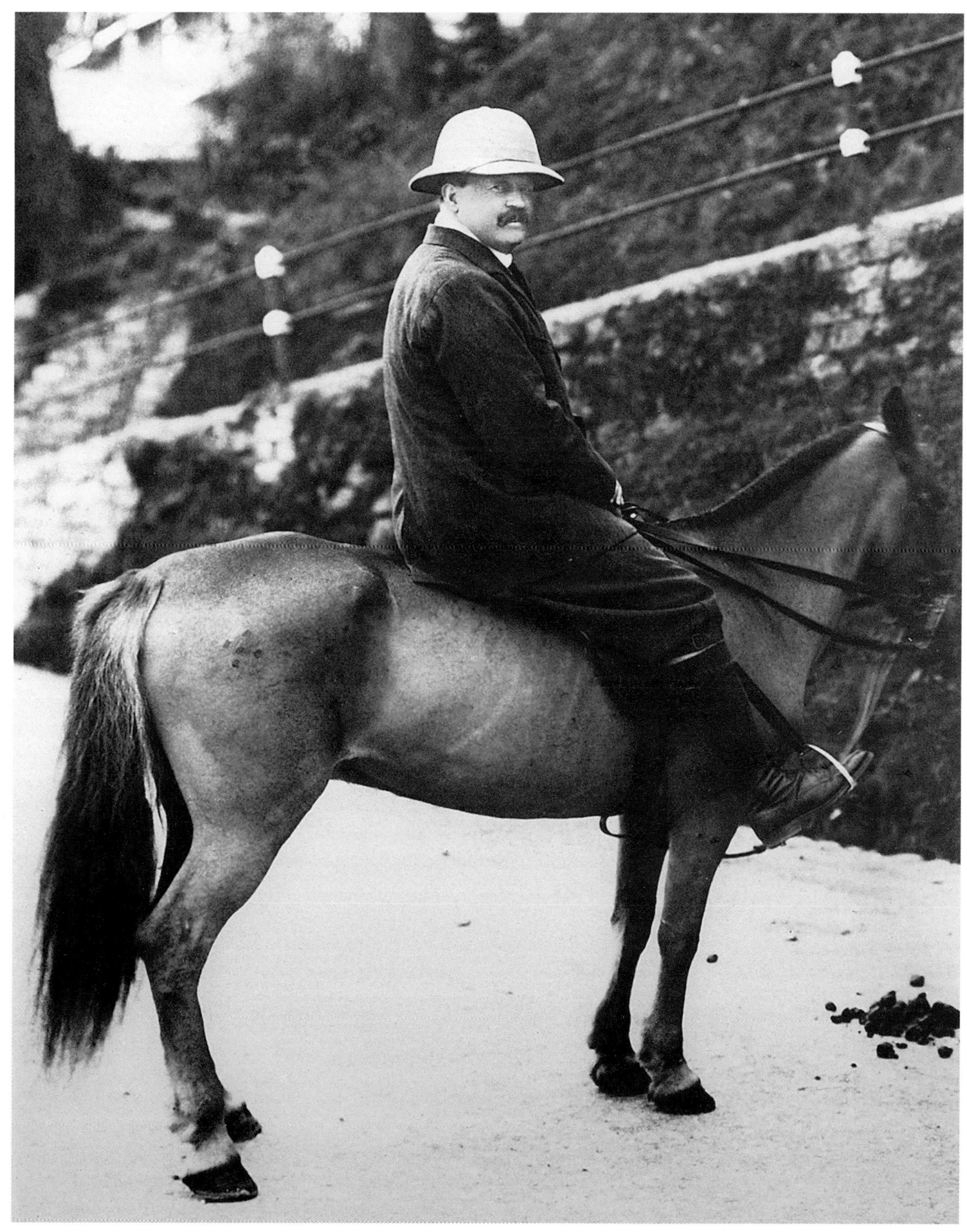

General Bruce on horseback. A regular Army officer, with years of experience living and working among the hillspeople of the region, he was an obvious choice as leader. He had not been able to get sufficient leave in 1921, but led the expeditions of 1922 and 1924.

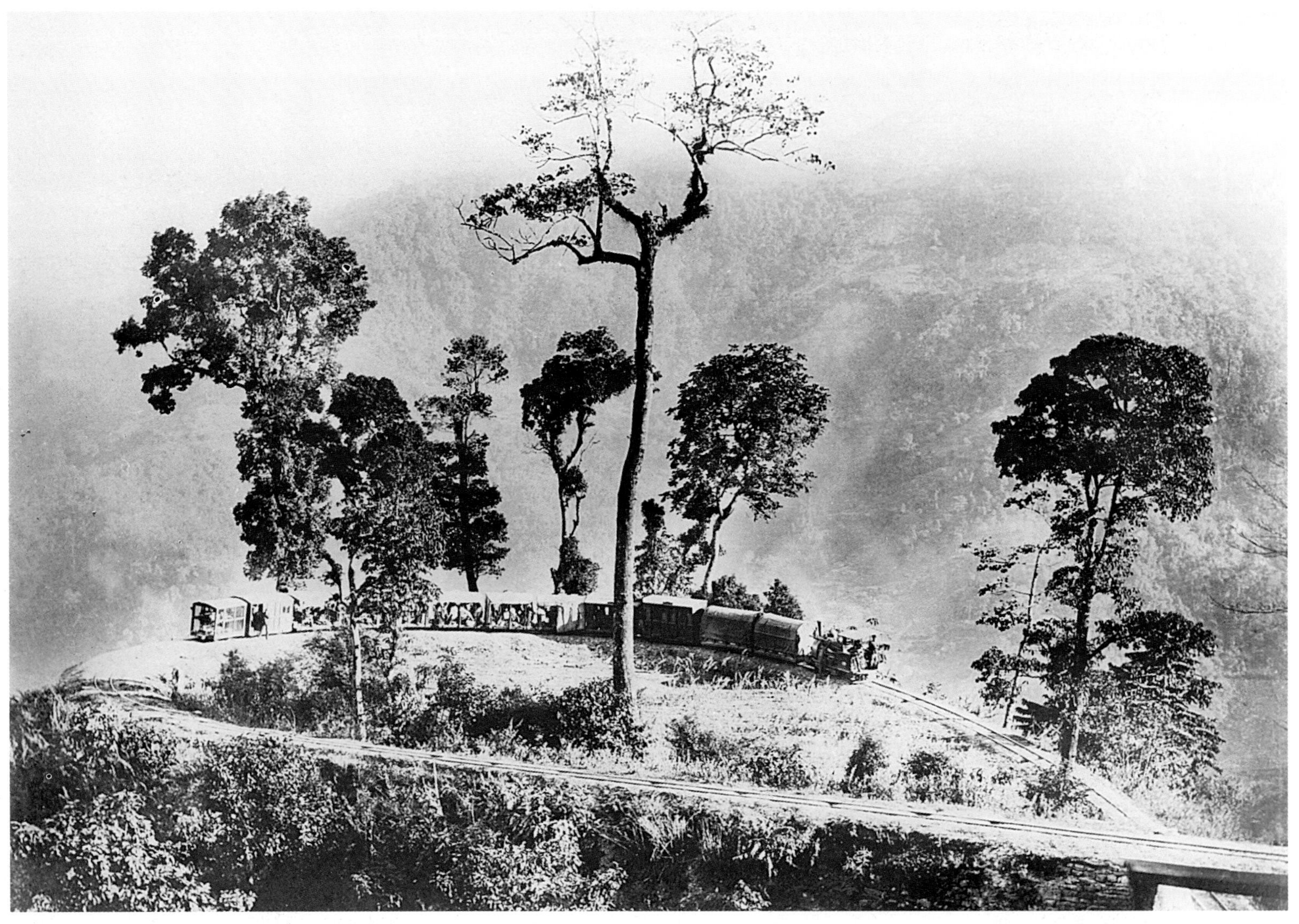

The miniature train which Noel used to travel from Siliguri to Darjeeling in 1924. It still exists, but the road is now so improved that the service is no longer very reliable.

Opposite: A view of bungalows in Darjeeling. 'As we approach in the train, we see the clearings getting larger and more numerous. The gentler slopes are shorn of their forests for tea-cultivation, which with its trim cabbage-like rows of tea bushes does not enhance the beauty of the landscape. The white villas of the hospitable planters dot the mountain sides.'

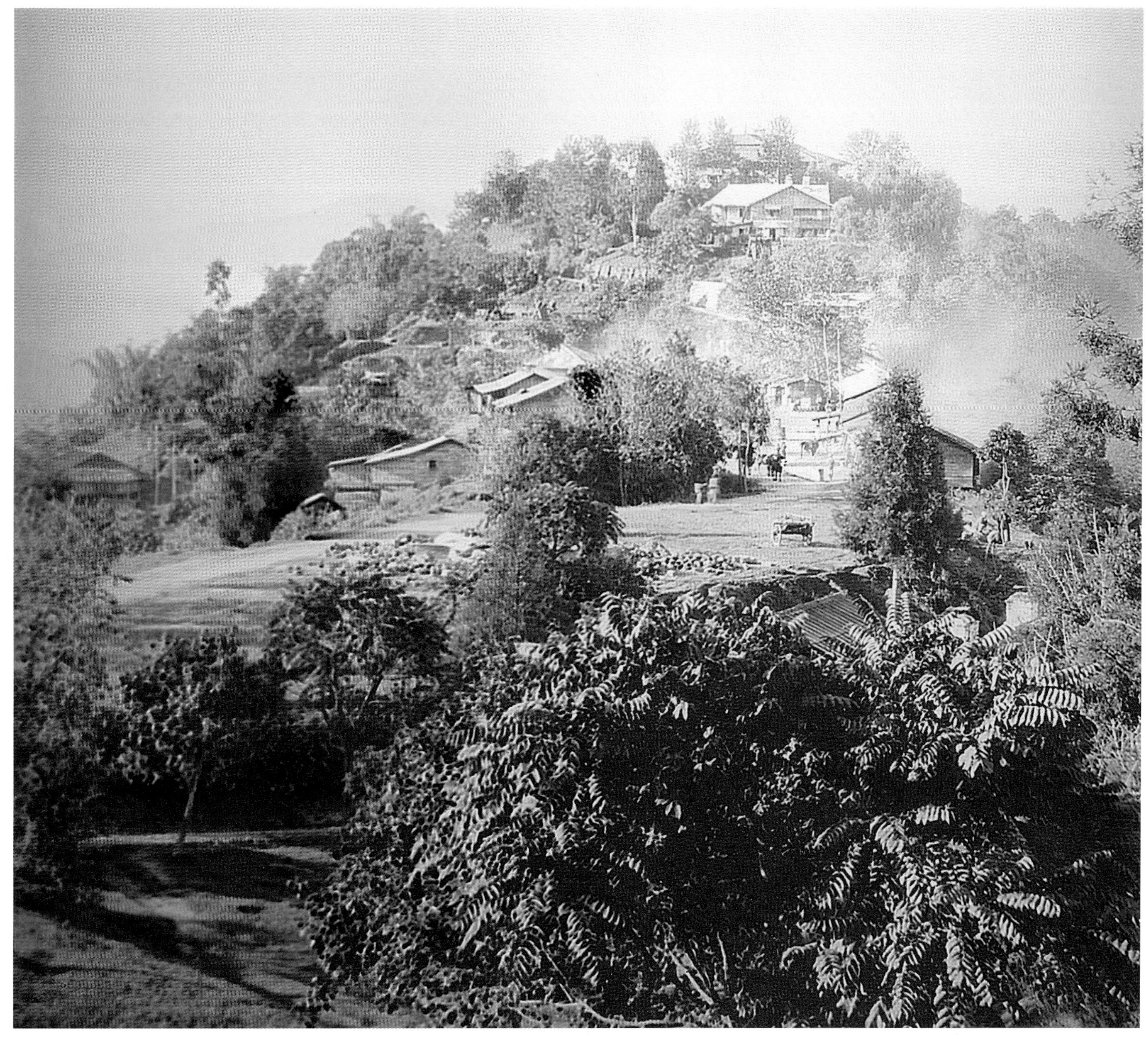

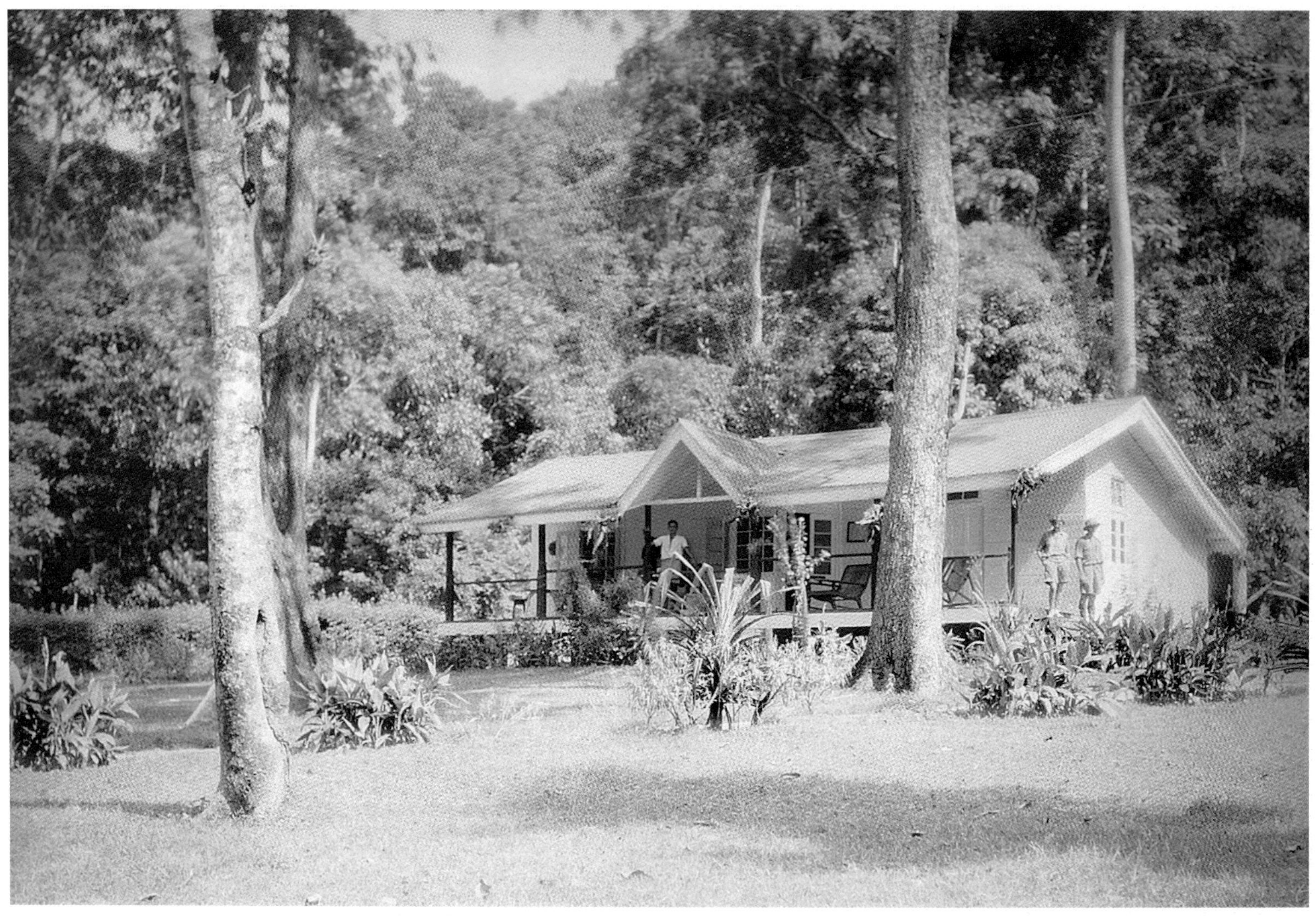

Away from the fierce heat of the plains of India, life in Darjeeling was comfortable for both Indian and British Civil Servants, and soldiers on leave. Cool, shaded and restful, the little town was always bustling with its ever-changing population of visitors.

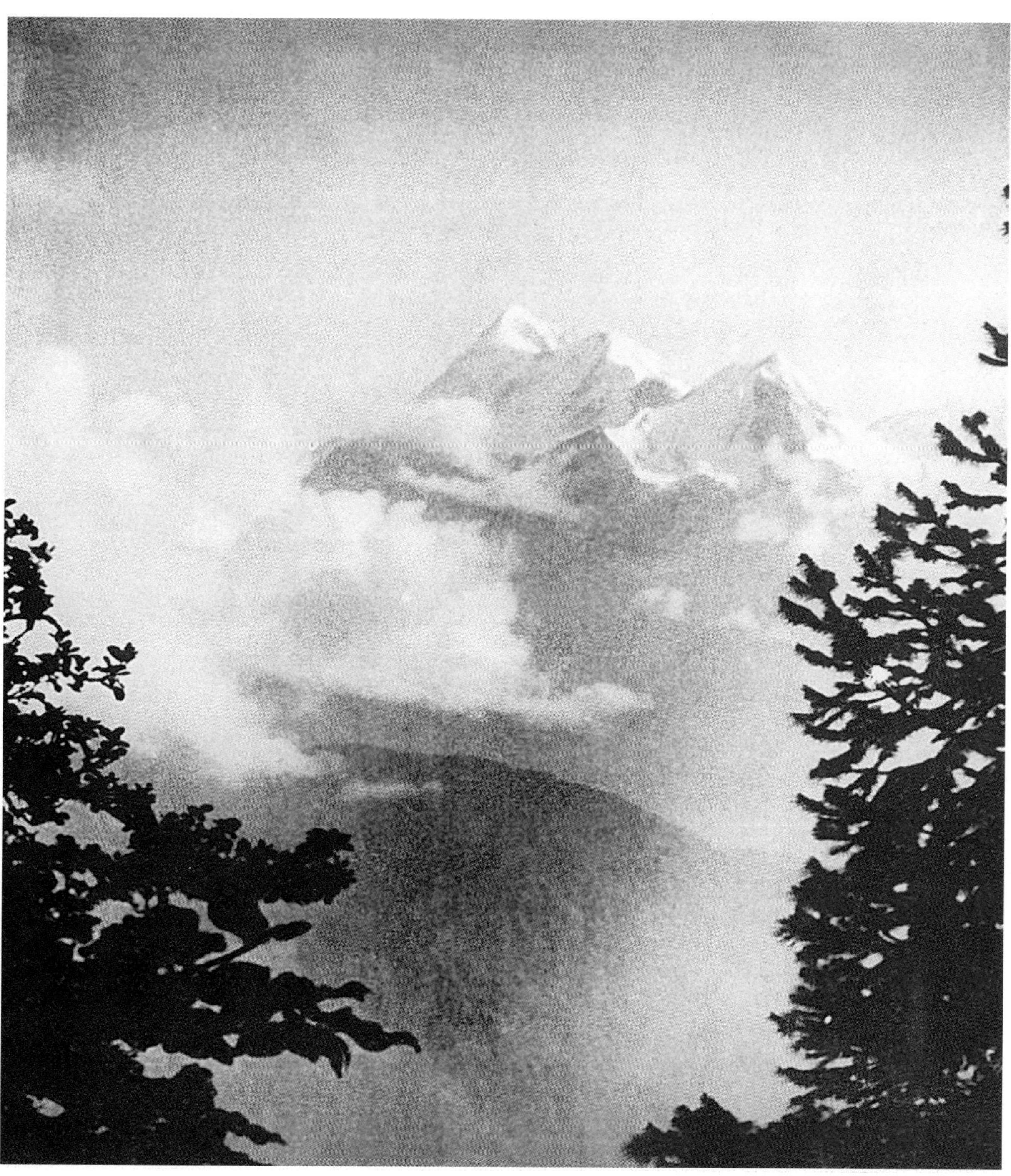

A clear view from the
hill station at the time of
the pioneer expeditions.

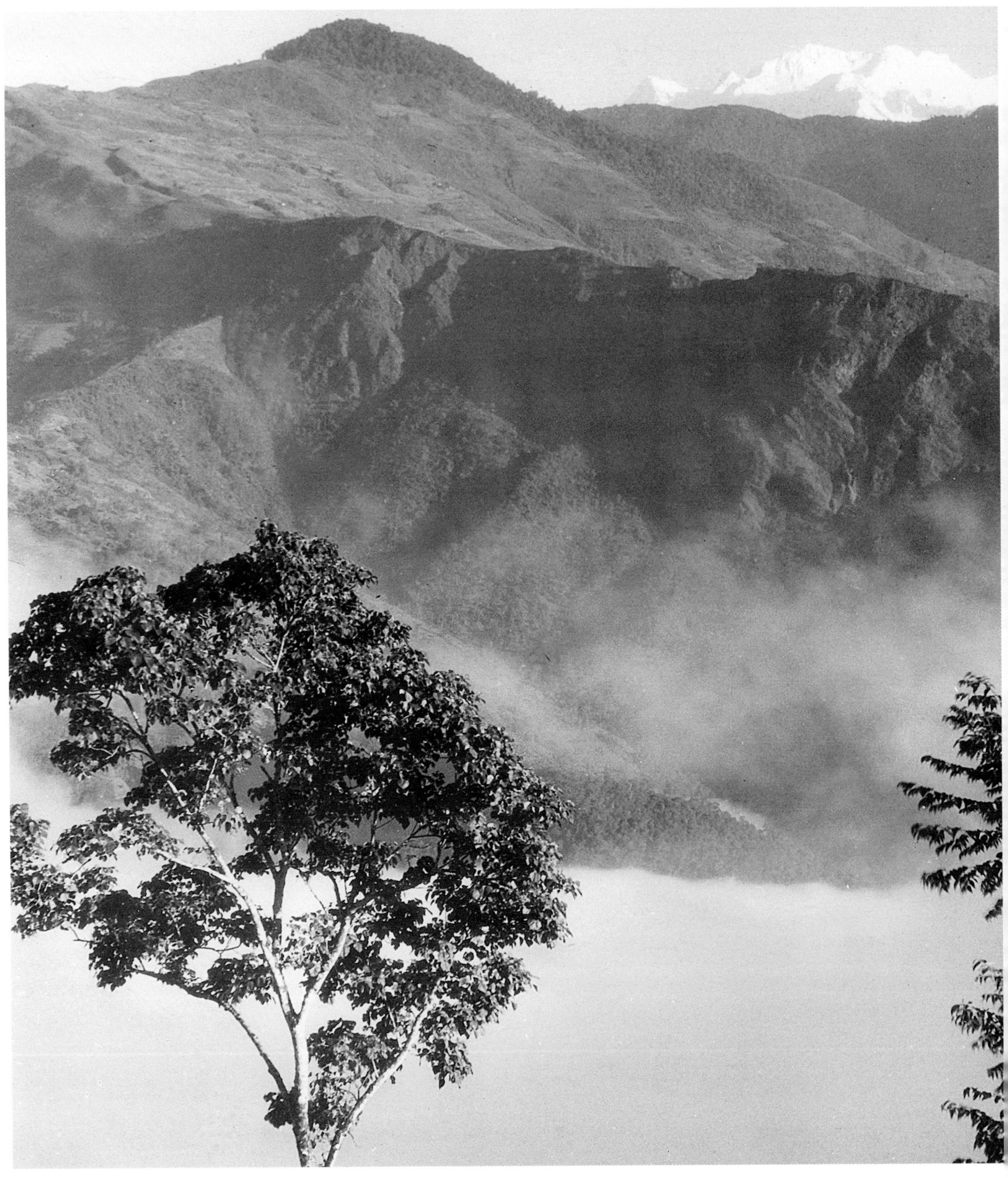

A view of the Himalayas from Darjeeling. Some 120 miles from Everest, it is 7,000 feet above sea level, and the trek from there to Base Camp covered 300 miles, as the expedition had to travel first north, then west and finally south to the great mountain.

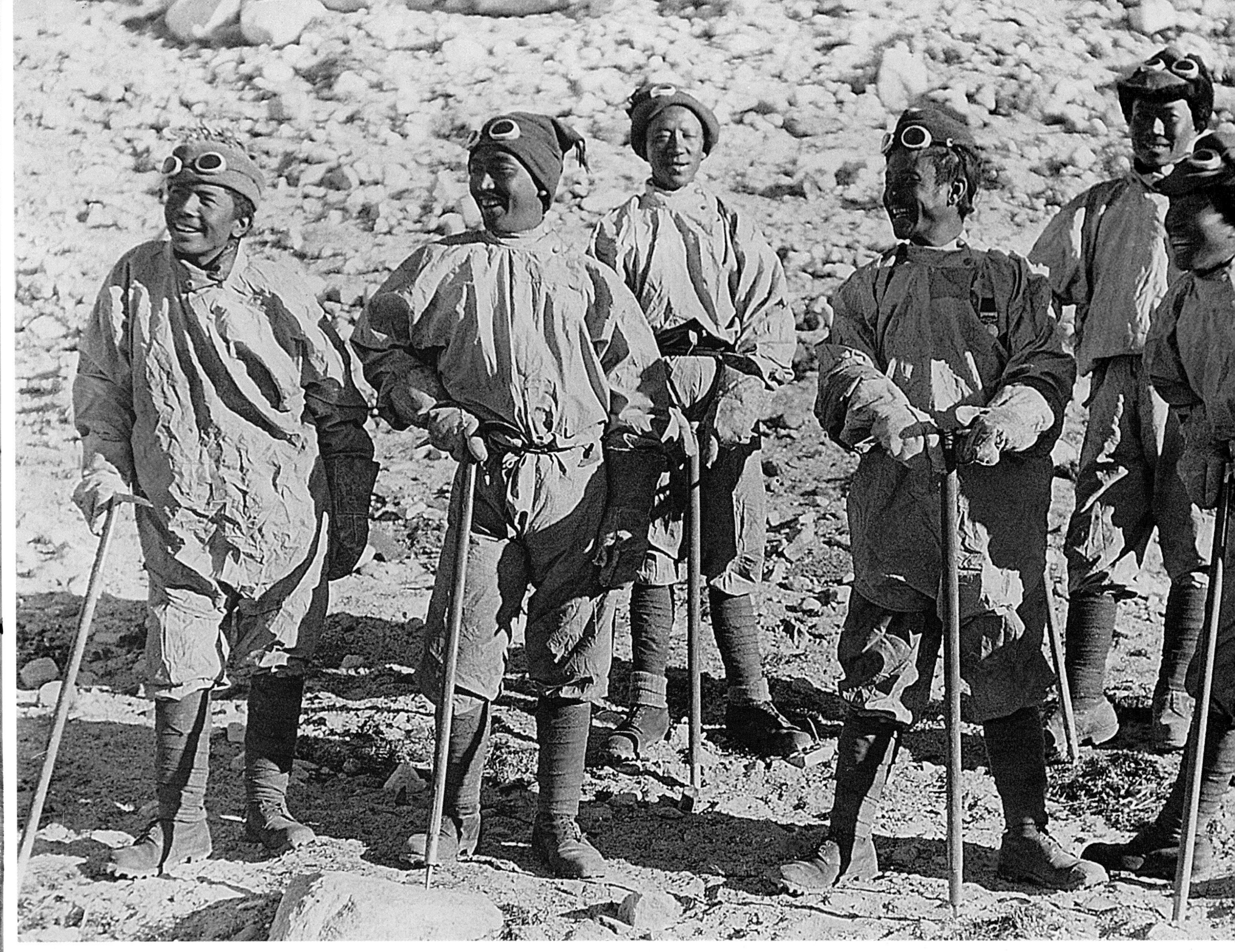

A group of sherpas, ready to embark with the European climbers. Early explorers had even brought Swiss guides with them to the Himalayas, as the power and usefulness of the sherpa had not been understood until Dr Kellas realized their potential, predicting that they would be able to carry loads to great heights.

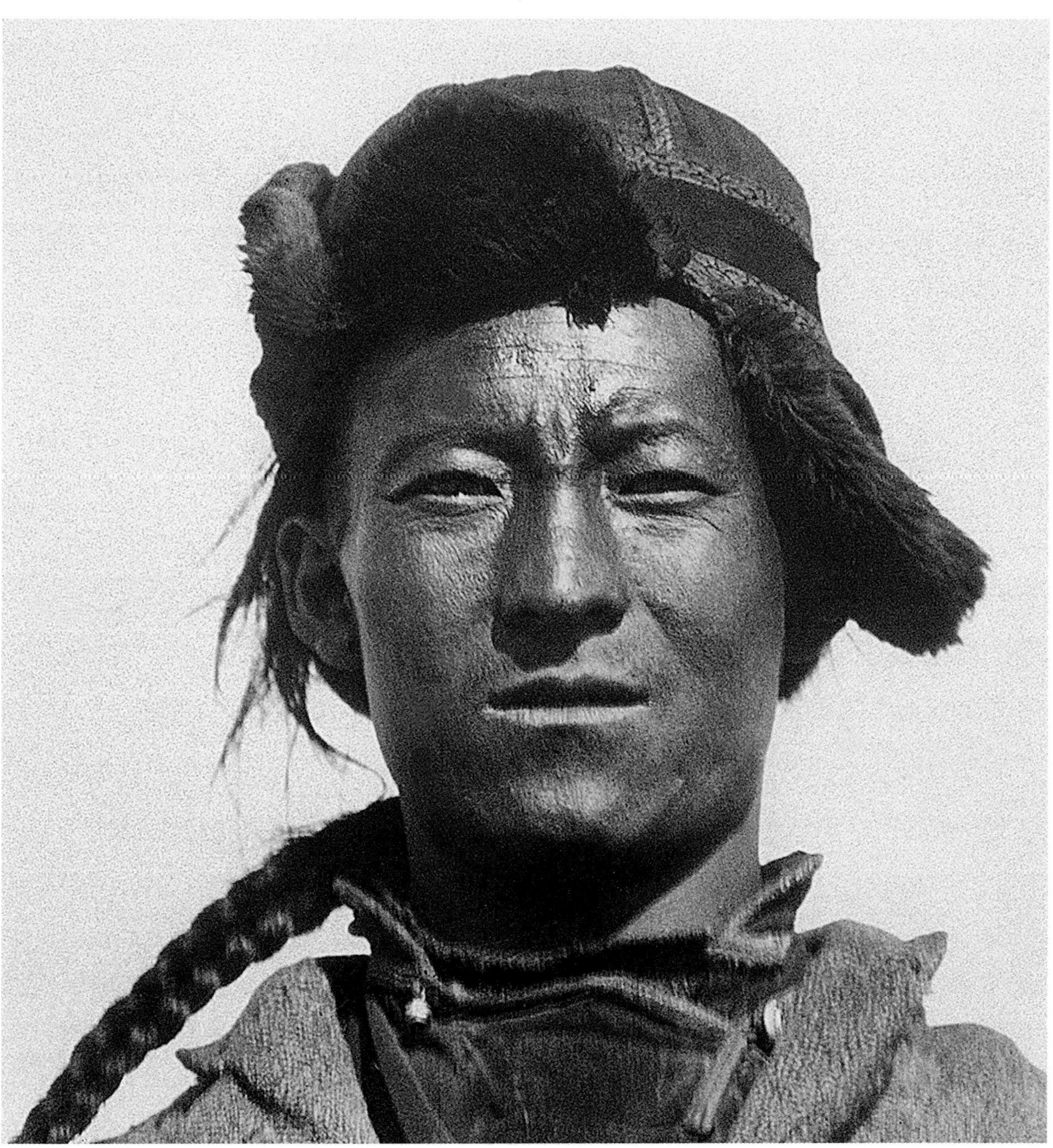

A typical mountain dweller, employed to carry the heavy loads on the mountain. From a selected group of 150, about 50 were to be chosen for their special strength and dexterity for altitude climbing.

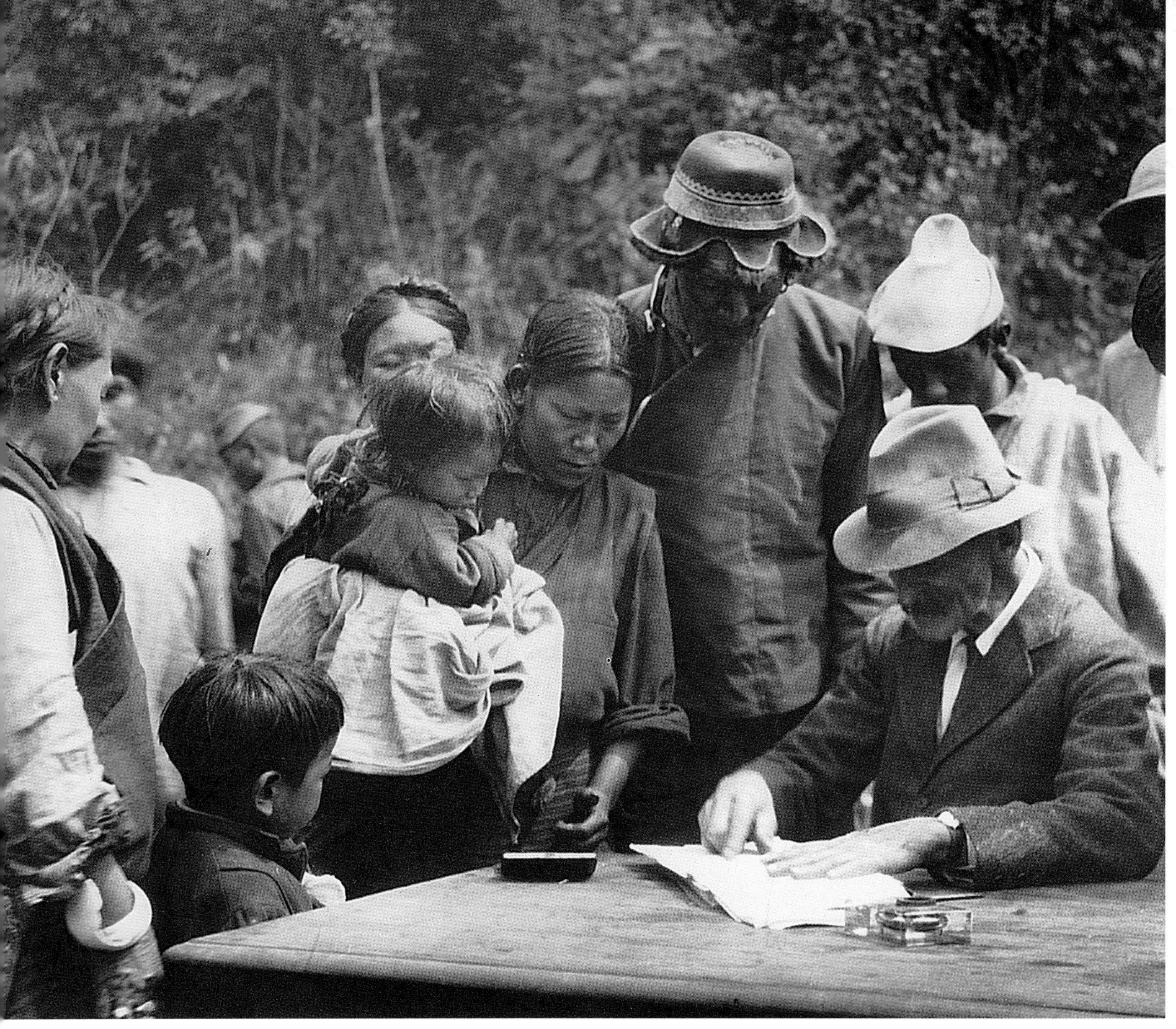

Once selected, the families of the porters – still called coolies in those days – had to be identified, in order that the pay would be given to the appropriate family. In such a close-knit community many families bore the same name and confusion easily arose, so family members had their thumbprint taken for positive identification.

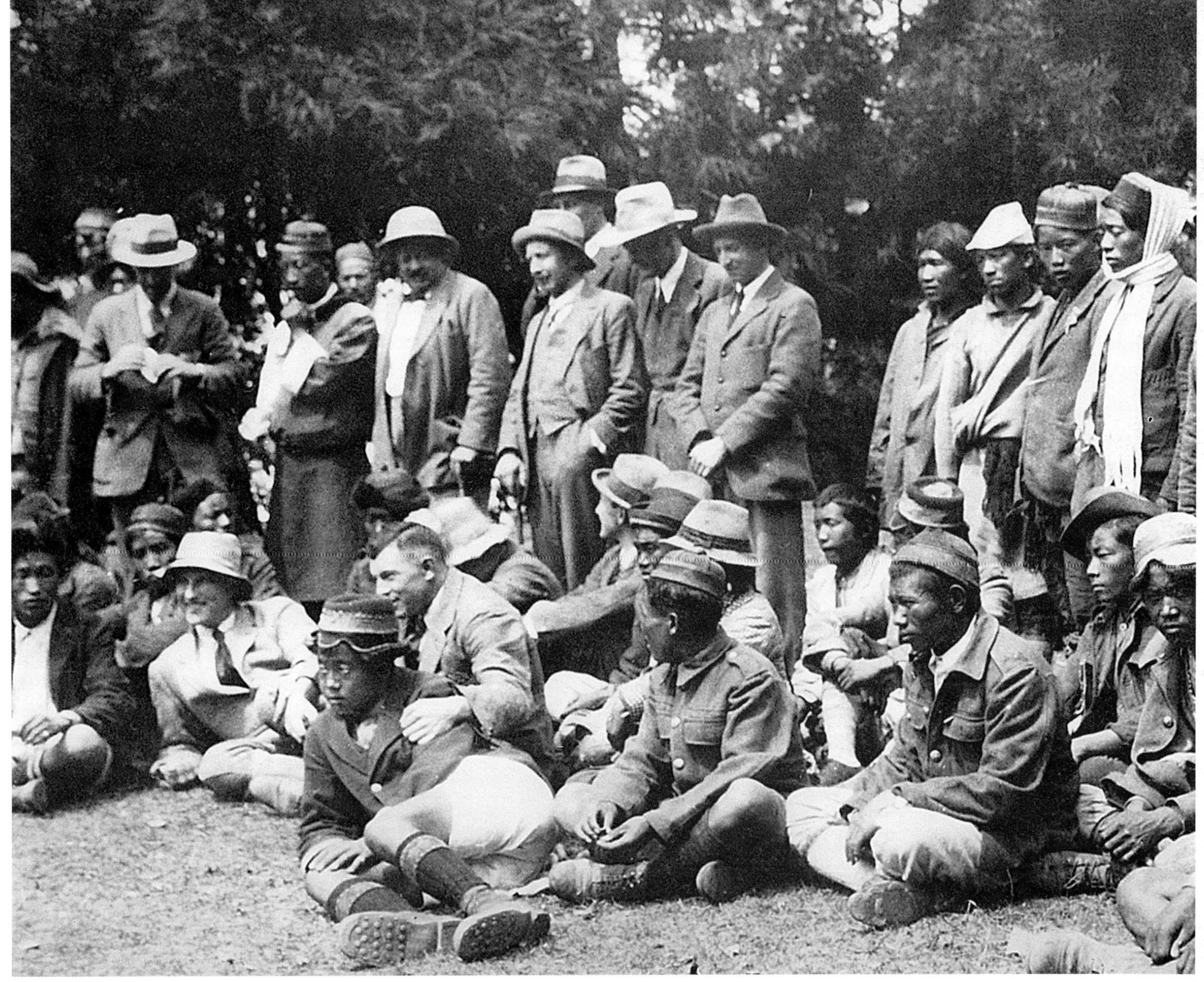

The group ready to leave Darjeeling, 25 March 1924. General Bruce is the prominent figure in the back row wearing a bow tie; Mallory and Irvine are sitting in the group in front of General Bruce. 'For me,' Noel remarked at the time, 'as I rode forward, the enterprise presented a singular blend of remembrance and emotion, for I could look back upon an adventure started ten years before, to which the experience came as a climax and completion.'

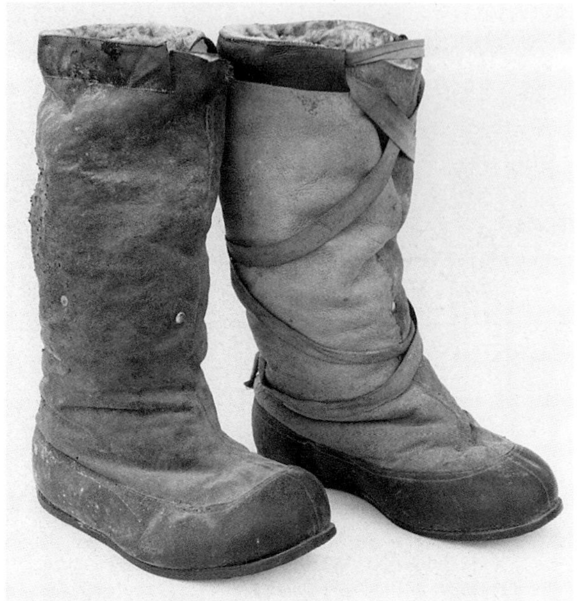

Noel's camp boots. Each member of the expedition was measured for a pair of leather boots, which were hand-made and then covered with sheepskin. The soles were hard and smooth, especially suited for camp life.

Some of the gear used by the expedition, which amounted to 350 yak-loads and 50 coolie-loads. Most of the gear had been designed and made in England, and was transported by sea and rail to Darjeeling, where the journey began with mule transport but later transferred to yaks.

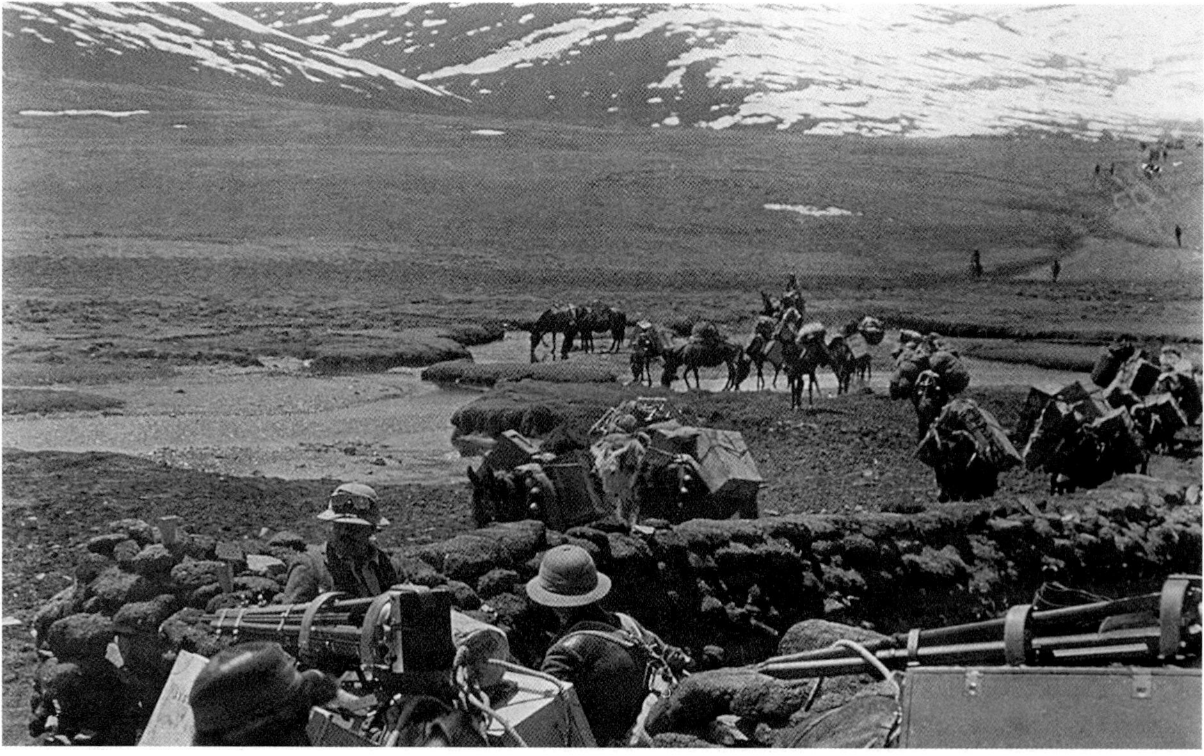

The postcard designed by Noel as advance publicity. It depicts Base Camp, and on the bottom line mentioned the film to be shown at the Scala Theatre in November 1924.

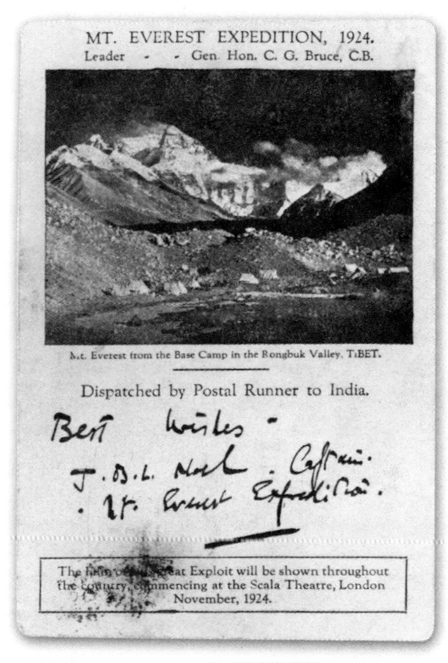

The front of the card, showing the commemorative stamp designed by the artist Francis Helps, depicting an ancient Hindu religious symbol in each corner. The cards were addressed in England, transported out with the expedition and sent back bearing an Indian postage stamp.

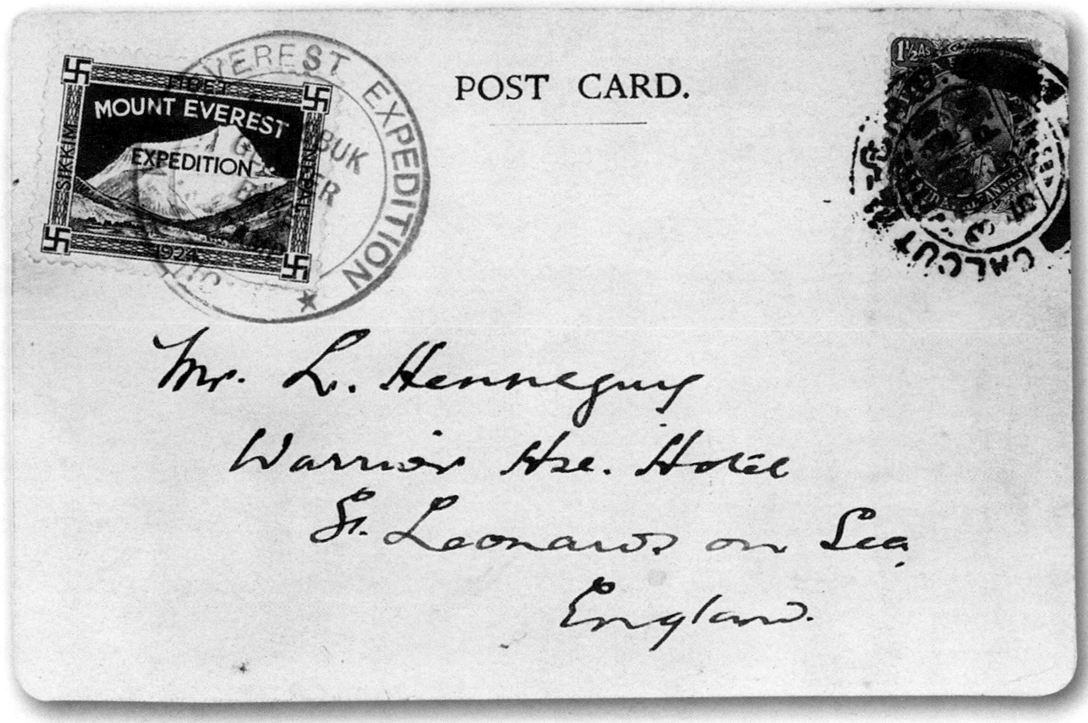

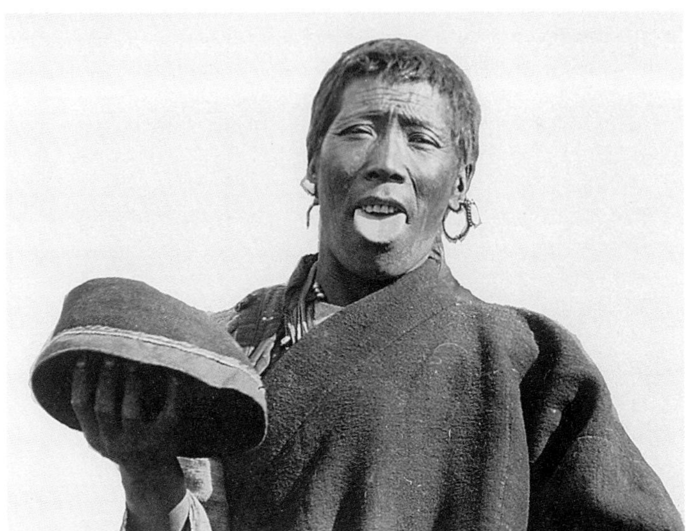

This may look like an obscene gesture, but is in fact a greeting. The Tibetan puts out his tongue and presses forward an ear in a sign of submission.

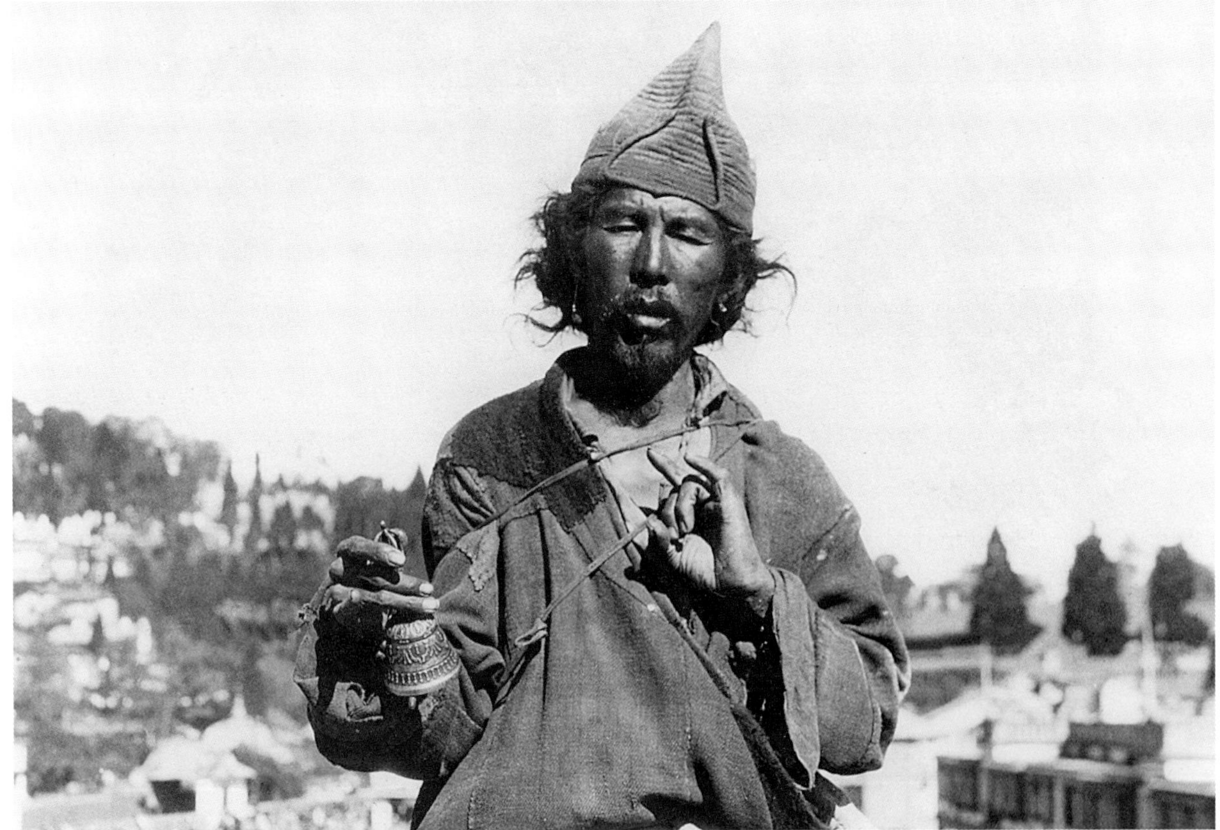

A typical visitor, who had crossed into India to trade, when Darjeeling was a thriving centre at the time of the expeditions of 1922 and 1924.

CHAPTER 2

PHOTOGRAPHY ON THE MOUNTAIN

The experience of photographing in 1922 had taught many lessons, and now, in 1924, Noel intended to do many things differently. Having staked a huge sum of his own money and the trust of some influential friends, this had to be an absolutely undeniable success: he needed to capitalize on what would be a great world achievement and recoup the financial investment which he and his business associates had made.

He decided that most of the undeveloped film – both still and moving – would be sent back to Darjeeling, where he had bought a plot of land and had had a photographic laboratory built and well equipped with developing tanks, drying apparatus, an electric generator and chemicals. He had engaged Arthur Pereira as director of photography in Darjeeling, who was to prepare for the runners, working in relays to bring despatches and photographs from the expedition down to Phari Dzong. Here the Indian postal service took over, and specially designed waterproof sacks, with their precious contents, were brought to the laboratory by further relays of runners, each covering his section at a trot to the music of bells tied to the short spear he carried as protection against wild beasts and other perils of the road.

Noel had also made modifications to the cameras and his photographic strategy. He needed to be mobile and independent, so that he could move ahead, or remain behind, but able to catch up quickly. The cameras were carried on chosen mules, fitted with special saddlery. They were contained in metal boxes, with clip handles, so that the lid opened in an instant. If it rained, the lid acted as an umbrella. The boxes were double-cavity, watertight, quite light and painted white to reflect the sun. He had two muleteers, who became expert in taking the camera from the box and setting it on the tripod in thirty seconds. Later, at higher altitudes, the mules were put out to graze and the cameras were mounted on metal rucksack frames carried by porters. Noel described their operation:

> When I wanted to take a picture, the porter turned his back, I opened the box, and took the camera out. Another porter carried the tripod and put it up. There was no screw in the tripod head. It had a special device which Mr Newman made for me in which the [cine] camera slid on in two grooves, so there was no fumbling about in the cold trying to find the screw head.

The air was so dry that the static charge would collect on celluloid film very easily, so Mr Newman had invented a retainer, with a sponge of water, inside the camera, which released a certain amount of humidity and introduced a magnet into the gate mechanism in the hope that it would attract the static charge away from the film's surface: 'the camera had magazines whose mouths opened when the camera door was shut, so the film came through an open gate and didn't rub against anything'. It was also fitted with an electric motor to permit time-lapse photography, a novel feature in those days. This cinematograph camera, constructed of Duralumin, was as strong as steel and as light as aluminium: fully loaded with 400ft of 35mm film, it weighed less than 20 pounds. It had been beautifully crafted to cope with the intense heat of the plains of India, the humidity of the forests, and now the notorious wind on the mountain and dryness at altitude.

The inability of the operator in the extreme cold was another matter, but, as Noel recounted, the worst problem was physical exhaustion from lack of oxygen:

> Your movements are very slow, and the trouble with high altitudes is that the lack of oxygen to the blood not only slows you down physically, but it slows your brain. You don't think quickly. You are muddled, and often appear to be drunk. The idea of using a camera is too much; your fingers fumble with a screw, and you drop the screw. You just don't care.

Above a certain height, there was no possibility of the motion-picture equipment accompanying the climbers. Anticipating this, Noel had made by Taylor, Taylor & Hobson a 20-inch Cooke telephoto lens. 'It had a six-power finder telescope, which clipped on to the camera, and was synchronised with the optical axis of the lens. So, the image in the finder telescope was in the aperture of the lens.' The long focus lens was the same one which had proved its value on the previous expedition, but now it had been provided with additional steadying supports. Noel used panchromatic film, not in standard use until later, in order to capture dark skies and cloud formations, with the help of red and yellow filters.

Although he climbed to 23,000 feet, Noel planned to position himself at his so-called Eagle's Nest at 22,000 feet; this camera position was set in rocks above Camp III, from where the pyramid of Everest was some three miles away in a straight line. In fact, he remained there for nine and a half days, ready, with the aid of the telephoto lens, to film the various attempts which would be made on the summit; he expected to be able to film the climbers at 26,000 feet, from a distance of two miles.

In addition to the specially designed Newman Sinclair cinematograph camera, he had other cine cameras and highly sophisticated still cameras, in which he used

Eastman film. Colour photography, however, was still not a feasible option, so Noel laboriously noted the colours of every still image by means of an American-designed chart and a system of numbers, so that he might faithfully reproduce the colours: once the negatives had been converted into glass plates he could hand-tint them, and then stick a cover glass on top to preserve both the original image and the delicate colours. But Noel was aware that to have good weather and a clear view of any summit attempt was a hope rather than a foregone conclusion, so he had small cine cameras specially designed, capable of taking two minutes of film, which he intended to give to the pairs of climbers as they prepared to make a summit bid, so that they could record the very moment they achieved their goal.

Having bought all the photographic rights of the 1924 attempt on the mountain, Noel was keen to attract newspaper coverage. Despite his feelings of animosity towards anything that smacked of sponsorship, Hinks, secretary of the Mount Everest Committee, had been persuaded to allow *The Times* to have access to a certain number of images, which were then syndicated to other newspapers, so keeping alive the drama as it unfolded. Noel had a separate agreement with *Pathé News* to supply film of the expedition's progress, which would keep interest in the project active, so that when he returned to England, and the film was ready, the public would be keen to see a photographic record of the adventure.

One of the few photographs taken by Noel in 1913.

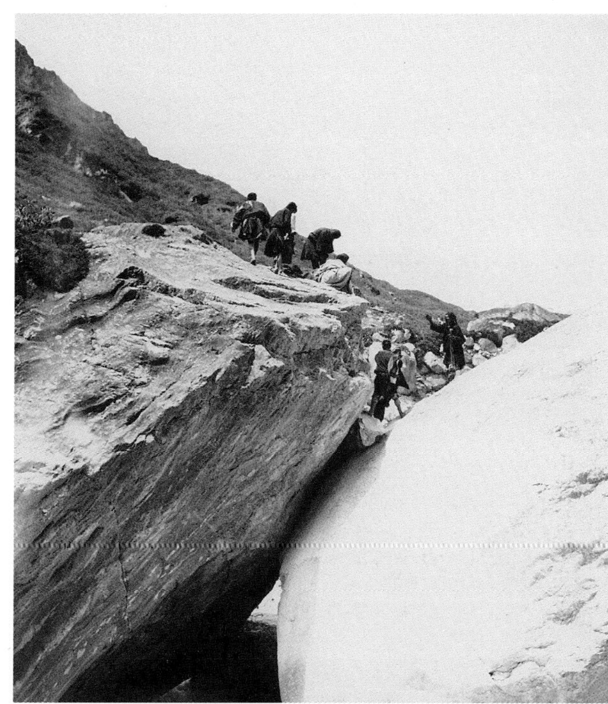

In 1913 Noel had to make the choice between hiring pack animals to carry more gear, or limiting the amount of equipment to be carried. Here is his trusted band of hillsmen with huge loads.

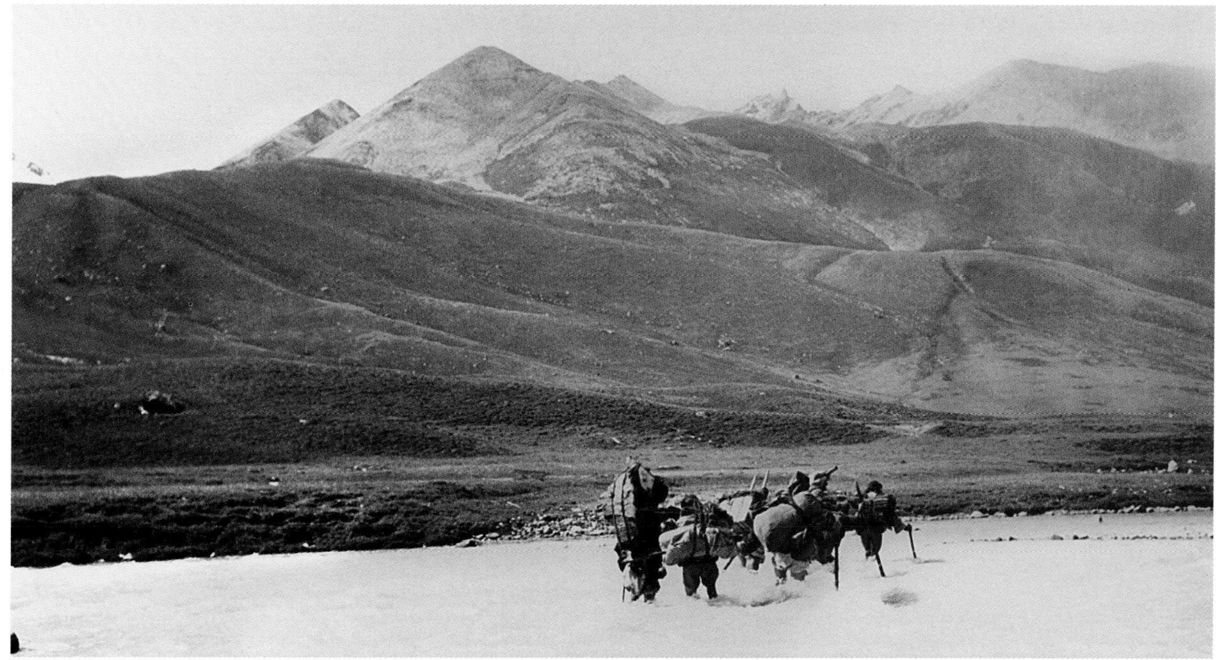

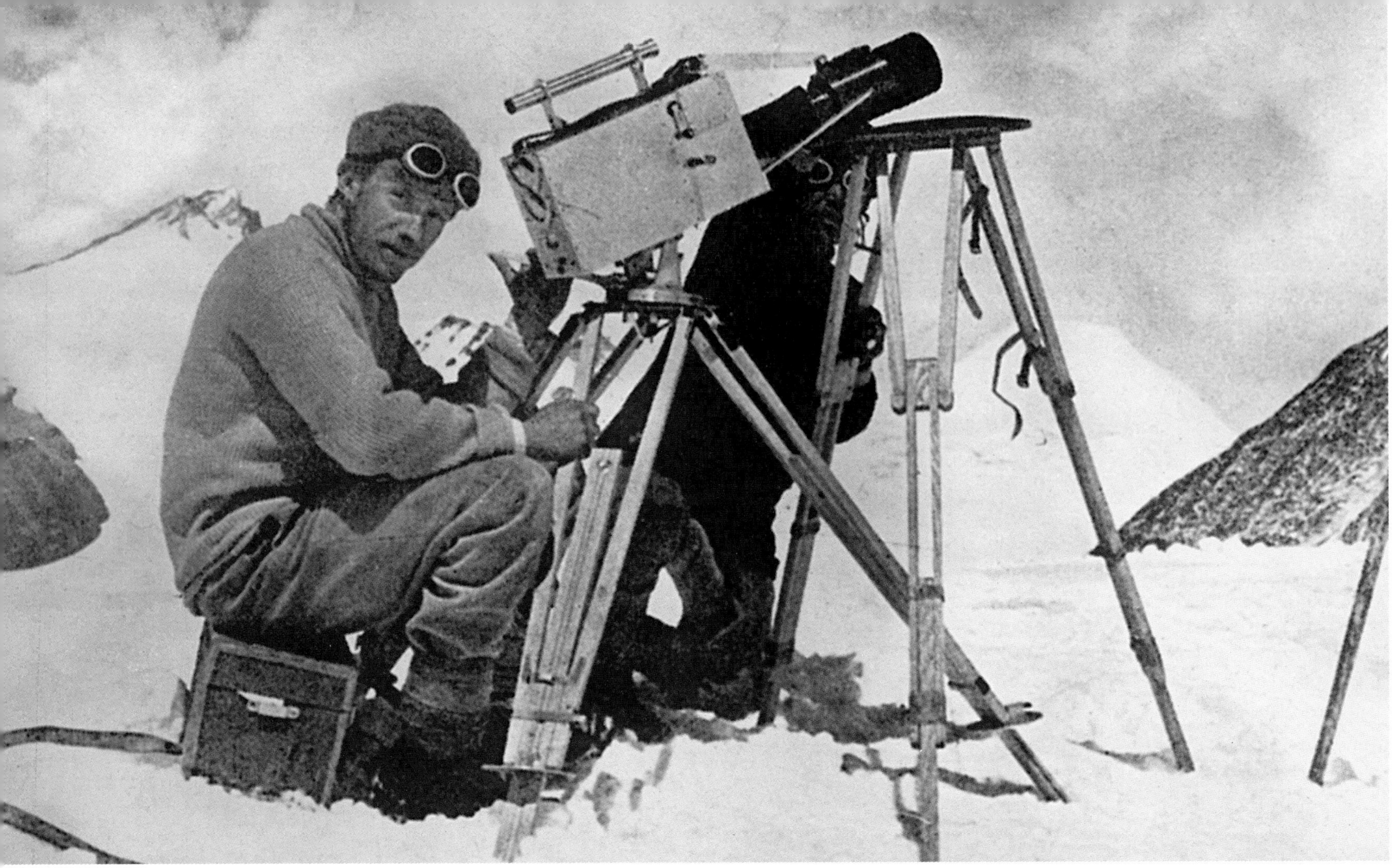

Noel with his cine camera in 1922. It was specially
designed and made by Newman Sinclair, based on the
designs used by Herbert Ponting, who had accompanied
Scott on the expedition to the South Pole. (© *Royal
Geographical Society*)

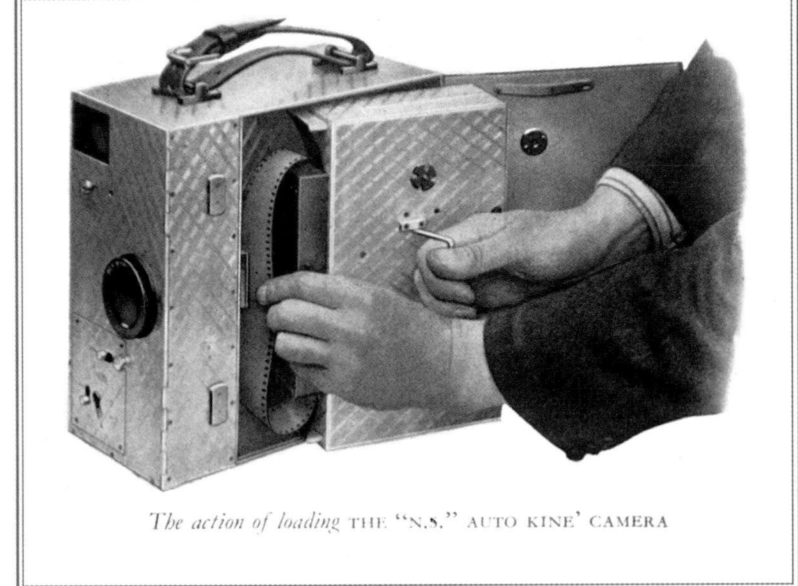

A page from the Newman Sinclair catalogue,
showing the action of loading the camera.

A page from a Sinclair Newman catalogue, showing the basic auto kine camera. In 1924 an electric motor was fitted, which enabled Noel to take time-lapse images. His equipment made use of many other modifications, very modern by the standards of the day.

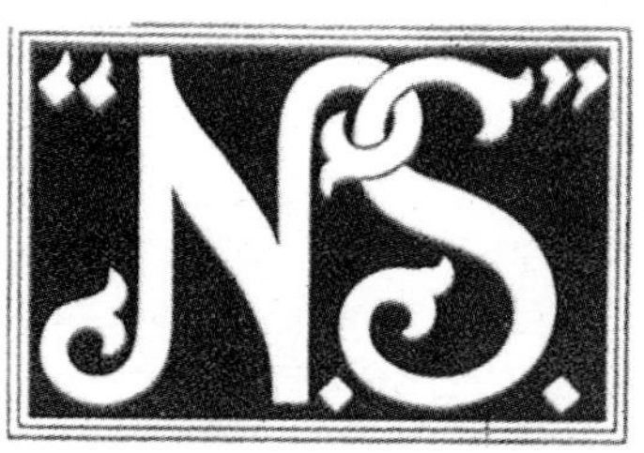

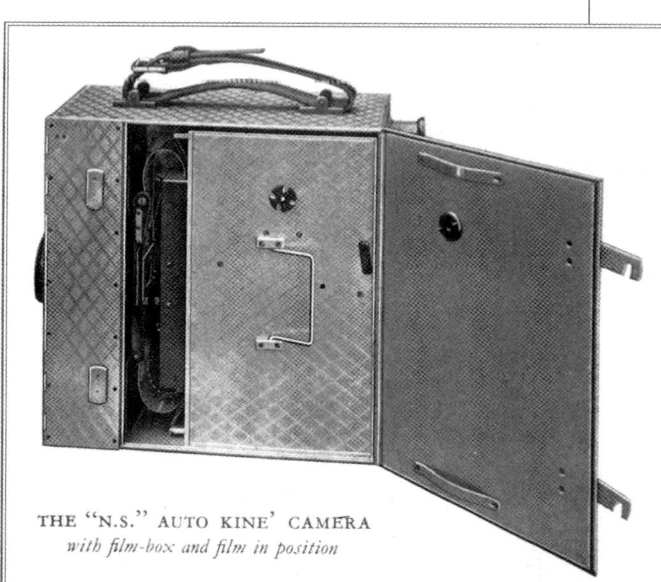

THE "N.S." AUTO KINE' CAMERA
with film-box and film in position

The camera with film in position. The date of the catalogue is unknown, and the firm no longer exists.

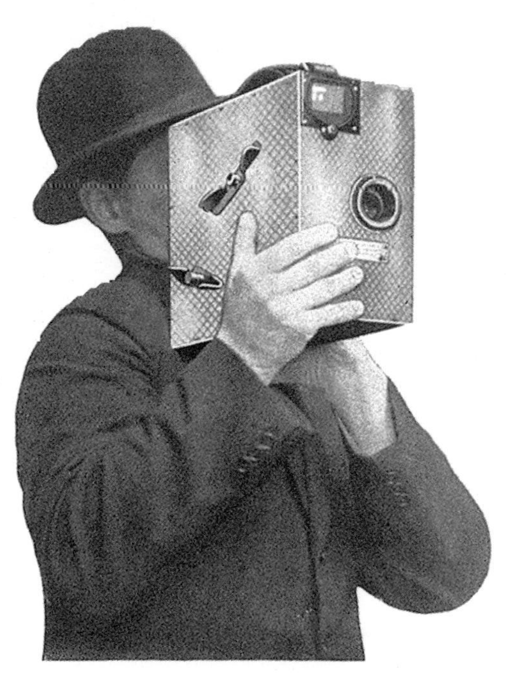

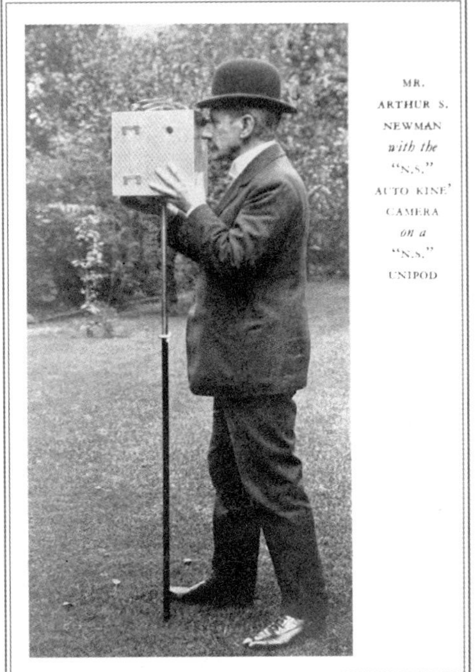

Another page from a Sinclair Newman catalogue, showing Arthur Newman demonstrating the monopod.

Noel setting up one of his still cameras to take photographs of Gurkhas, with General Bruce sitting on the right. The tripod was made of mahogany, and the camera was fitted with brass screws and leather bellows.

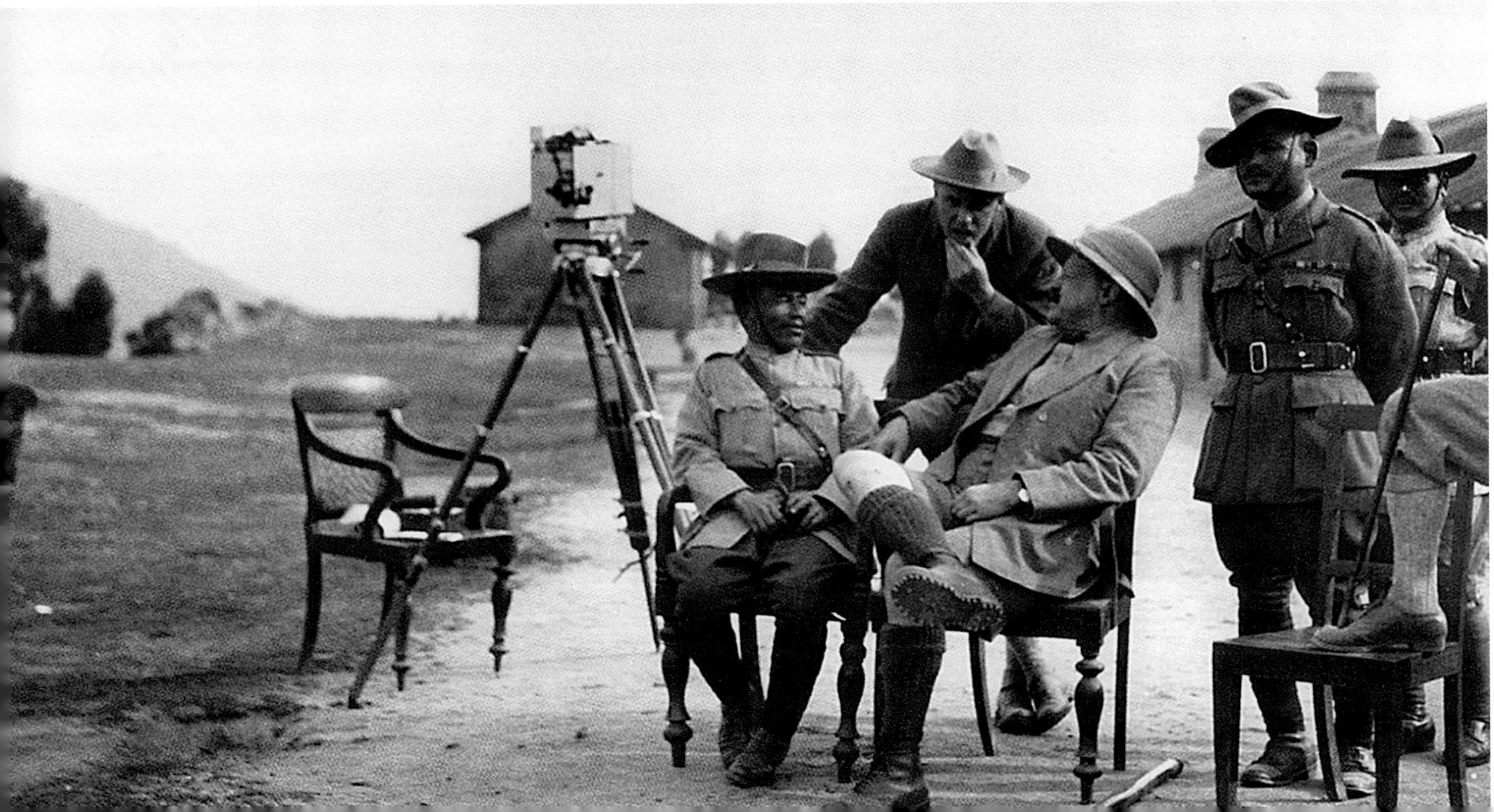

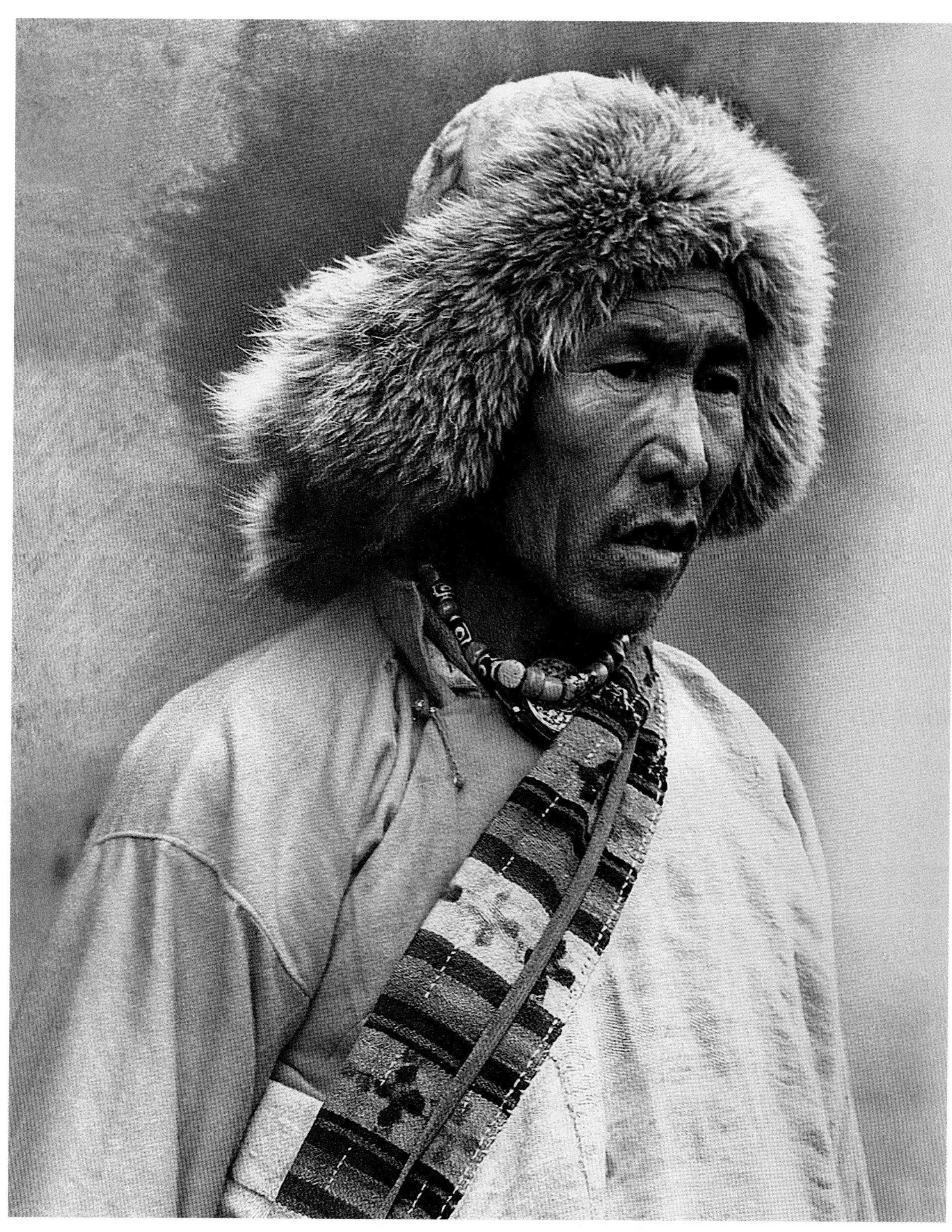

Noel's favourite muleteer. His porters were trained to open the metal boxes and mount the camera in minutes, all while the apparatus was being carried on mules, so that he would always be ready to capture a scene. Yaks were not suitable, being too capricious, so porters were used to carry the cameras in the higher regions.

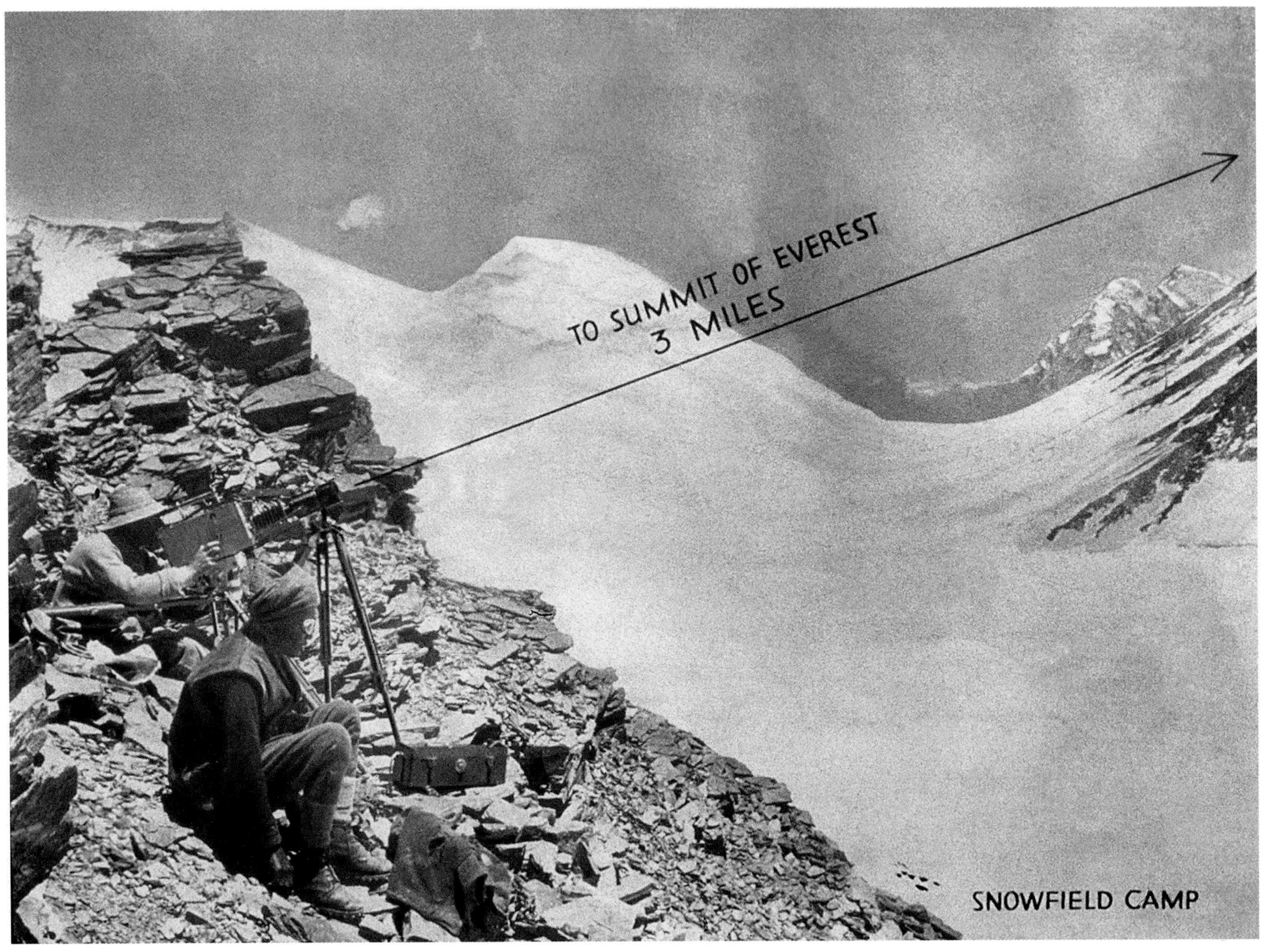

Noel's photo station at 22,000 feet, which he selected to enable him to view, weather permitting, the various attempts to be made on the summit. He called this perch 'Eagle's Nest' because it was fairly inaccessible, but it afforded a view of the summit of Everest, three miles away as the crow flies. The position of Camp III, known as 'Snowfield', is clearly indicated below.

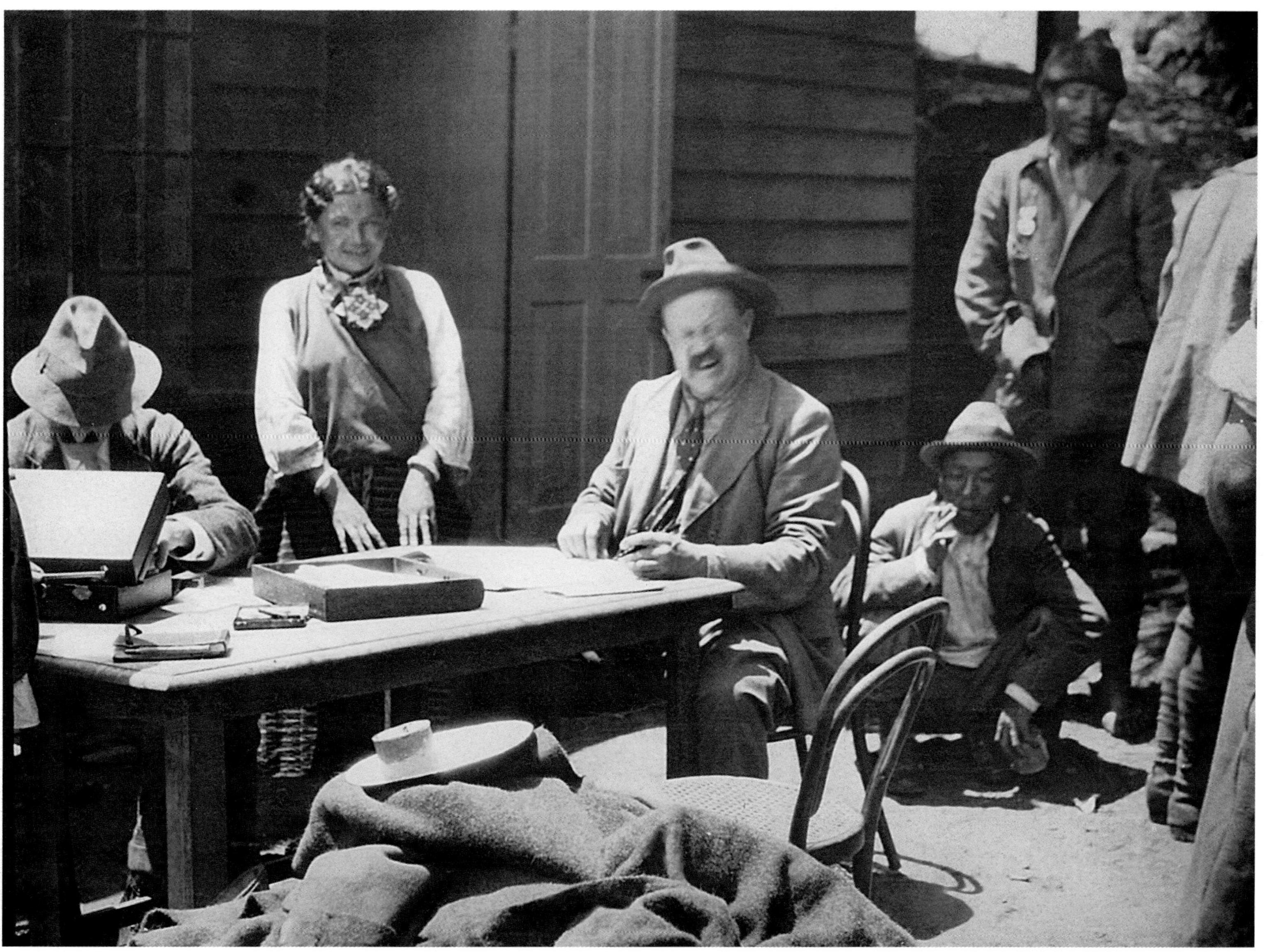

General Bruce outside the photographic laboratory. Noel had bought land in Darjeeling and engaged staff to set up sophisticated equipment for developing and processing the photographic material which was sent down from the expedition.

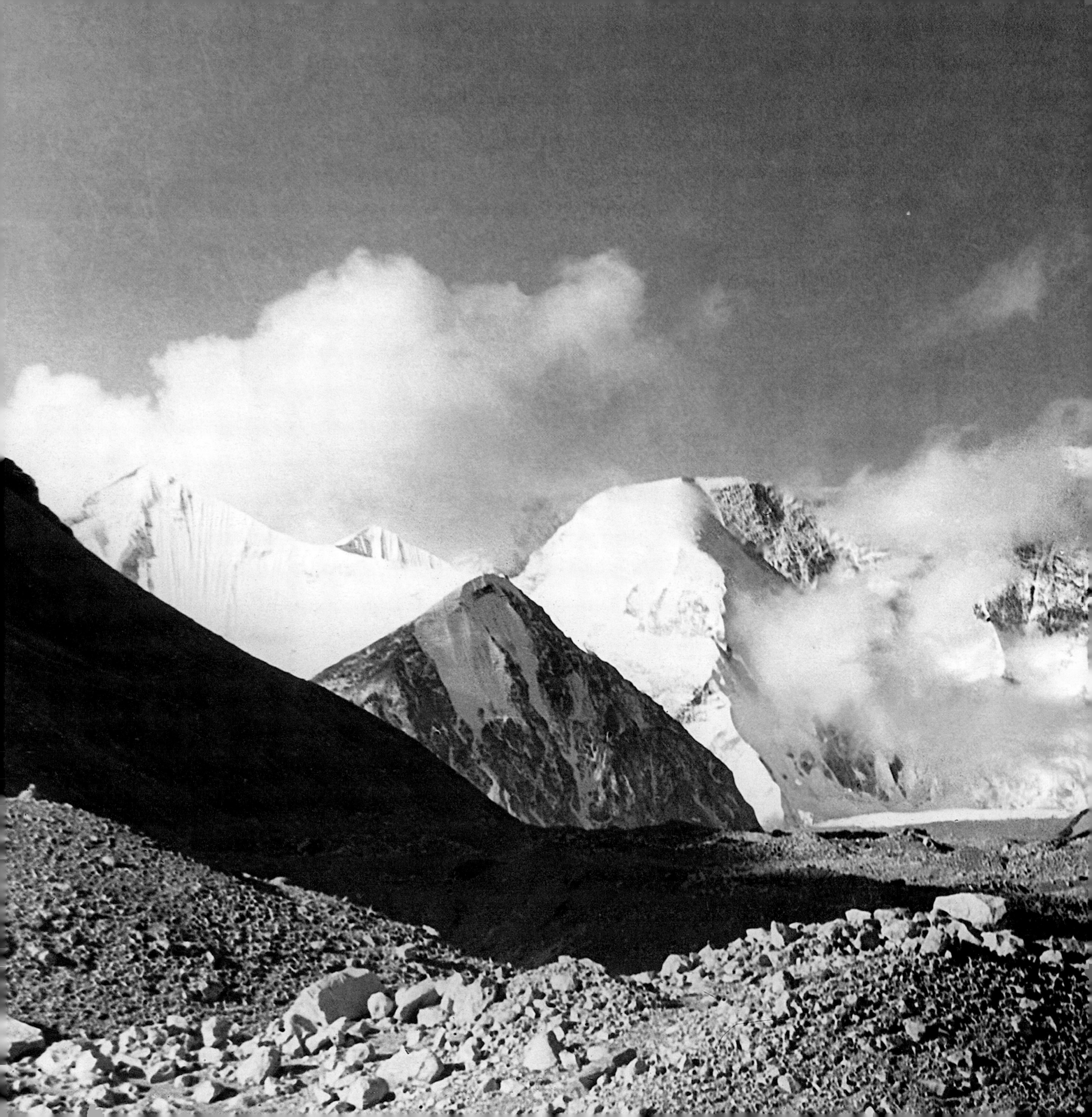

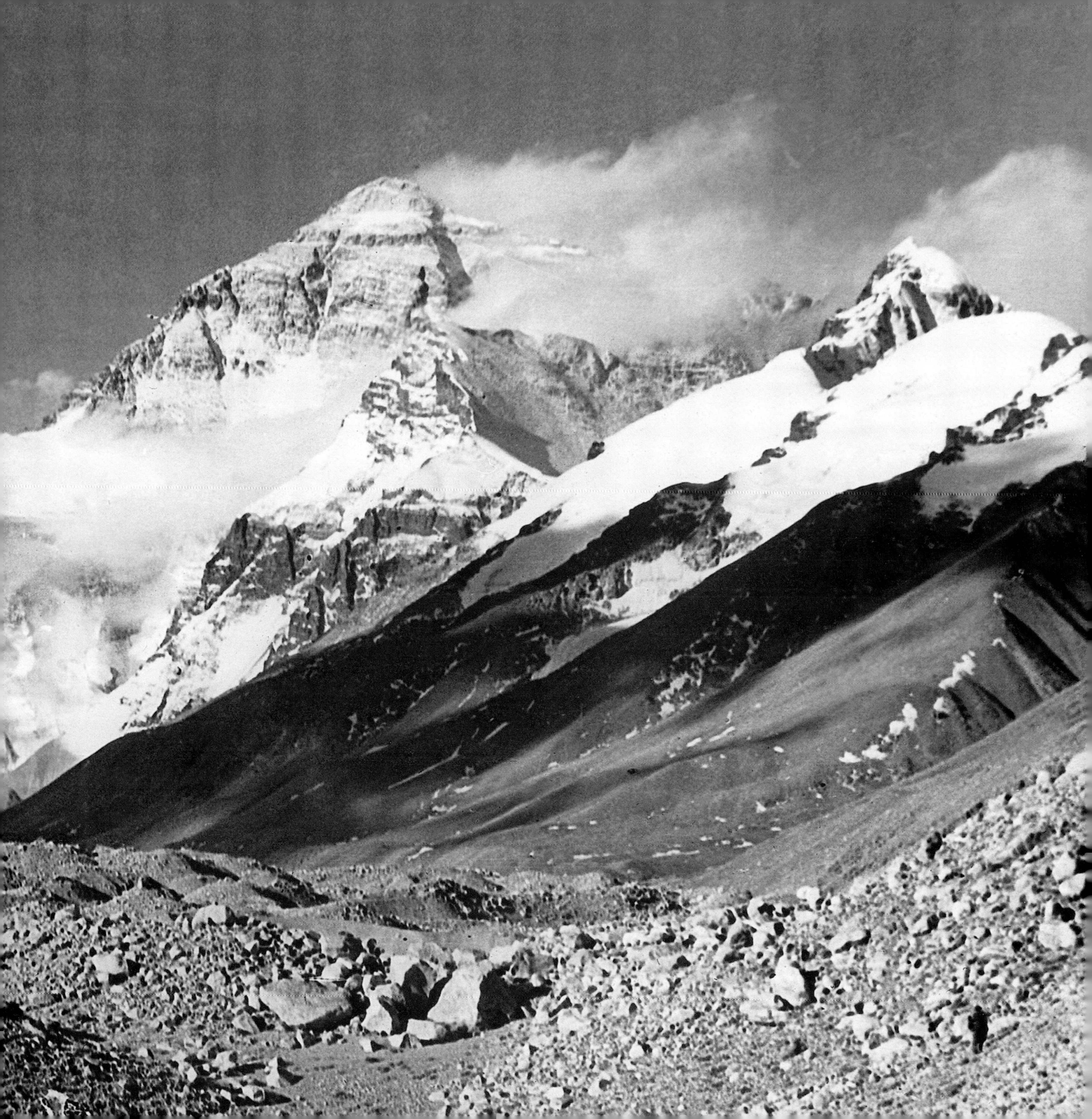

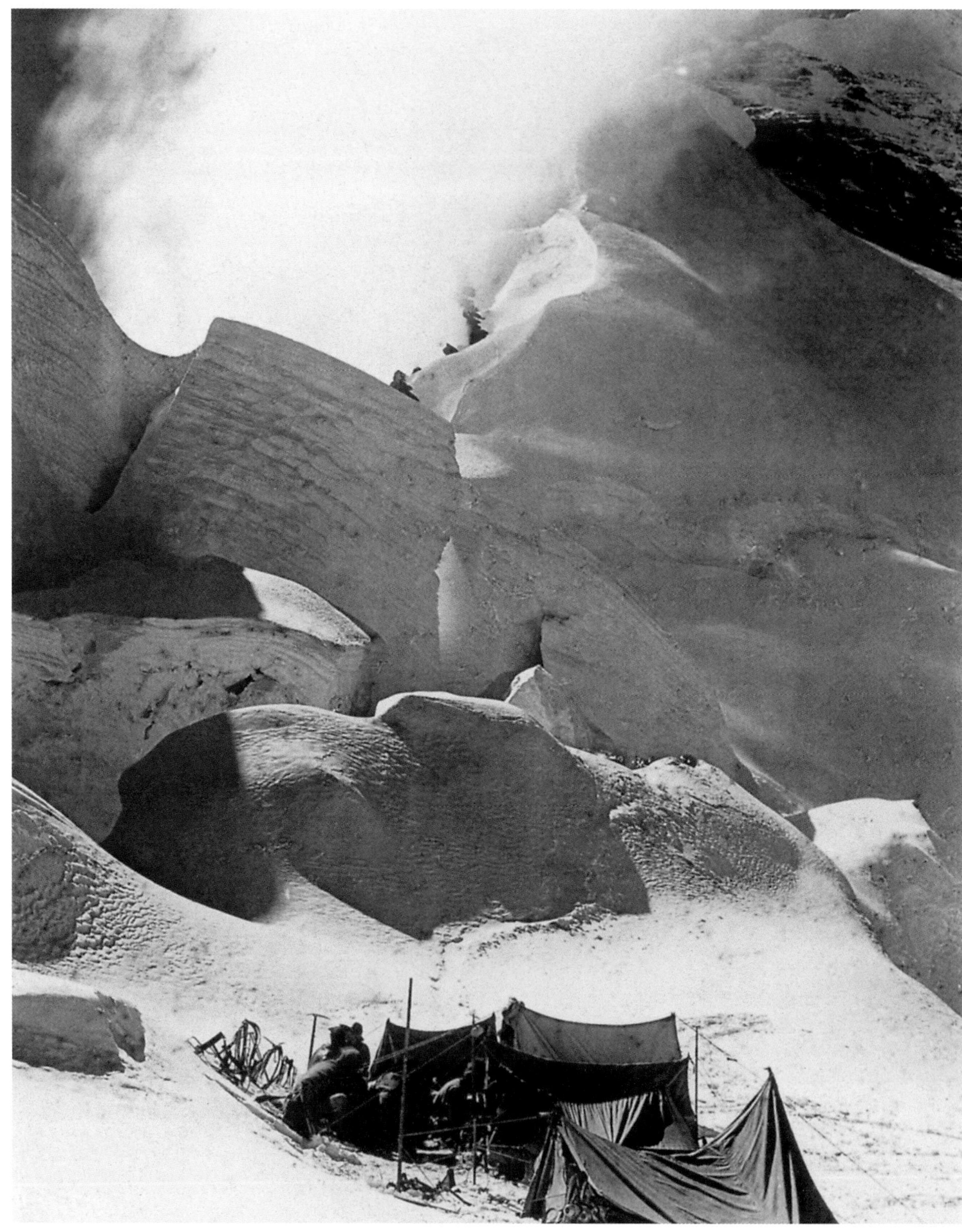

Previous photograph: For the 1922 expedition Noel developed much of the material on the mountain, using yak-dung as a source of heat for drying the film. He had a special tent designed and made by the tent makers Benjamin Edgington of London. The developing process was performed at night, despite temperatures below freezing, as the only suitable period for drying the film was just after sunrise, before the incessant wind became a huge threat by blowing particles of dust around in the rarefied atmosphere. Base Camp was the best position, as river water was essential for the developing.

The highest point that Noel reached with his cameras was Camp VI at 23,000 feet. Although the cine camera weighed less than 20lb, fully loaded with 400 feet of 35mm film, it was unrealistic to expect that the camera and necessary paraphernalia could be carried higher.

Noel selected a 20-inch Cooke telephoto lens to
enable him to view and, he hoped, capture
the climbers on their summit attempts.
The cine camera has been donated
to the Science Museum. This is the
image using the telephoto lens.

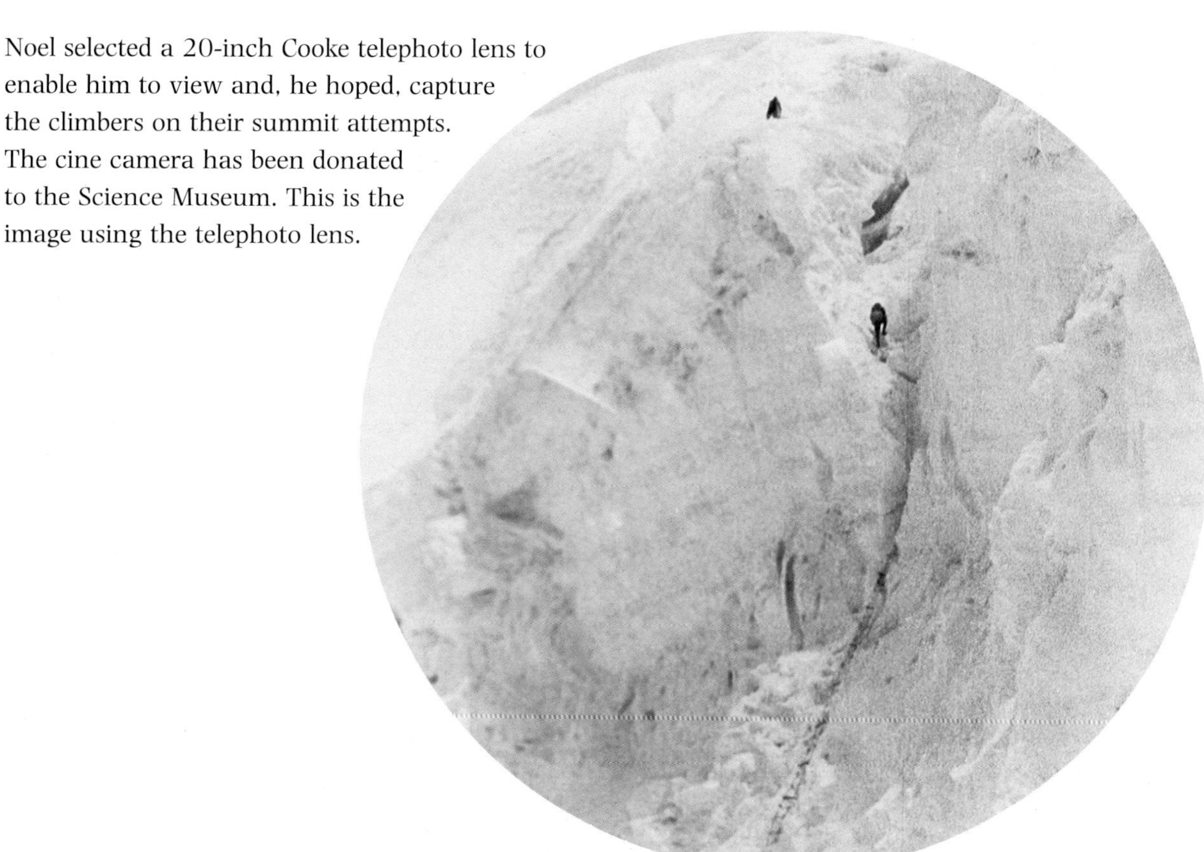

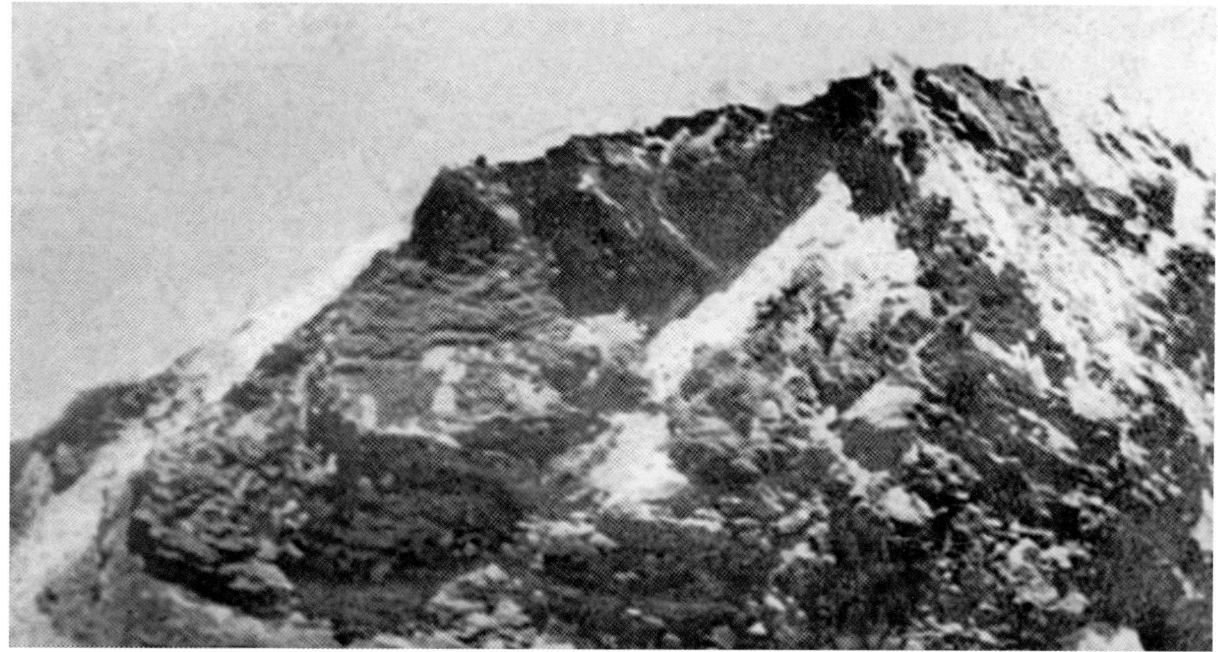

The view Noel had of
the summit from Eagle's
Nest, at 22,000 feet in
June 1924.

In 1922 Noel concentrated his photography on the Tibetan landscape, the people and their customs, for fear of upsetting the climbers, who had originally resented the presence of anything which smacked of popular filming. This is a *dzongpen*, the civilian leader of a community, whose high position is indicated by a single pendant earring of turquoise and gold.

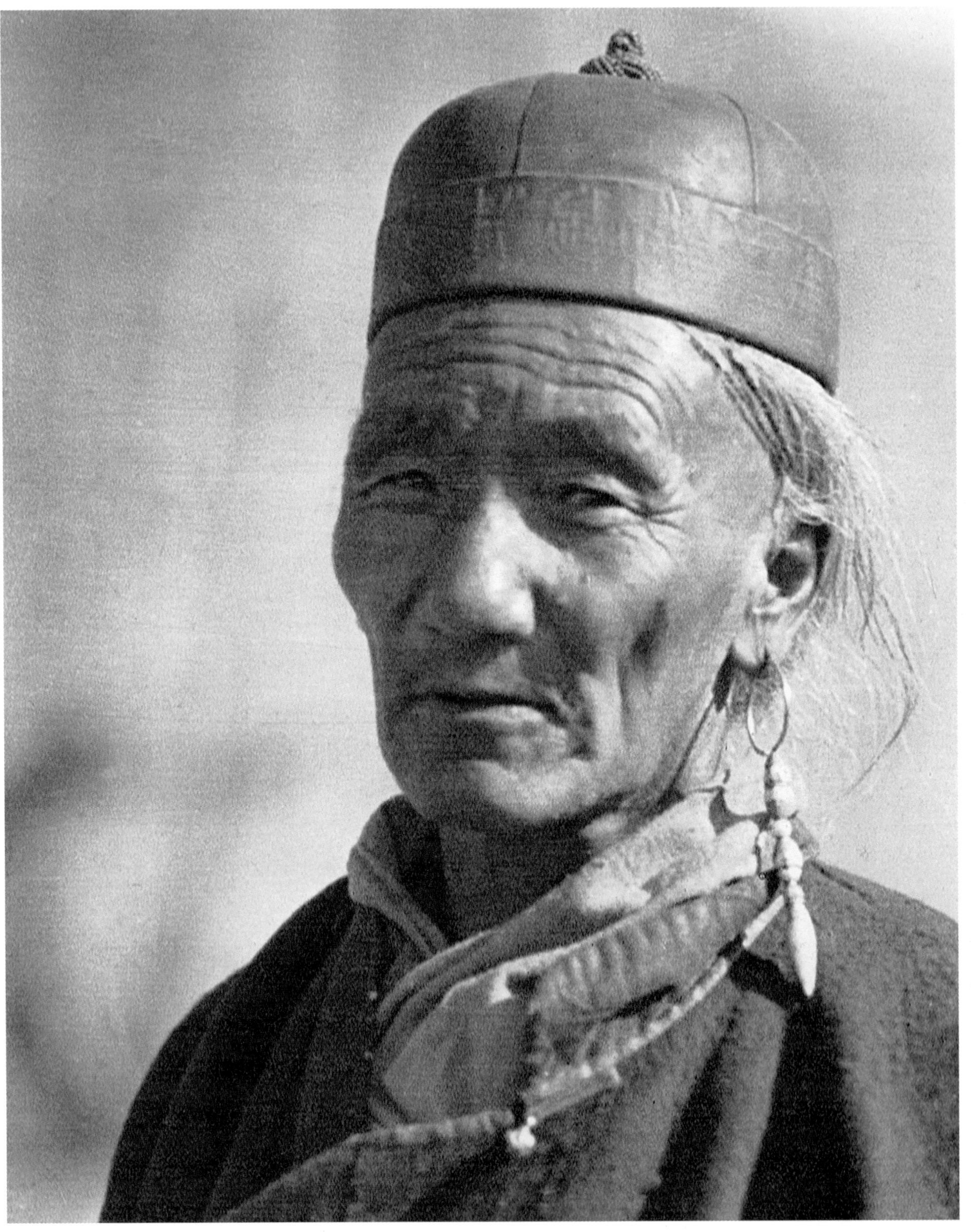

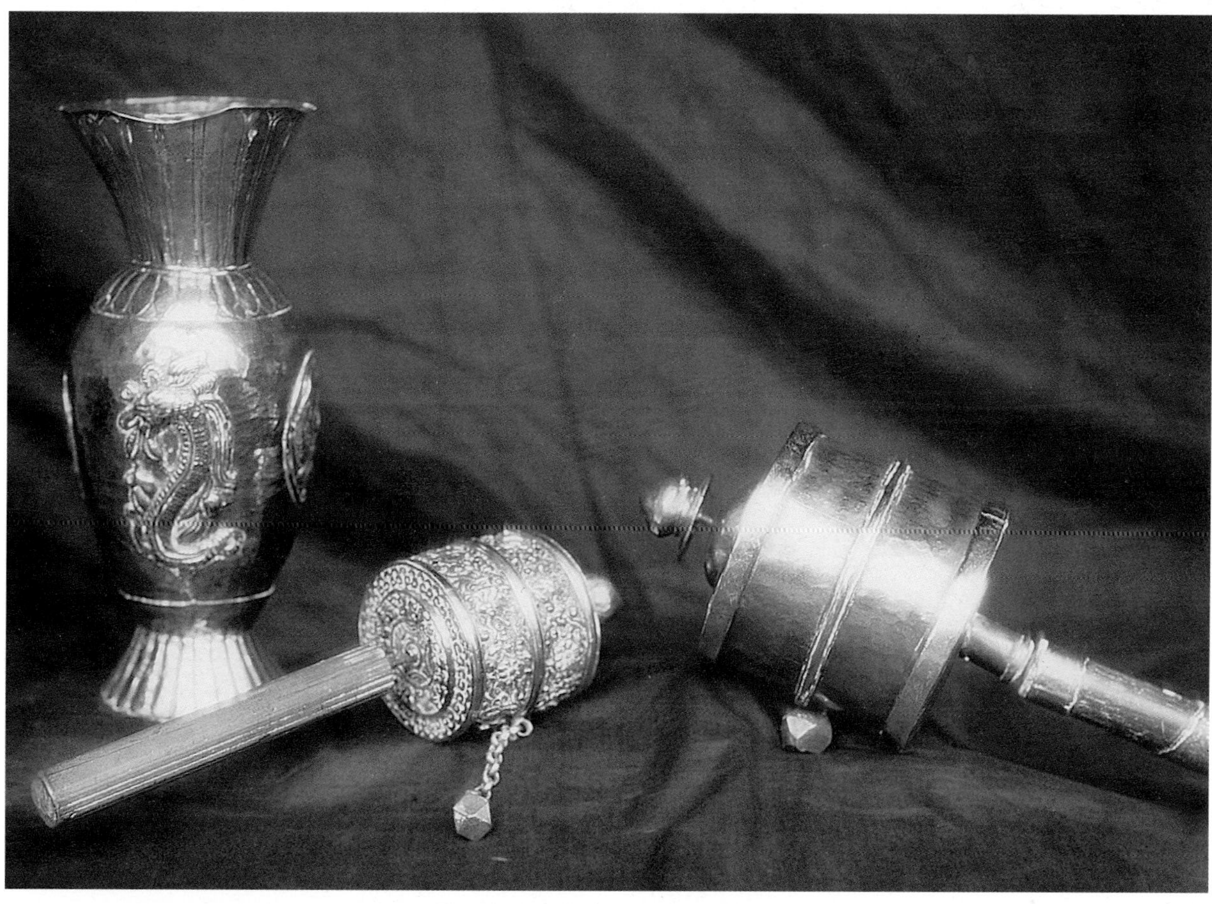

A vase and two prayer-wheels of copper, brass and silver – the natural resources of Tibet.

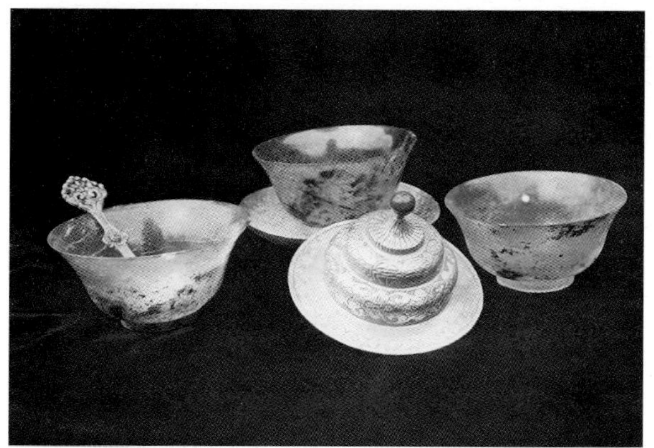

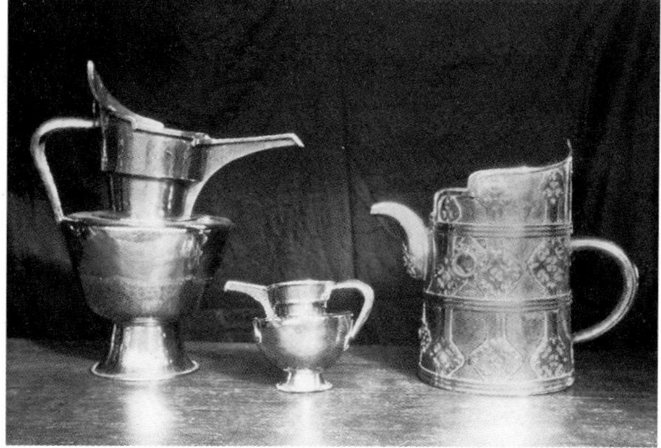

Left: Onyx drinking vessels, so thin they are almost transparent.

Right: Water pitchers of brass and copper.

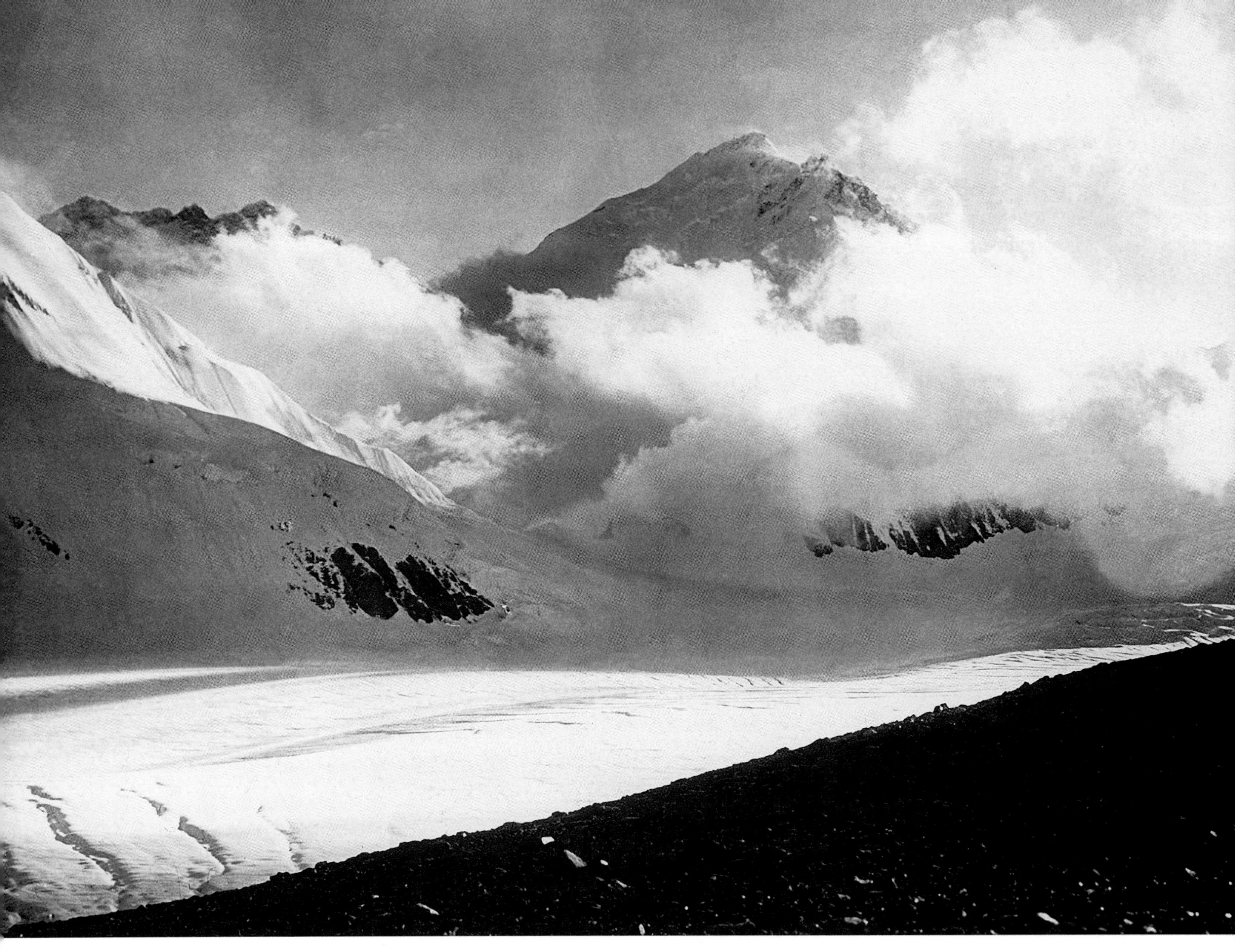

Noel was fascinated by the ever-changing cloud formations, and by the constant plume of cloud on the mountain, created by the ferocious, incessant wind. Here the mountain chain is almost obscured by the driving clouds.

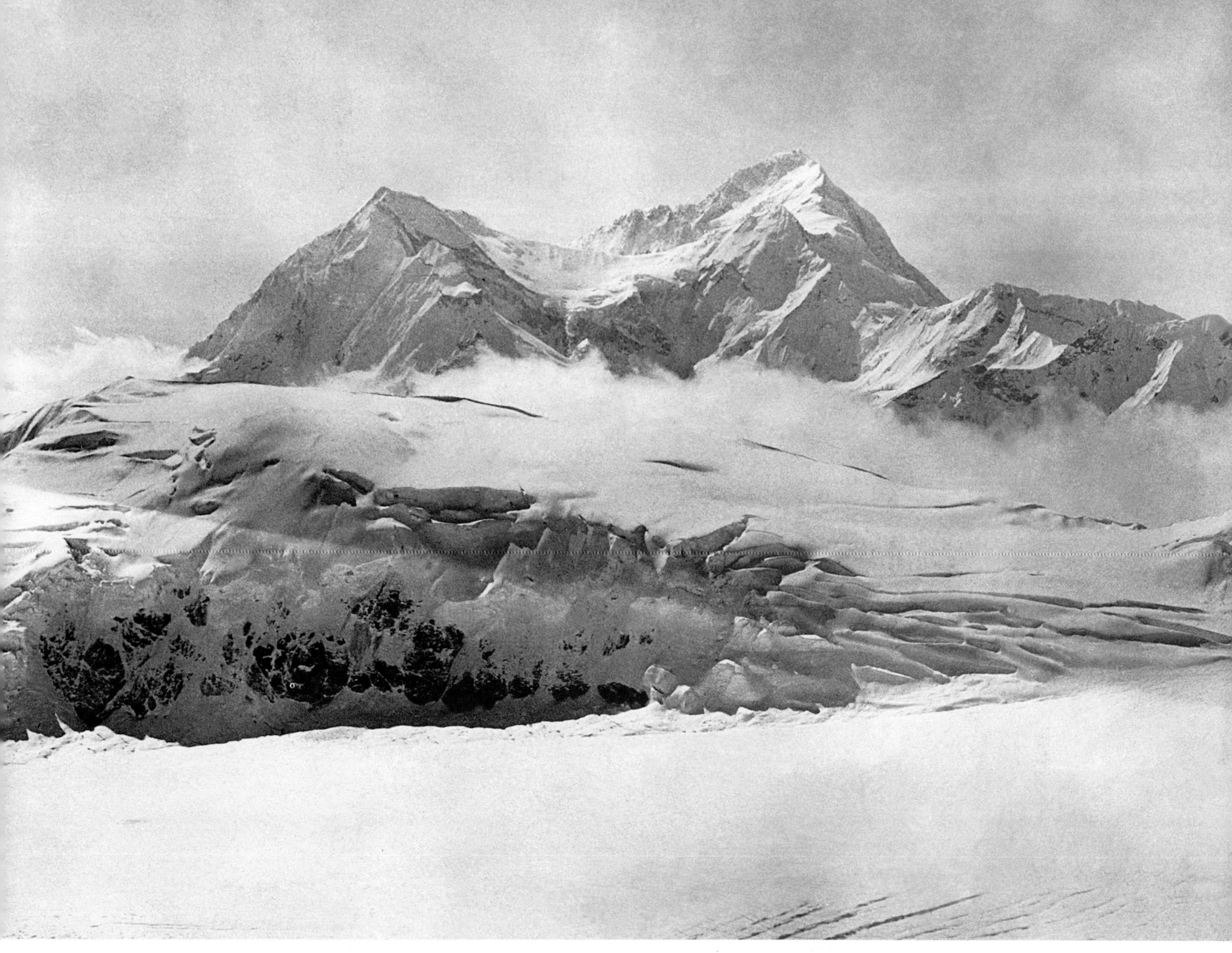

Another cloud formation.

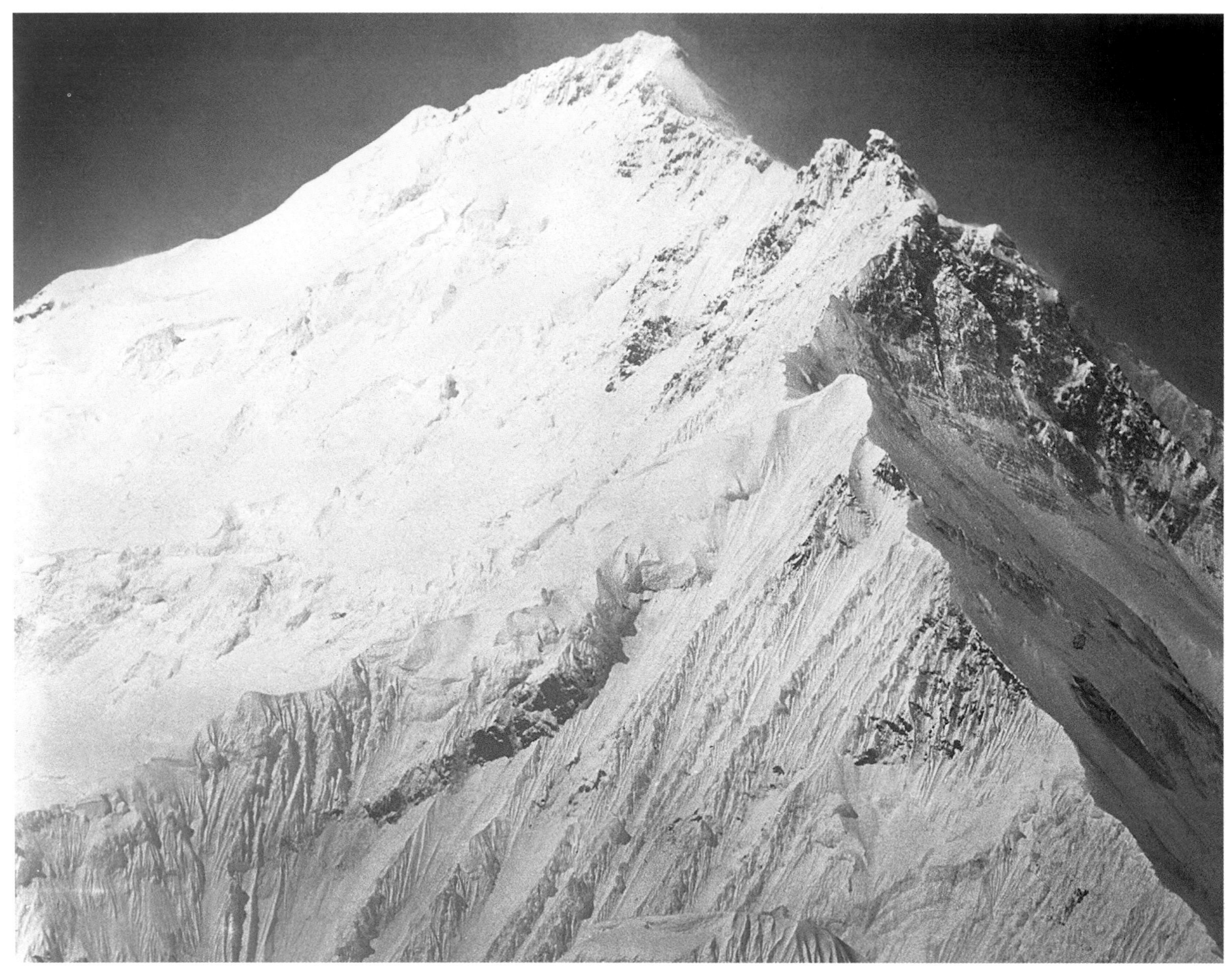

A clear view of Everest.

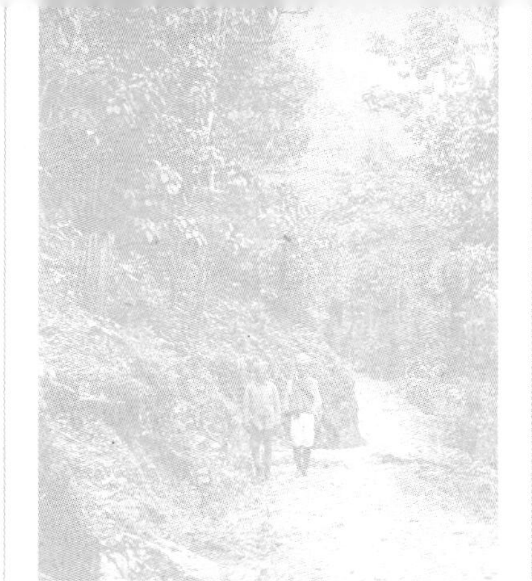

CHAPTER 3

FOOTHILLS AND FORESTS

The Himalayas, meaning, in Sanskrit, 'the Abode of Snow', form a mountain chain stretching 1,500 miles, separating the lowlands of the Indian subcontinent from the high, dry Tibetan plateau. Here rise the three great rivers of the region, the Ganges, the Indus and the Brahmaputra, and, in addition to the towering peaks reaching to 29,000 feet, there are broadleaf and conifer forests which provide homes for a diversity of plant and animal species.

Darjeeling, at 7,000 feet, was established as a hill station during the era of the British Empire, allowing diplomats and soldiers and their families to escape from the fierce heat of the plains of India and take refuge in the cooler foothills among the tea plantations. Until Partition, Assam was easily accessible from Calcutta, but now West Bengal, in north-east India, is almost divided into two, so that Darjeeling and the tea plantations are virtually cut off from the main part of India; this, combined with the withdrawal of the vast numbers of civil servants and servicemen, has reduced Darjeeling from its position as a major hill station to a centre for walking and climbing, and there remains but a trace of the faded elegance for which it was once renowned. In addition, since Nepal has opened up and many expeditions now approach Everest from the south, it is no longer the only base from which to set off in a quest for the great mountaineering goal.

In the 1920s Darjeeling was a thriving trade centre, comprising bungalows dotted on the hillsides and a bustling centre, where many local nationalities and tribes came to sell and barter their wares. Noel wrote:

> Swarms of sprightly little chattering Nepalese, who have immigrated in enormous numbers to settle as well-paid workers in the tea gardens. The bright-eyed Nepalese women, gaily parading their best attire, are neatly dressed in bright colours; some of the piquant faces of the youngest would be almost pretty, were their owners not addicted to the unsightly practice of chewing betel-nut. Most picturesque of all are the mounted Tibetans, dashing along on sturdy ponies with jingling harness bells, and their scarves red and blue, streaming in the wind. Few Tibetans are conspicuous for personal cleanliness, most of them wear constantly the same suit day and night for months without changing, and often until it is a thing of shreds and patches; and both here and along the road it is no uncommon sight to see, as in India, both men and women seated on the ground reciprocating kind and necessary attentions to each other's hair.

The expedition left Darjeeling on 25 March. The track took them to Kalimpong, where they stayed in the home of the Macdonald family. David Macdonald had accompanied the Younghusband mission to Lhasa in 1904 as interpreter, and was then posted to Tibet as a British Trade Agent, later serving as British Political Officer in Sikkim, in charge of Britain's relations with Tibet, Bhutan and Sikkim. When his large family had grown up, the family home was turned into a hotel, where all expeditions originating in Darjeeling stopped off. His son John accompanied the expedition in 1924 as postal officer, and eventually came to England with Noel to look after the lamas.

Kalimpong was once the headquarters of a Bhutanese Governor (the word 'Kalim' means king's minister; 'Pong' (or Dzong) means stronghold). Before the Chinese take-over of Tibet, it was the centre of India's wool trade with that country, with Tibetan caravans wending their way down from the Tibetan plateau to trade wool for manufactured goods. Now, thanks to the experience gained in 1922, Shebbeare, the transport officer, was sent ahead to Kalimpong to take delivery of the stores and arrange the onward journey to Tibet: it was decided to earmark the stores according to the intended position of the high camps on the mountain.

From Kalimpong the track followed the Teesta river up to Gantok, the capital of Sikkim, the home of the Lepchas, the timid, placid native population of these mountains. Noel was clearly fascinated by the people, and observed them keenly with both pen and camera:

He is, indeed, with his distinctive traits, physical and moral, very much what his environments have made of him. Living in a country which yields to him, without husbandry, a profusion of wild fruits and edible roots and other jungle products, the Lepcha is naturally indolent and easy-going. His close companionship with nature has made him a naturalist, a tender lover of flowers, and something of a philosopher, though his narrow gorges have narrowed his views. His solitary life in the peaceful depths of the great forests makes him timid and shy of strangers. His hard experience of the forces of nature, the storms and floods which wreck his home and scanty crops, and scatter desolation and death around him, has made him a worshipper of malignant devils, and intensely superstitious. His exposed bivouacking at night in malarial gorges has sapped much of his vigour and enervated him. His roving life has made him love liberty and hate restraint, leading him to shun service, and preventing him ever combining with his fellow-tribesmen against a common foe. And this unwarlike spirit, crushed under generations of Tibetan oppressors, has left little of the heroic in his composition, when he is pitted against disciplined masses of other tribes. But he is a keen sportsman, a born naturalist, sympathetic, frank and generous to a fault, and none can be braver than he is in facing danger in the forest.

> Notice how these Lepchas specially associate themselves with their ubiquitous bamboo, whose stout stems supplies them with their huts for shelter, with fuel, bows and arrows; its larger joints afford water-jugs, cooking pots and pans; its smaller joints bestow bottles, smoking pipes and flutes; its branches make a springy couch; its bark supplies ropes to span their raging torrents, also baskets and umbrellas; and its tender young shoots are eaten as food.

He marvelled at the natural beauty of the forest:

> Its giant oaks, chestnut and magnolias thickly draped with moss and wreaths of aerial orchids, ferns and festooning climbers and parasitic plants, which hang in great tufts and pendants, waving over the blue hydrangeas of the undergrowth. Some of the branches of these trees are perfect gardens in themselves. In the soft drapery of moist moss that thickly clothes these branches, and in the beds of fine mould from the decaying leaves that fills their crevices, are to be found not only luxuriant clusters of exquisite orchids. A gorgeous feature of the forest is the blaze of crimson blossoms of the Magnolia Campbelli; here it is a forest monarch over 80 feet high, and its huge flowers, like those of the cotton tree below, appear curiously on its bare branches before its leaves. White magnolia also abound, scenting the air with their fragrance. Delicately pink hydrangeas, 18–20 feet high, are common, and ferns so numerous that over 60 species may be found along this forest road within a few miles.

At Gantok, capital of Sikkim, there was time to visit the gardens of the Residency, and admire the rich vegetation and the profusion of flowers – which in our climate need careful nurturing – achieving vast heights and luscious blooms.

The beauty and wonder of the forest, however, were always tempered by the presence of leeches, so it was with mixed feelings that the party, after just a few days, left the forests to embark upon the long march across the 'roof of the world'.

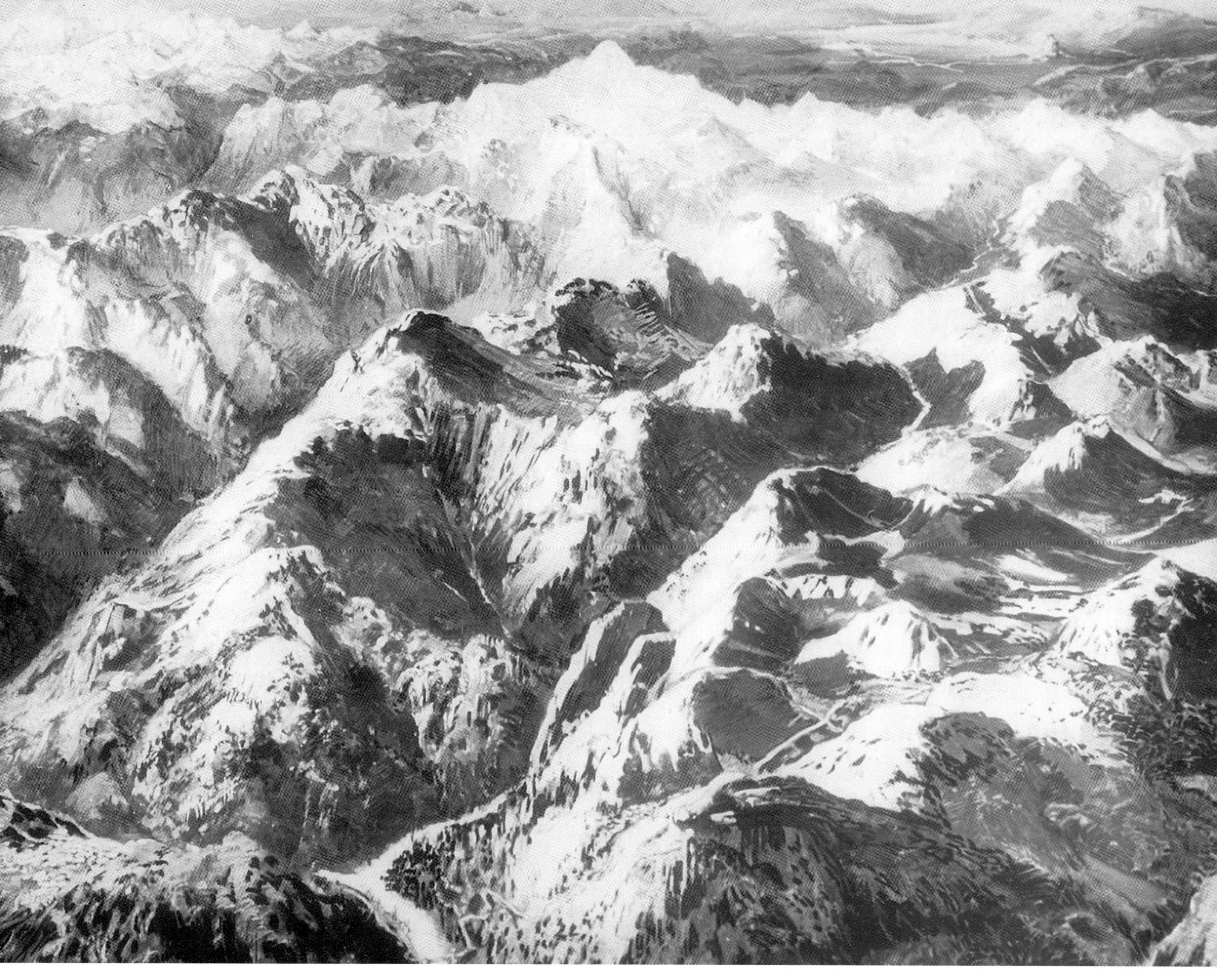

Pictorial representation of the route from Darjeeling at 7,000 feet, in the bottom left-hand corner, to Everest, in the top left-hand corner.

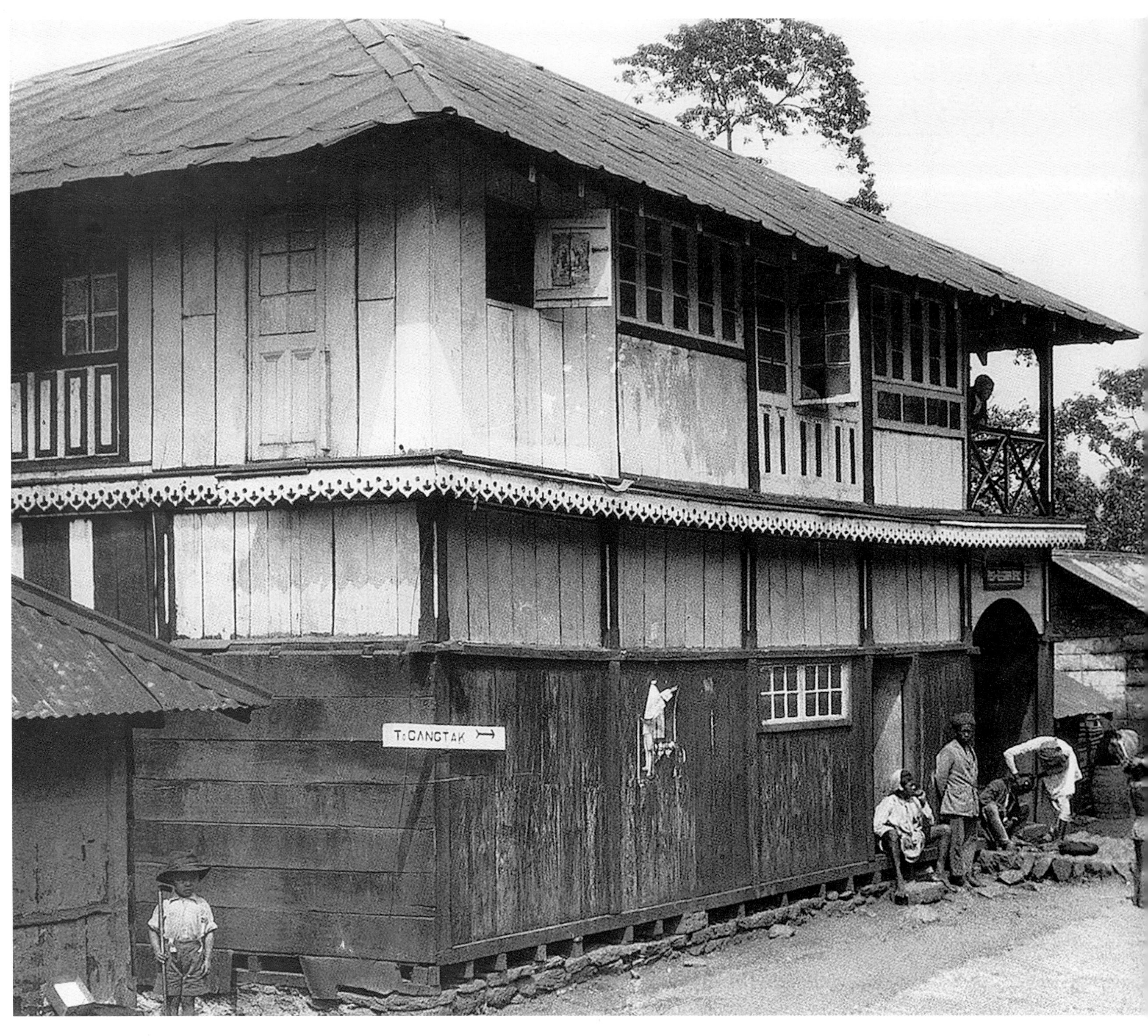

To GANGTAK →

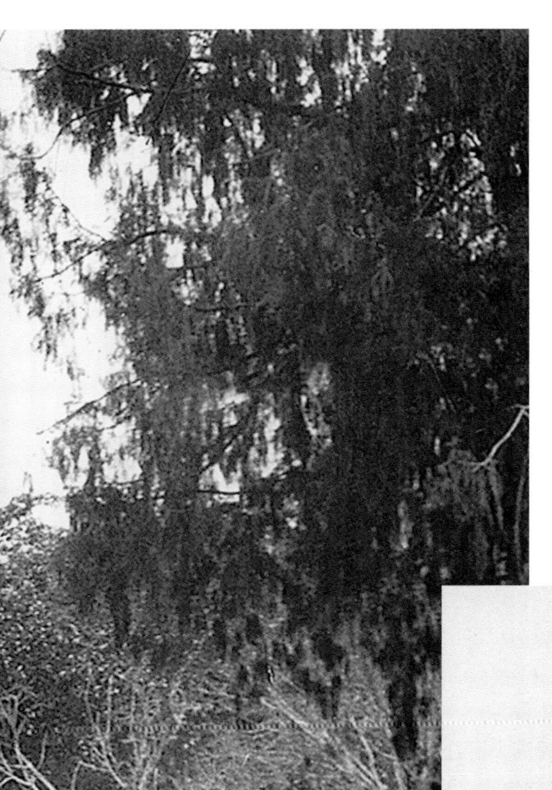

Kalimpong crowns an open, cultivated spur. It has a much milder climate than Darjeeling, and boasts a considerable mart to which Tibetan traders came.

The Tibetan traders were encamped in yak-hair tents and other improvised shelters. They bring for sale or barter ponies, wool, coarse blankets, furs, yak-tails, musk, turquoise, gold-dust, Chinese silk, brick tea and salt.

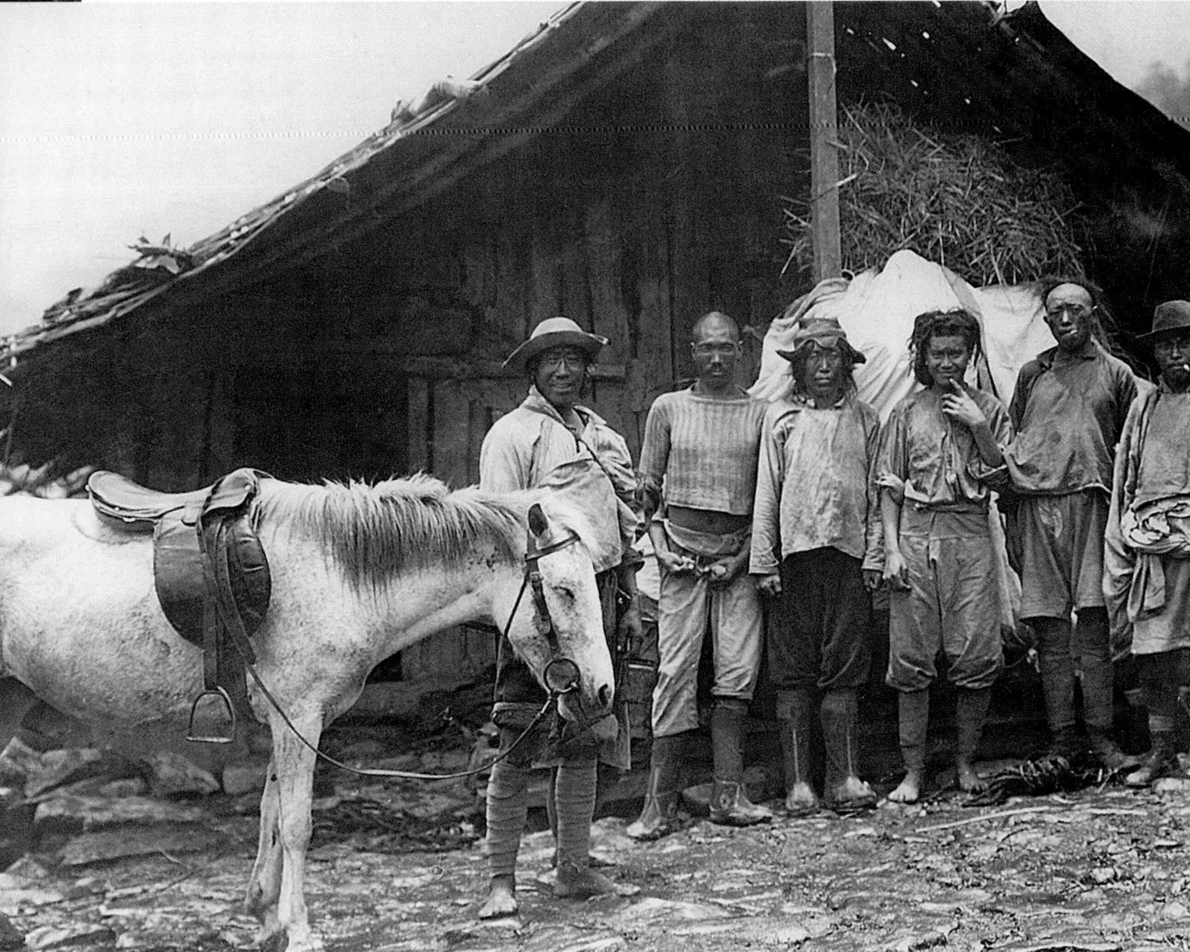

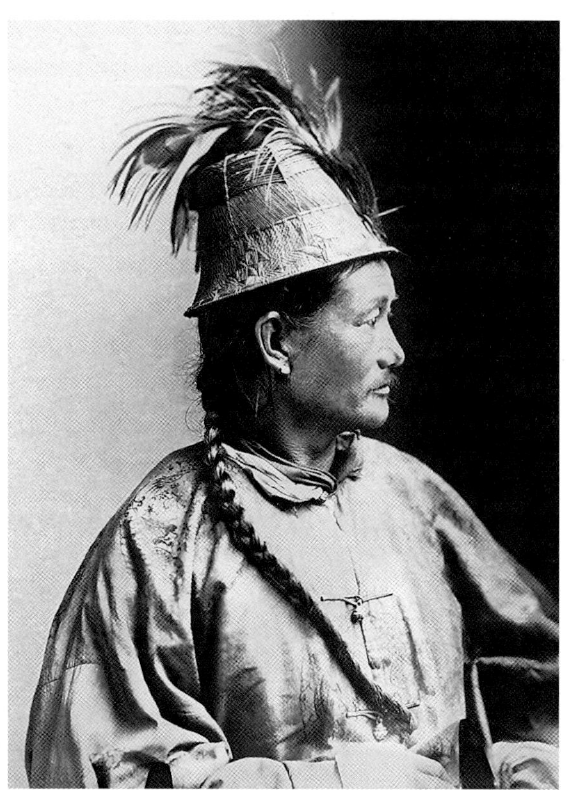

A Lepcha, one of the indigenous people of the forests. 'His mild Mongolian features, hair parted down the middle, scanty beard and moustache . . . and the happy look in his honest eyes stamp him as the simple contented child of the forest.'

Bamboo grows to massive proportions and is extensively used in the everyday life of the Lepcha. This is a bridge made entirely from the larger stout stems, perfectly strong enough to carry men and pack animals across a river up to 300 feet wide.

Opposite: The bridge is formed by two suspended ropes of cane strung across a gorge, lashed together with knotted palm, with bamboo slings attached to the parallel suspension ropes, and filled with a line of bamboos, end to end, on which to find a footing! This simple structure sways and jerks with every movement, like a ship in a storm.

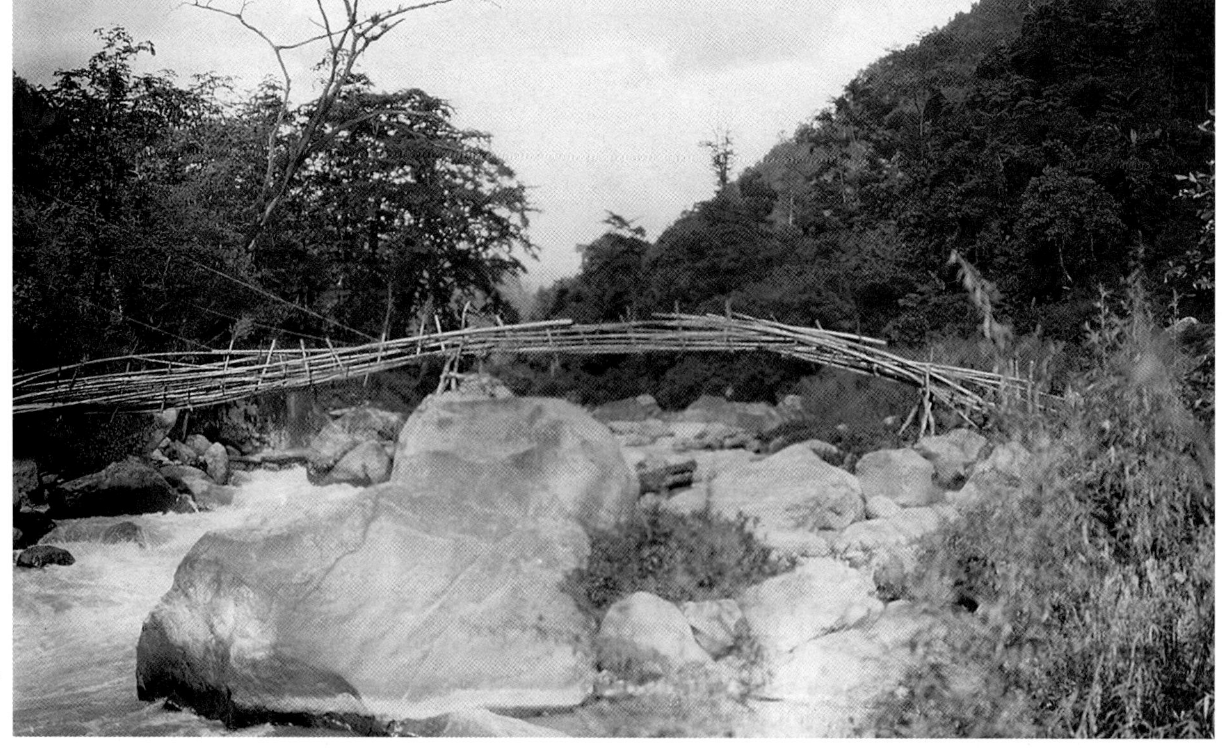

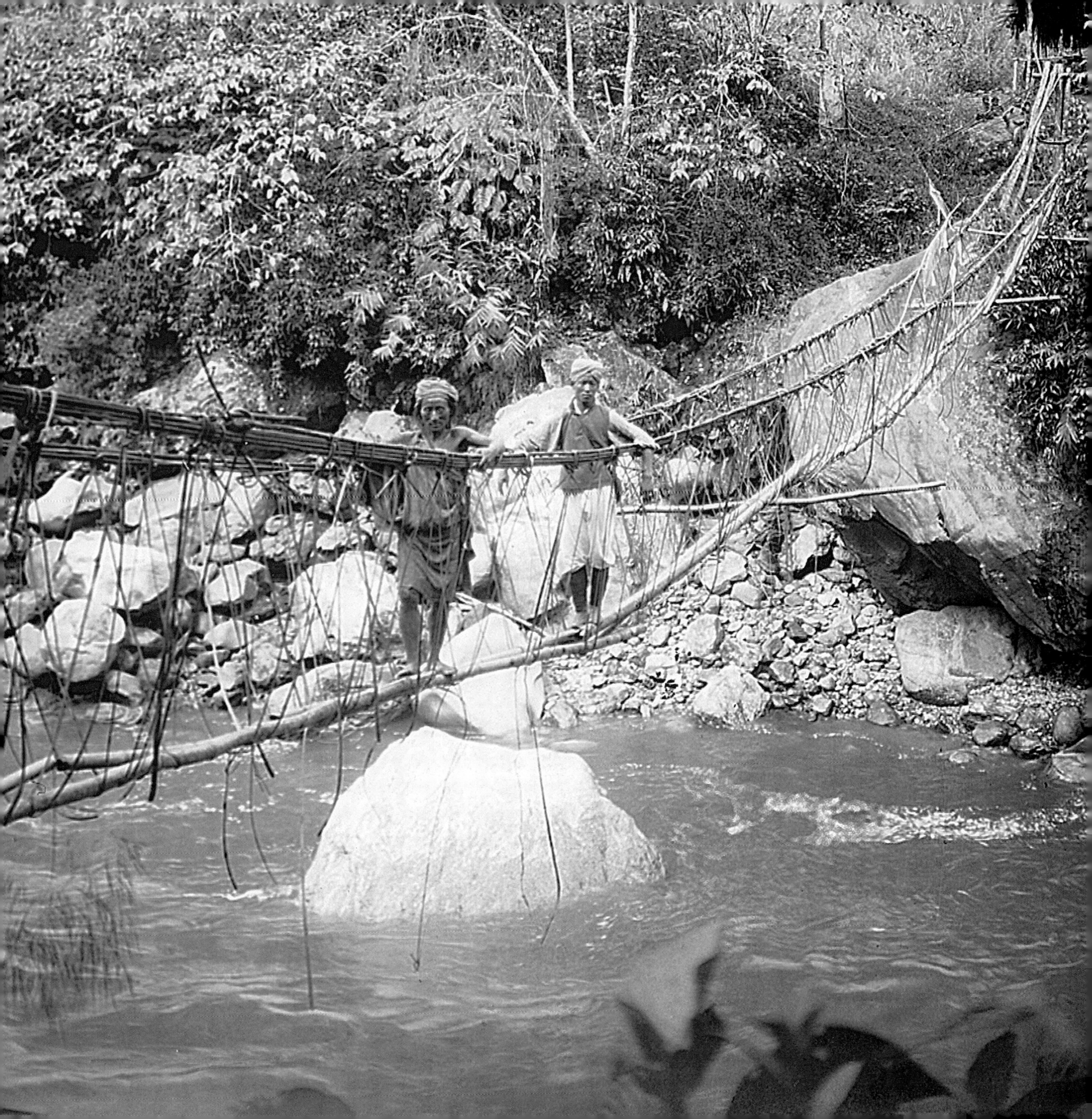

Lush vegetation. The
Lepchas live in harmony
with the forest and use
all that nature provides;
they are masters in the
art of identifying the
safe from the dangerous.
Noel wrote, 'Their
alertness, their capacity
to glide through the
forest almost as
stealthily as an animal,
their keenness of sight,
their acute sense of
hearing, their
knowledge of jungle lore
and of the habits of
animals, and their
ability to stand long and
hard physical strain, are
the envy of us civilised
men when we find
ourselves among them.'

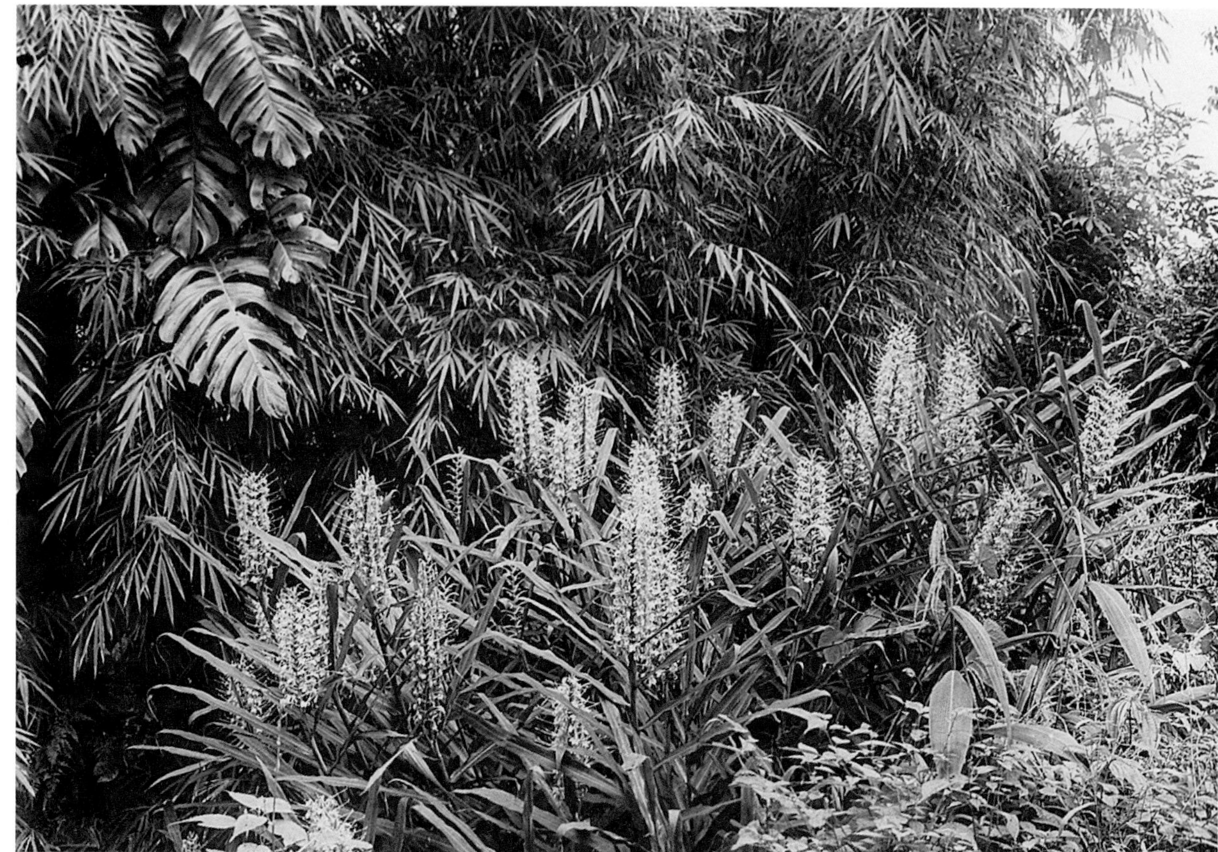

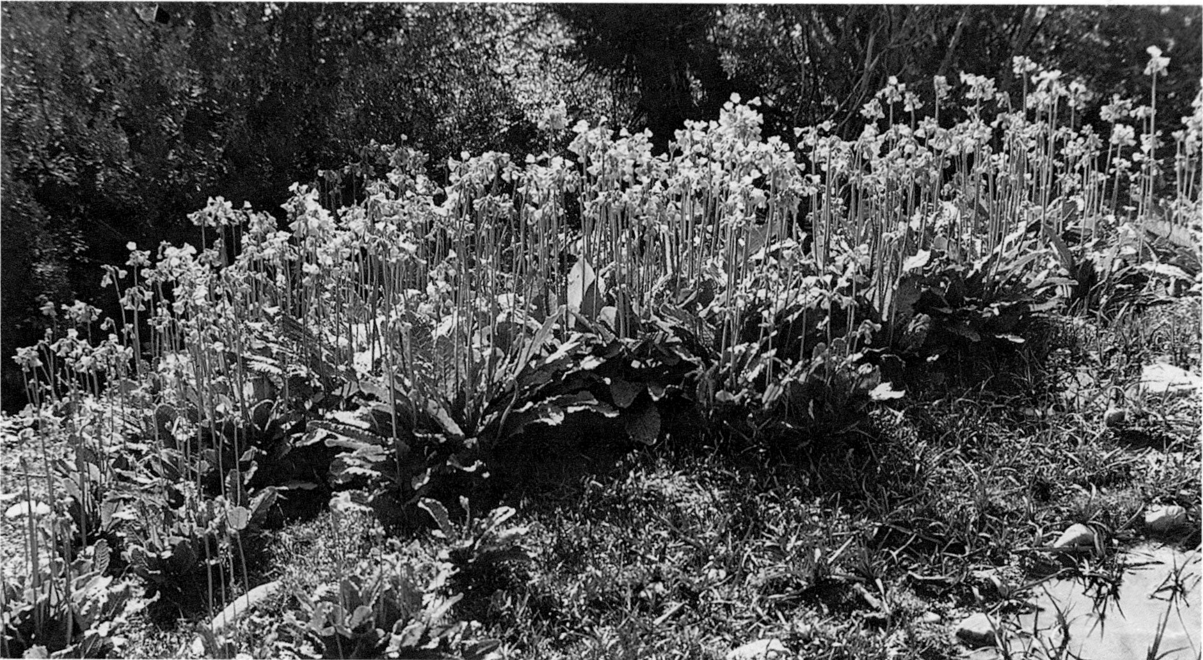

Primulas growing in
profusion.

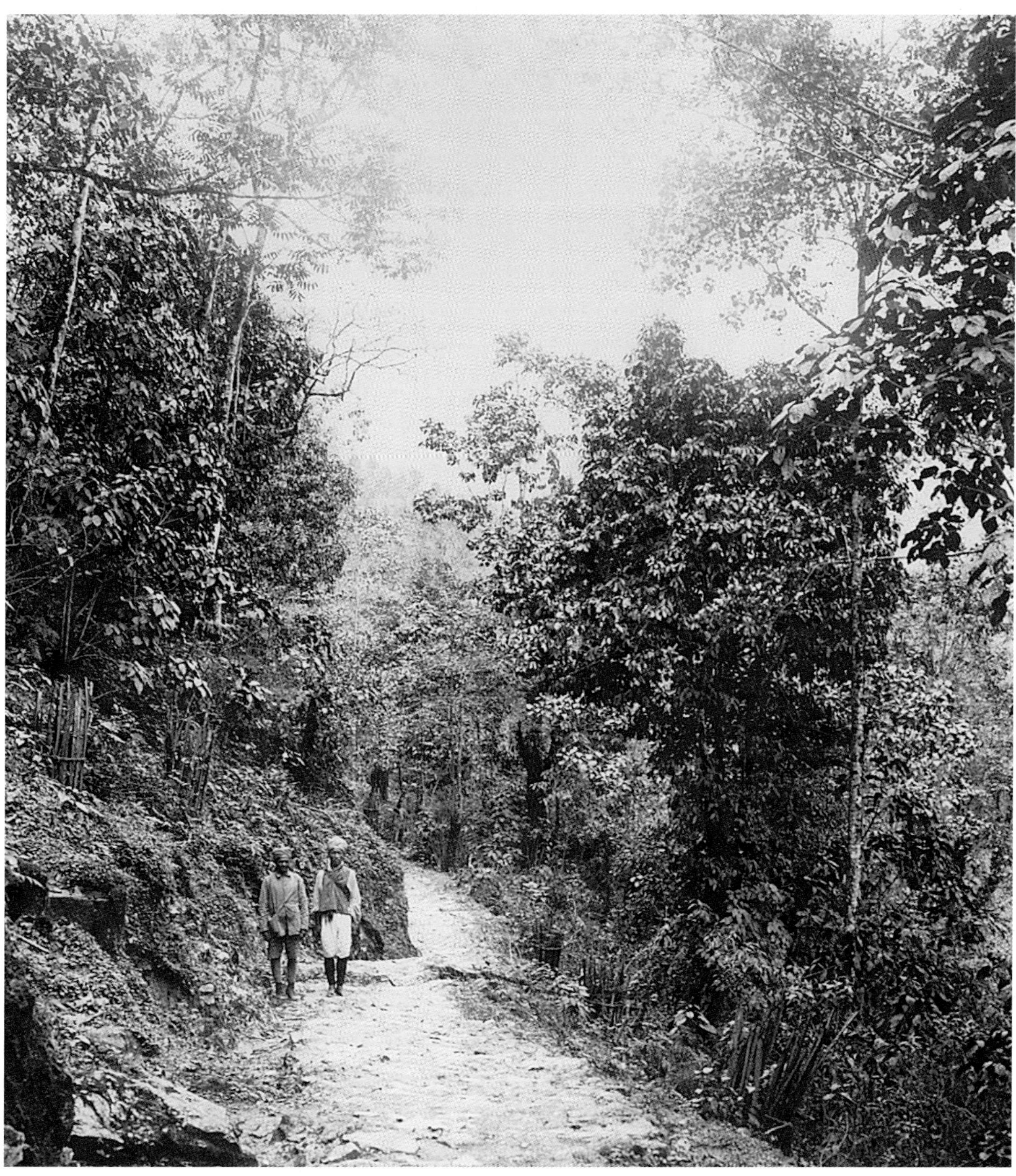

Two people dwarfed by the trees on either side of the path. 'In these forests, perhaps near enough to see us, though their forms are hidden by their likeness to their leafy surroundings and the dappled sunlight, are animals as various as elephants, tigers, leopards, foxes, squirrels, and bats: birds as various as hawks, parrots, and finches; and insects from butterflies, bees and wasps to crickets, beetles and ants.'

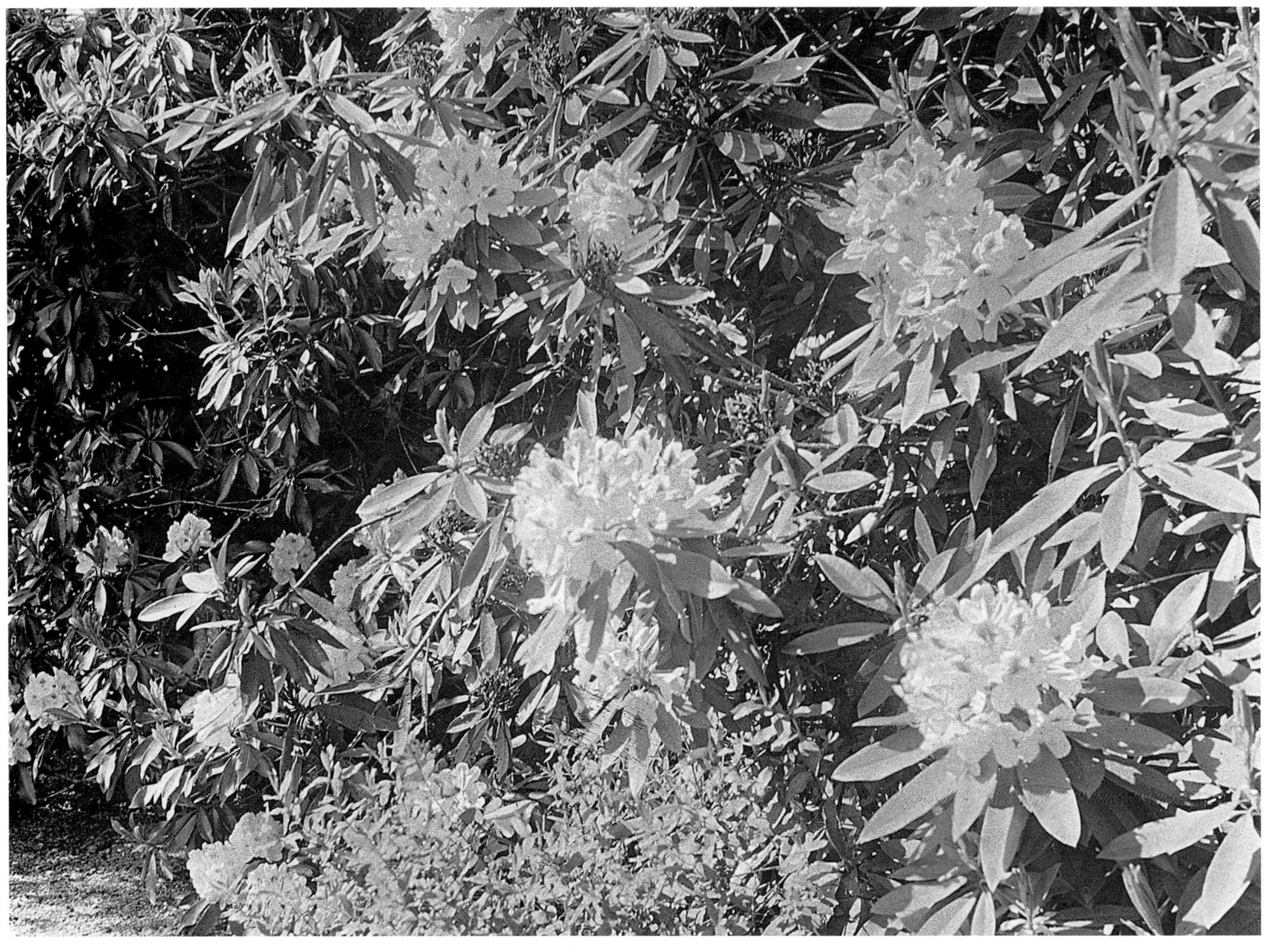

Rhododendrons, which grow up to 30 feet in height. The Lepchas are hunter-gatherers and use vegetation for roofing and flooring; they eat fruit, berries and fungi, as well as wild animals and birds, which they deftly catch.

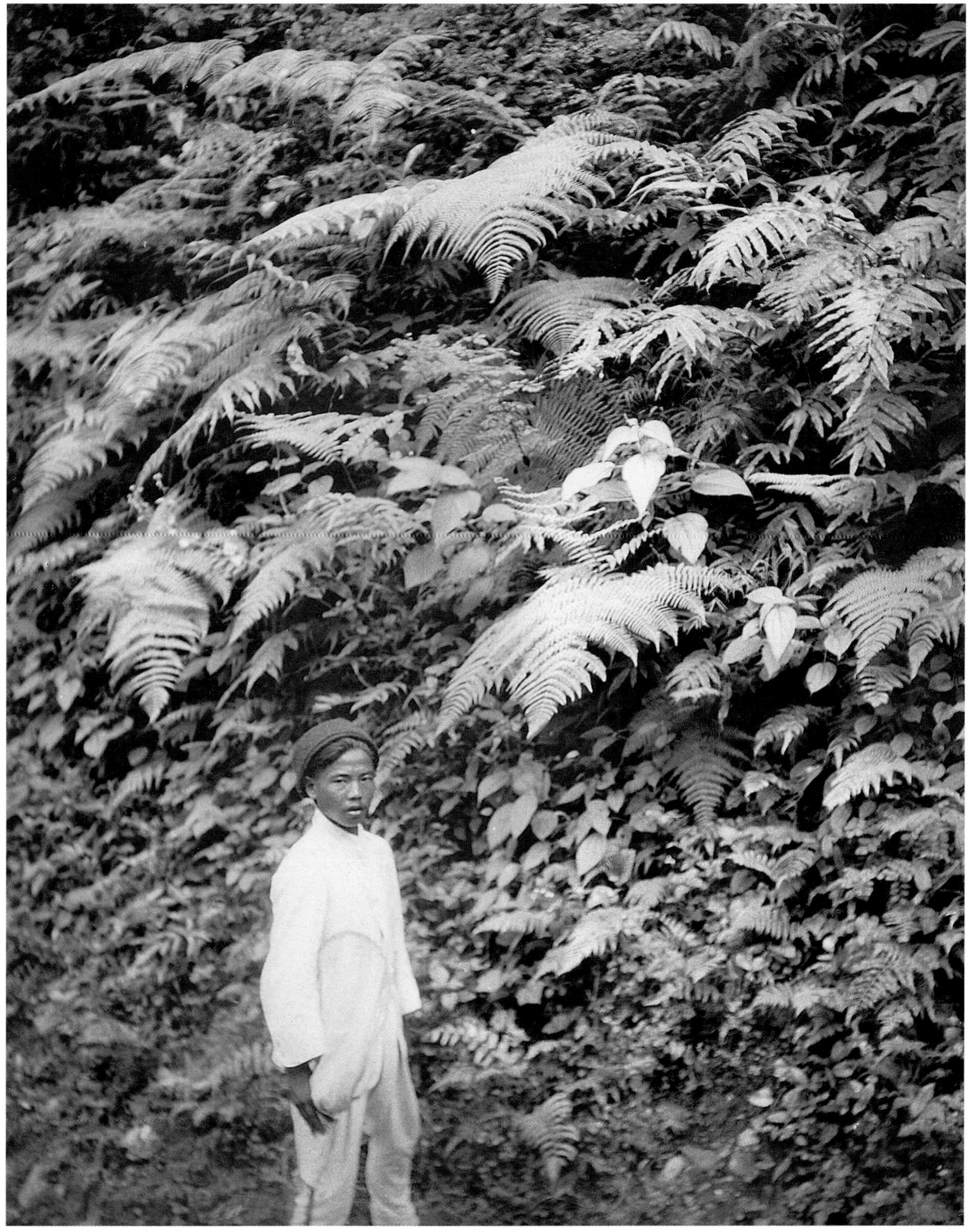

Ferns grow to five times the height of an adult. They provide dense growth, are used for shelter and bedding, and the tender shoots are a staple food.

Overleaf: Hunter-gatherers.

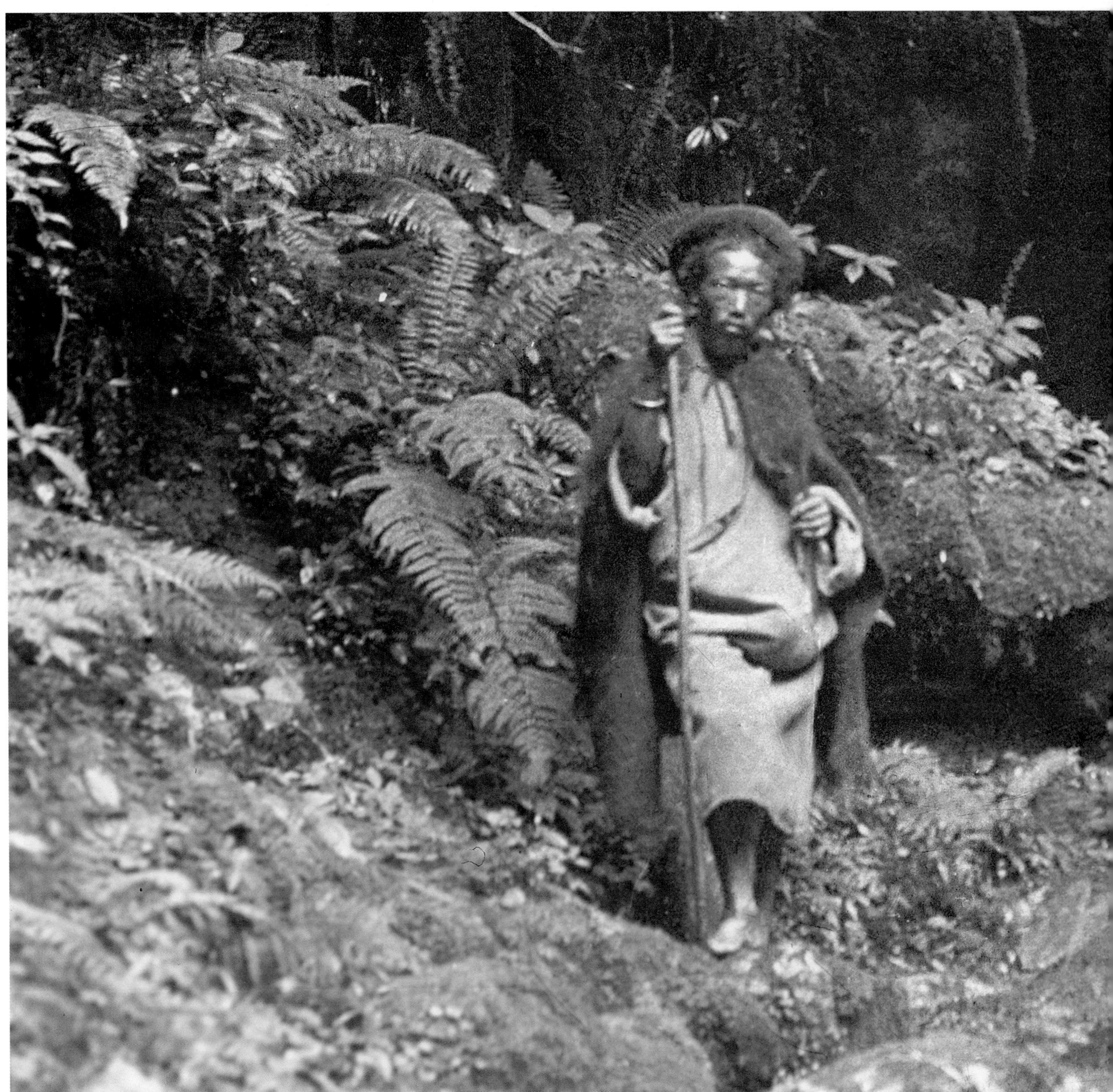

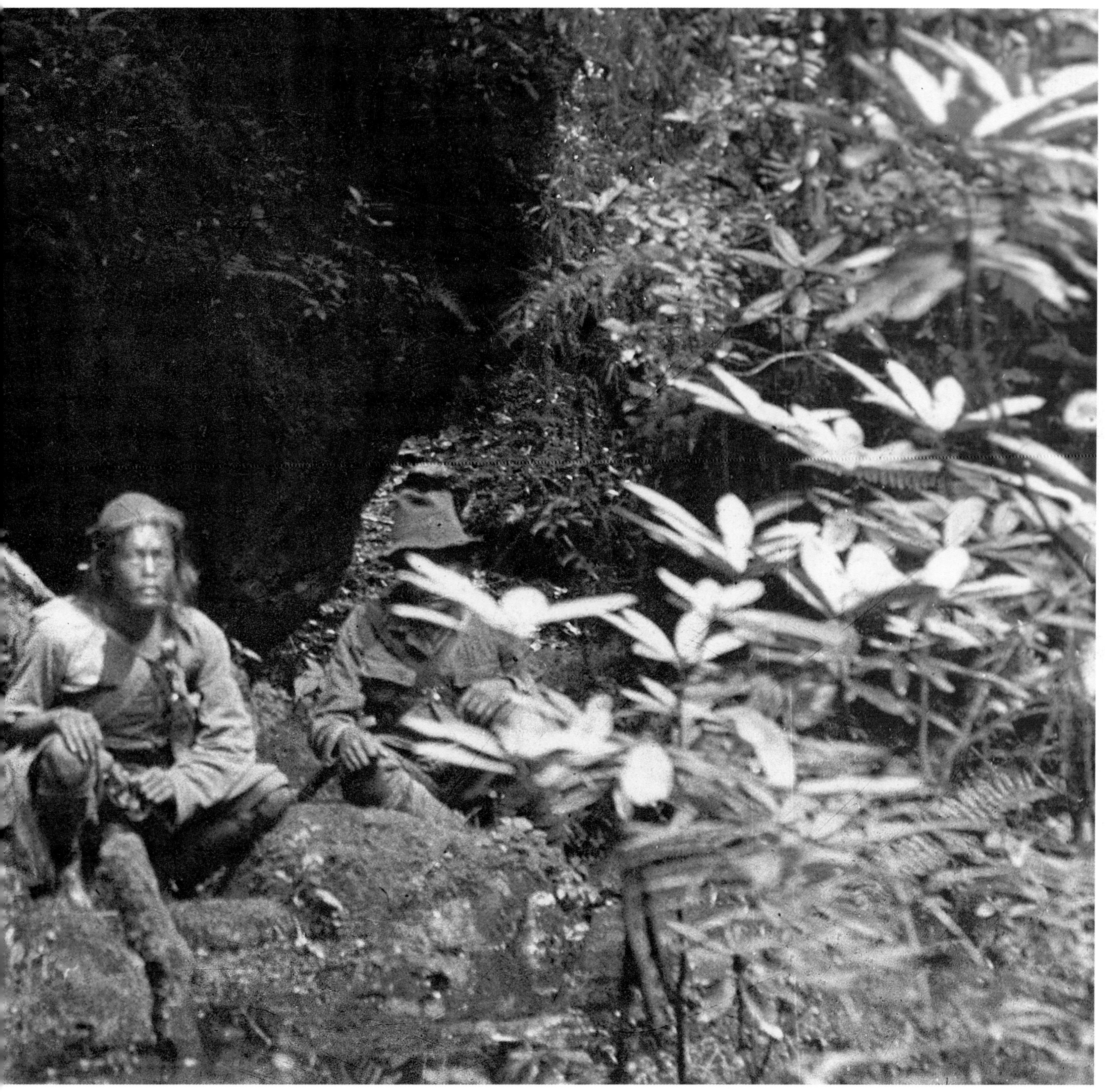

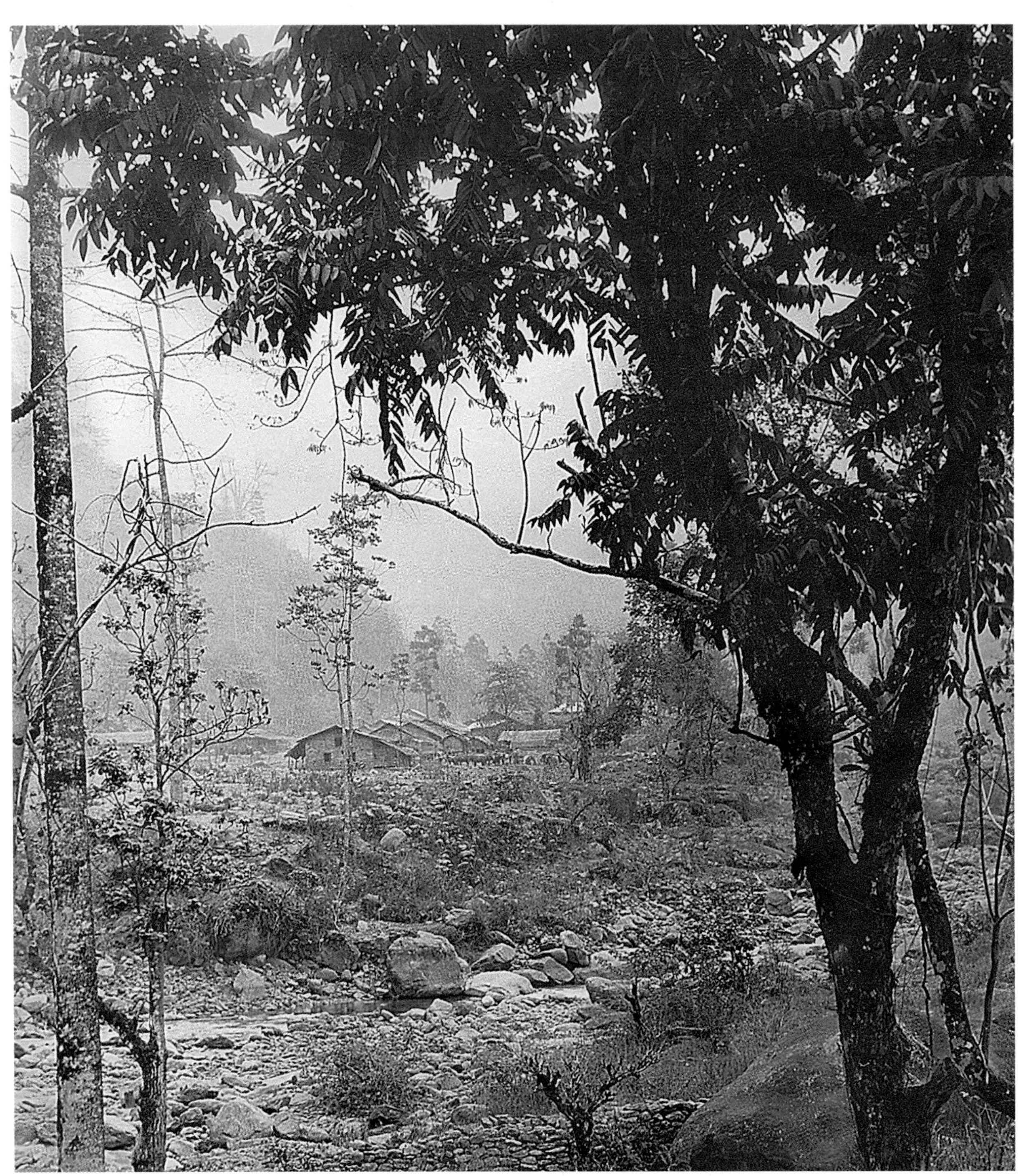

A typical village in the forest, always built close to a river.

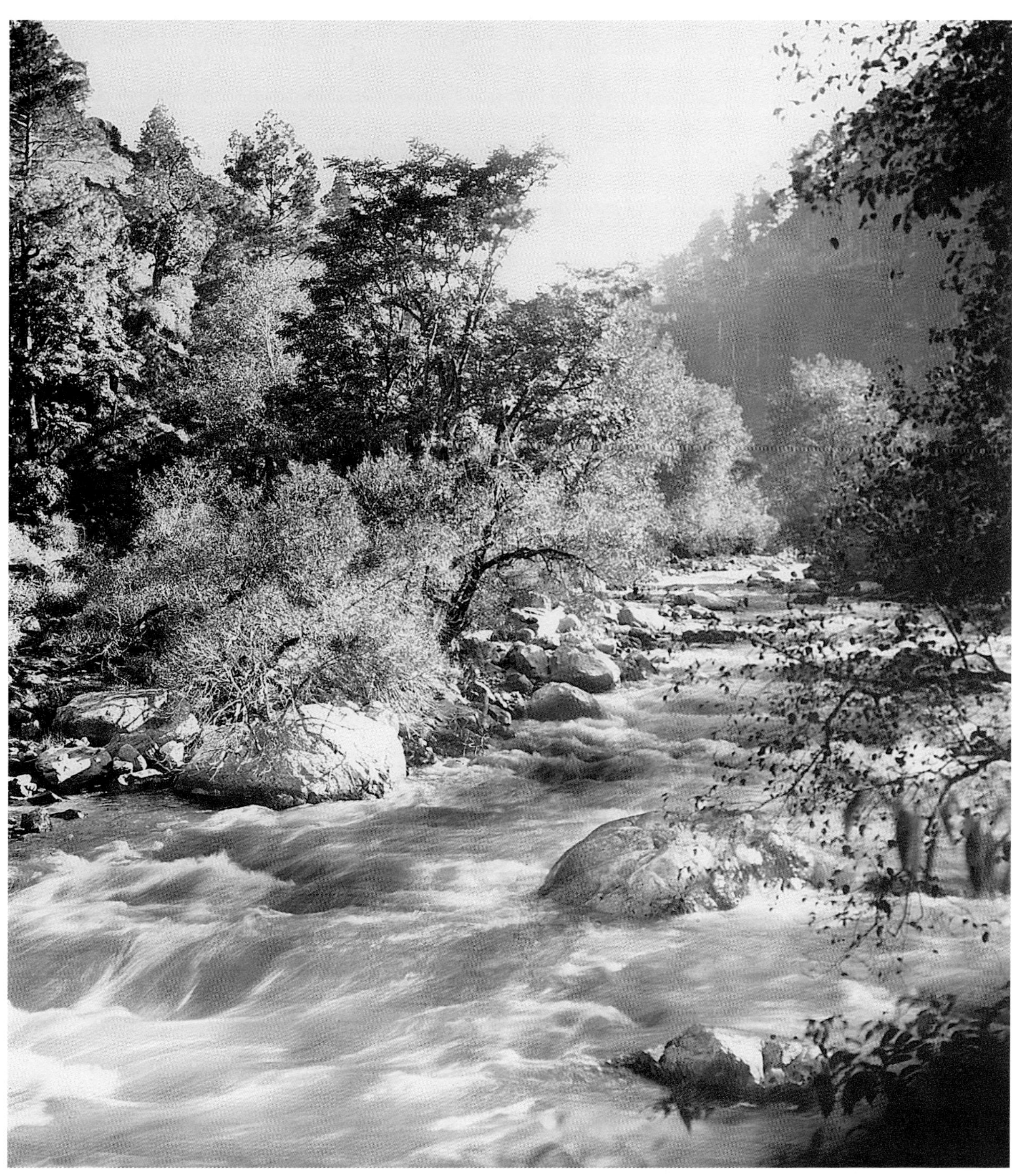

A rushing river, heavy
with the melting snow
water.

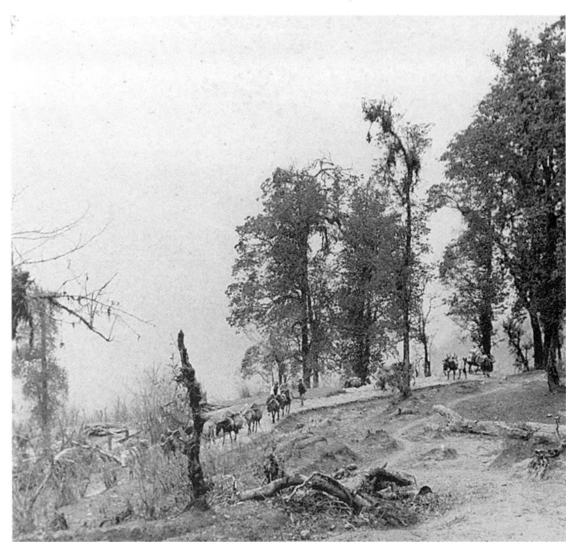

The caravan of mules carrying loads through the forests as far as Phari, where they were exchanged for yaks. The mules were provided by the Indian Army and, despite their sure-footedness and tenacity, were often difficult and stubborn.

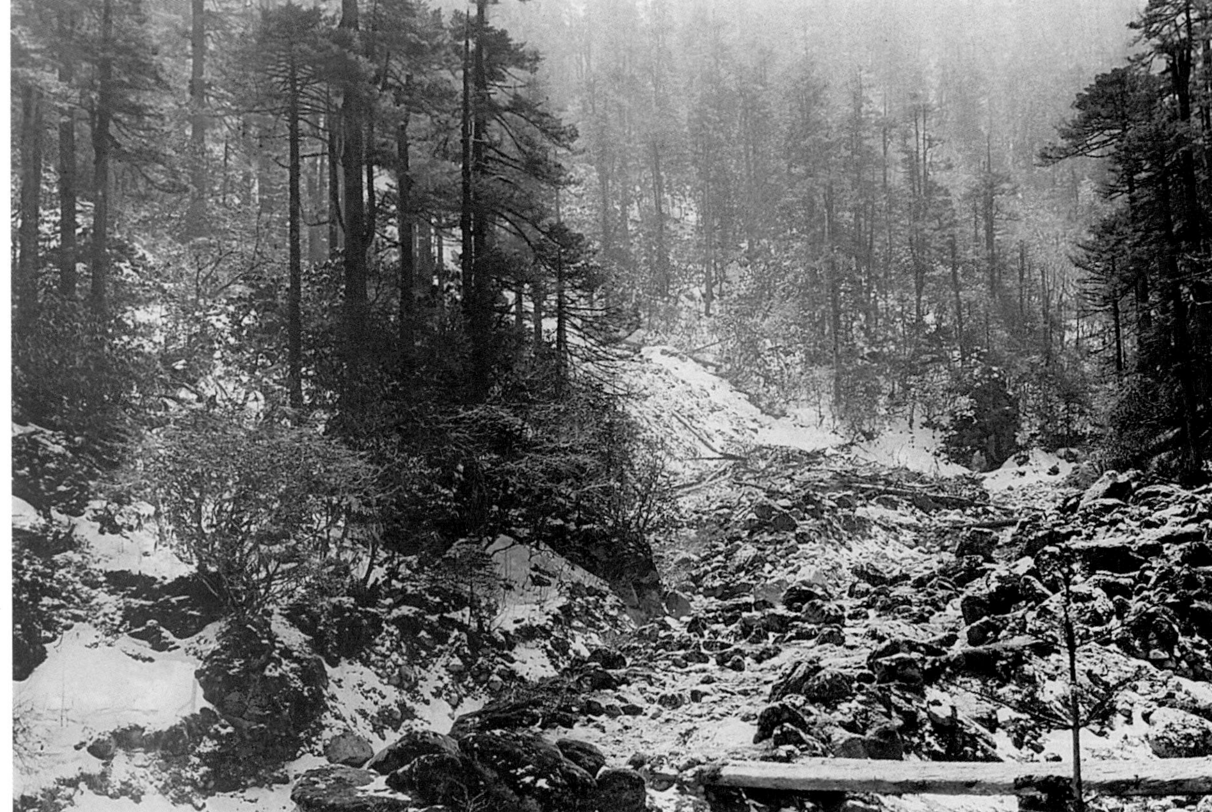

The tree line: here the lush vegetation of broadleaf and evergreen trees straggles to an end, above which rises the barren plateau of Tibet. The lack of trees means that the nomadic Tibetans must resort to tents made from wool, as there is no wood available for construction.

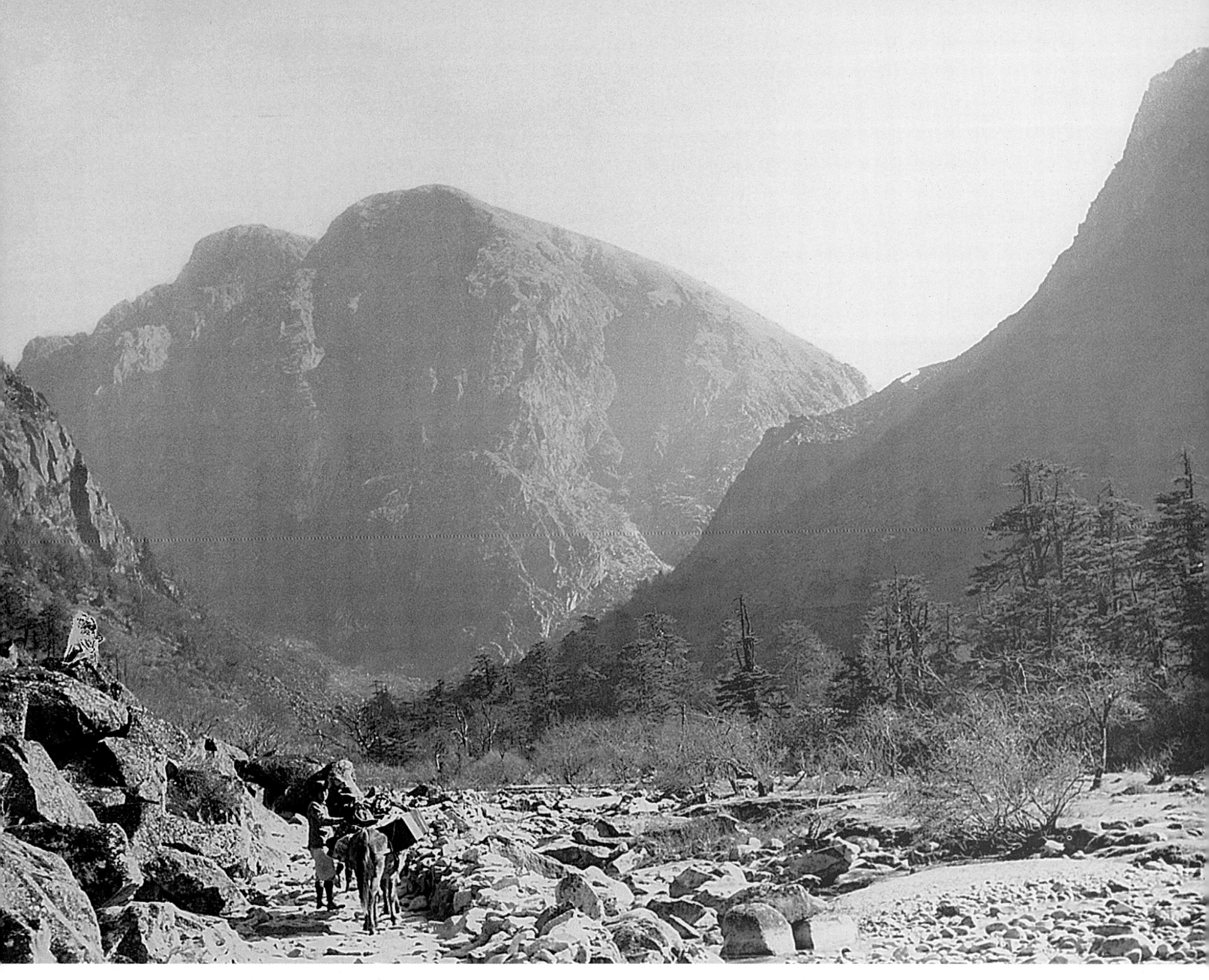

The rough path along which the loaded animals, porters and climbers made their way.

Overleaf: The pack animals grazing after a long day's walk.

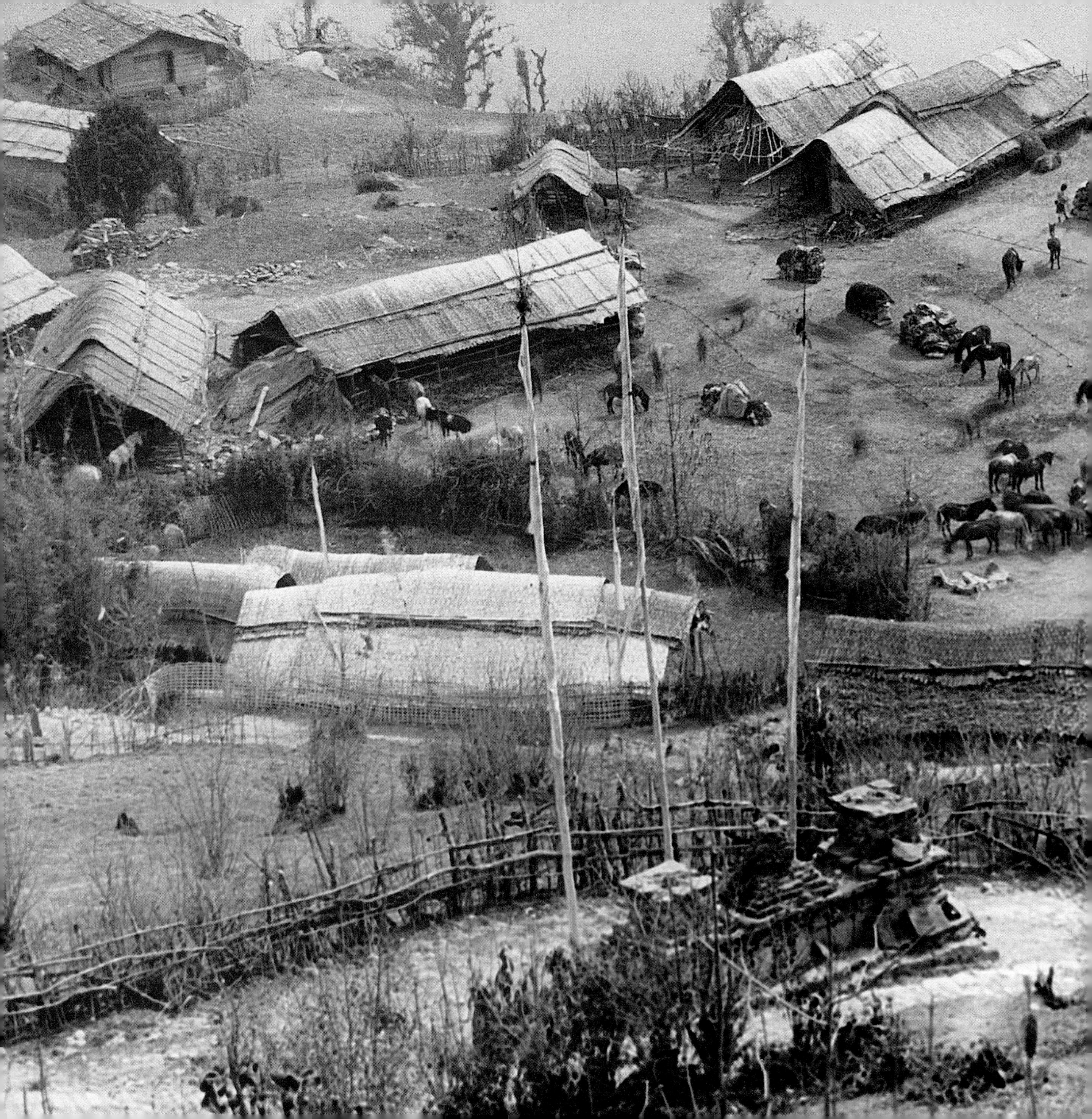

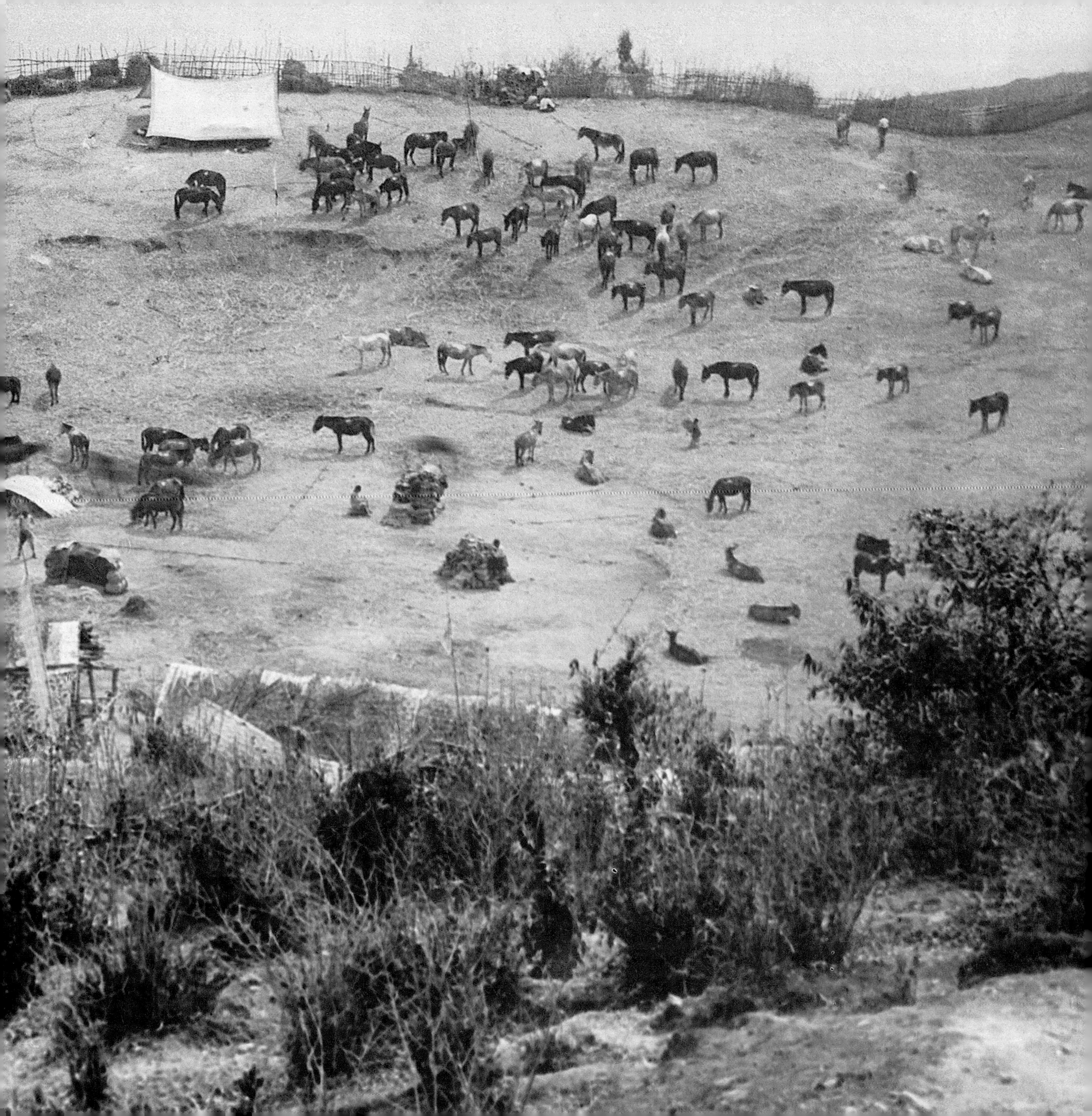

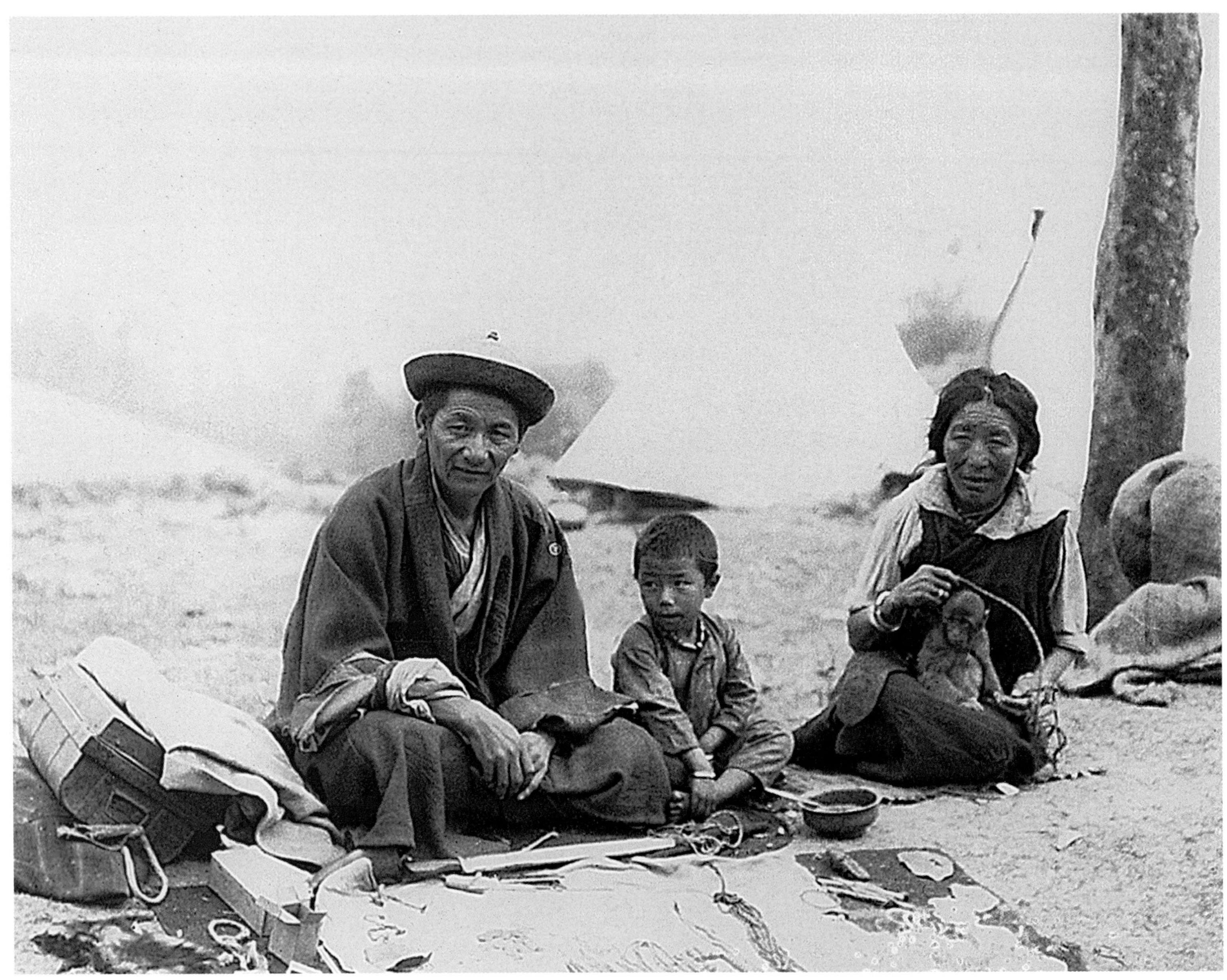

A nomad family with their tent and pet monkey, living as mendicants, on money given to them by travellers.

CHAPTER 4

THE ROOF OF THE WORLD

Although Everest is only 120 miles in a direct line from Darjeeling, the journey to Rongbuk Monastery and Base Camp covered 300 miles and would take the expedition members up to six weeks. They left on 25 March 1924.

After the dense forests of Sikkim, they crossed into Tibet and embarked upon the 200-mile across the 'roof of the world', a plateau at over 15,000 feet, as Noel described it:

Tibet, in spite of its charm, is unquestionably the most frightful and desolate country in the whole world. No other land can be so harsh and forbidding as that vast tableland raised 15,000 feet, where stone and ice and mountain seem to conspire against all life. The people live in the most extreme poverty and discomfort. It is so cold and the land so poor that the only crop they can grow is barley. There is even a scarcity of air to breathe. Yet the icy winds blow endlessly with a biting velocity.

Indeed, no one who has not been in Tibet knows what wind can be. I cannot better describe a gale than by likening it to myriads of knives thrown at one with great force. It cuts into one through any kind of clothing, and penetrates to the marrow of one's bones. The skin, particularly where exposed, chaps and cracks and becomes a mass of sores, unless the constant precaution is taken in keeping it well soaked in butter, grease or Vaseline. The women manage to preserve their complexion slightly better than the men by smearing their cheeks, nose and forehead with a black ointment.

At 15,000 feet above sea level, manual labour is tough and a strain on the heart. What does time matter in Tibet? When tending herds of grazing yaks, men and women sing and spin. From the pure wool of the sheep and the hair of the yaks, they weave the material to make tents of the *Dok-pa* – the shepherds – and the *bokkus*, the loose blanket coats girdled at the waist, that the people wear – coats so voluminous, that bags of *tsampa* – oatmeal – wooden bowls, cooking pots, bladders of milk, and prayer wheels may all find storage place therein. In the winter, over the woollen *bokkus* they will wear a raw-cured sheepskin coat, the wool inside and the leather outside. It stinks, but it is warm!

The Tibetans import all their food from India, Nepal and China during the summer months, while the snow passes are open, and store it in sufficient quantities to last all through the winter. Wheat, rice, *tsampa*, *ghur* – a sweet paste – and sugar are bartered in large quantities in exchange for Borax, salt, sheep and yak wool.

Salt is extracted from the great lakes, and is an indispensable commodity for preserving food. The Tibetans have their own peculiar system of cold storage, as Noel discovered at a special meal prepared at Shekar Dzong for the climbers, when they were allowed to partake of some old, smoked vintage mutton, killed forty years before. There were two favoured beverages – *murwa*, a beer brewed from millet seed, which is drunk cold and served up to grandees at feasts in the horns of the wild-yak; and brick tea, which is a concoction of tea leaves stewed in a brass vessel, then transferred to a wooden churn in which have been deposited several balls of butter with copious sprinklings of salt. A piston which passes through the movable lid is then vigorously set in action, and when well stirred and steaming, the mixture is served all round and avidly drunk from wooden bowls, one of which everyone carries about the person. To the European palate, this drink was impossible to take, but, to comply with the custom of their hosts, they attempted to drink the bowl empty. Imagine their dismay on discovering that local custom never allowed for the bowl to remain empty: it was quickly and deftly refilled. General Bruce was fortunate in finding an excuse to get out of the tricky situation – he told his Tibetan hosts that he would never drink more than one bowl at a time until the group had climbed the sacred mountain. Noel also managed to avoid most of the rancid drink by announcing that he must hurry to catch the beautiful sunset or a passing cloud formation on camera.

He was also struck by the polyandry. Noel had noticed this in 1913, when he wrote in a journal:

It is rather regarded in this pastoral country as an arrangement to protect the joint family when its head is away for weeks, herding the cattle; and it is also viewed as a device to keep the common property within the family, in a country which cannot support a large population. The women are seldom separated from one or other of their husbands. When one man goes for some days to take the yaks or sheep to a distant grazing ground, another fills his place in the tent. Occasionally, more than one of her legal husbands live together happily under the same tent, but usually not more than one at a time.

The Indian Army had supplied mules for the early part of the journey, but in Phari, the first important trading post in Tibet, 400 yaks were taken on to carry the expedition baggage. A beast can travel at about a mile an hour, grazing as he goes along. The animals could be capricious, however, so Noel relied on eight porters to carry the cameras, and to have them ready at a moment's notice. He had intended to take an artist as part of his team, but this had not been permitted by the Tibetan authorities, already anxious that even the climbers were about to desecrate their mountains. Francis Helps, a talented portrait painter, and Noel's wife Sybille stayed in Chumbi, Helps to record members of the expedition as they passed through, and the native Tibetans, and Mrs Noel to write a book about Tibetan folklore.

At Phari, Bruce remarked that the canny Tibetans had increased their prices by 25 per cent since 1922; but it was still a filthy place, as every traveller has irresistibly remarked. None the less, Noel cautiously wandered through the fort and noted the construction of houses, built to resist the cold and wind – mud is strengthened with horn, hair and skins of dead cattle to provide insulation. From here, the yak caravan, some five miles long, set out north and then west to the great goal.

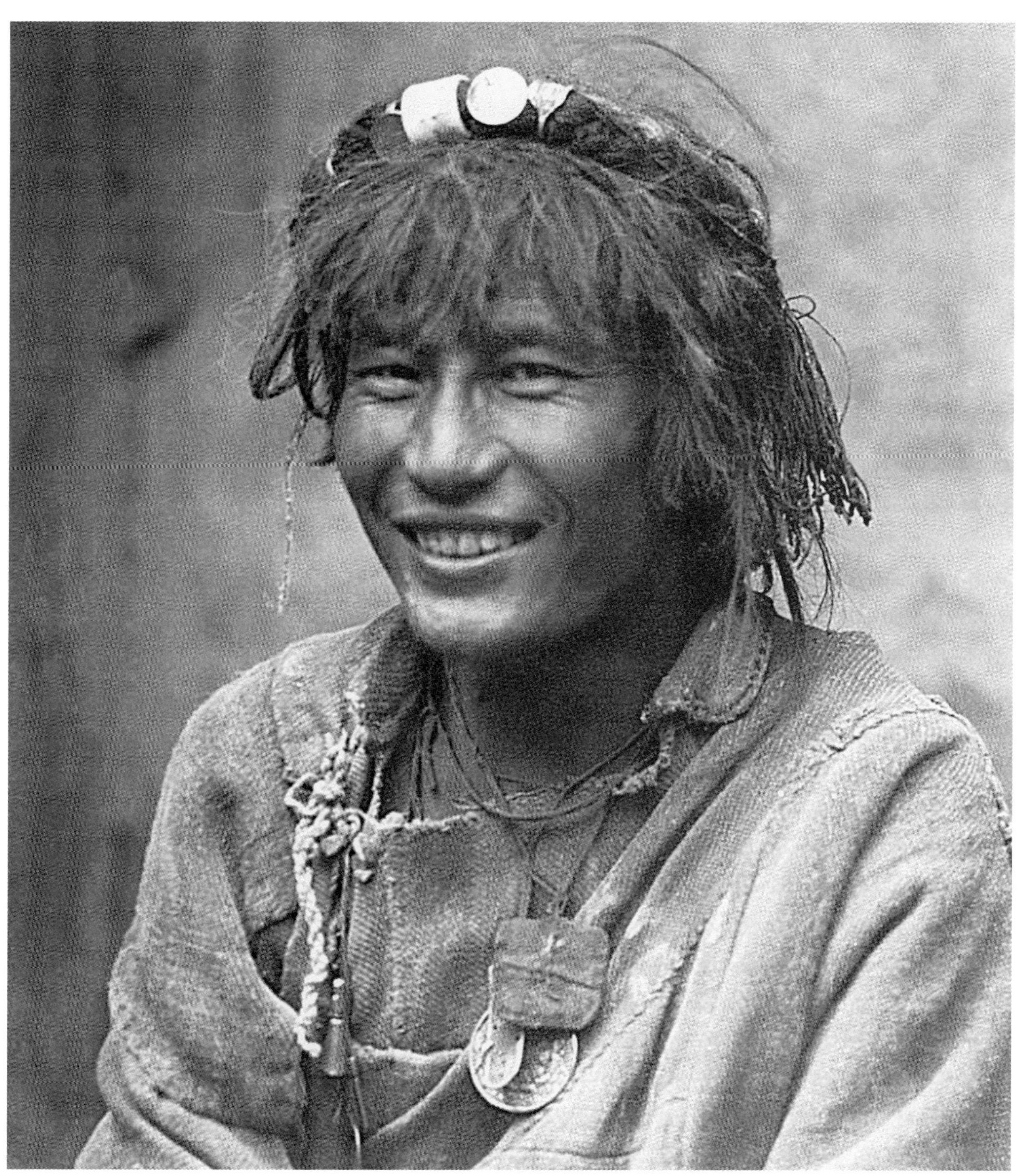

Tibetan youth, servant
of the ruler of Shekar.
Both boys and girls wear
masses of jewellery,
made of coral, turquoise
and silver.

At 15,000 feet above sea level life is difficult. The climate is inhospitable, and outside villages the nomad has to live in a tent made of the coarse and waterproof fabric of yak-hair, and survives by raising a few yaks and sheep. The tent is open at the top, to allow the smoke from the fire to escape and yet to limit the ingress of cold air.

Child mortality is high and medical care scarce. Babies are smothered in butter to protect their skin against the fierce, incessant wind. They would not have had a bath in their entire lives, but they were adorned with charms from their earliest days, to protect them against evil.

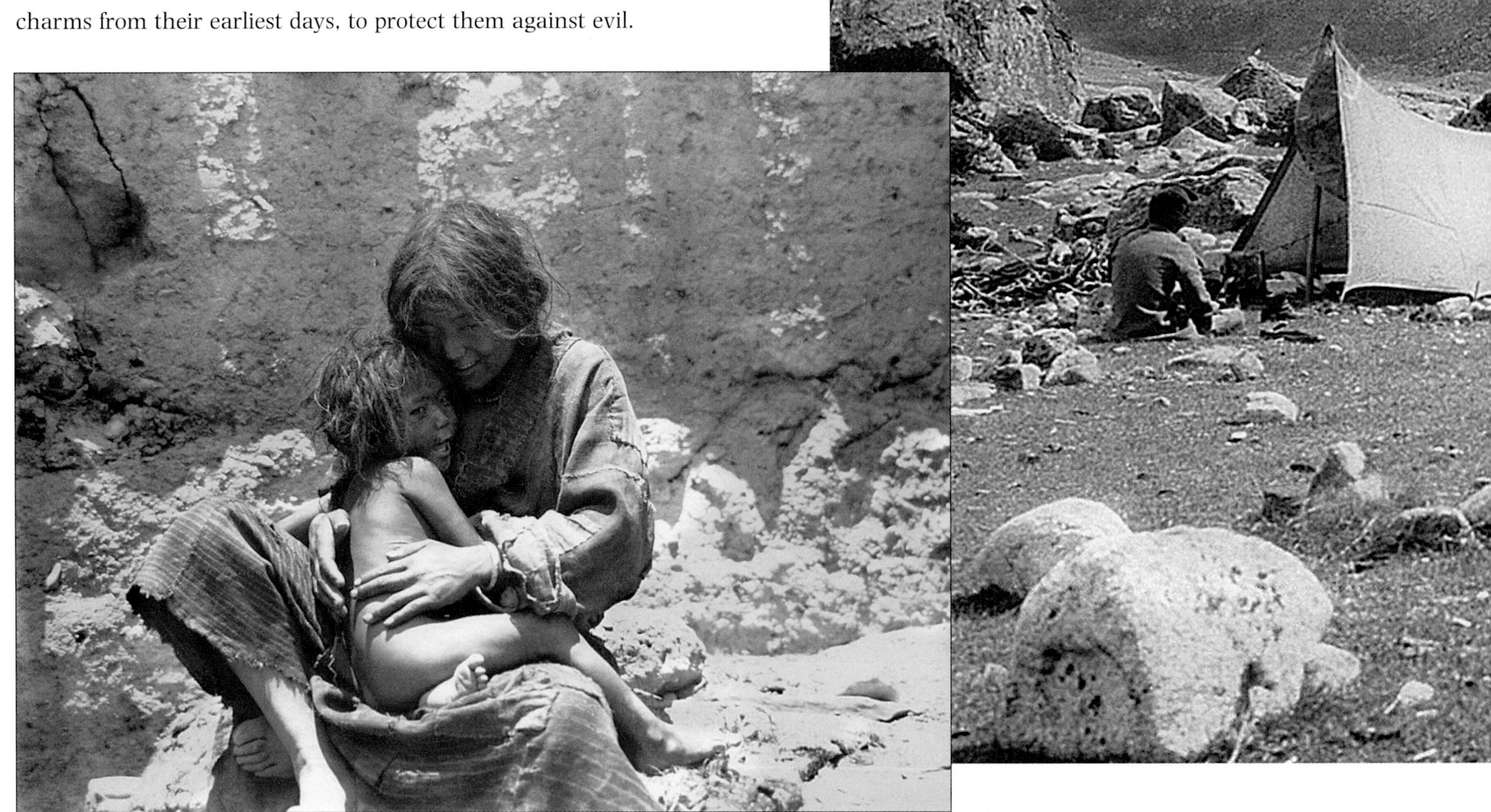

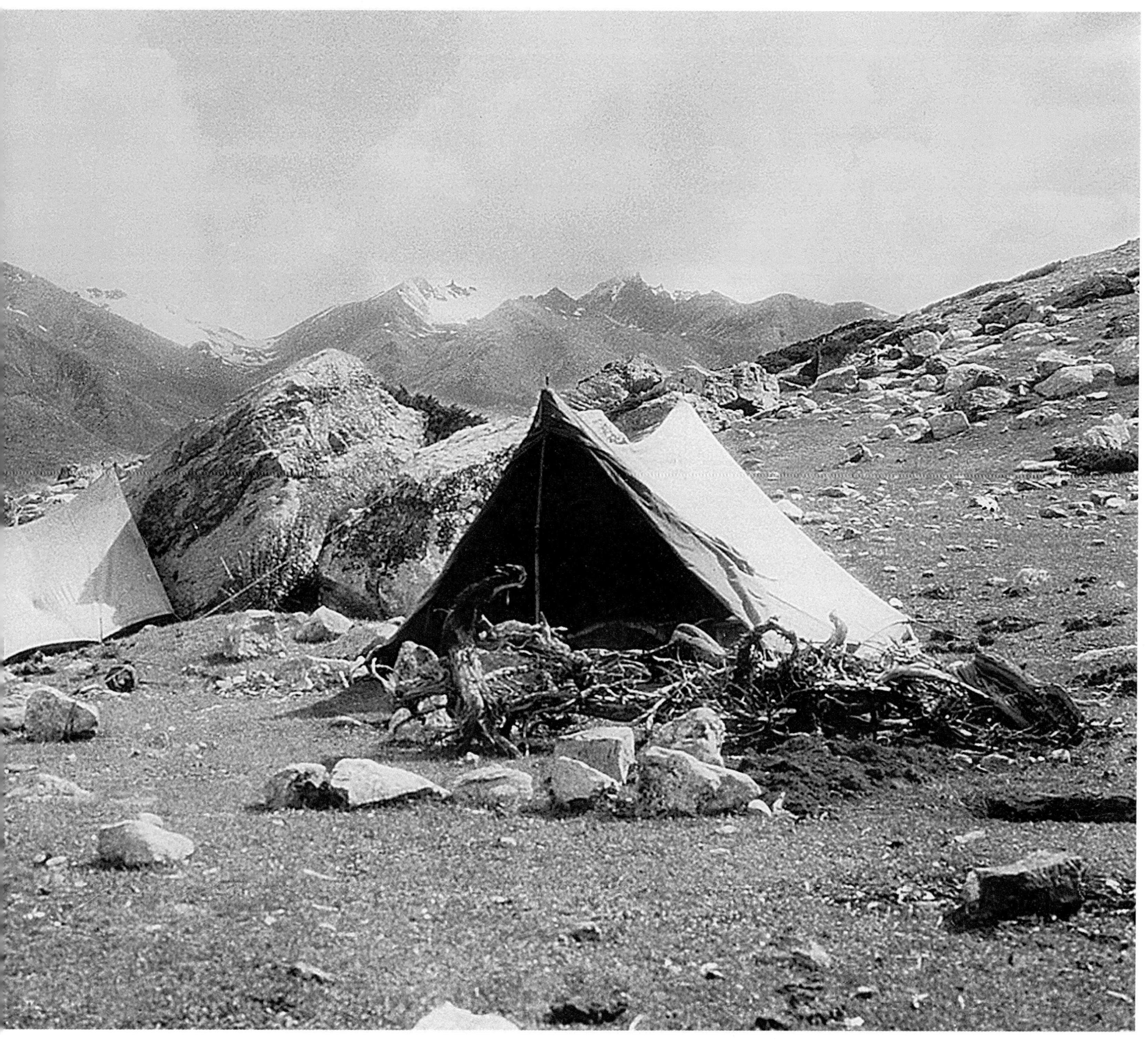

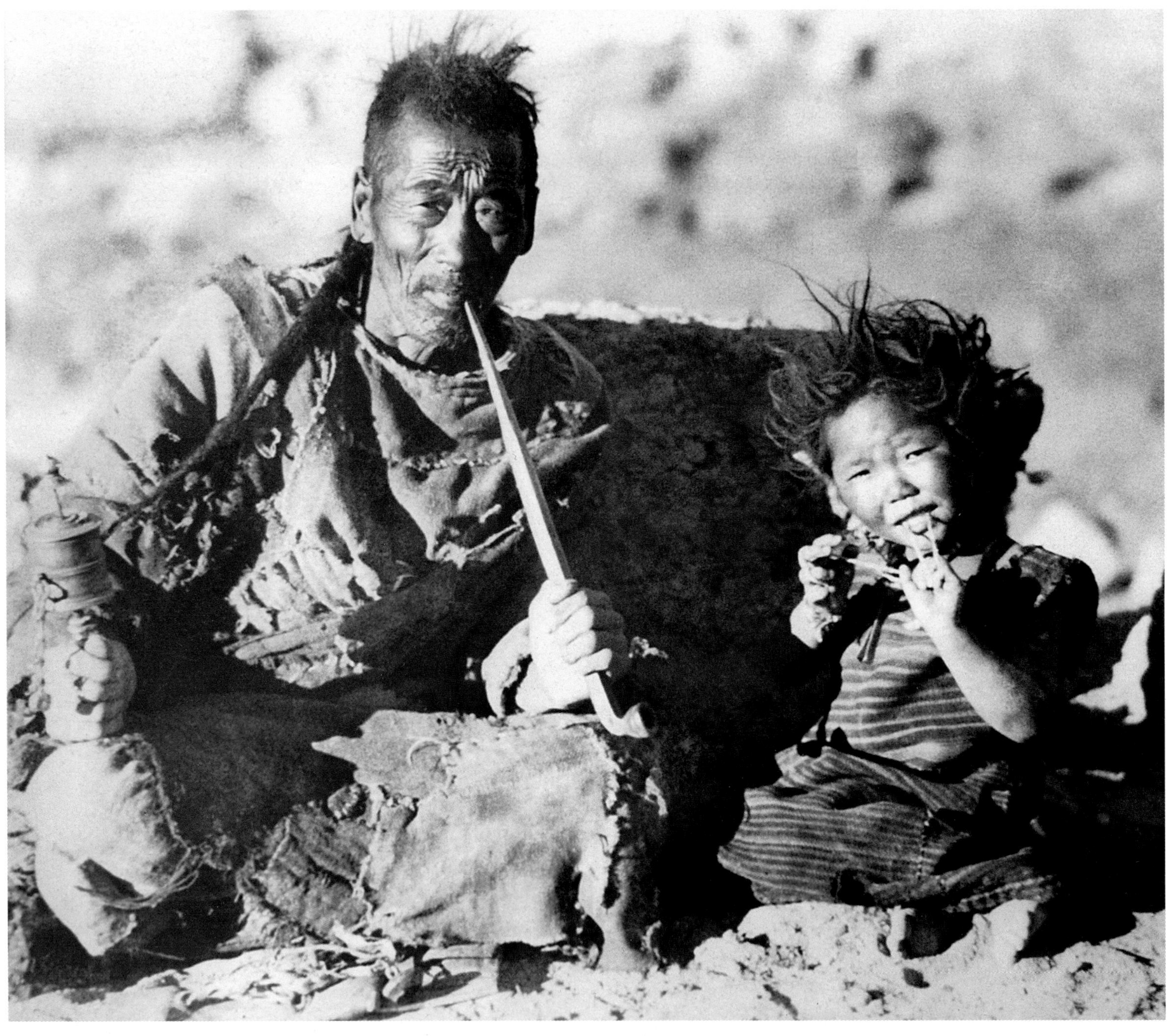

The Tibetan is a happy person, while working his yak and plough or tilling the barley fields, but nothing is done quickly. Manual labour is tough and a strain on the heart. Besides, what does time matter in Tibet?

Camp in the lush tropical forests of
Sikkim at about 2,500 feet. This
dense forest has approximately 250
inches of rain per annum, and
formed the first part of the trek from
Darjeeling into Tibet. One of Noel's
still cameras is visible on the tripod.
Note the gigantic azalea and
rhododendron trees.

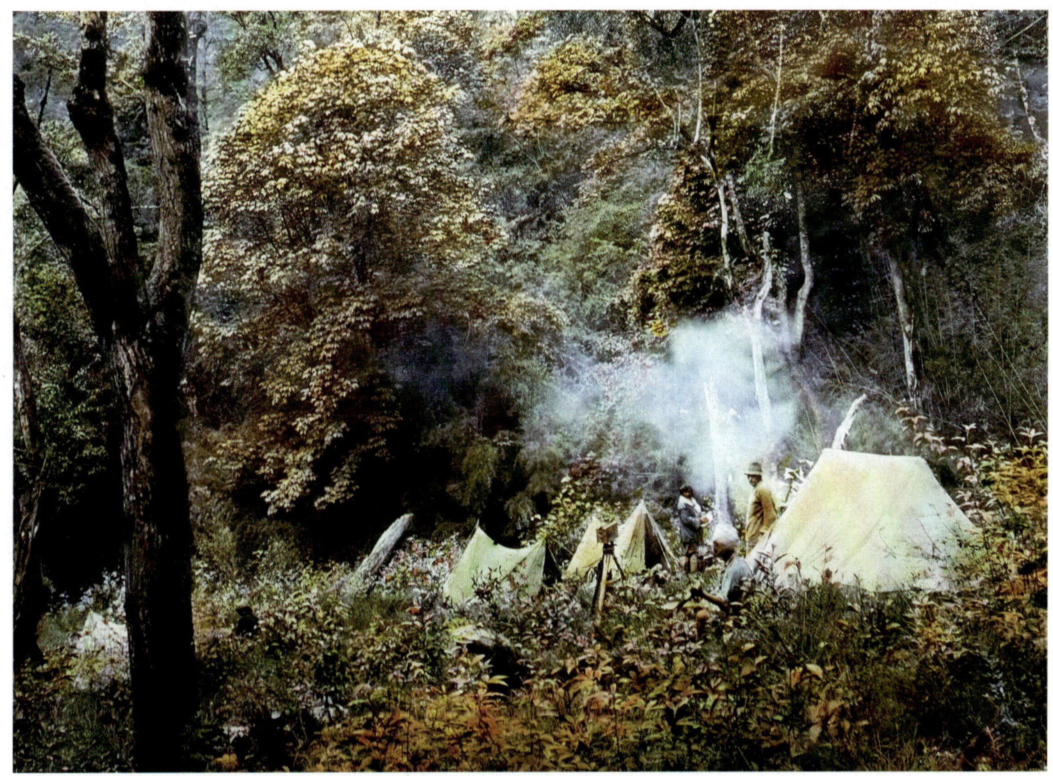

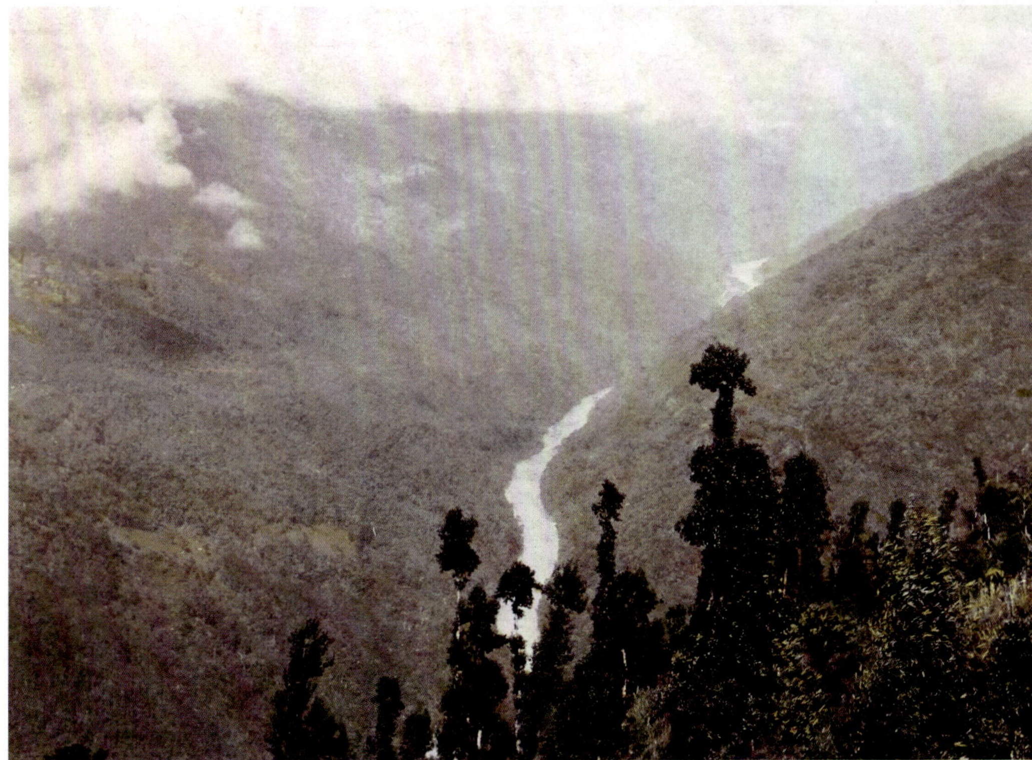

The valley of the River Teesta in
Sikkim.

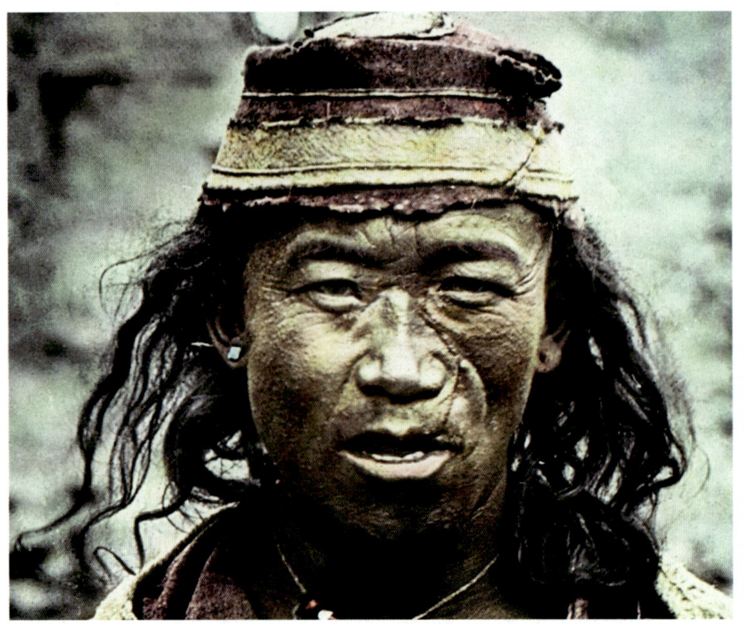

The rugged Tibetan.

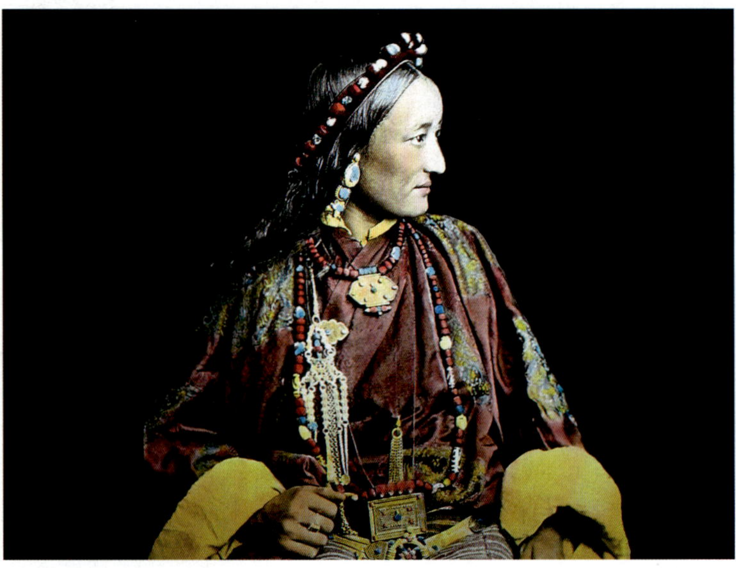

A Tibetan lady from a city, showing off her silk garments, massive earrings and amulet box, and an ornate belt clasp, all made of coral and turquoise.

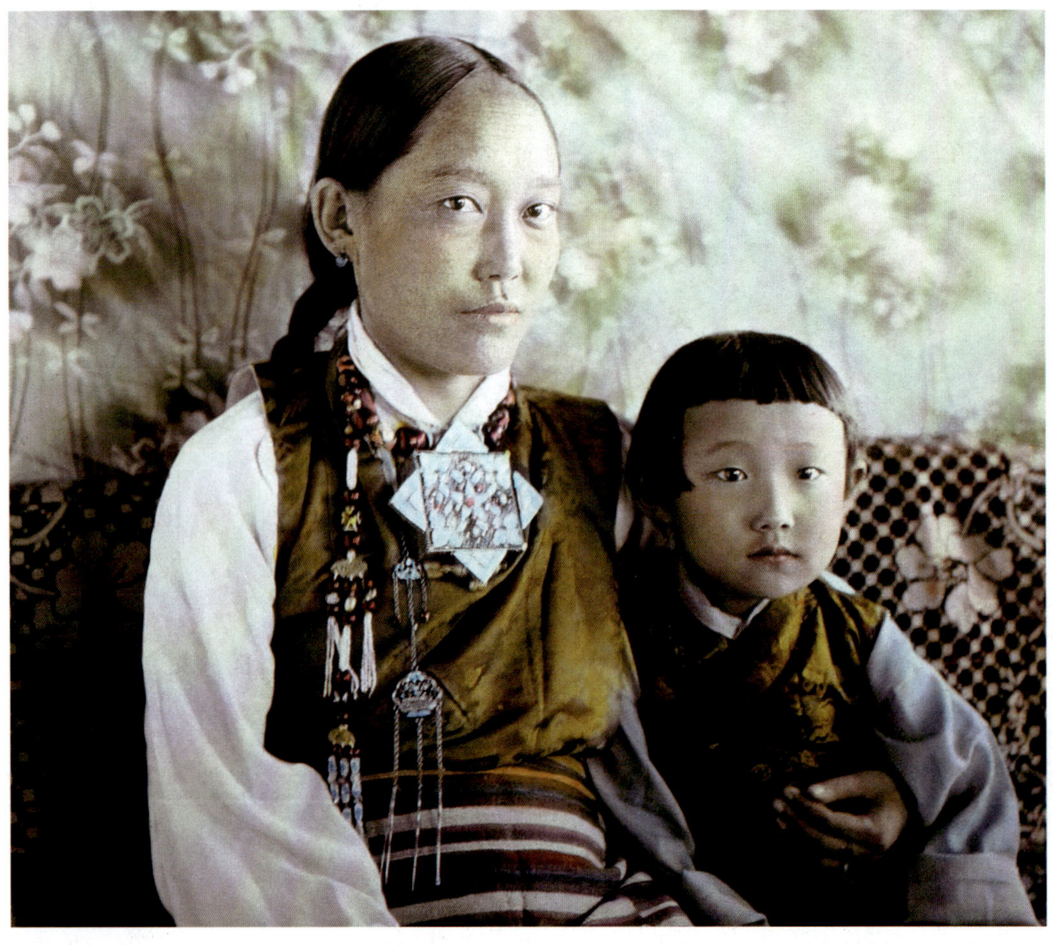

A lady of high rank and her child: her amulet box contains holy relics, almost the only 'medical' help available to the Tibetans at that time.

Interior of a monastery, showing the intricate buildings which house not only the head lama, the religious chief, and the monks but also the *dzongpen*, the civilian leader of the community.

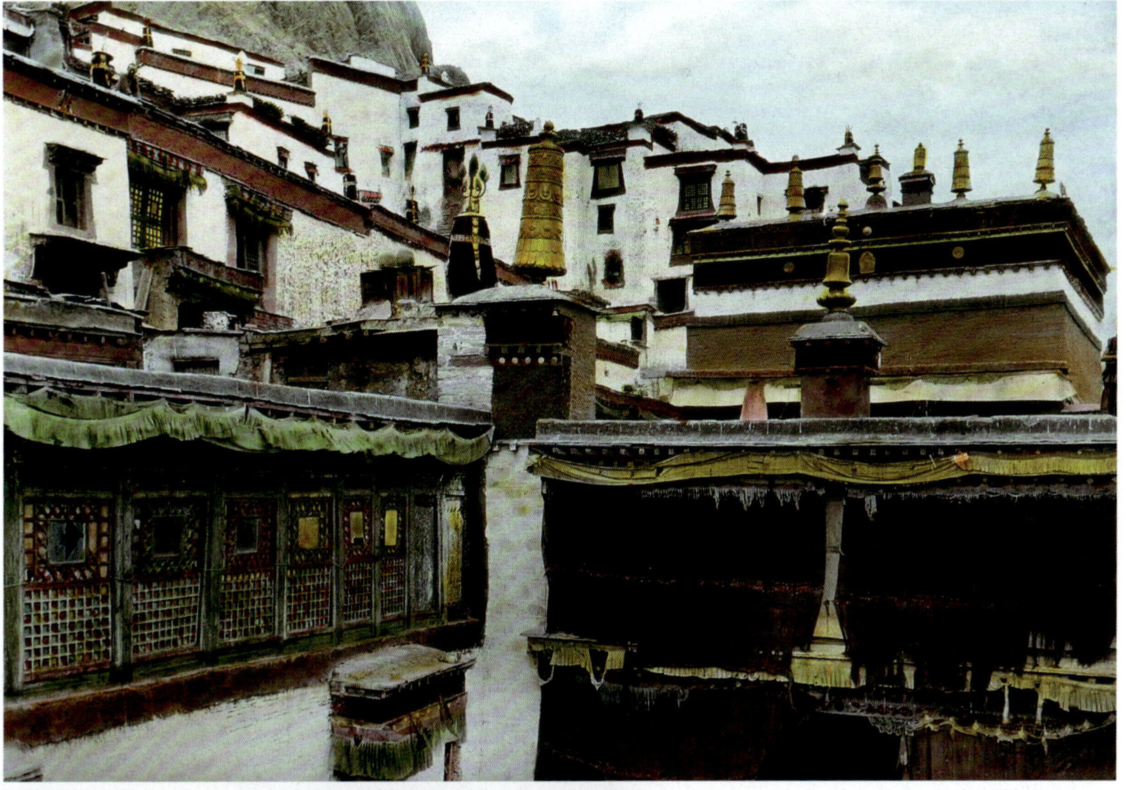

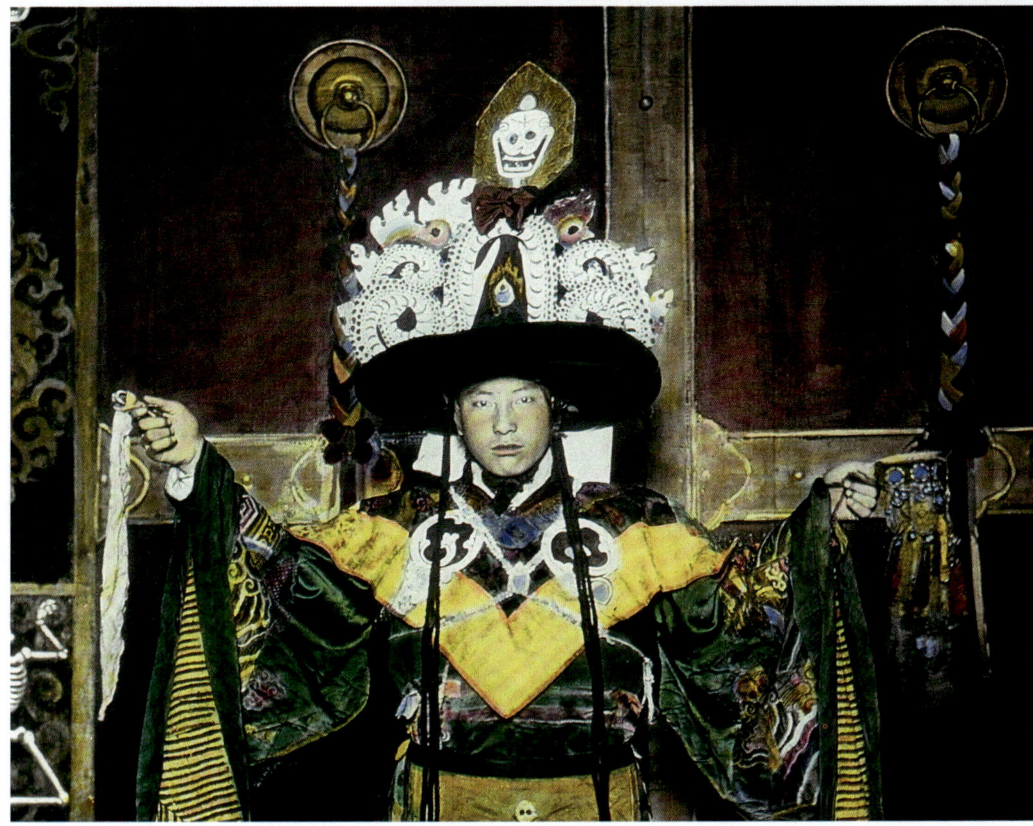

Tibetan lama in ceremonial dress.

A detail of the rhododendron. These grow to a
height of 30 feet.

A field of irises in the Kharta Valley, on the
approach to Everest.

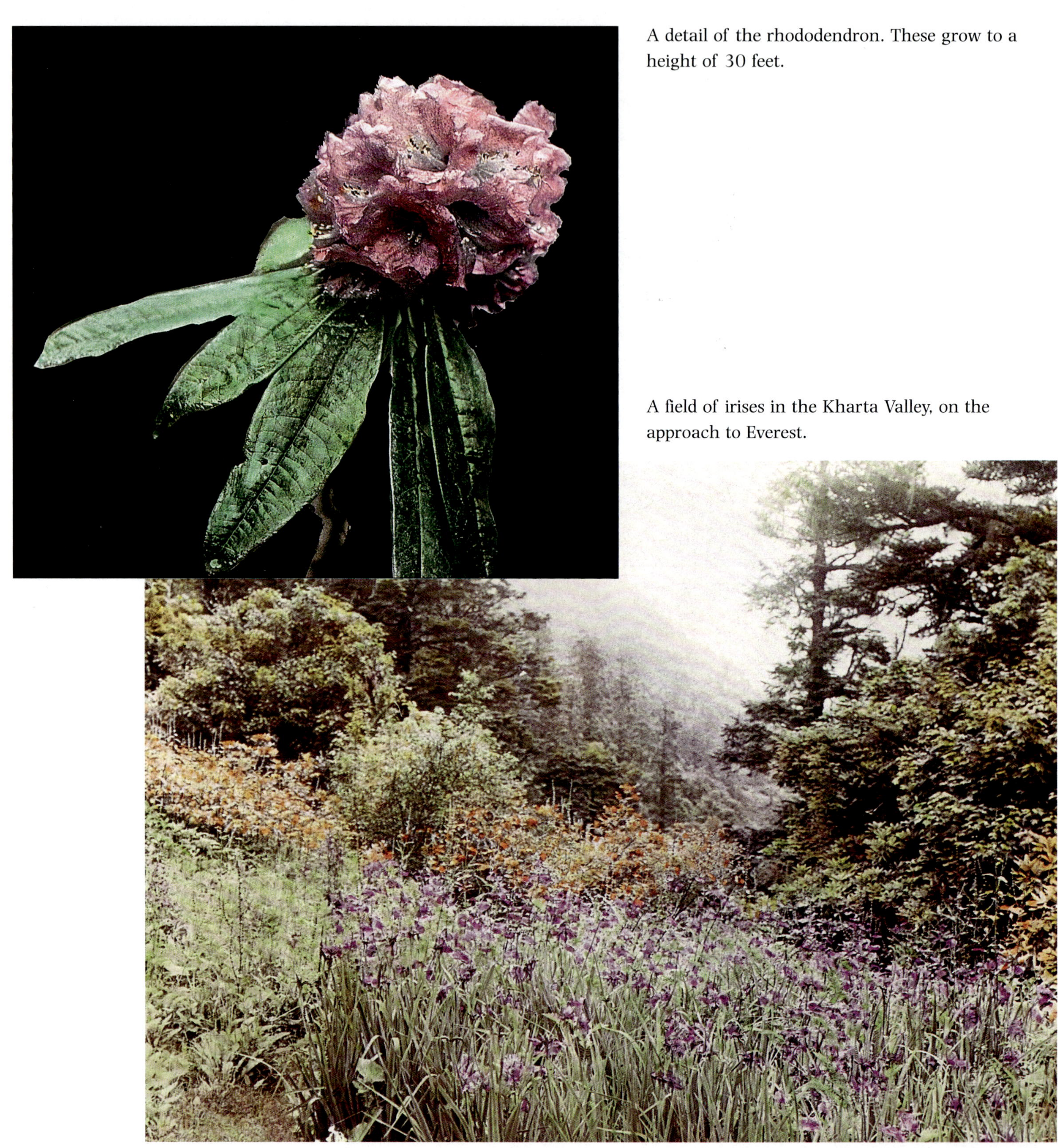

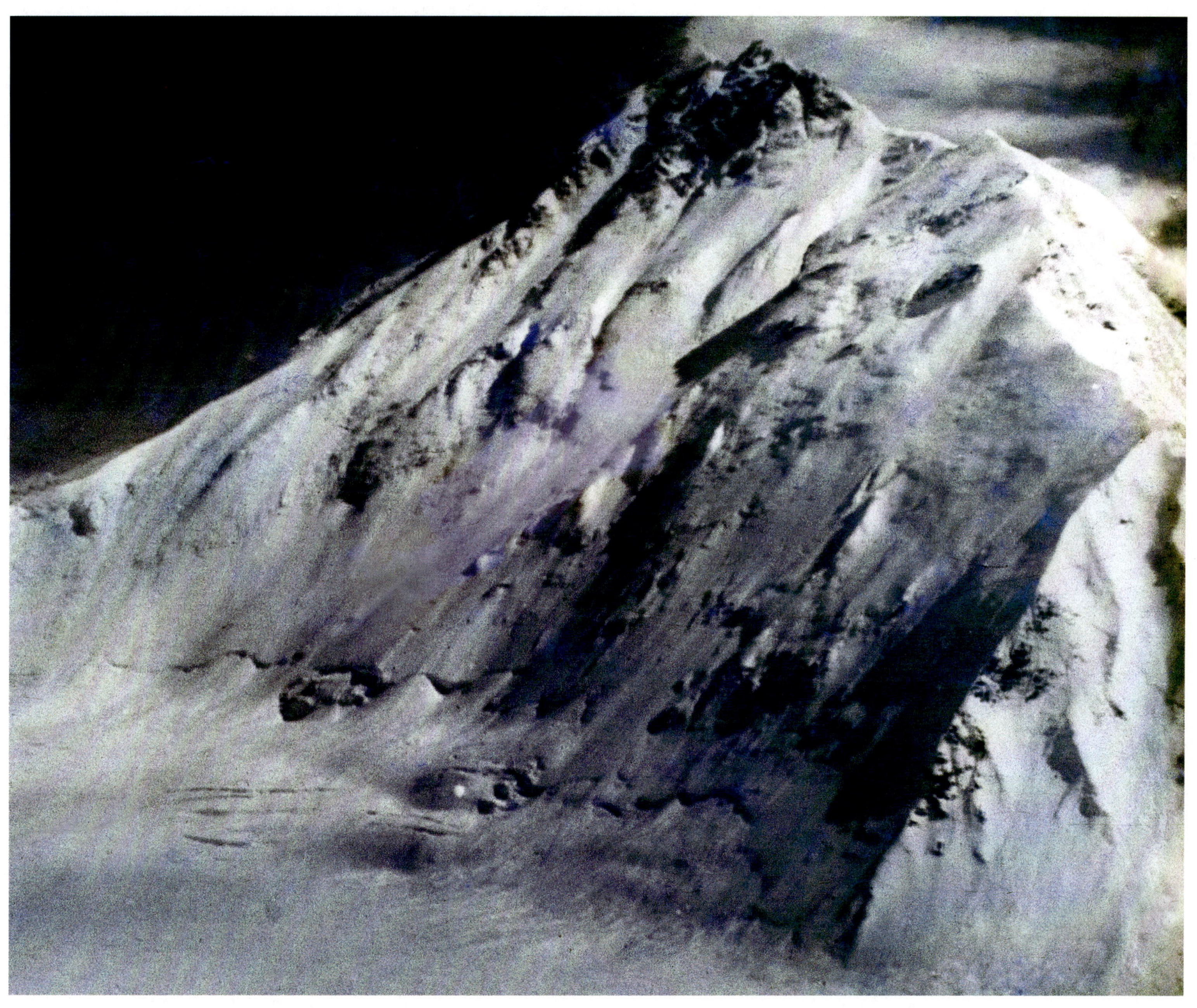

The north-east ridge of Everest, showing the menacing cloud which indicated the ever-present wind.

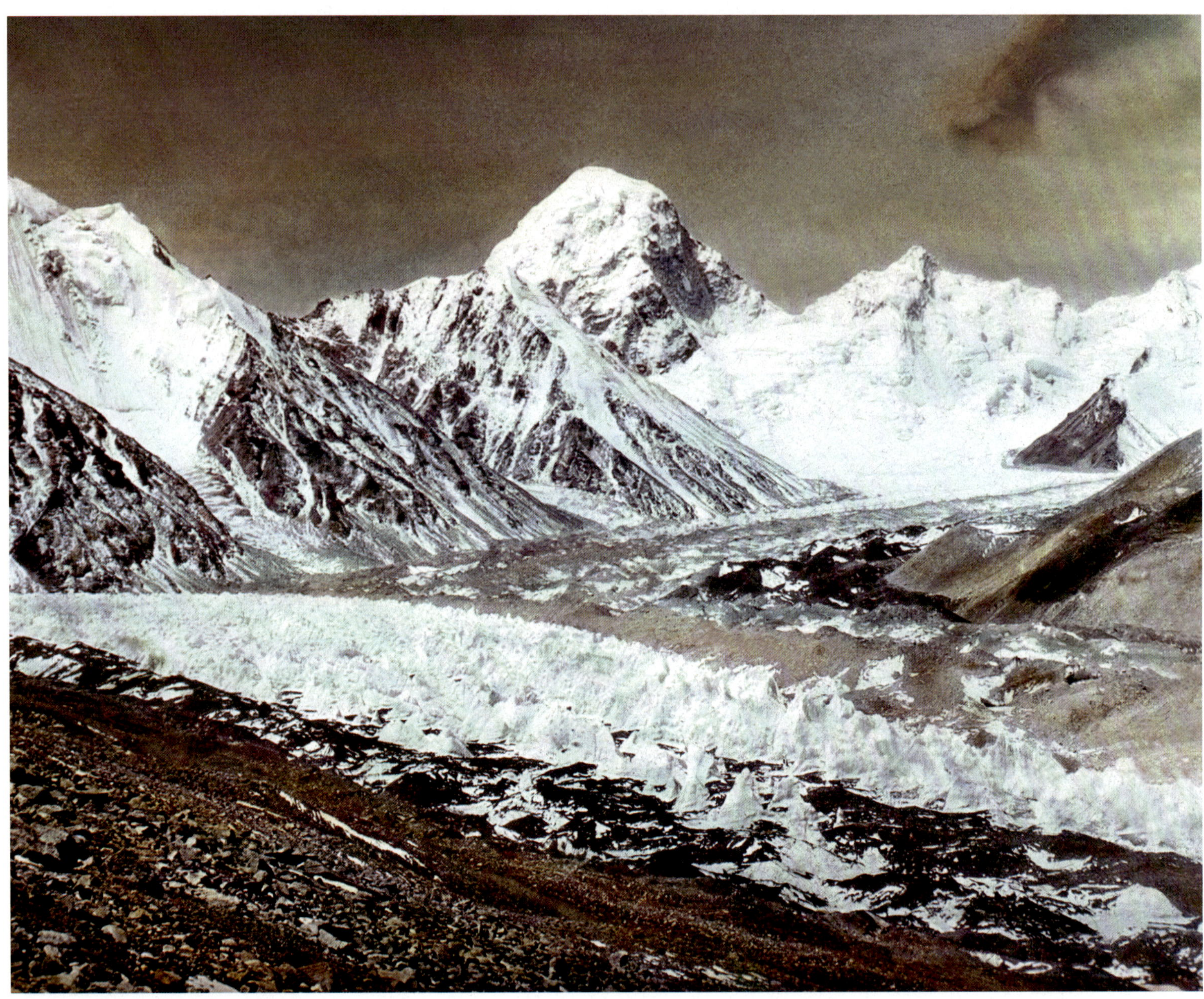

The main Rongbuk glacier.

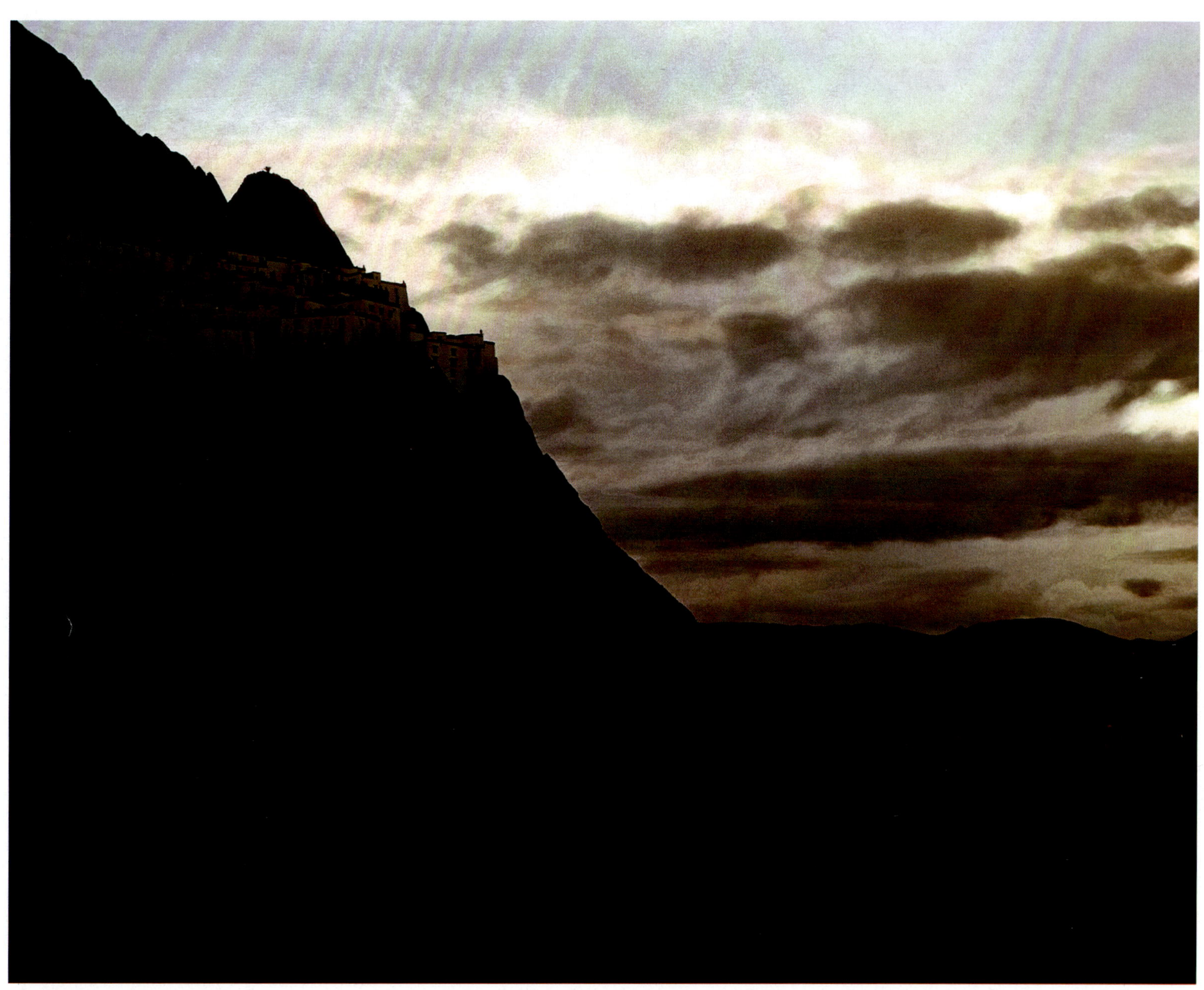

Shekar Dzong at sunset.

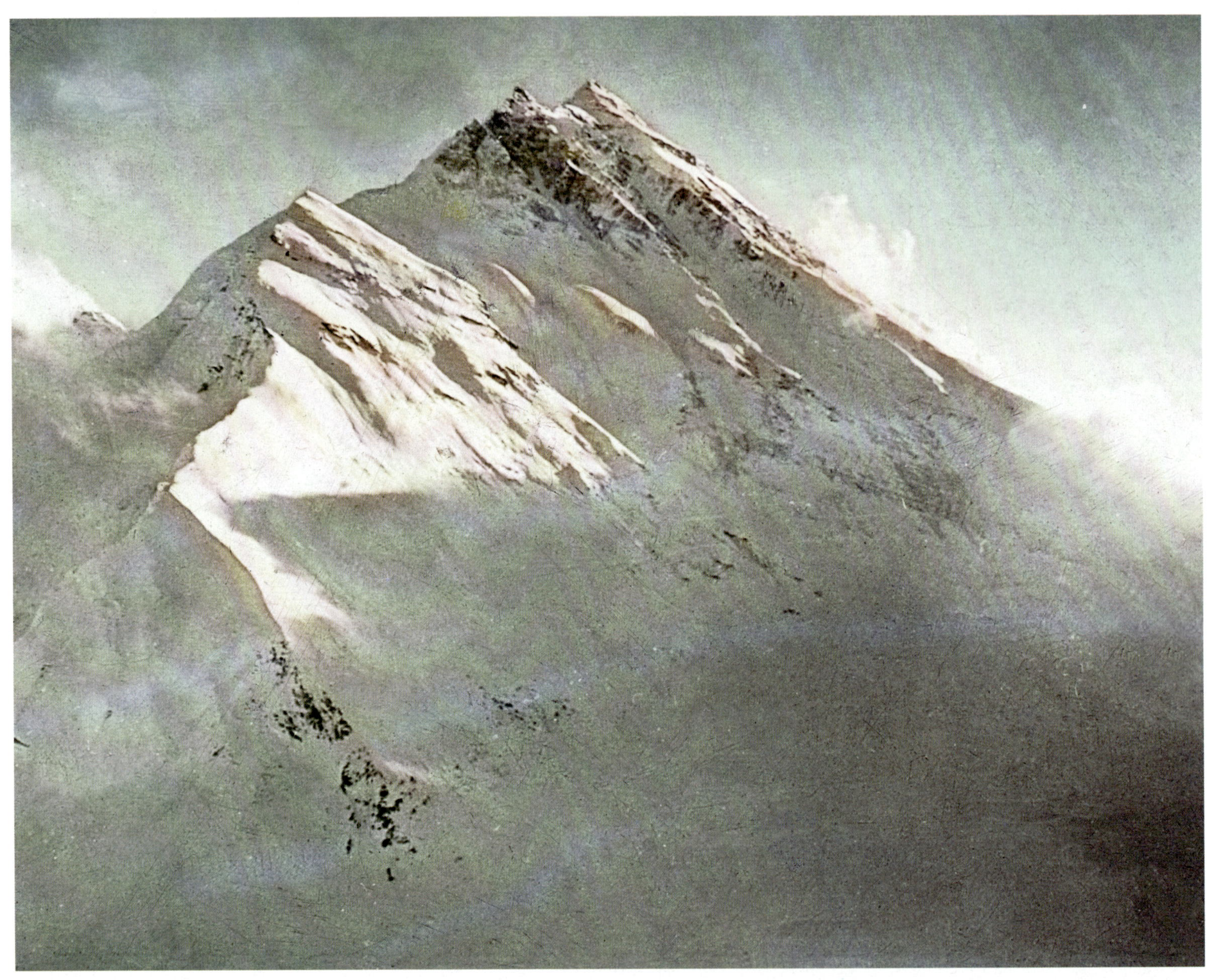

Sunset on the summit.

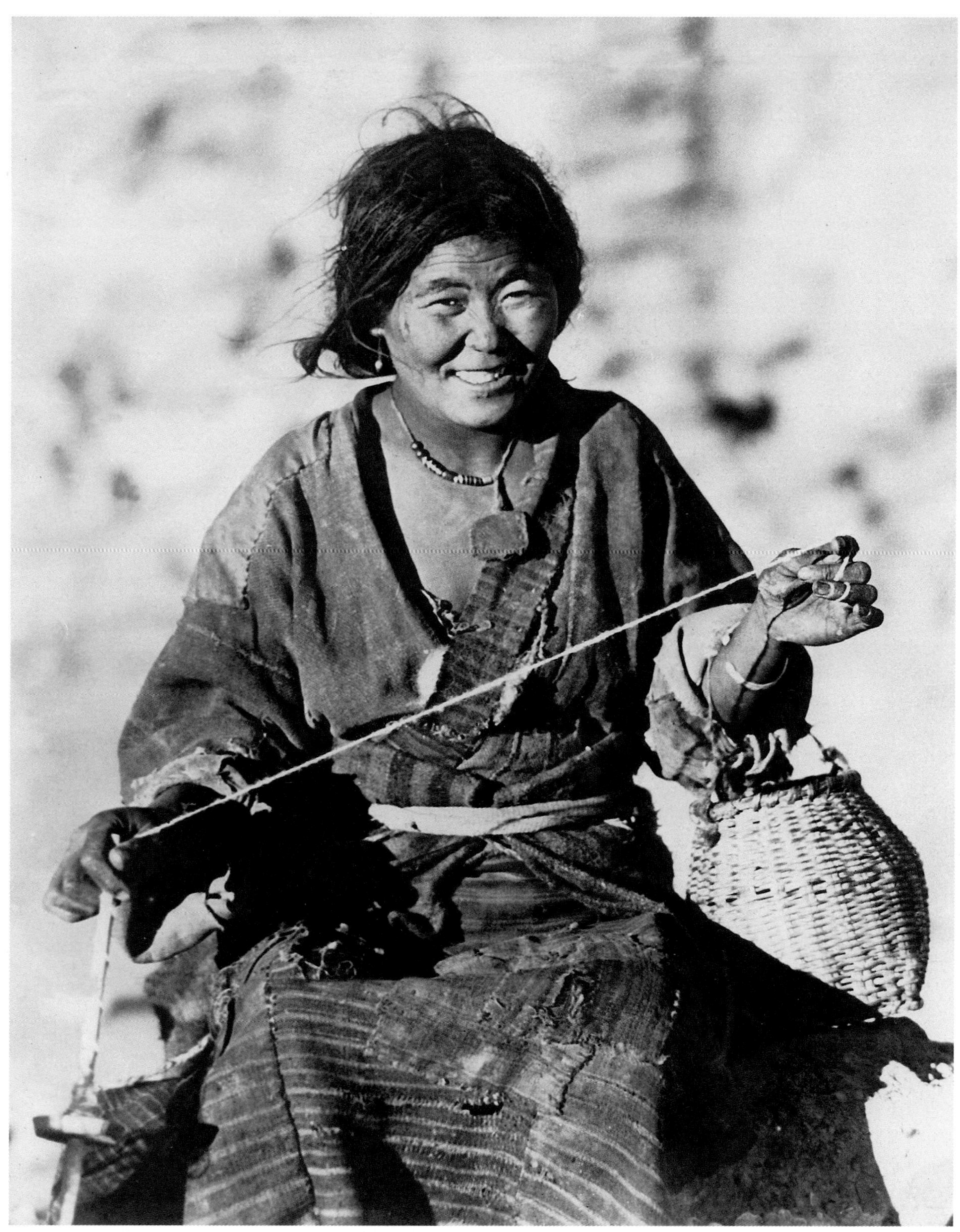

When tending herds of
grazing yaks, men and
women sing and spin
wool, which they will
weave into material for
tents and loose blanket-
coats, girdled at the
waist.

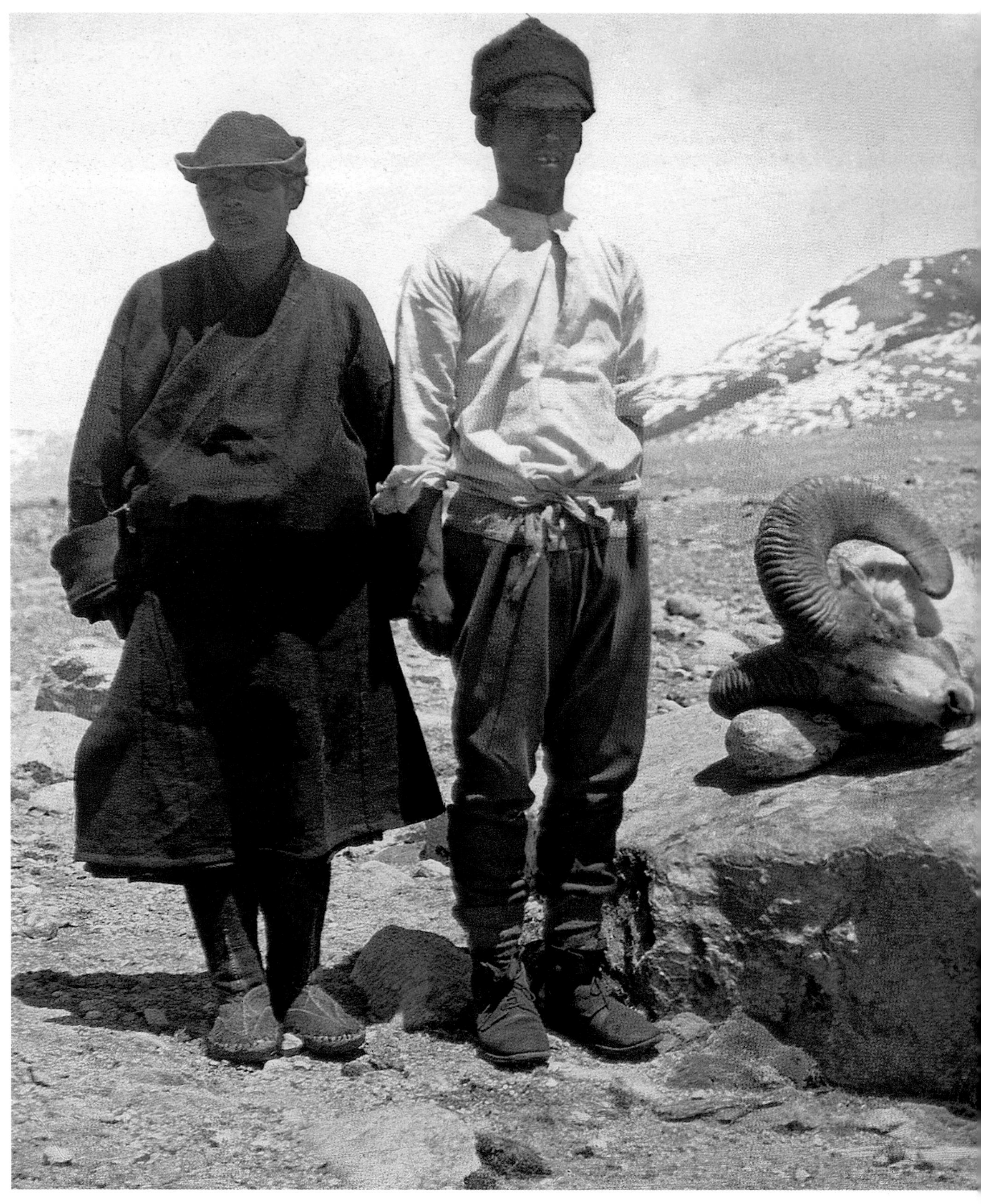

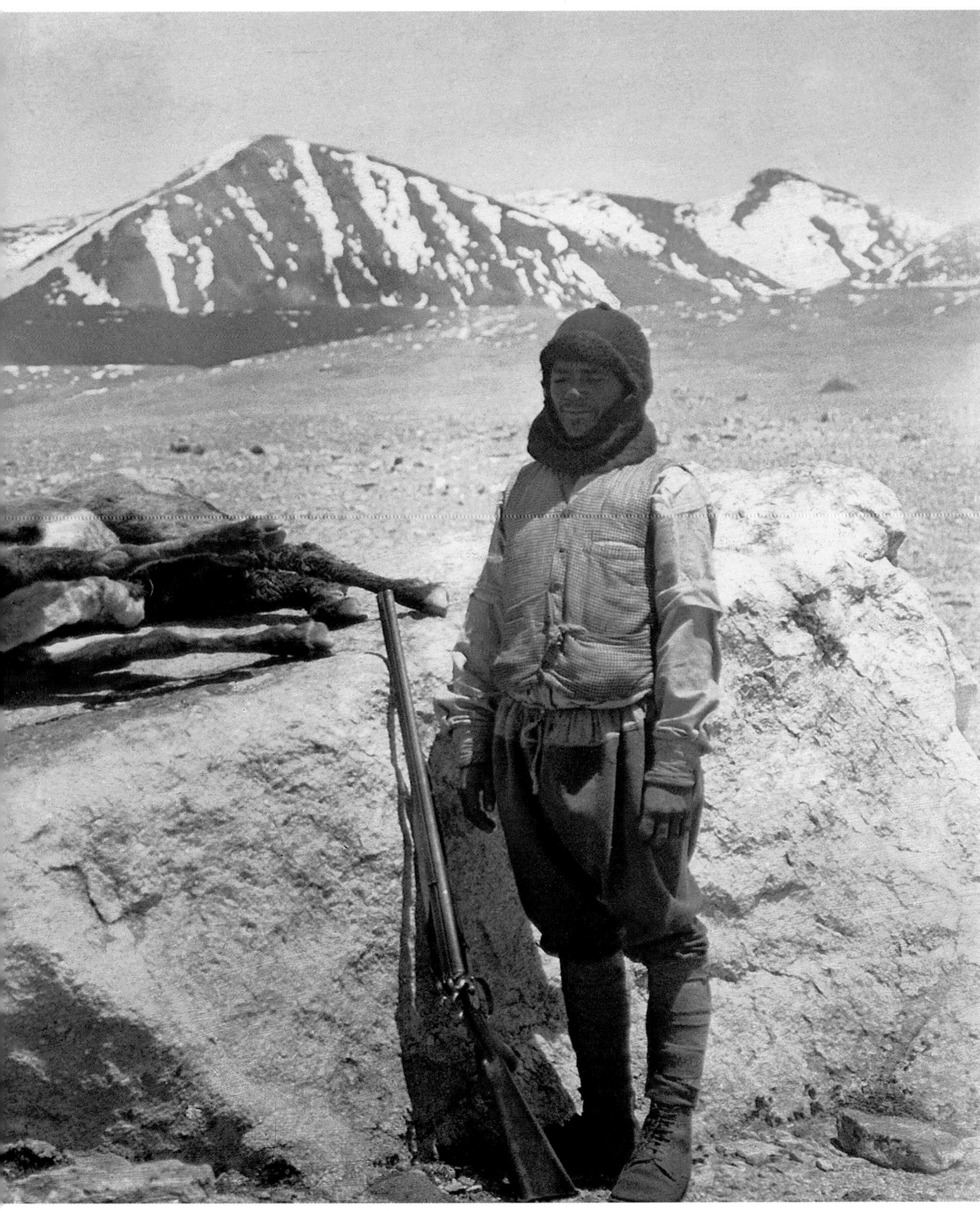

Three hunters with a kill – the man on the left is wearing a typical blanket-coat.

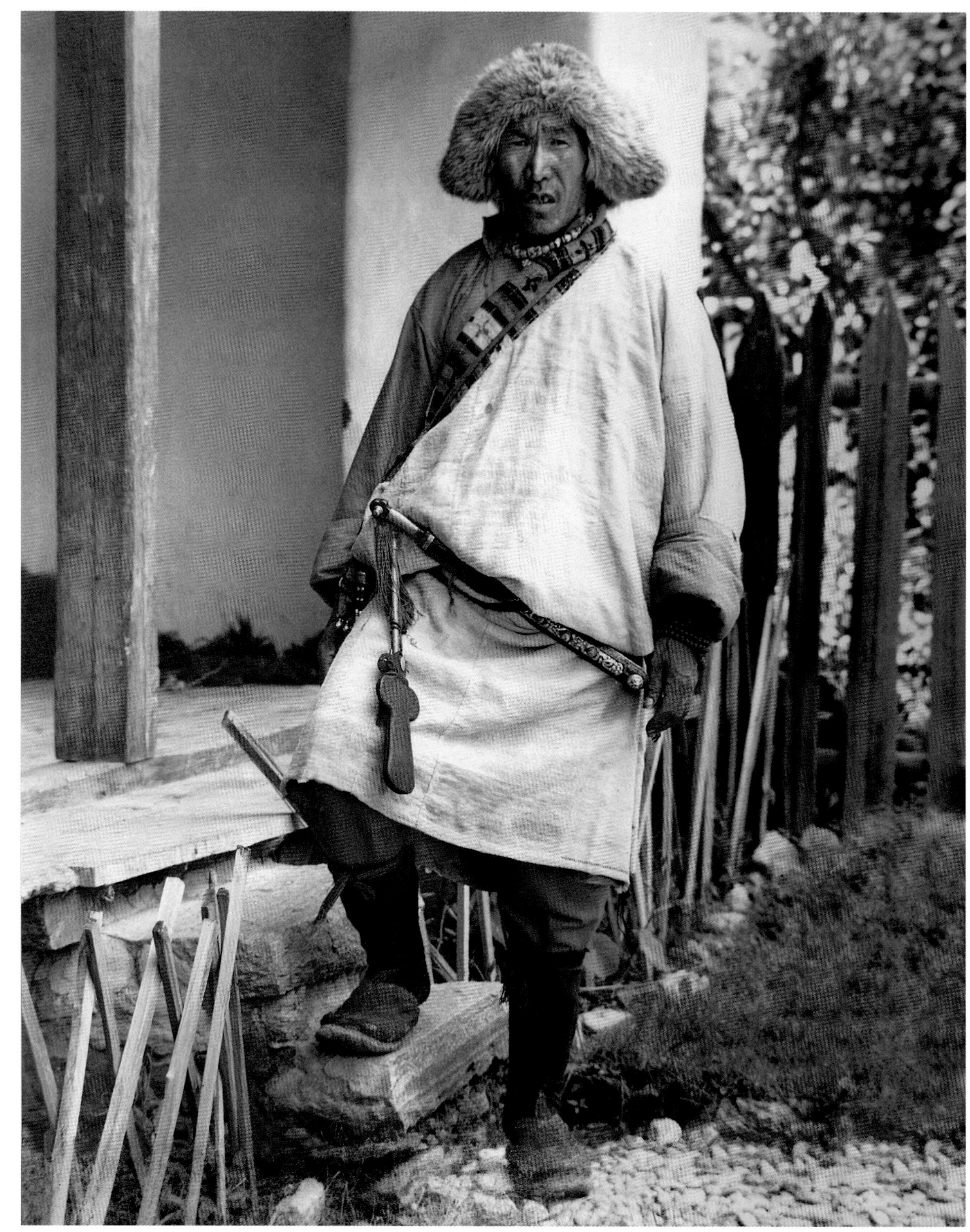

The blanket-coat has no pockets; instead a pocket is created by pulling up the front of the garment above the girdle, which is used to carry a long knife.

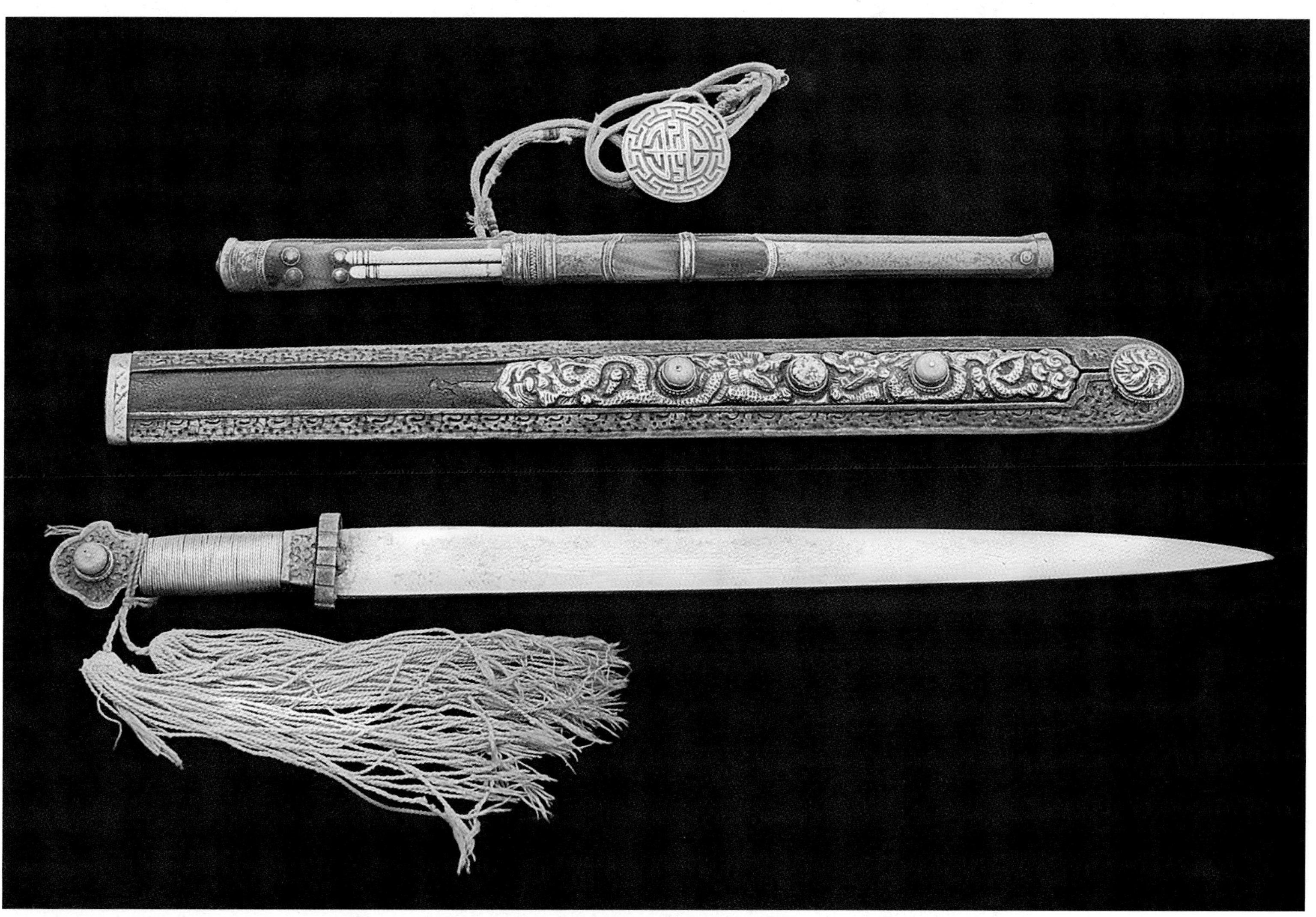

Examples of ceremonial knives.

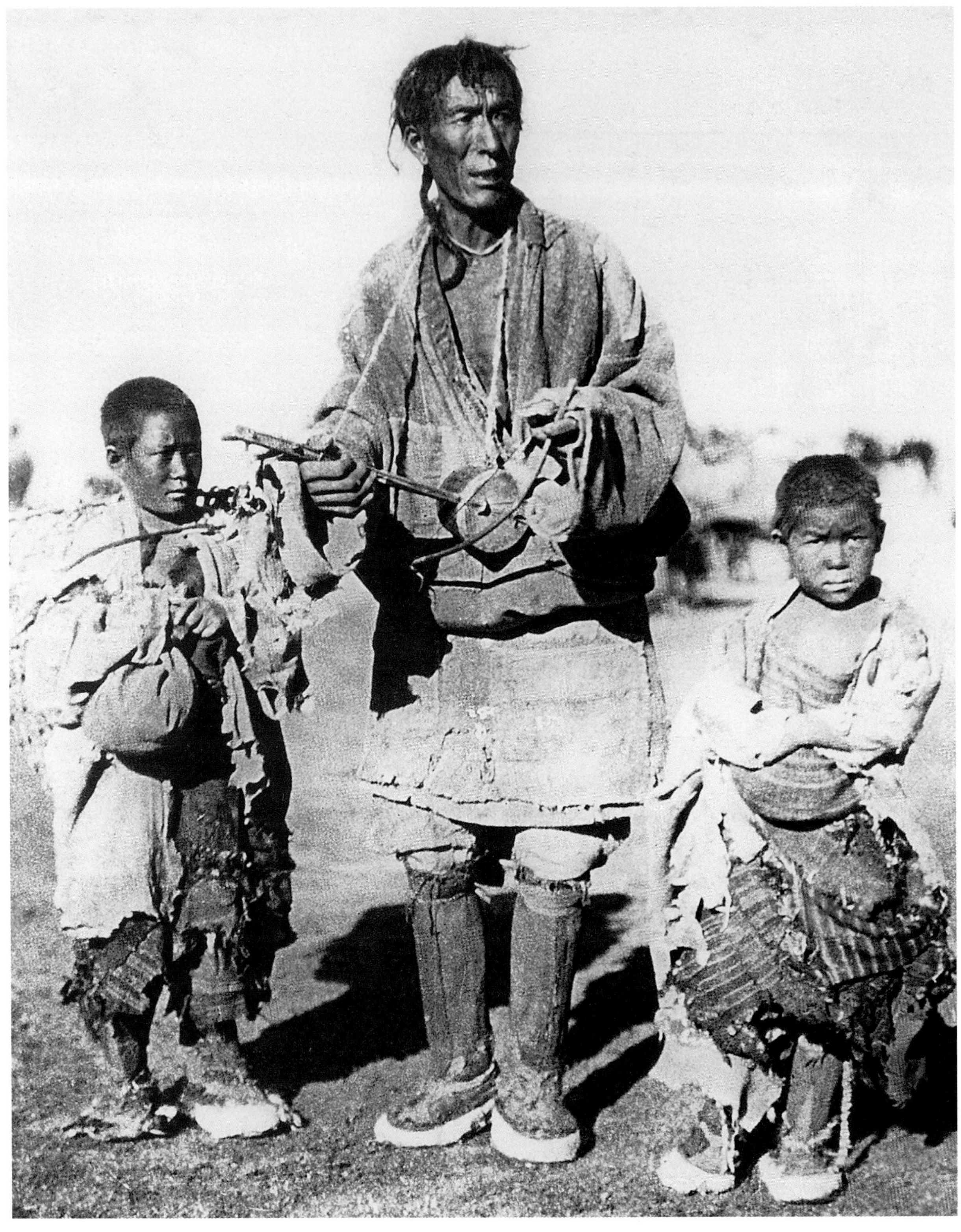

A family of wandering minstrels, all wearing typical long boots which were usually hand-made, with heavy rope soles.

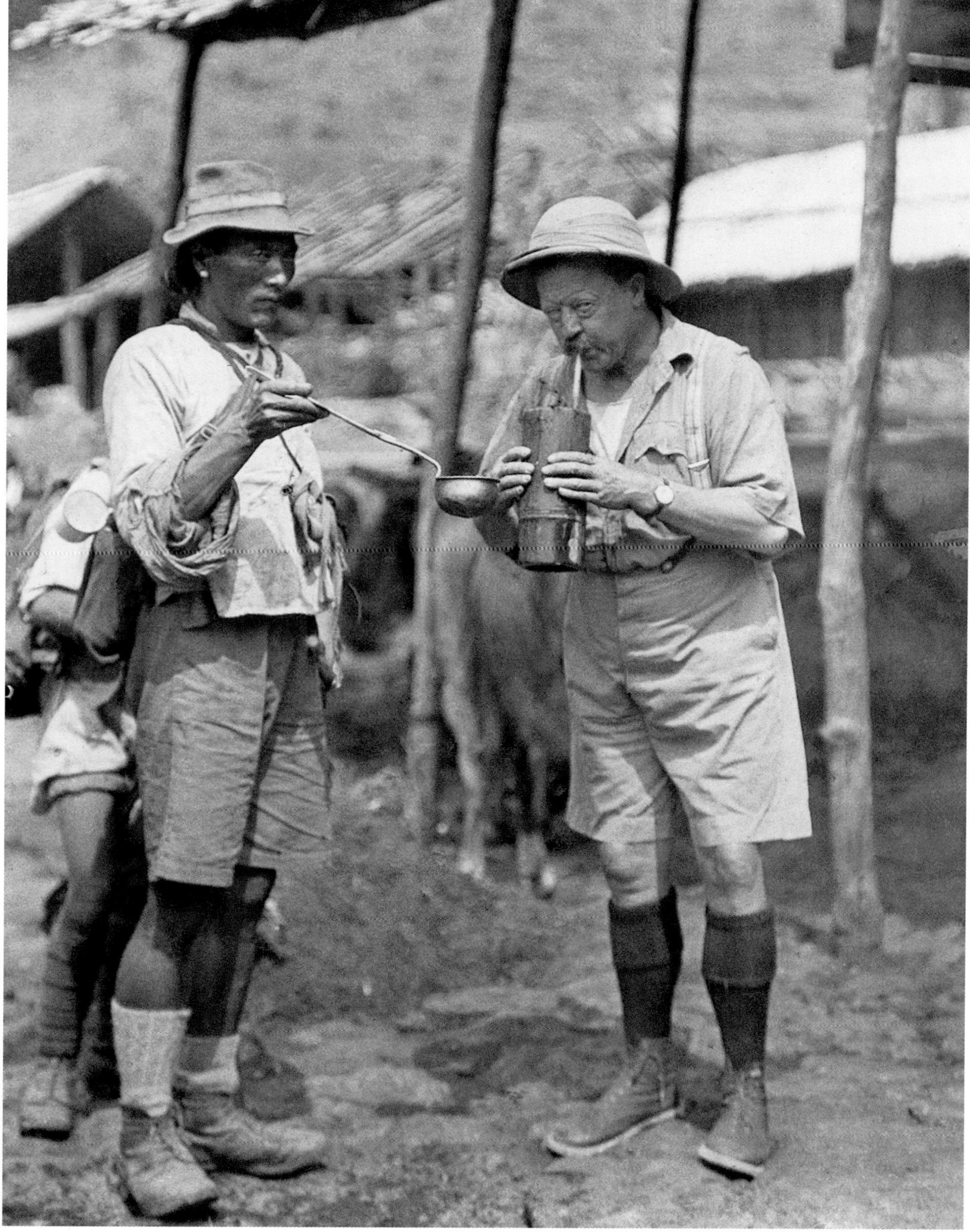

General Bruce drinking beer, which the Tibetans brewed from fermented barley and strained off from the seeds into vessels. It could be drunk hot or cold.

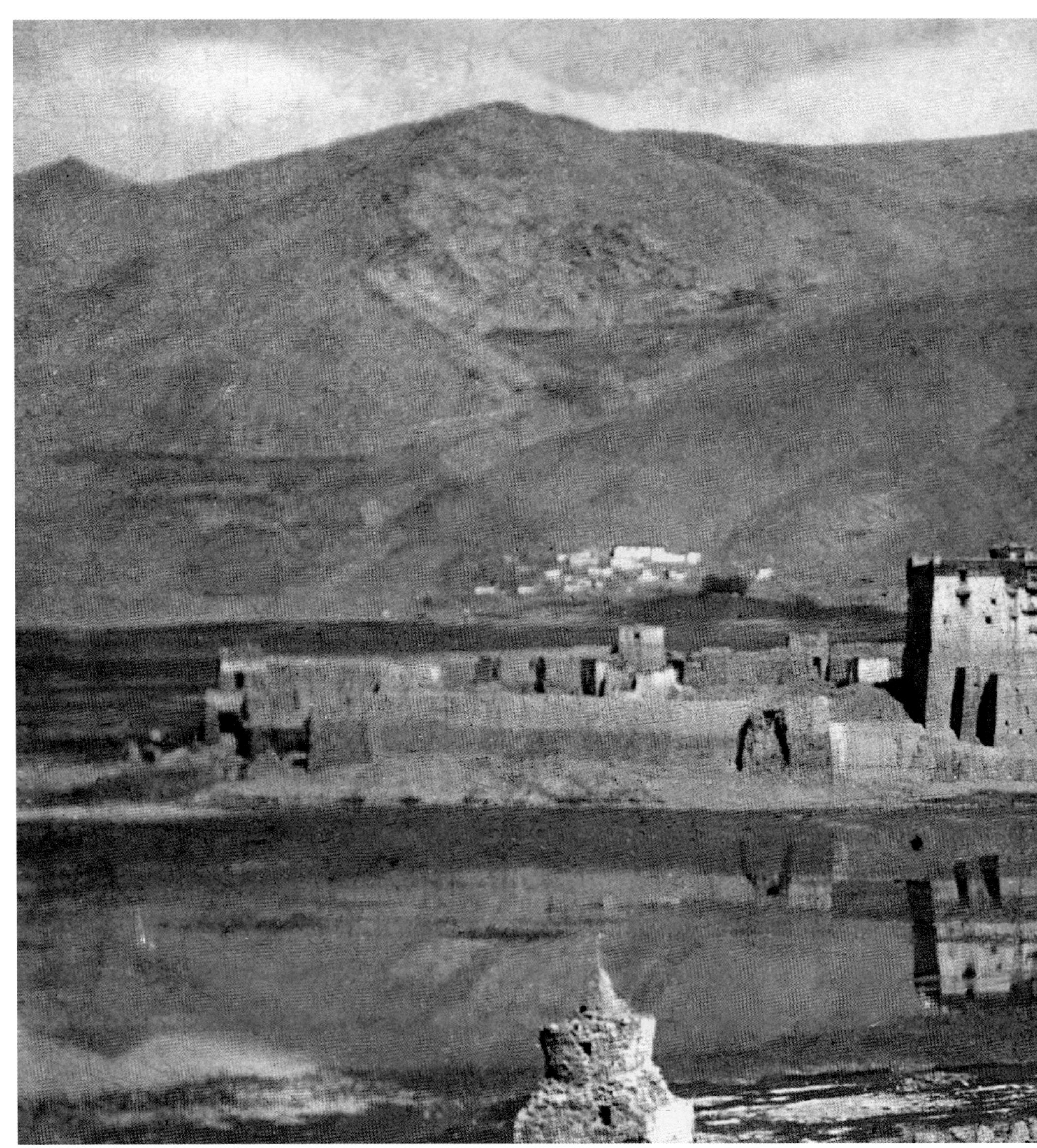

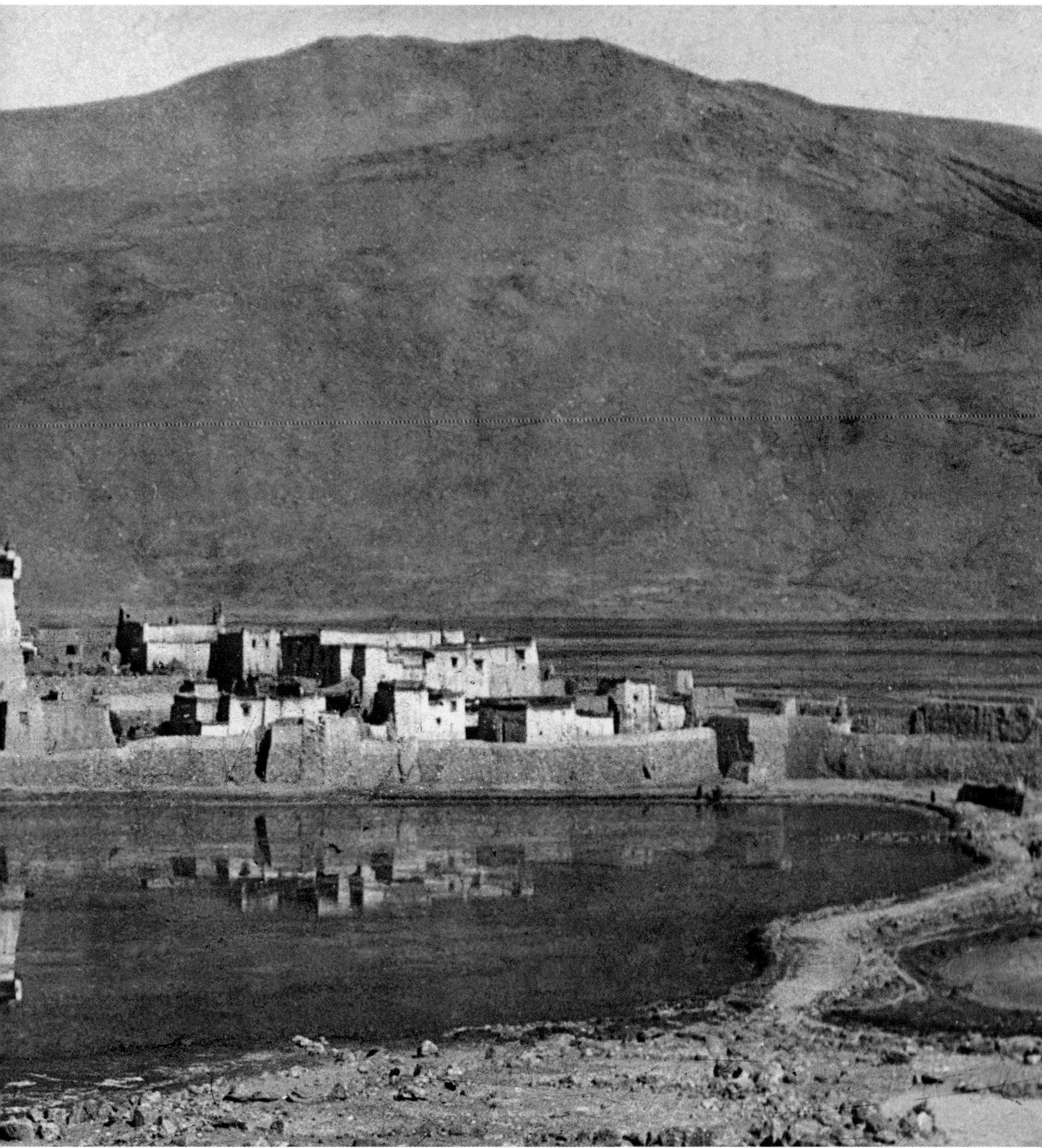

A typical walled village: 'at least one son from each family would join the religious community, which is enclosed within the *dzong* (fortification) also the residence of the local civil leader (*drongpen*)'. Ideally there is a source of water nearby, often a lake.

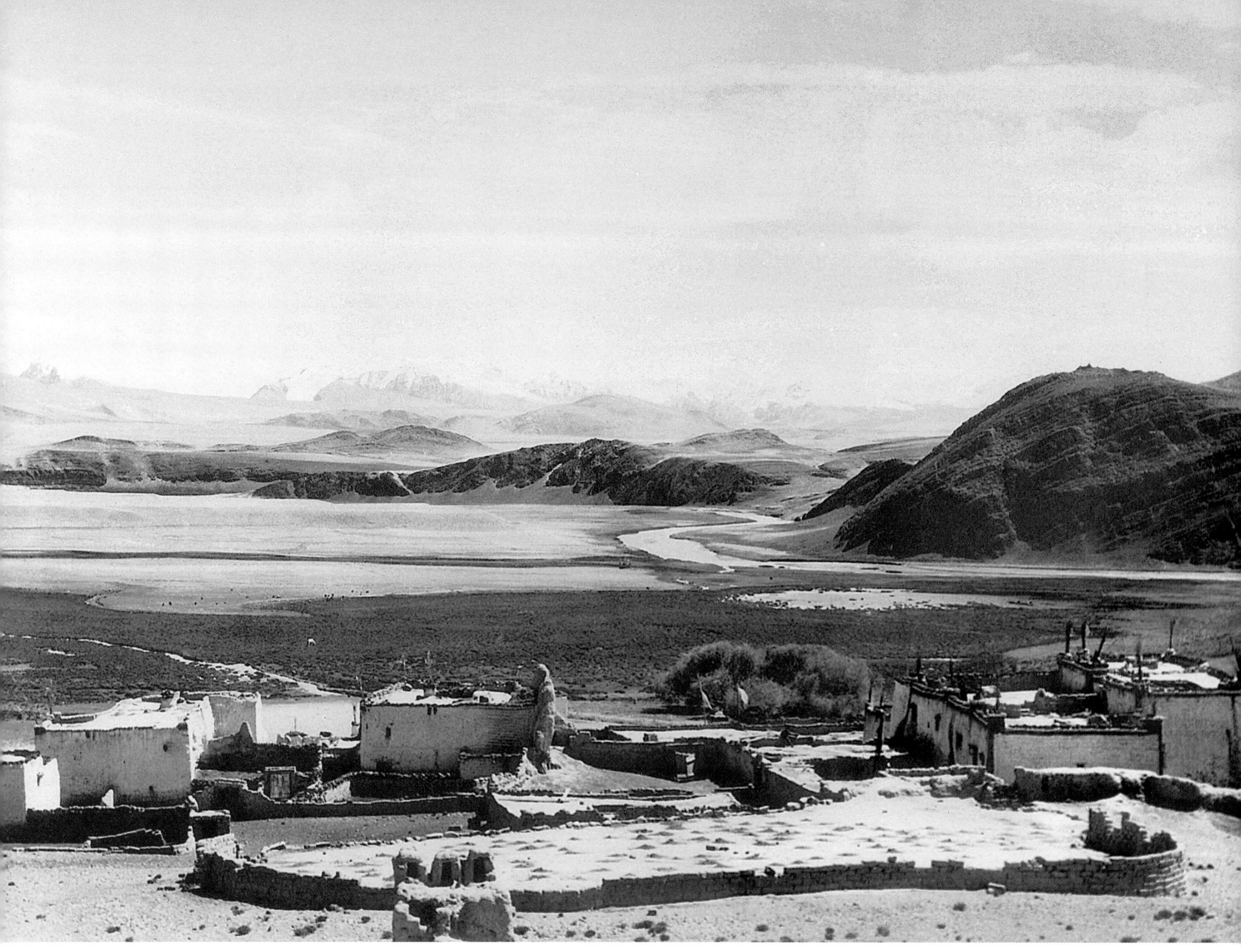

A typical village scene: the house is built of mud, strengthened with horn, hair and skin from dead cattle. The rooms were only 7 feet high, with little slits for windows, and an ill-fitting door. Yak-dung is used on the open fire, as the only form of heating.

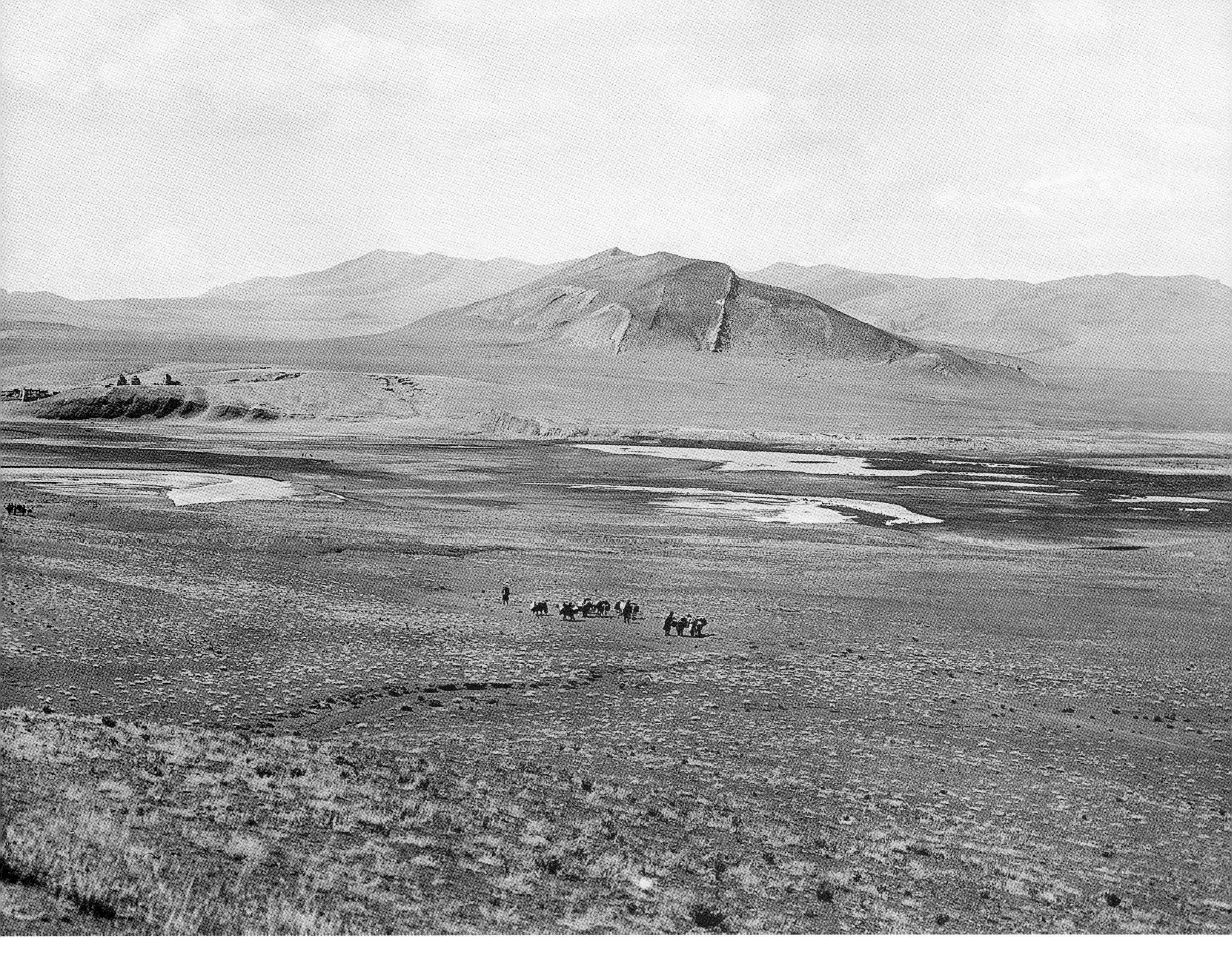

The expedition crossing the desolate plateau: a baby donkey was born en route, but soon got to its feet to take part in the great march.

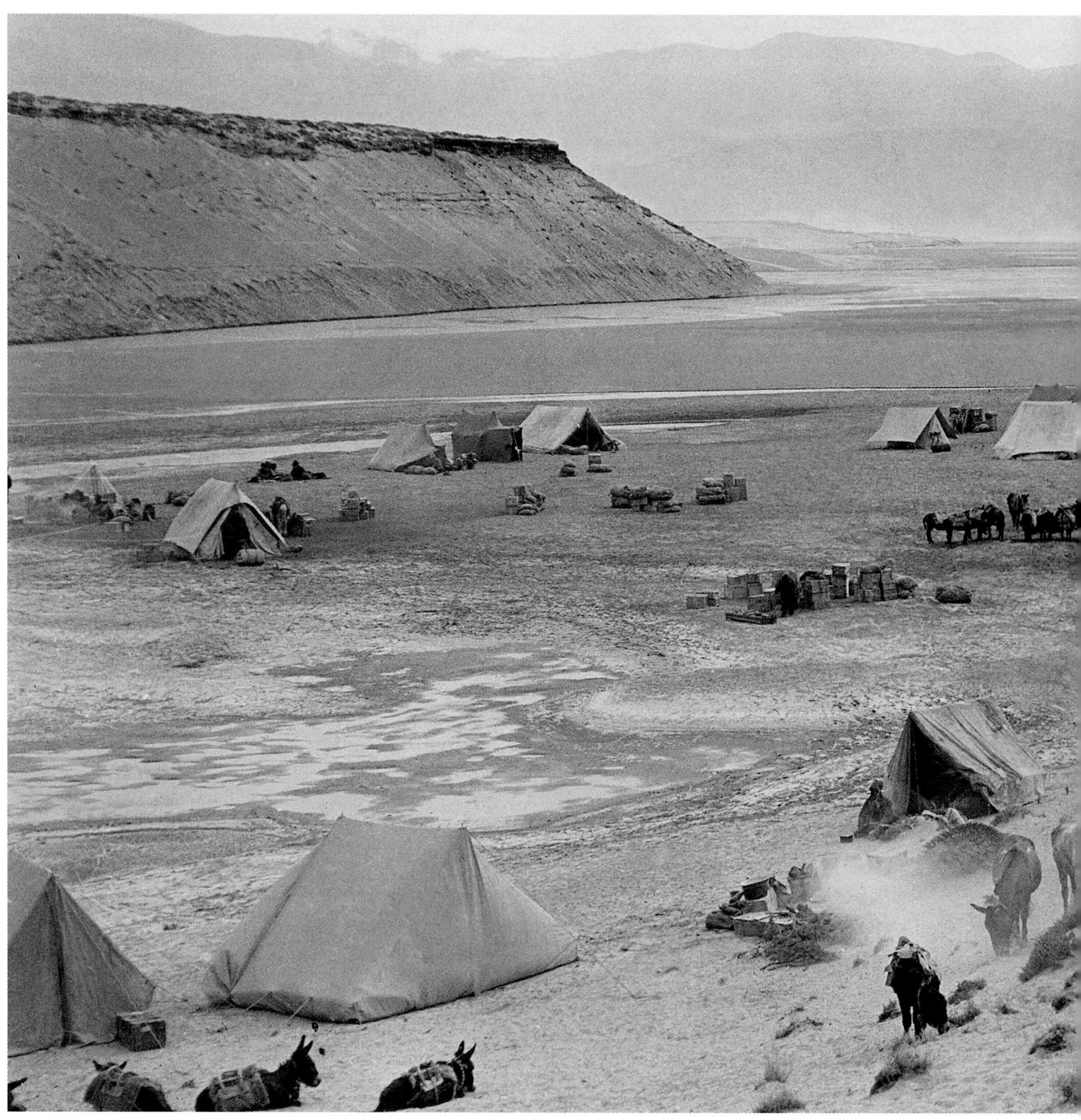

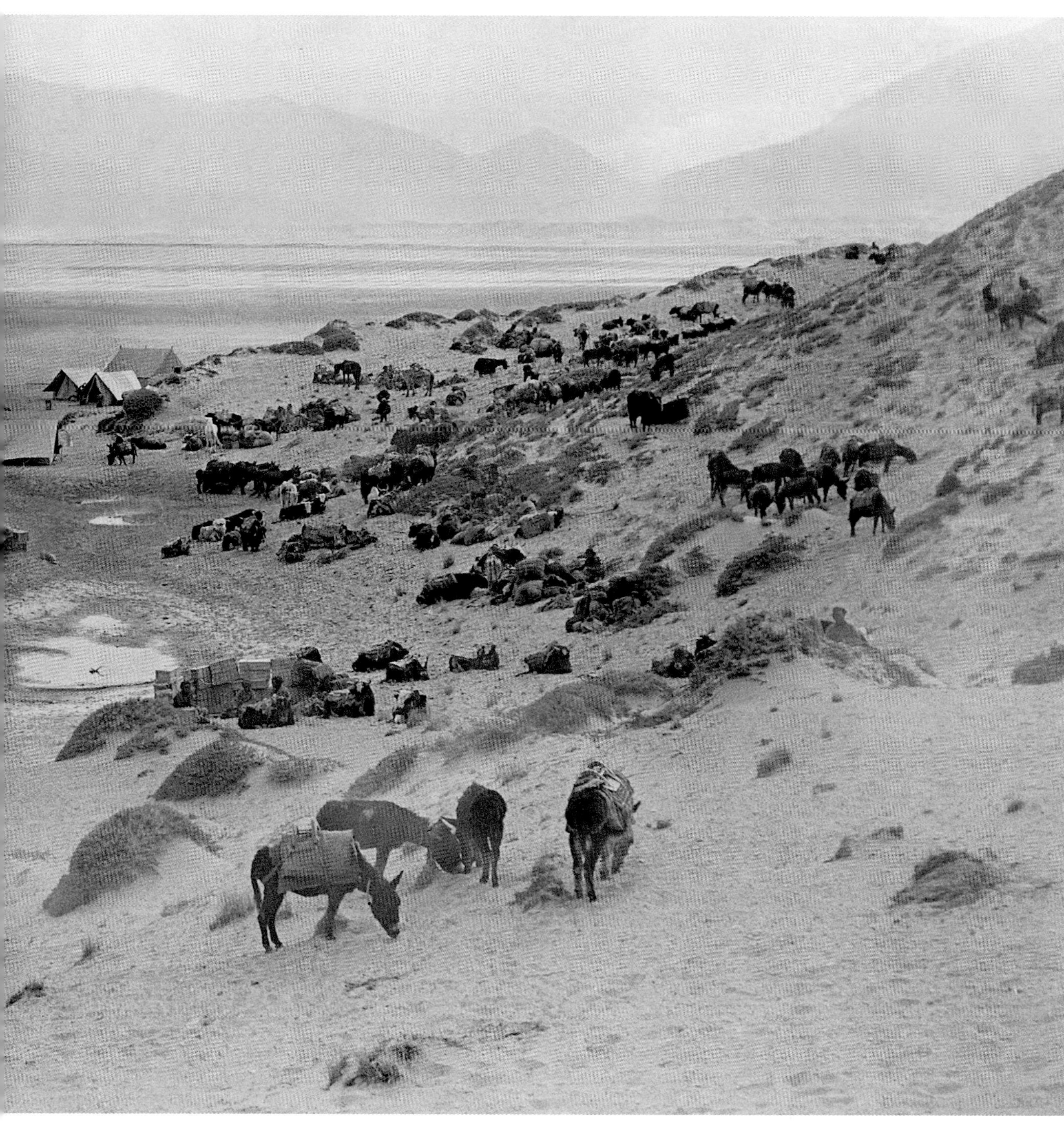

Pack animals grazing
after a day's work
carrying the loads.

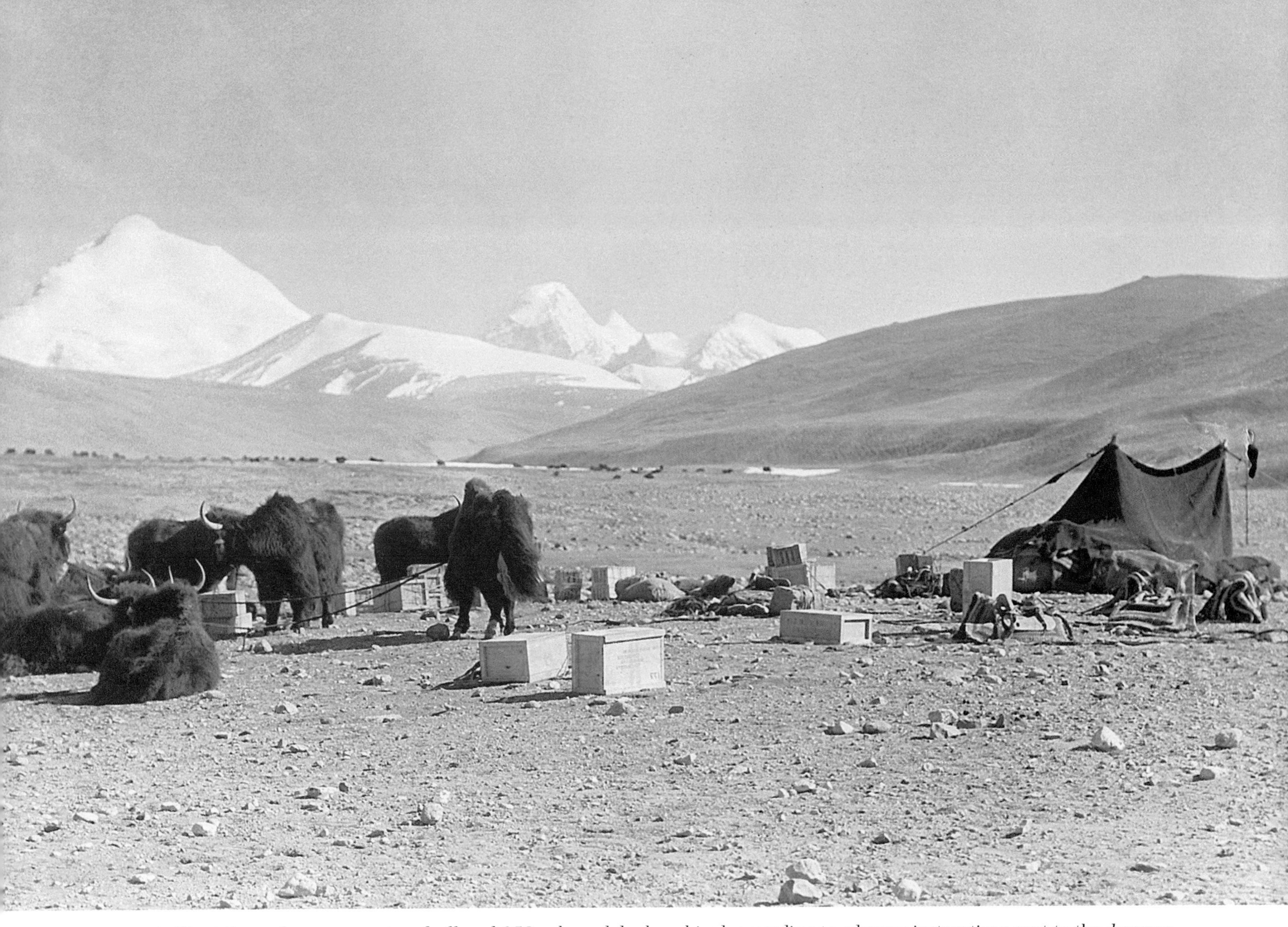

At Phari the mules were pensioned off, and 350 yaks and donkeys hired, according to advance instructions sent to the *dzongpen* from Lhasa, for the onward journey. Local taxes were imposed on all the Tibetan traders who passed this town on their way down to Kalimpong and Darjeeling to sell their wares.

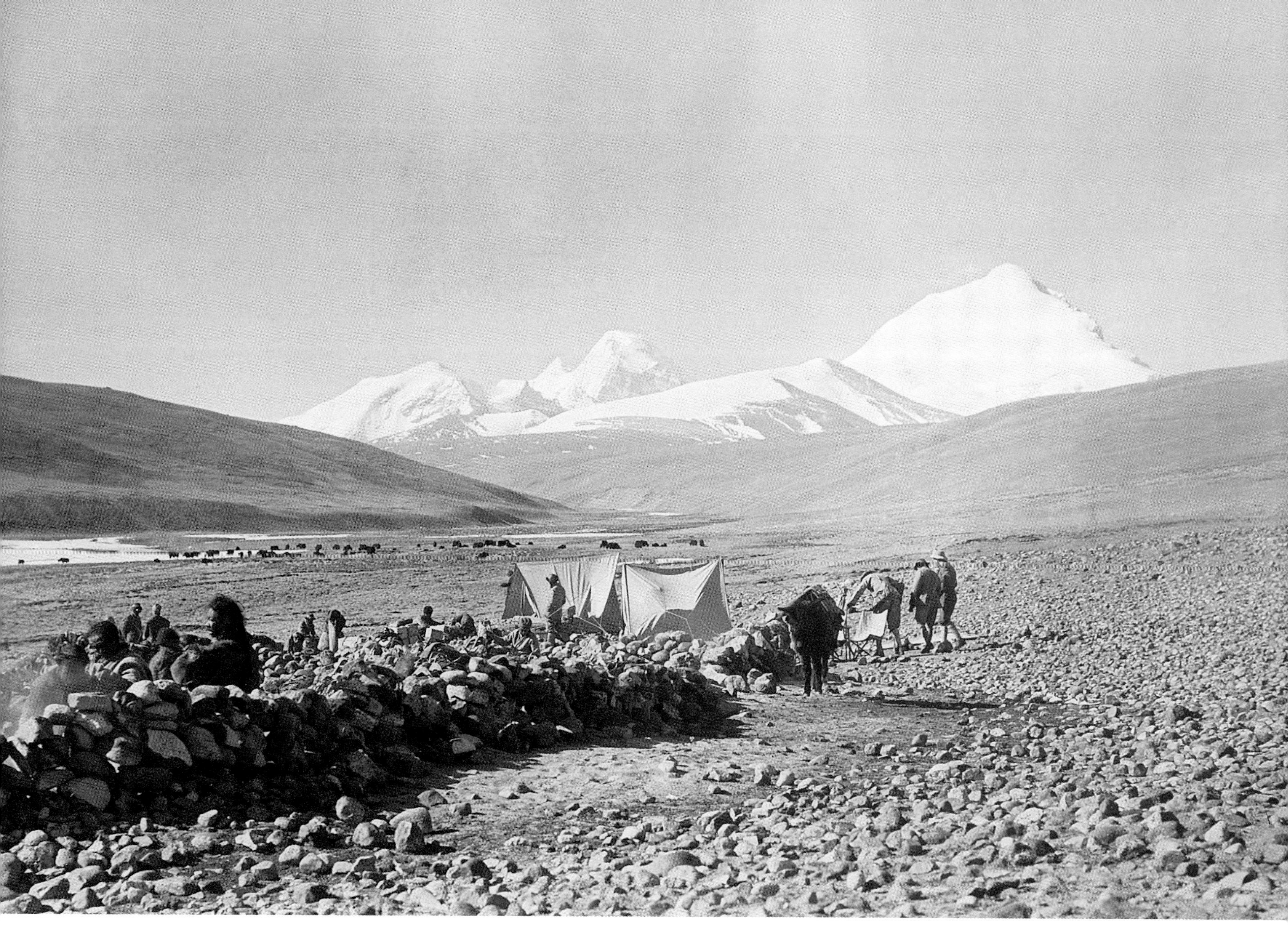

Yaks taking over – they are massive, hardy, surefooted beasts, with broad, straight backs, short legs and long silky hair, which in older animals almost sweeps the ground. Their scientific name is *Bos grunniens*, a reference to the curious grunting call. More than 350 yaks formed a caravan five miles long.

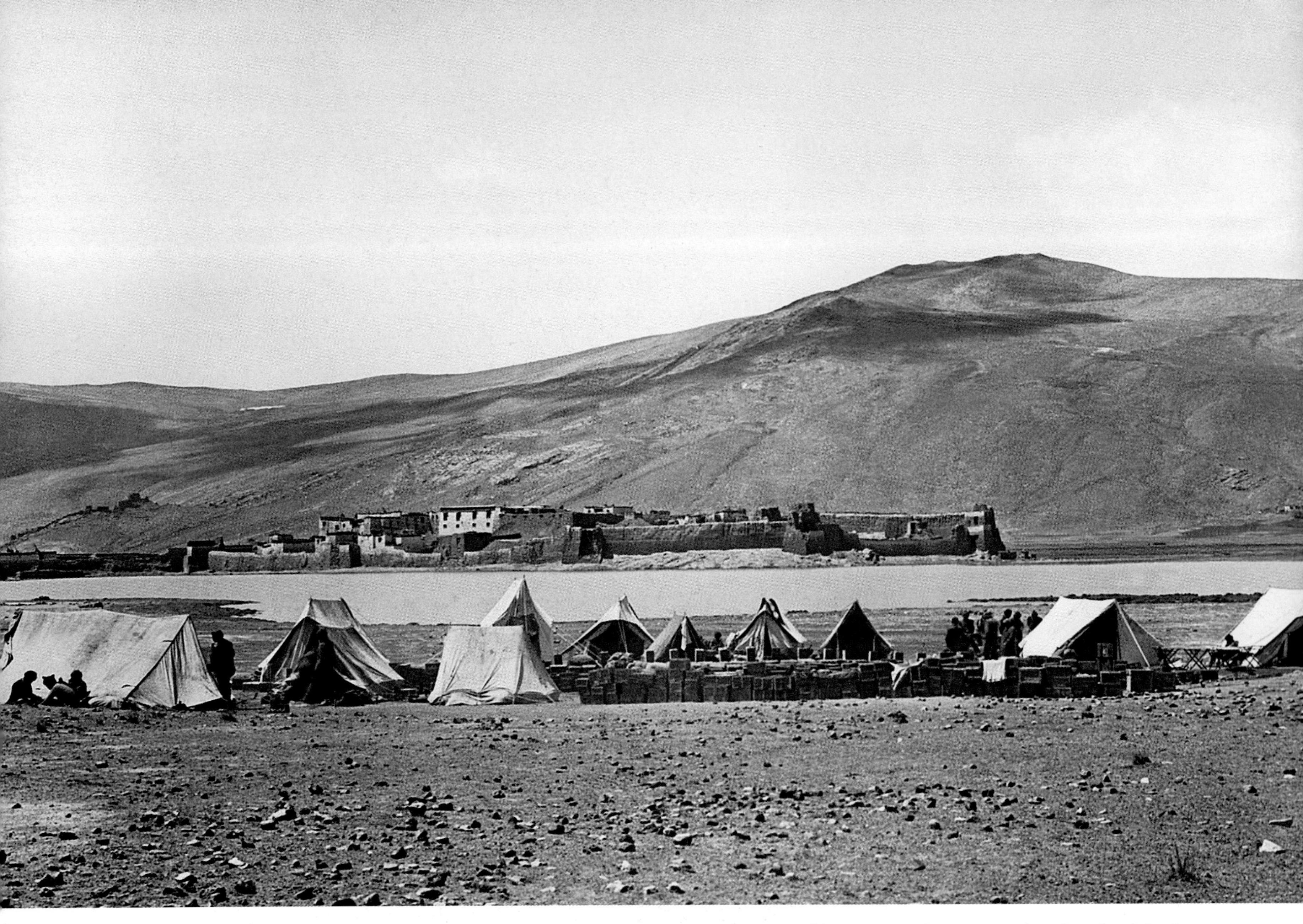

Gear beside the tents. The expedition camped just outside the small towns, to enable the animals to graze after their hard day's work transporting the equipment.

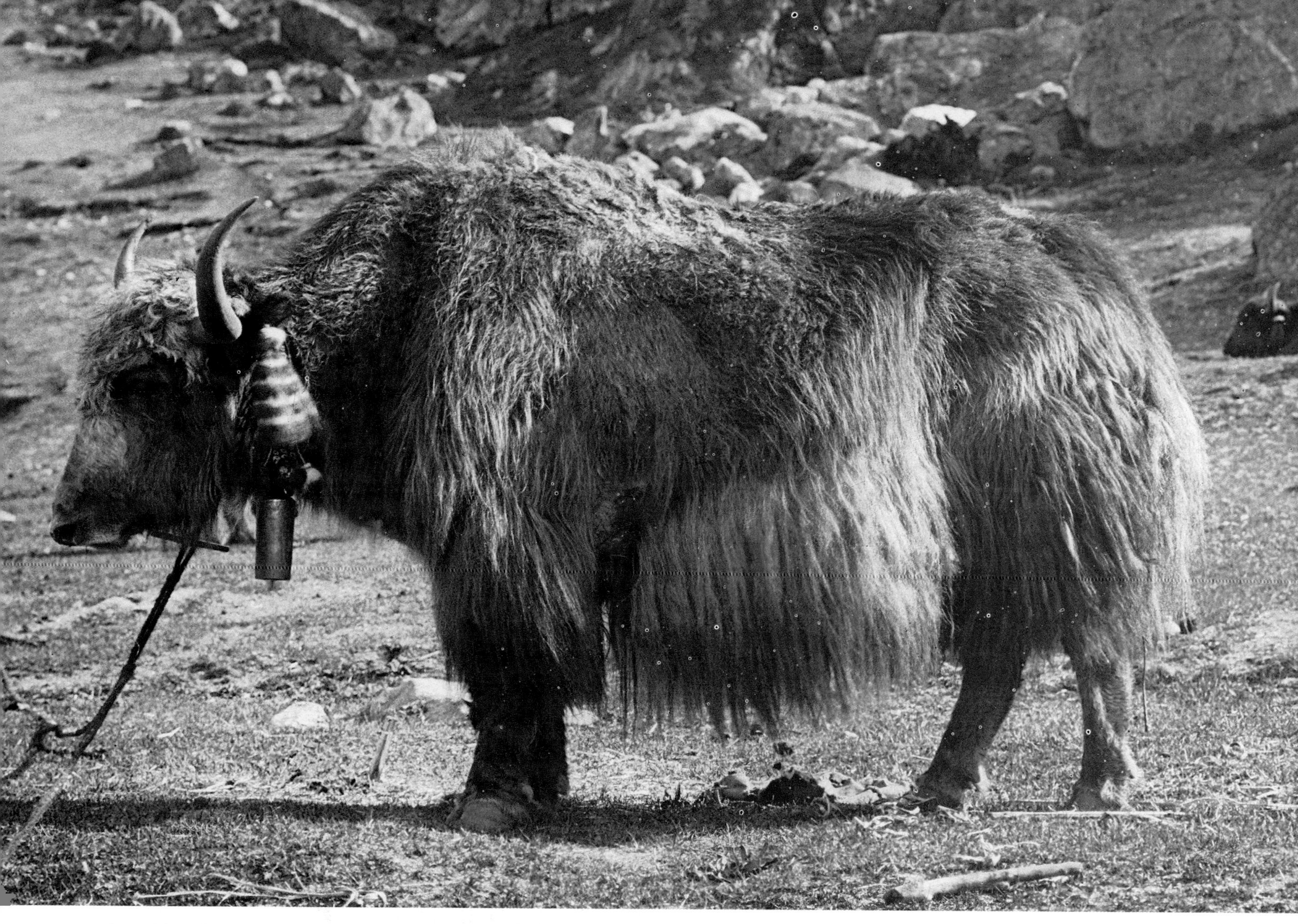

The yak's tail ends in a great, bushy tuft, which is curled over the animal's nose to protect it when sleeping. Most yaks are black or dark brown, but inbreeding and domesticity have introduced some white markings.

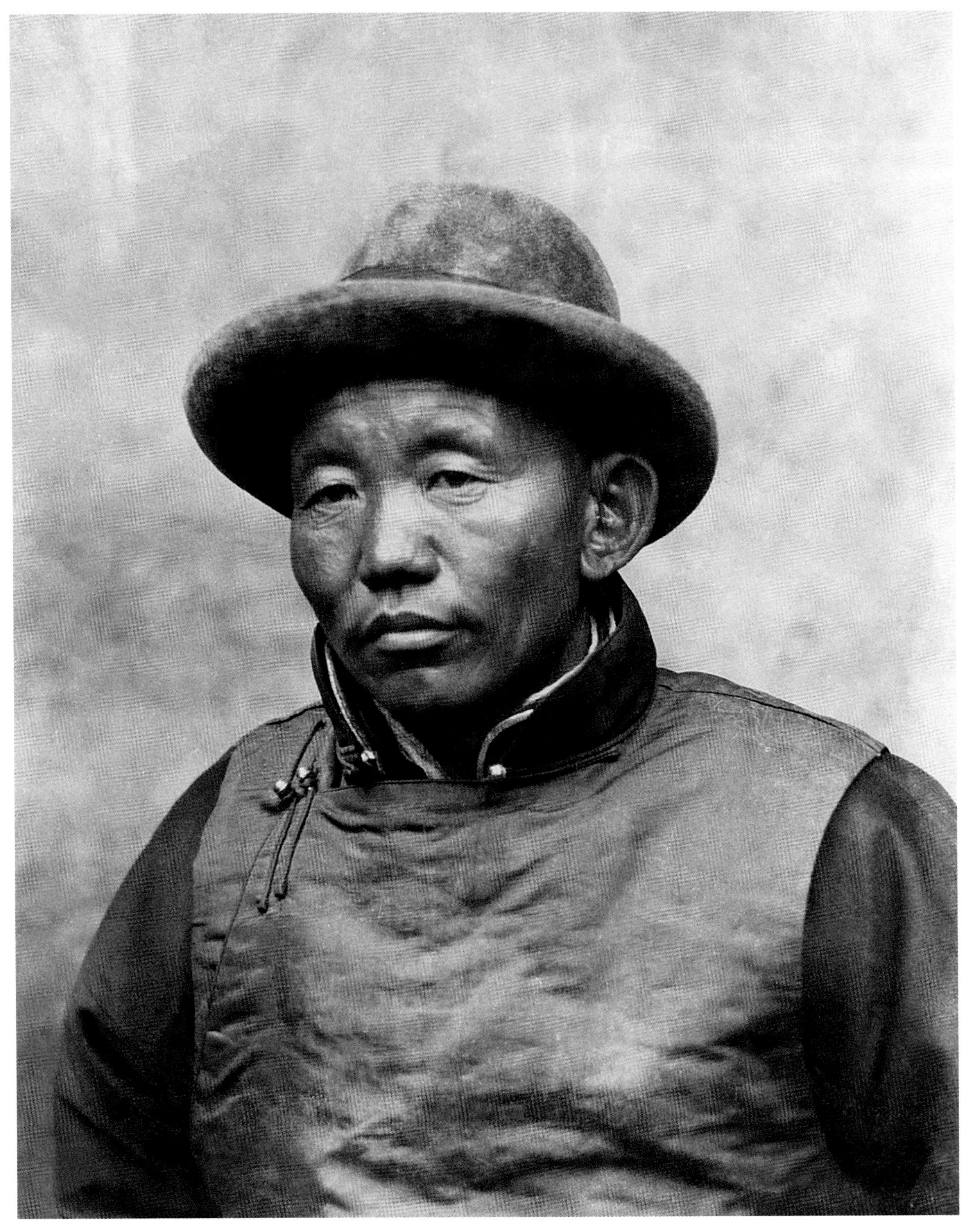

The *dzongpen* of Shekar. It was essential to meet the local governor at each stop, and the expedition leader was required to discuss niceties and drink butter tea.

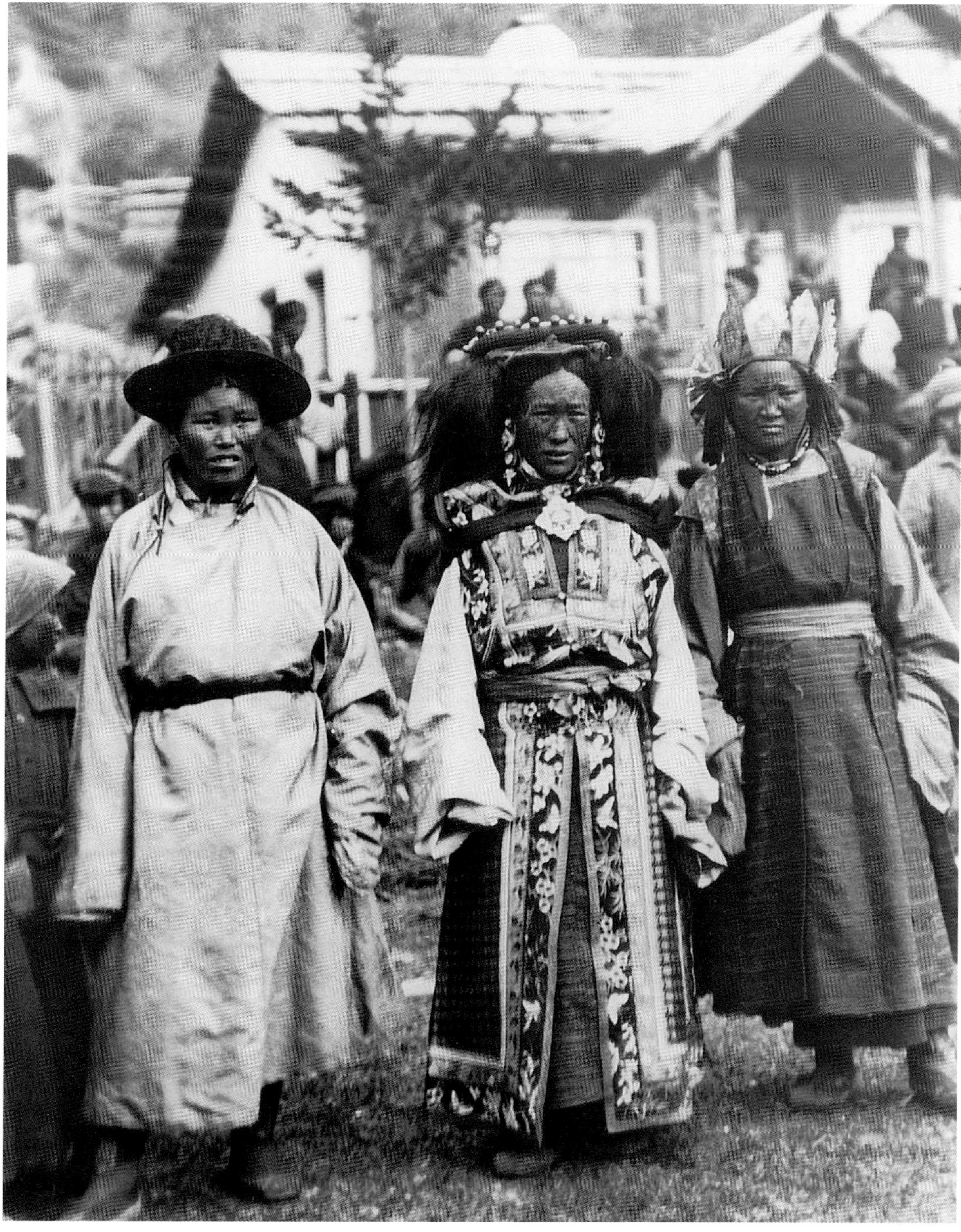

The townsfolk were more prosperous. The ladies have typical ornate headdresses and masses of colourful jewellery, notably an amulet box to ward off evil; the man is wearing a long silk robe and loose trousers and a bowler-style hat.

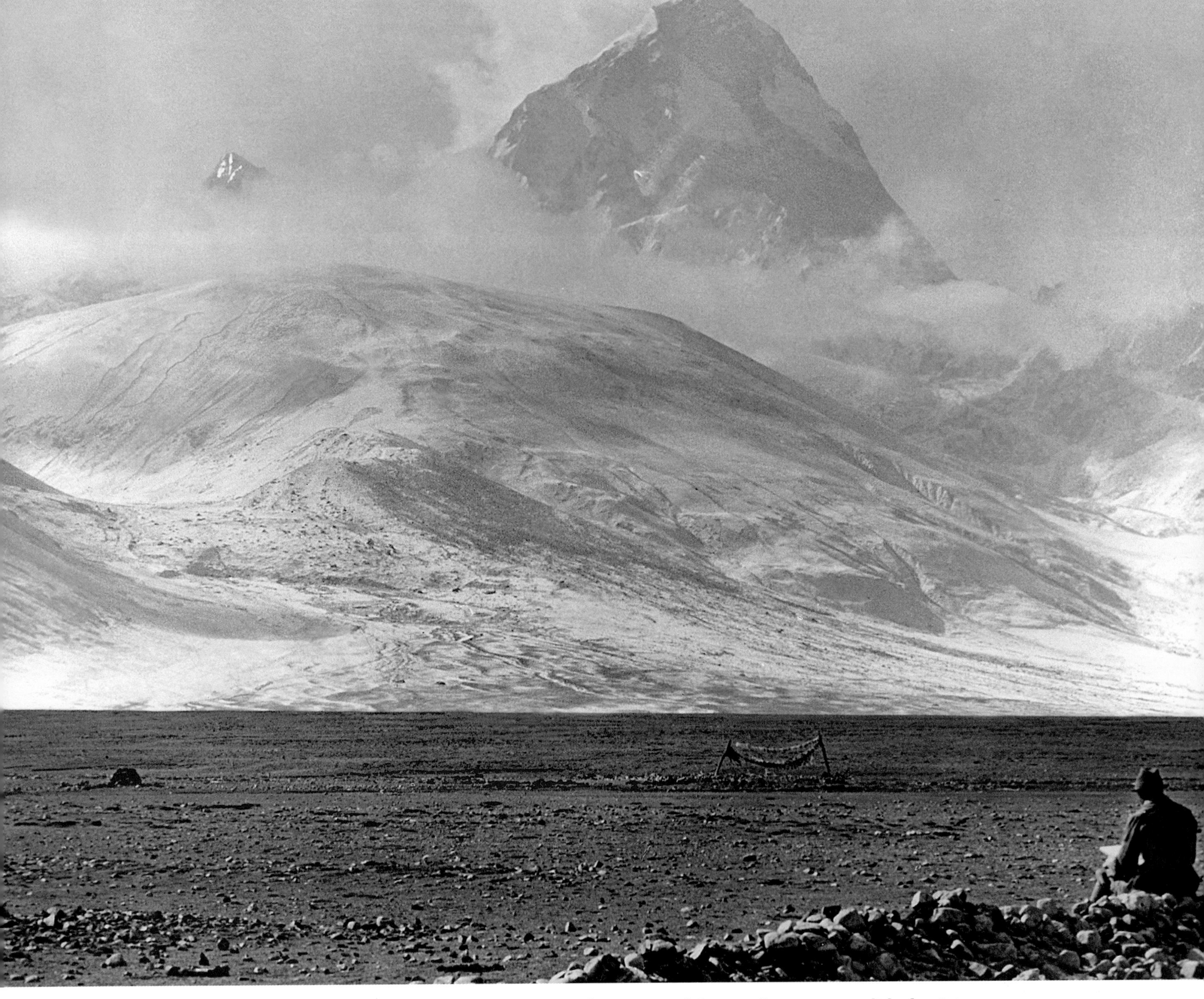

Norton sketching the majestic scenery. Both Norton and Somervell were accomplished artists.

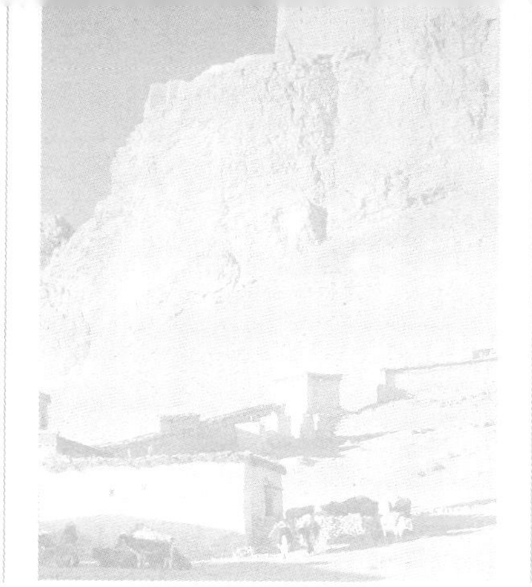

CHAPTER 5

TOWARDS THE GREAT MOUNTAIN

With a vigorous team of pack animals, the expedition set forth, still more than 100 miles from the mountain. Across Tibet were scattered numerous monasteries, where men spent much of their lives in the pursuit of religious enlightenment. Because this veneration had for so long been of the utmost importance to the Tibetans, the lamaseries were among the first establishments to be destroyed, both literally and symbolically, by the Chinese after their invasion in 1950. Today these buildings have largely been reduced to piles of rubble, but at the time of the early explorers great edifices arose from the desolation of the plateau of Tibet as monuments to the skill of the builders and the strength of the religious followers. Some seventy-five miles from Everest, in a direct line, is Kampa Dzong, a massive fortress built sheer out of the barren rock. Closer to Everest is Shekar Dzong, which translates as the 'Monastery of the Shining Crystal', whose uppermost pinnacle is 17,000 feet above sea level. The word *dzong* means castle or fortification, as indeed these buildings were: the *dzongpen* was the district's civil leader, but the great armies of lamas were the absolute rulers of the land and every Tibetan was required to give a third of his produce to the monasteries.

When the expedition arrived at Shekar Dzong on 23 April the *dzongpen* rode out to meet them, agreeing to provide fresh transport and a further team of porters, rugged men and women who would carry the loads from Base Camp to the first camps. In addition, since Everest lay in his district, arrangements were made with the *dzongpen* for the provision of grain, meat and fuel to be regularly supplied to Base Camp. The *dzongpen* was very polite and the exchanges were conducted in an orderly manner, usually on orders from Lhasa. The customary gifts of ceremonial scarves were exchanged and copious amounts of butter tea drunk, and, after a two-day well-earned rest beneath the ramparts, the tents were dismantled and the group moved on.

Four days after leaving Shekar the expedition arrived at Rongbuk Monastery, ten miles from the mountain, where another ceremony awaited – a 'devil dance', a colourful display that Noel was able to photograph. An awe-struck crowd of poor, superstitious peasants received a blessing from the lamas, who chanted and scattered rice-grains over the pilgrims. They extended a blessing to the expedition members, but it was hardly auspicious: 'Chomolungma, the awful and mighty Goddess Mother, will never allow any white man to climb to her sacred heights. The demons of the snow will destroy you utterly.' With these unnerving words ringing in their ears, the group left to set up Base Camp, four miles further on. So far, the trek from Darjeeling had taken four and a half weeks, and there had been one serious casualty. General Charles Bruce had fallen ill with malaria near Phari and had to be taken back to Sikkim. For Bruce it was a bitter blow. At the age of fifty-eight he could never have been among the climbers at great heights, but he could still cajole and encourage; and he had desperately hoped to be there when success came.

The leadership was taken over by Edward Norton, a good, experienced climber, who also had an intimate knowledge of the area, since he had been there in 1922. The climbing party was now stronger – Norton, Mallory and Somervell were joined by Noel Odell, a geologist with vast experience in Alpine mountaineering, who had been unable to take part in the previous climbs owing to prior commitments. Now, this calm, fit, enthusiastic member was keen to be part of the assault party. Another schoolmaster,

Bentley Beetham, and John Hazard, an engineer with much experience of life in India, in addition to a great mountaineering record, were joined by Andrew Irvine, aged twenty-two, an Oxford University student. Although lacking in Alpine experience, Irvine had been on the Oxford Spitzbergen expedition in 1923, and his superb physical condition – he had twice rowed in the University Boat Race – and mechanical aptitude would outweigh his inexperience of altitude climbing. Major R. Hingston was Medical Officer, E.O. Shebbeare of the Indian Forest Department was in charge of transport and Captain Geoffrey Bruce was again available.

From the Rongbuk Monastery the expedition moved to the first camp on the mountain, Base Camp, at 16,500 feet, and began depot-laying. There were almost 300 yak-loads of provision boxes, rolls of bedding and stores of every kind to be sorted into orderly lines. The yak-drivers refused to go further, claiming that the yaks would die and devils would harm them, and some of the local porters were reluctant to go very high, fearful of the mountain devils. This reluctance could have seriously jeopardized the plan to sort out all the provisions and arrange for them to be carried higher up the mountain. Anticipating such an eventuality, bribes were distributed – Noel had taken 25,000 cigarettes for his own porters, knowing their enjoyment of smoking – and so the depot-laying continued. The intention was to transport from Base Camp the needs of each higher camp exactly as required, and from there a smaller quantity of stores were taken higher, so that the absolute minimum was carried to the top camps, thus conserving energy in the rarefied air at high altitude.

Mallory and Beetham were in charge of the Alpine equipment and the provisions for the high camps; Odell and Irvine, the oxygen apparatus; Somervell, the scientific and medical stores; Hazard, the mess; and Shebbeare and Geoffrey Bruce the large convoy of 150 Tibetans who had been taken on at Shekar to help in establishing the first camps. There were both men and women, each capable of carrying loads of 40 pounds, but with no tents for shelter to sleep in, no blankets and none of the equipment which was being kept for the sherpas recruited in Darjeeling. Some of the woman carried small children on their backs, as well as the loads.

It was now time to decide upon a climbing strategy. Norton and the main climbers decided that attempts on the summit would be made in pairs, with or without oxygen depending upon the physical condition of the climbers and their ability to acclimatize. However, before any attempt could be made, terrible blizzards drove the temperature to 30 degrees below zero Fahrenheit. There was soft snow, which interrupted the system of convoy parties and the chain of supply; the result was chaos, and demoralization set in. Stores and food had failed to arrive from lower camps, tents were blown down in the high winds and two of the porters were seriously ill. Due to the atrocious weather, Norton gave the order to retreat to Base Camp, where they spent a week: seven precious days of climbing were lost.

The suggestion was made that the entire group should return to the Rongbuk Monastery and seek a blessing from the head lama, who had not been able to meet them when they had passed through a few days earlier. On the appointed day, 15 May, the group proceeded four miles down the valley for the audience with the High Priest of the Mountain. The impact on the Europeans was as great as that on the natives, for the serious nature of the blessing upon these profoundly religious people was easy to see – after the usual ceremonial exchanges of messages and respect, each man went before the head lama and presented a *Kata*, a long piece of silk, the ends trimmed with fringe, a gift traditionally given and accepted as a symbol of love and friendship.

The expedition returned to the work of laying depot camps up the mountain in earnest, with hopes and morale high. From Base Camp at 16,500 feet there was a constant stream of humanity making its way up and down the mountain, laying depots, setting up camps, testing equipment and always trying to find the easiest way up, since the conservation of energy was a prime objective.

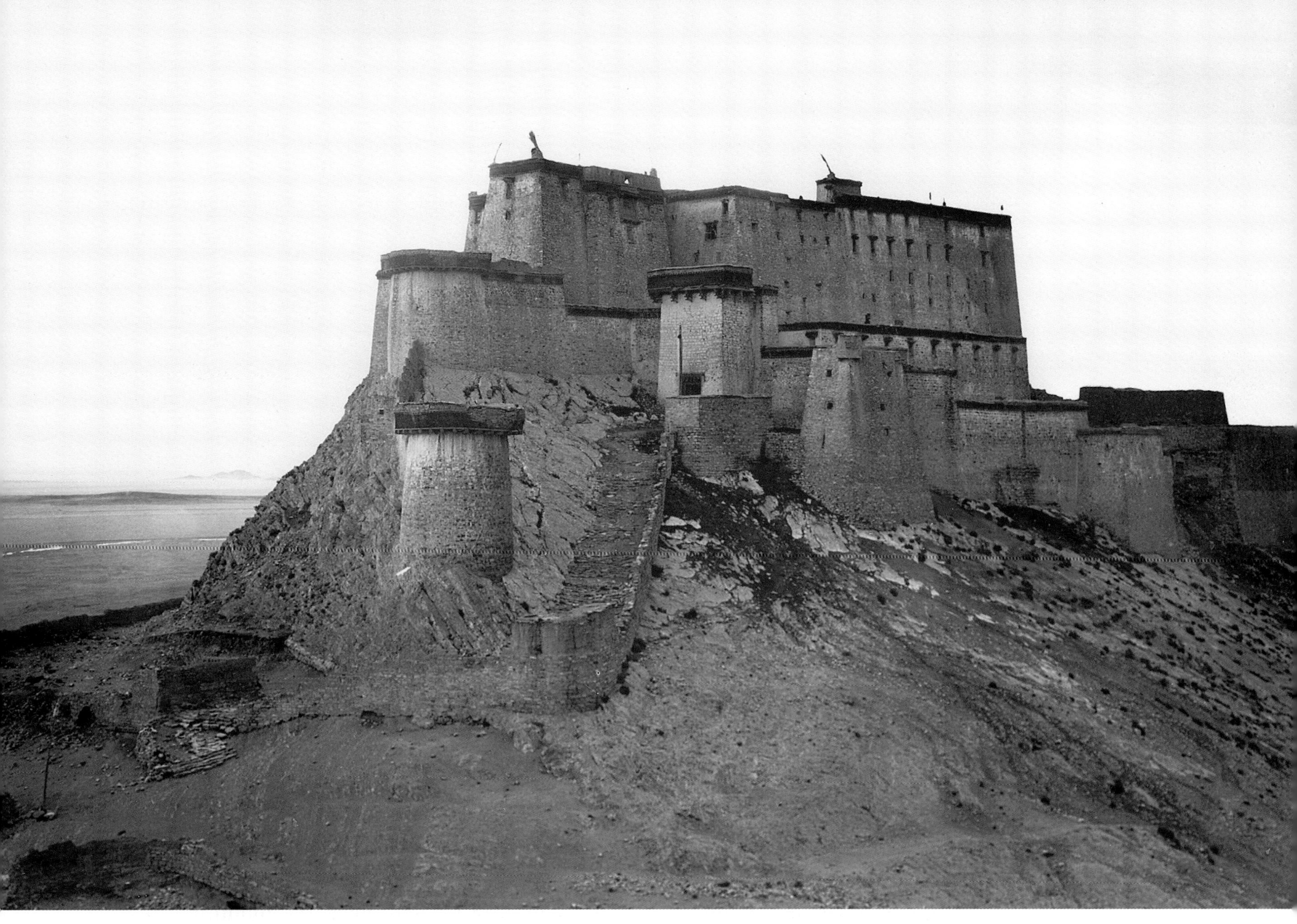

Kampa Dzong: a magnificent fortress built on a rock 15,000 feet above the sea. Villages are few and far between. The people are mostly collected in settlements under the protection of a fortress monastery.

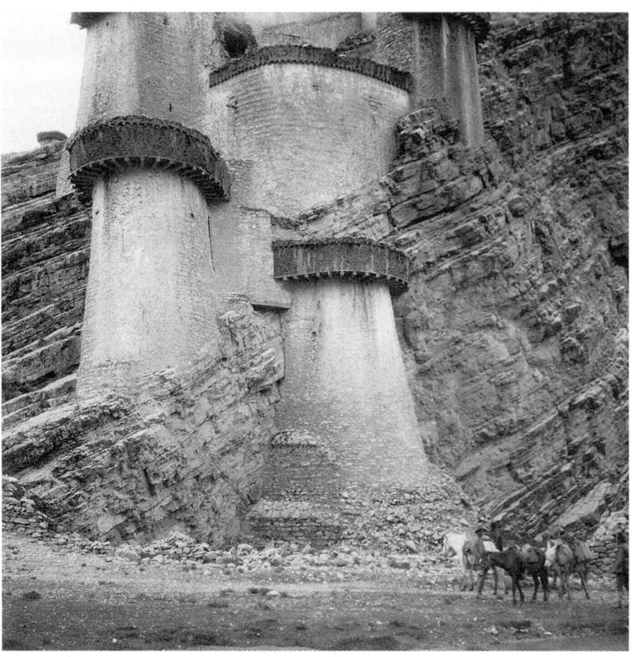

Kampa commands a view for a hundred miles of the snowy mountains, so was a vital defence as well as a shelter; the towers lead to wells, an essential source of water. This is a detail of the image below and the pack animals give an indication of the scale of the structure.

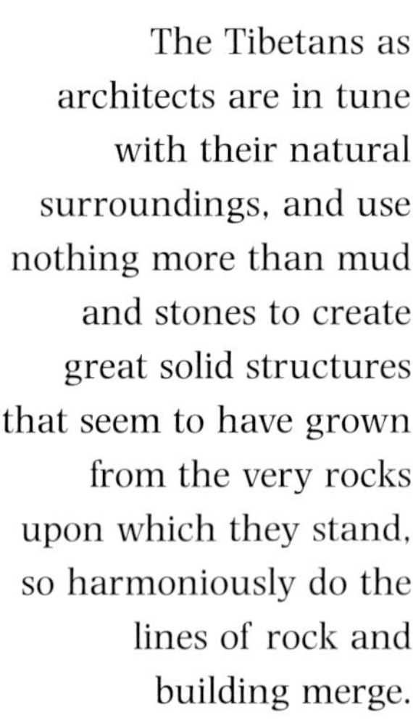

The Tibetans as architects are in tune with their natural surroundings, and use nothing more than mud and stones to create great solid structures that seem to have grown from the very rocks upon which they stand, so harmoniously do the lines of rock and building merge.

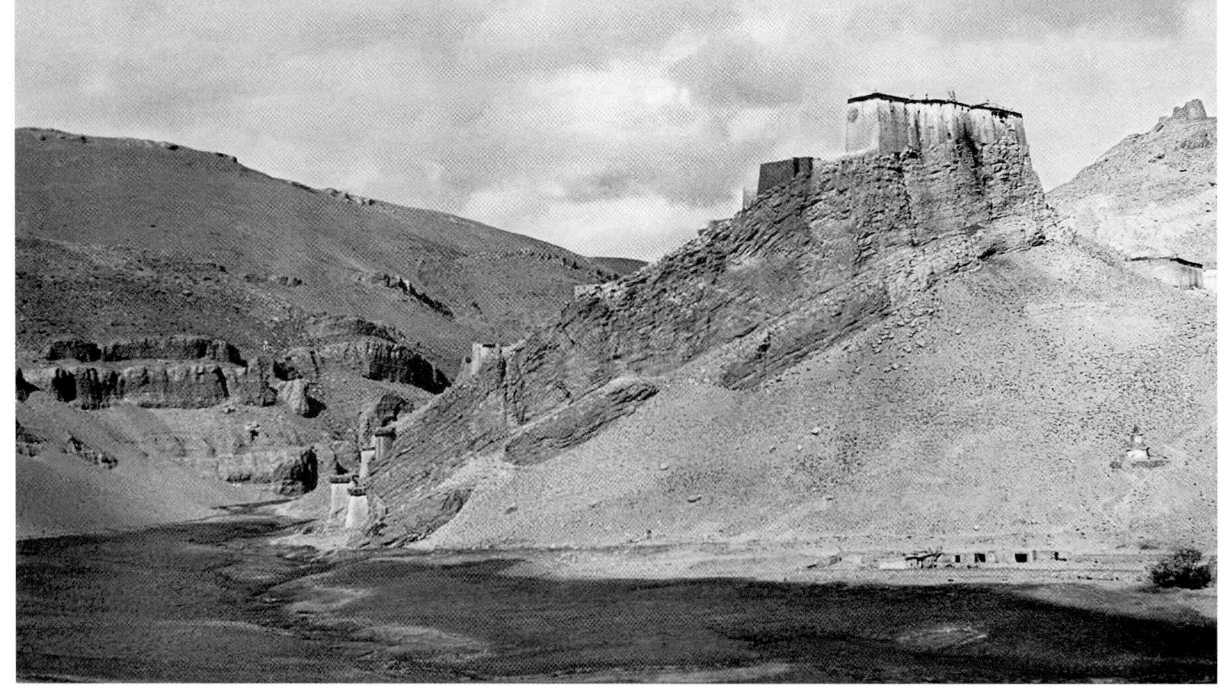

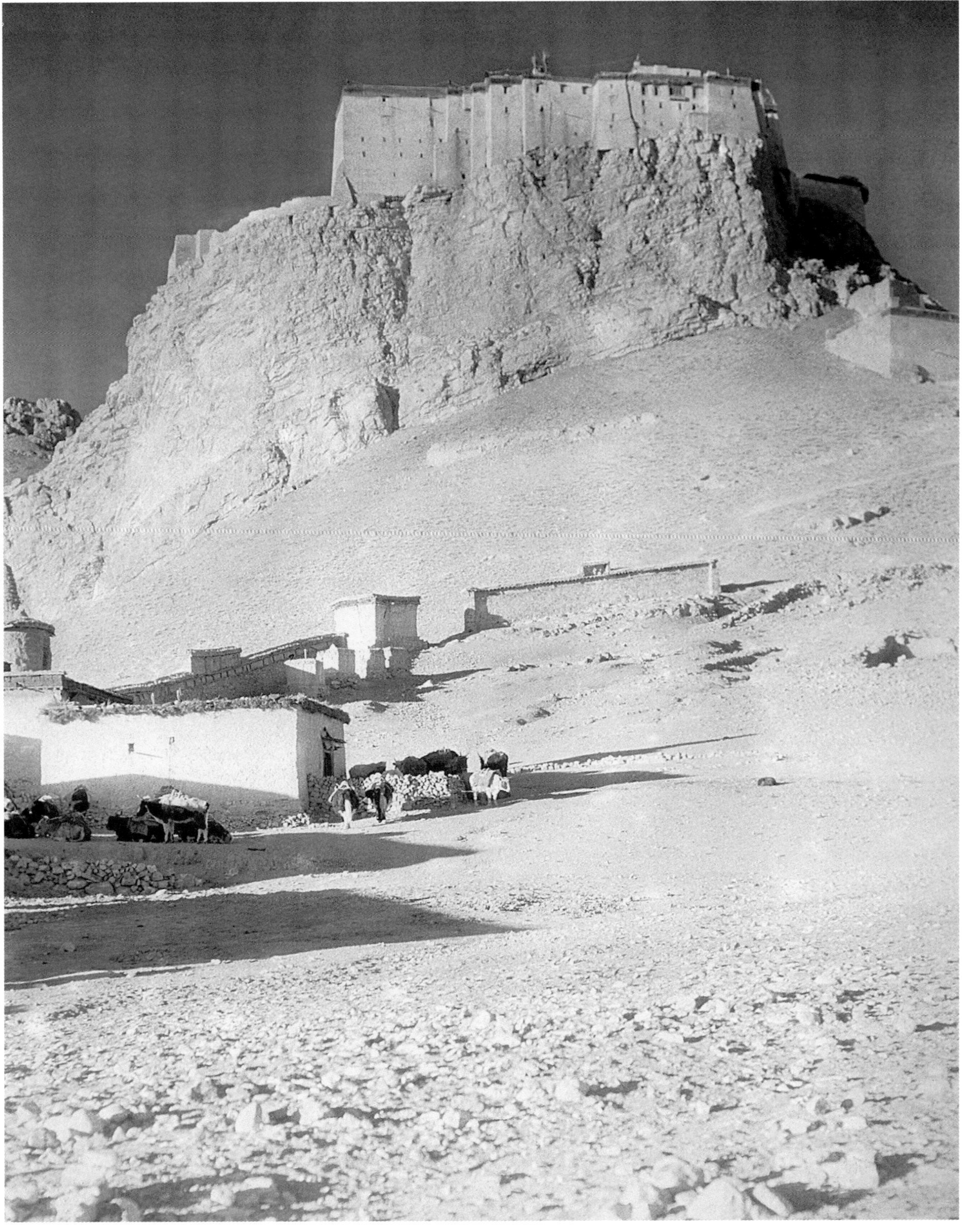

The expedition camp 500 feet below the fortress of Kampa, by full moon.

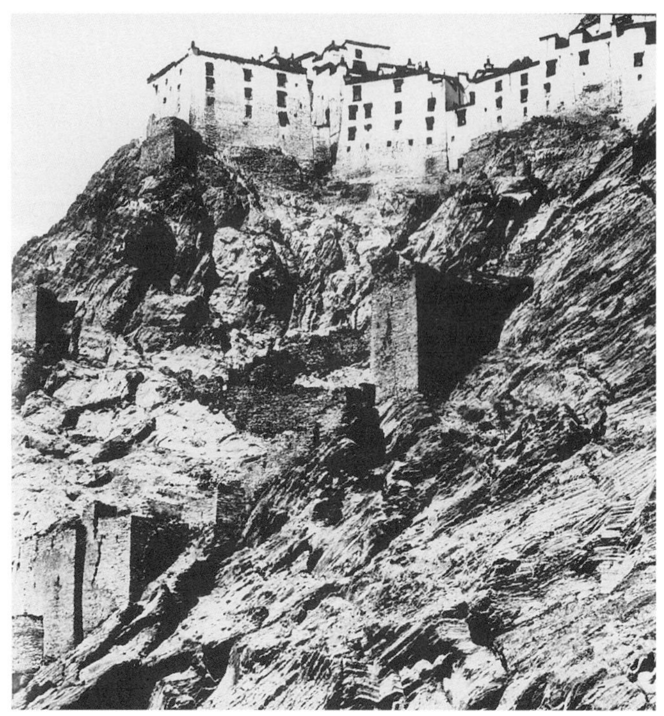

Shekar is 17,000 feet above the sea, and is an example of how the Tibetan builder is inspired by the immense surrounding spaces and heights, as well as being influenced by superstition and fantastic fears.

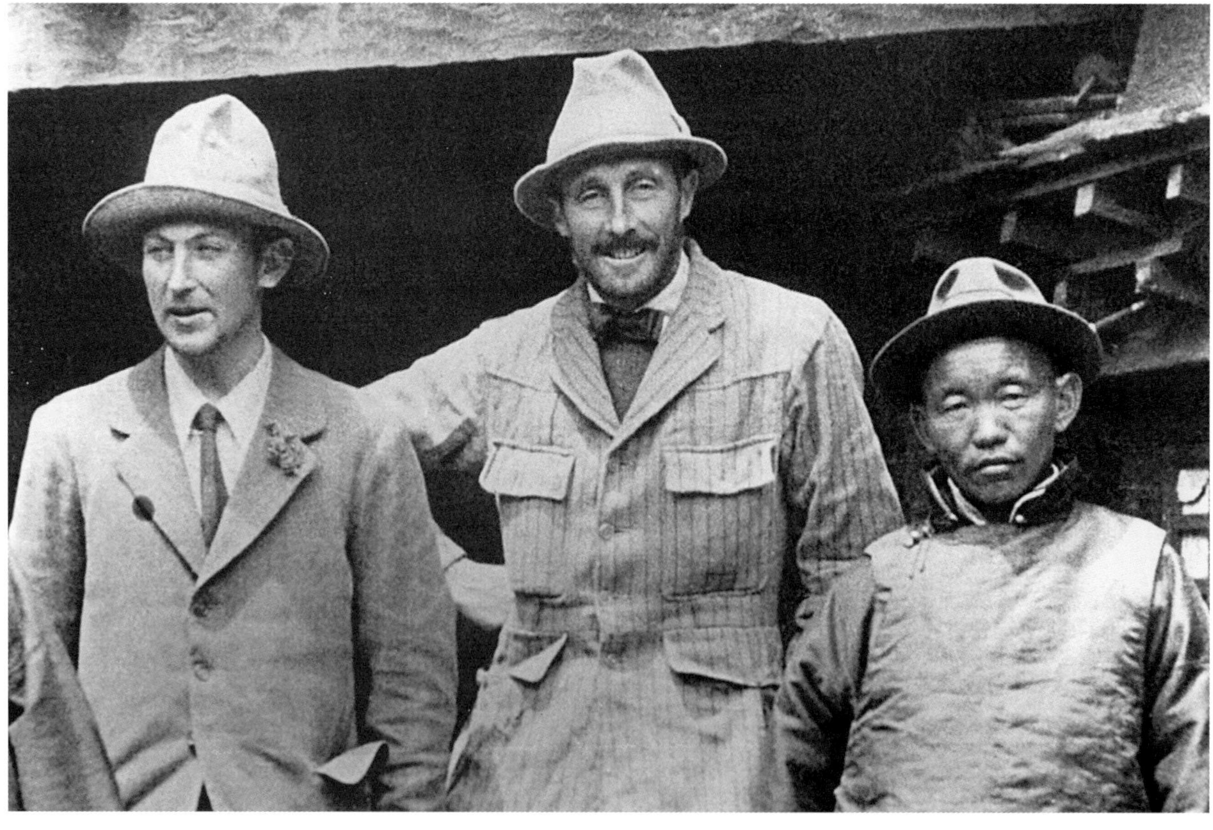

A meeting with the governor or *dzongpen* of Shekar to discuss the additional transport. From left: Mallory, Norton, the *dzongpen*. As the *dzongpen* is the civil leader so the head lama is the spiritual leader, and both customarily live within the fortifications.

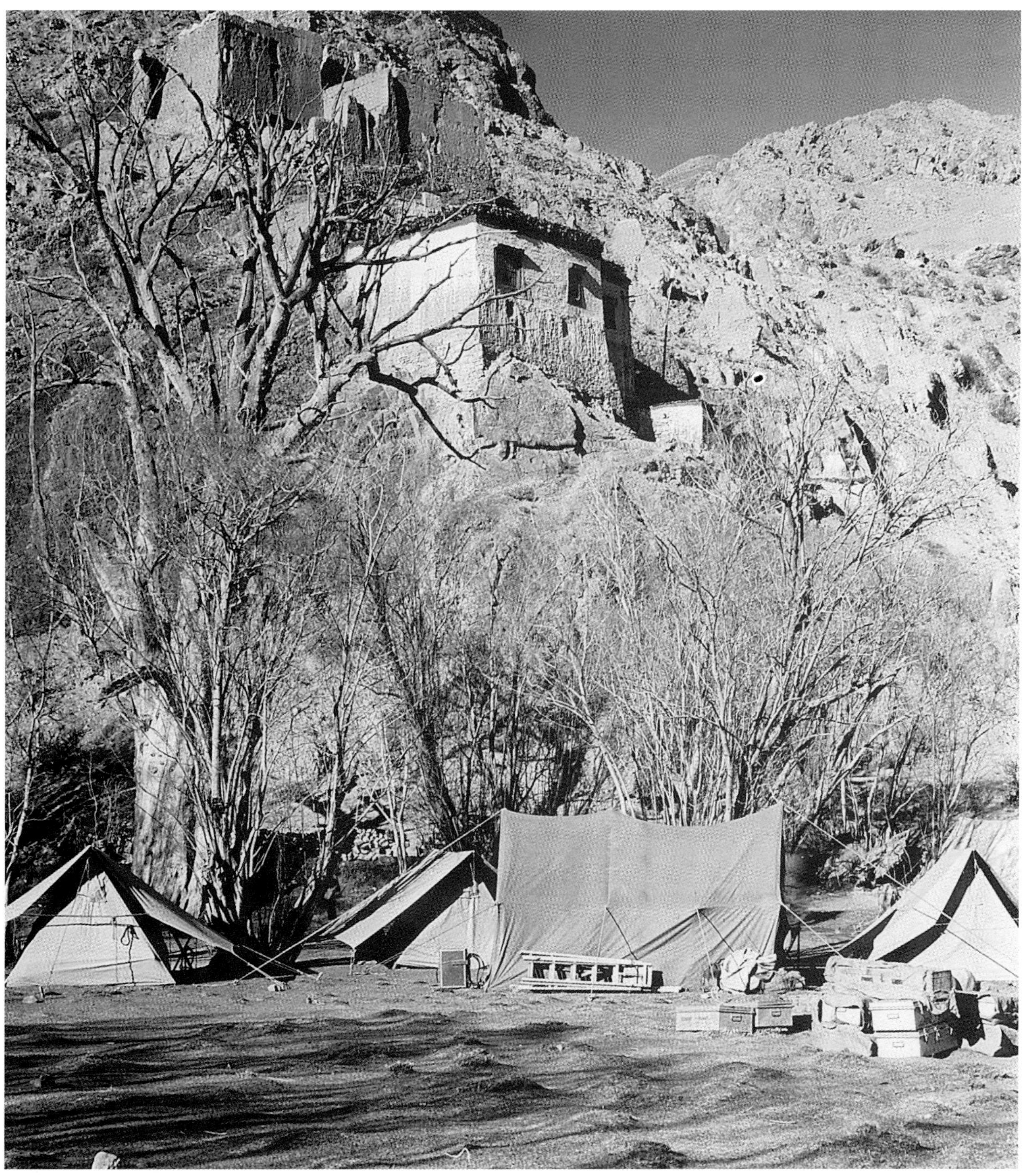

Camp below Shekar. The early mornings were usually still and gloriously sunny, and the men took breakfast at about 7 o'clock, while the larger tents were taken down, packed and dispatched ahead by a pair of fast pack animals. The party set off, usually by 8, taking a break at about 11.30 for a light lunch of biscuits and cheese, chocolate and raisins. They expected to reach the next camp by mid-afternoon, where the mess tent would already be operating and tea would be ready. Dinner was served at about 7.30, and by 8.30 the camp was closed for the night.

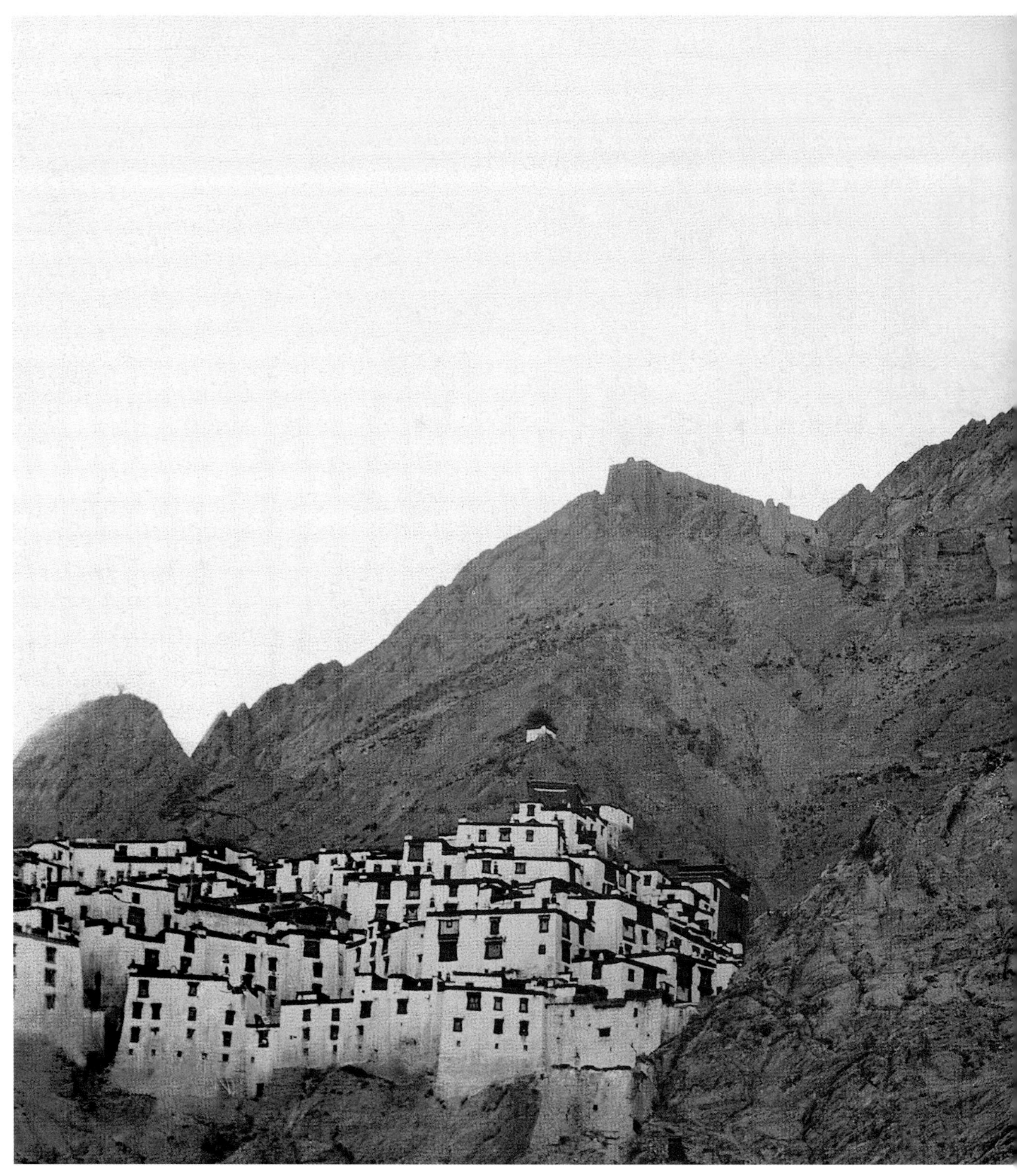

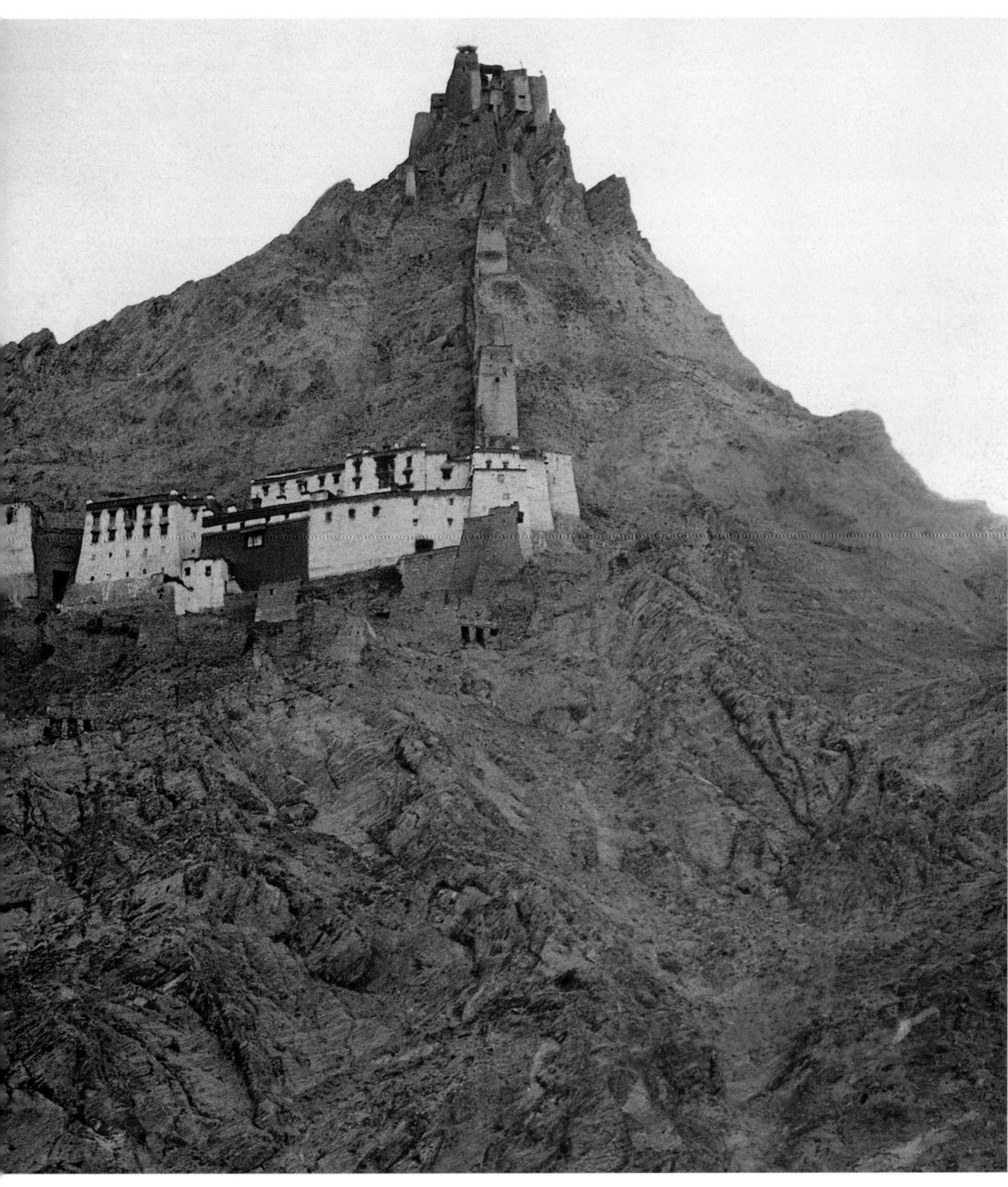

Shekar Dzong had never been seen by Westerners until the British expeditions arrived. This is an example of the artistry of Tibetan design – the marvellous sense of line and the lofty flights, inspired by the majesty of the surroundings.

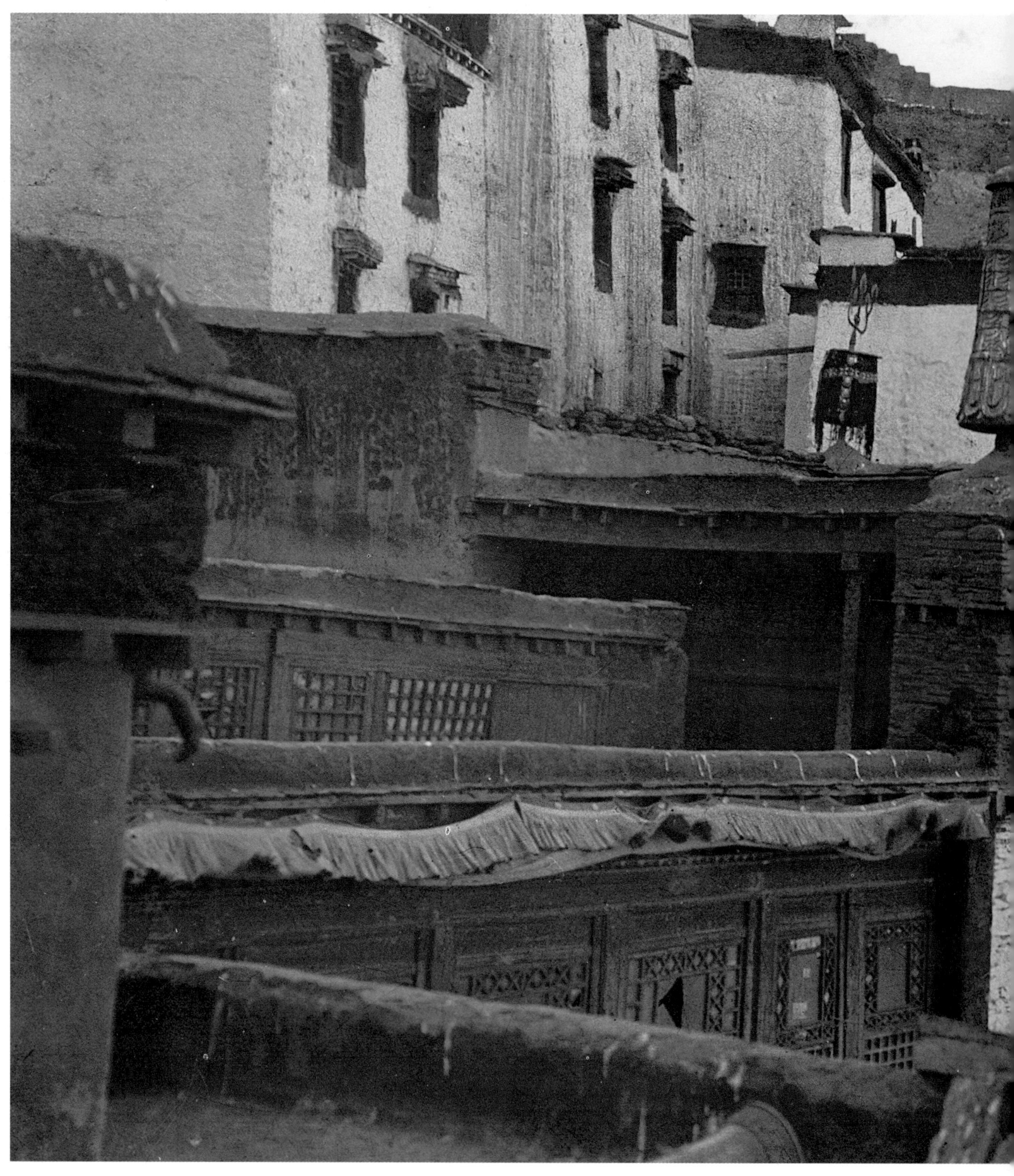

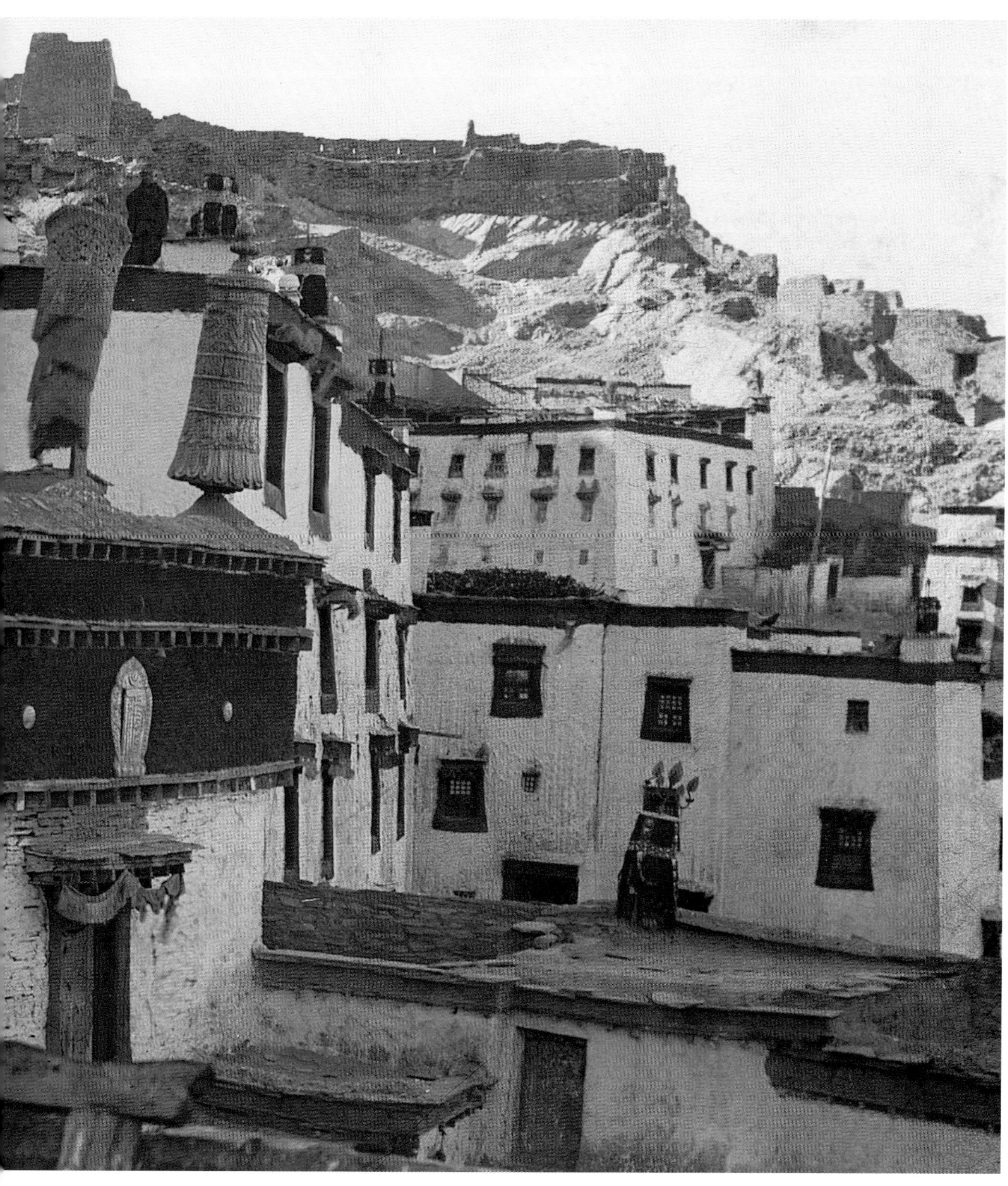

Monastery interior: the tightly packed dwellings are simple structures, built with the only available materials – mud, yak-hair, skin and horn – which protect the huddled people from the icy blasts of the northern winter wind. Some 400 monks live within Shekar, which translates as 'shining crystal monastery'.

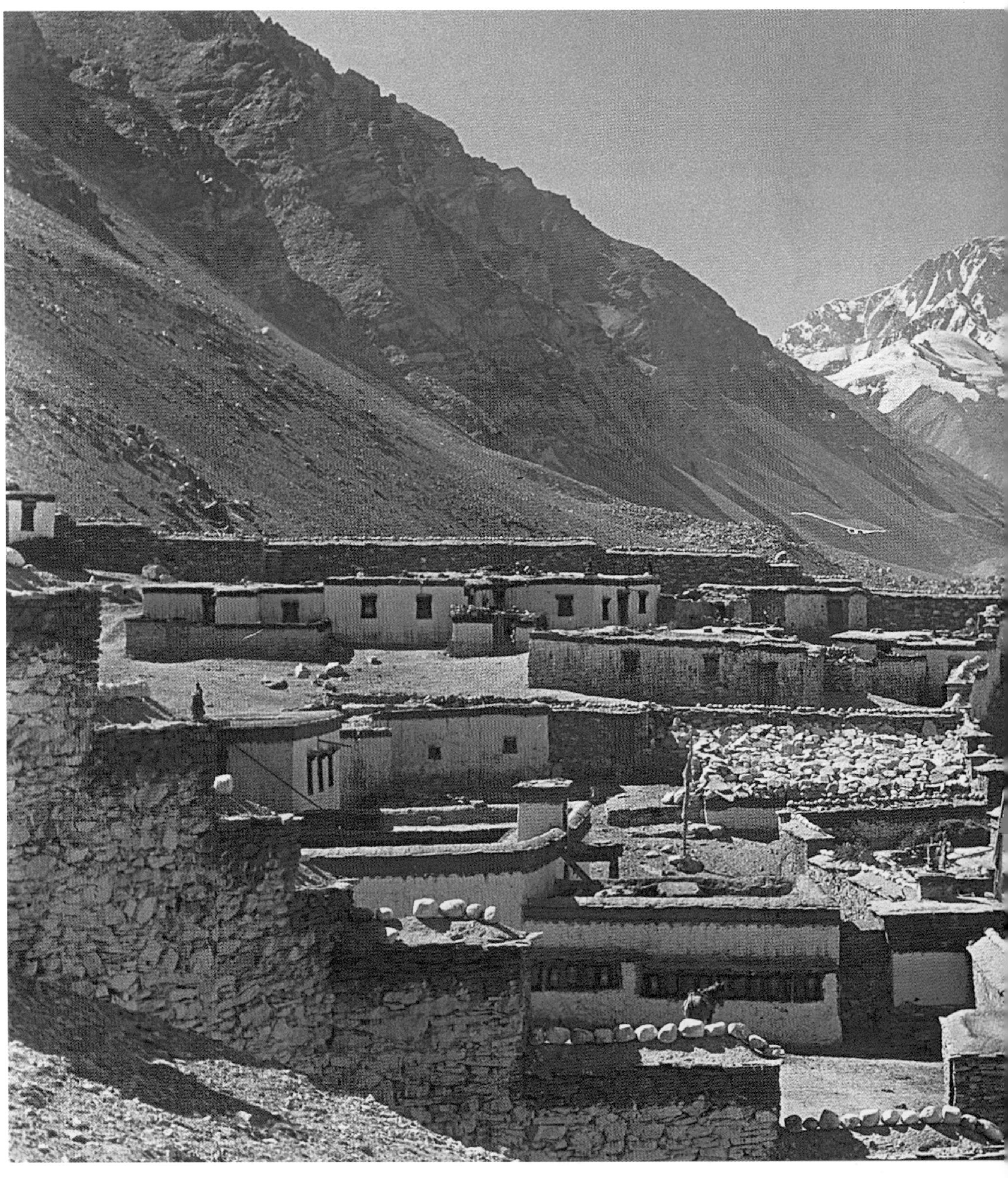

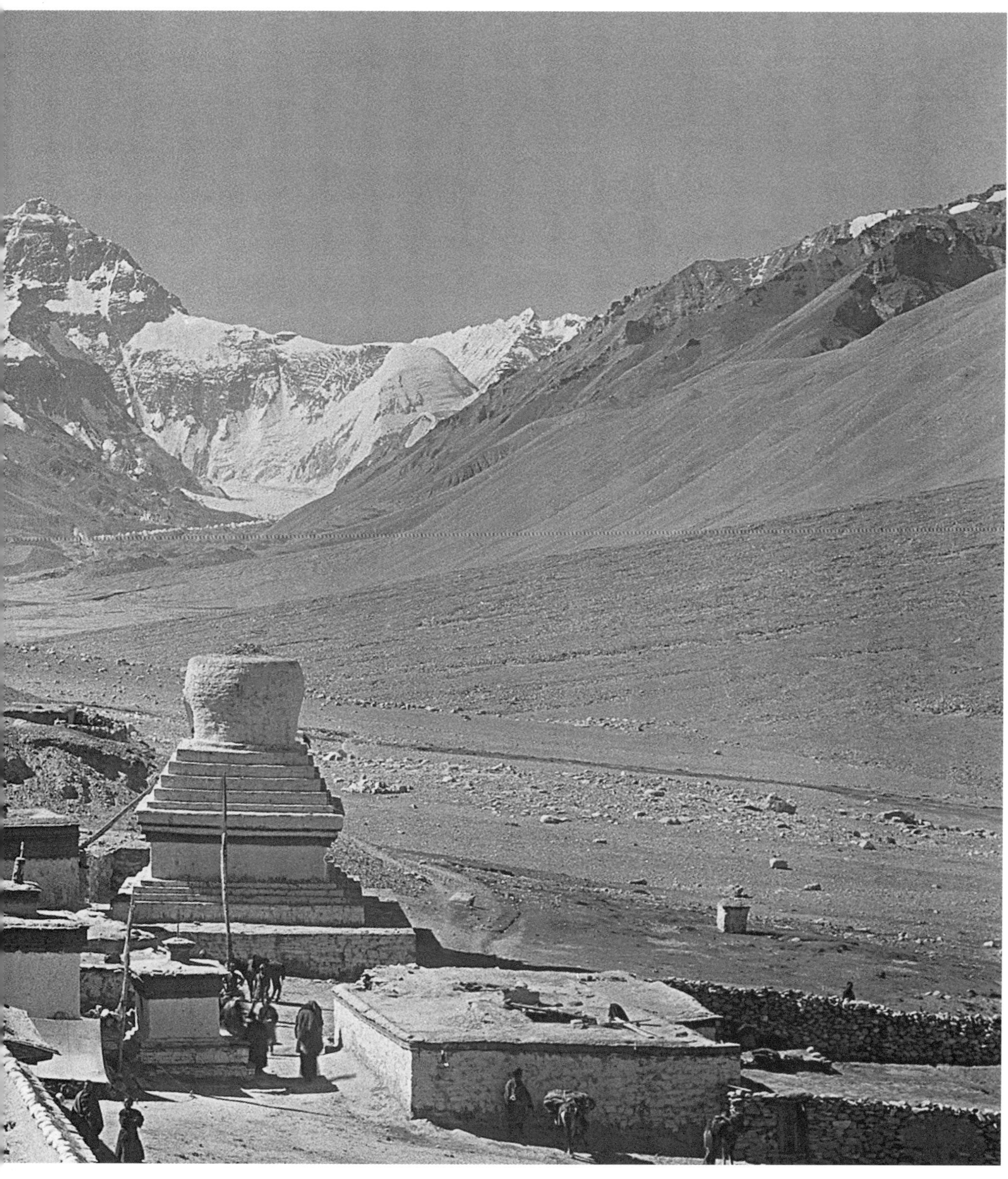

Rongbuk Monastery. At 16,000 feet above sea level, this is the highest monastery in the world, and offered the first view of Everest, which is more than fifteen miles away. The monastery was originally built 2,000 years ago as a shrine dedicated to the highest mountain known to man. 'It is a collection of low, flat buildings, and in front stood an immense chorten, a cupola-like monument built in terraces and crowned by emblems of the sun and moon, symbolising the light of Buddha's teachings illuminating the world.'

The temples were ornately decorated: this Buddhist deity is covered in gold leaf. Temple interiors are dark, have a heavy perfume of incense and are filled with colourful ornaments, semi-precious stones and peacock feathers, which are highly esteemed.

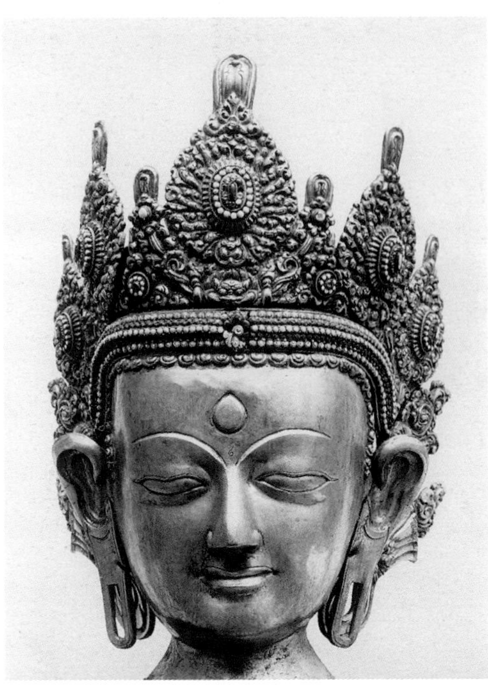

Below: When the expedition first passed the Rongbuk Monastery, the head lama was living as a hermit. Cells are built into the rough stone walls, where those seeking religious enlightenment are incarcerated, and given a bowl of water and a handful of barley meal each day. Noel witnessed a brother monk bringing the daily rations to this isolated priest. He noted '. . . through a hole in the wall on the hermit's cell, [I saw] a hand steal out and take in the water and bread. Even the hand was muffled, because not only no one must see him, but the very light of day may not touch his skin.' It is known that one hermit lived thus for twenty years, never exchanging a single word with the outside world. In the absence of the head lama, his representative accepted gifts, particularly a load of cement, which had been requested when the expedition passed in 1922.

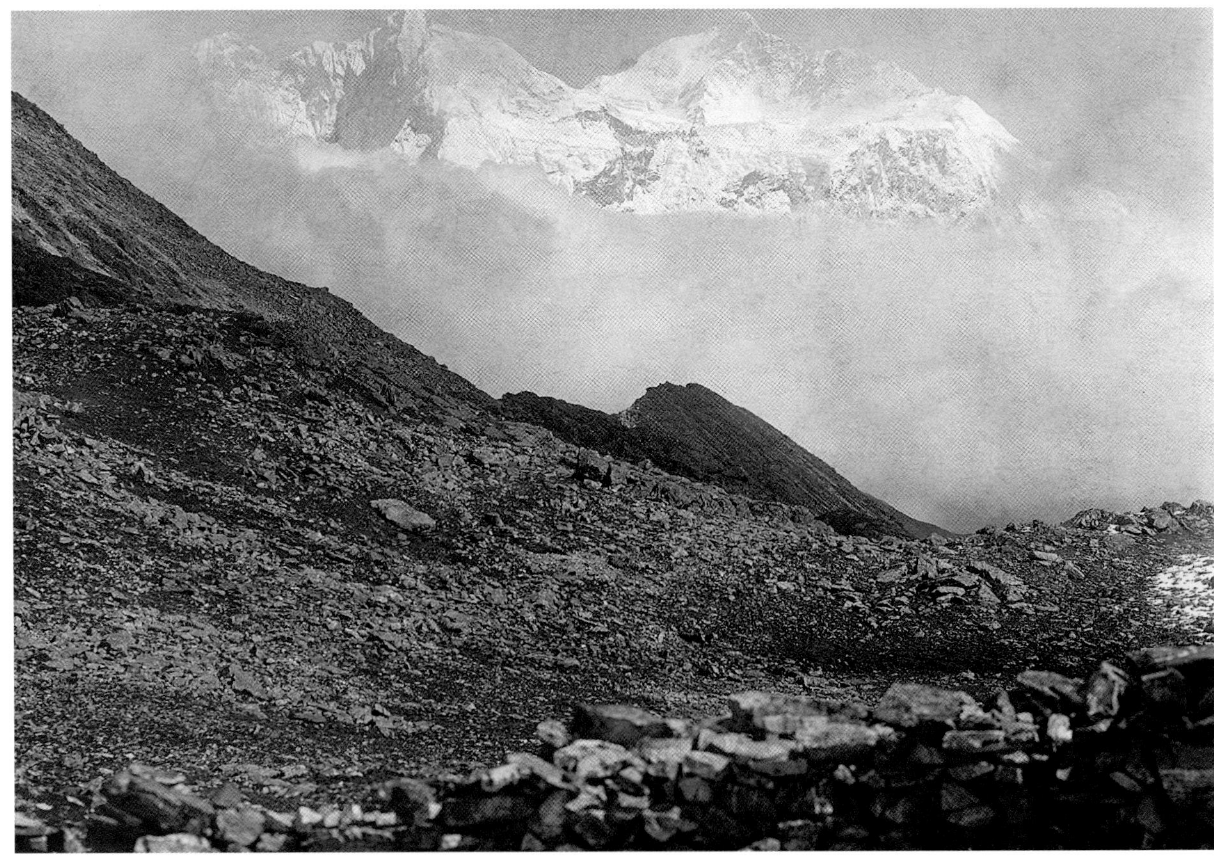

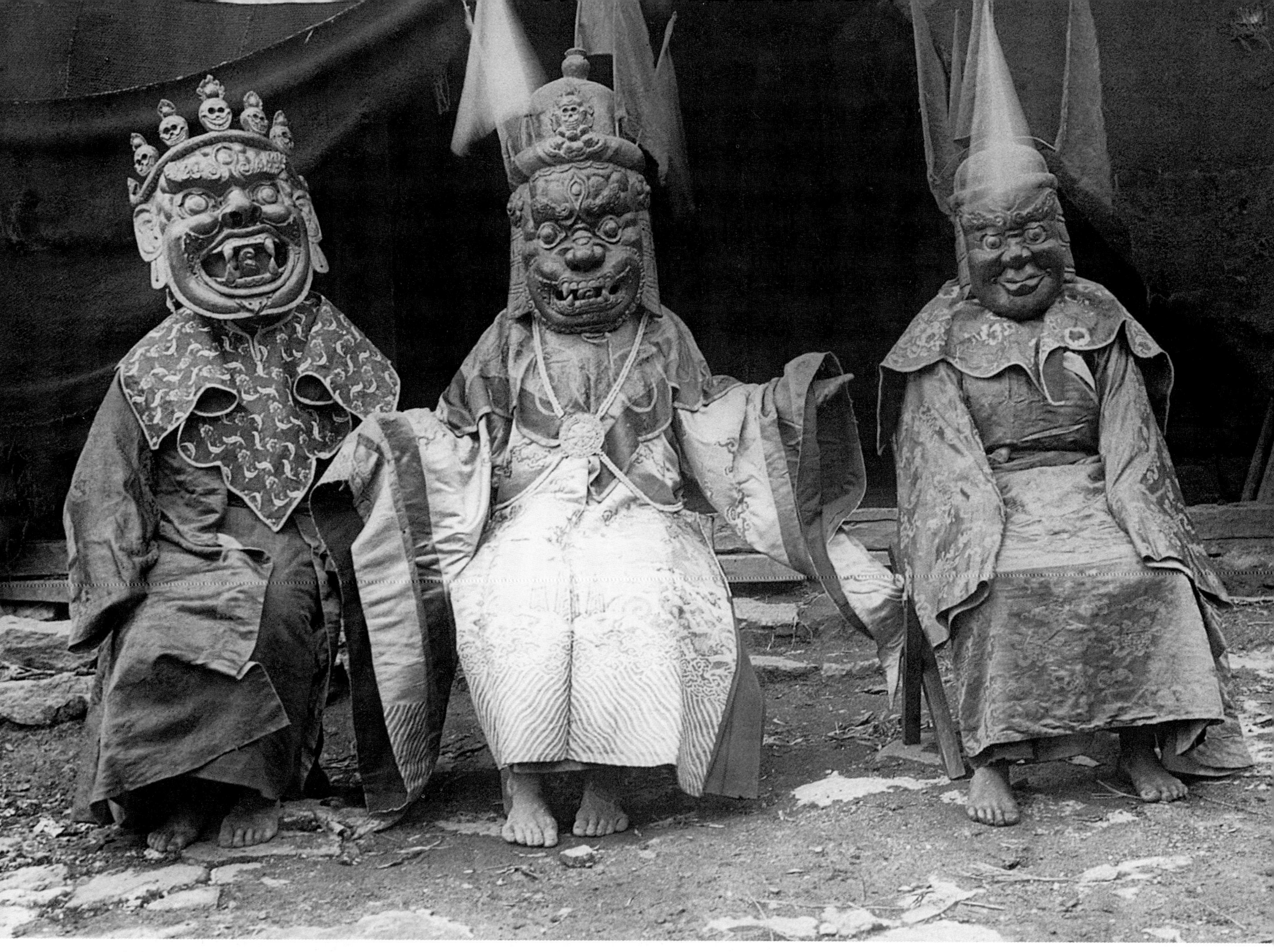

'A troop of demons, fantastically clad, flinging themselves into the struggle for possession of the poor little white soul about to be reincarnated and embark on a new weary life in the world. The drums and gongs and cymbals rolled, rumbled and clashed, while droning notes from the horns blown on the temple roof resounded incessantly.'

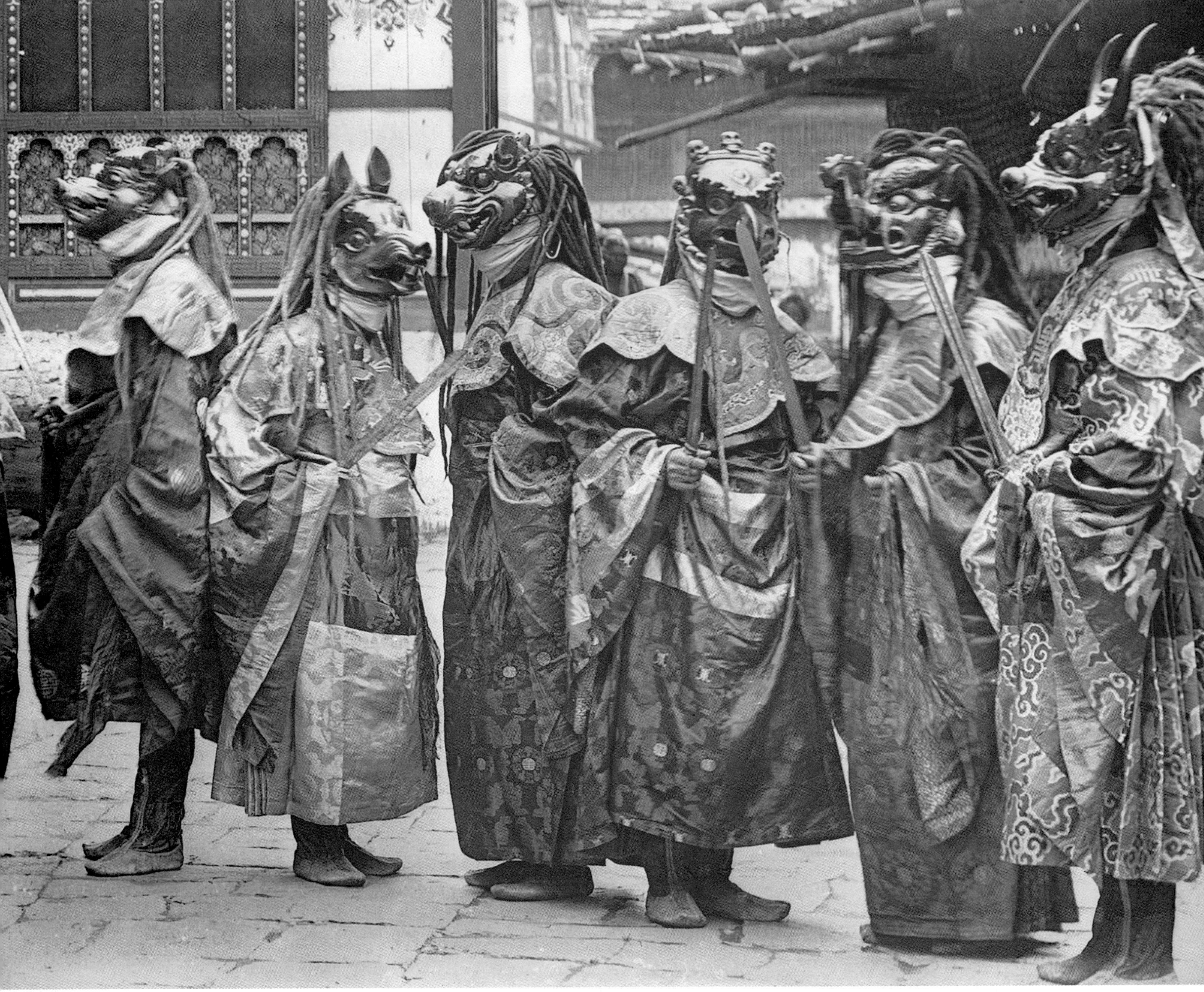

Noel wrote, 'We witnessed a "devil dance". The priests were blowing gigantic horns, beautifully made in copper and silver. They had other trumpets and human thigh bones, and drums made of humans skulls with drum heads of human skin. In the centre of the dancing-place, the courtyard of the monastery, a human protagonist fought and was slain by grotesque monsters.'

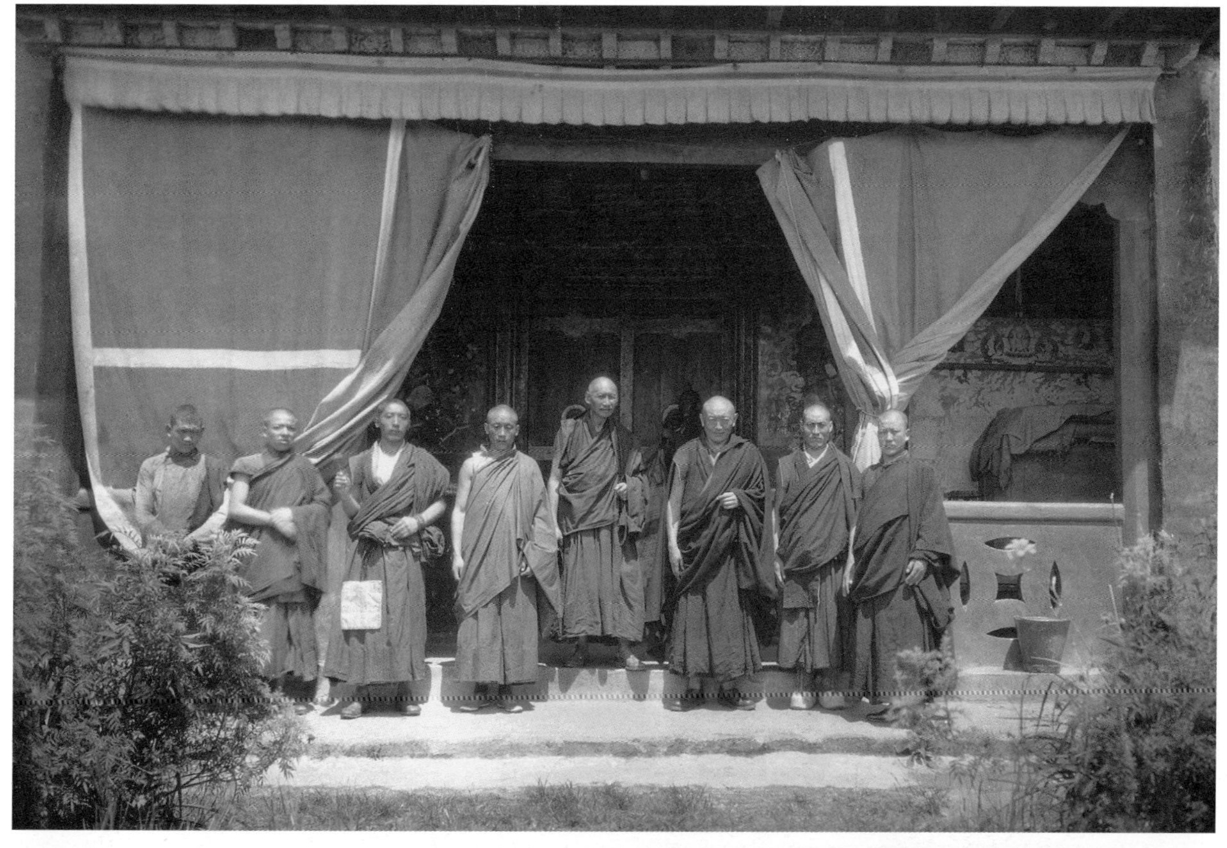

Group of monks. 'What an amazing life these Tibetan monks lead – a life of seclusion and peace. They are one of the most contented and happy of people, devoted to their gods, revelling in the multitude of their demons. They avoid intercourse with other nations. They live in their mountains, despising machinery, science, and all that is Western. It is their ambition to live in isolation from the outside world, without change or progress, in the future as they have lived in the past.'

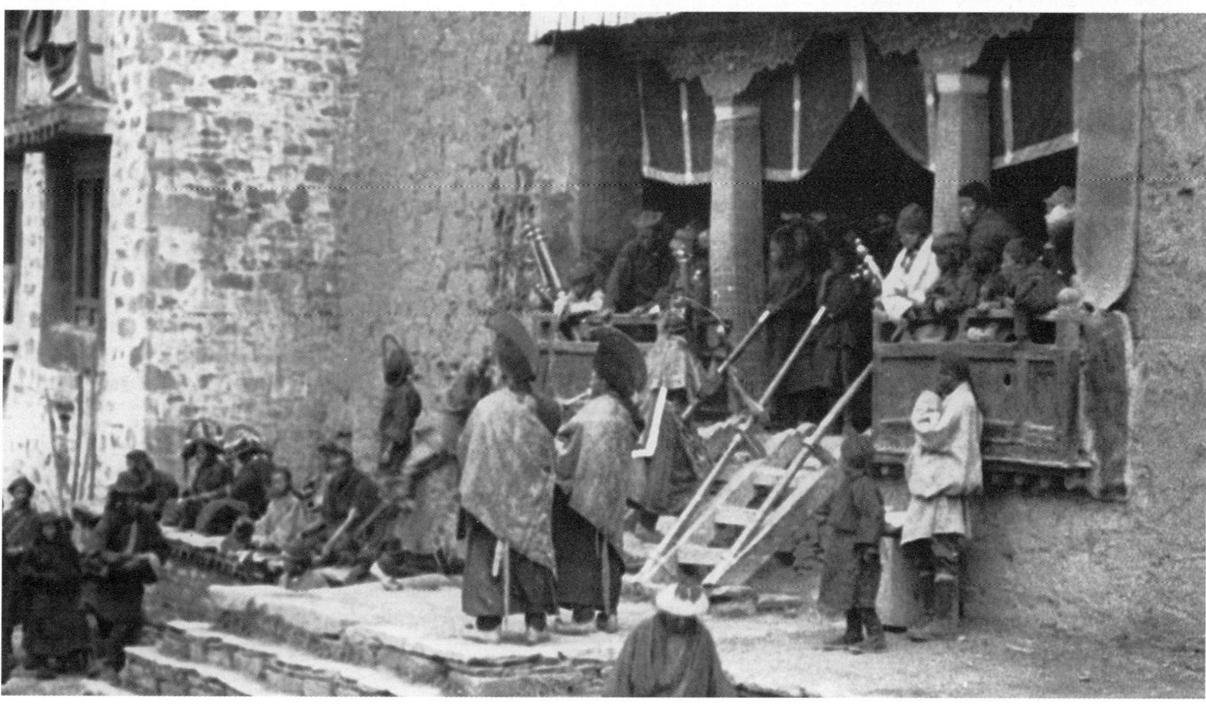

A long procession of gowned monks paraded around the monastery courtyard, and the expedition members were given a send-off. Noel recorded their blessing: 'Chomolungma, the aweful and mighty goddess mother, will never allow any white man to climb her sacred heights. The demons will destroy you utterly.'

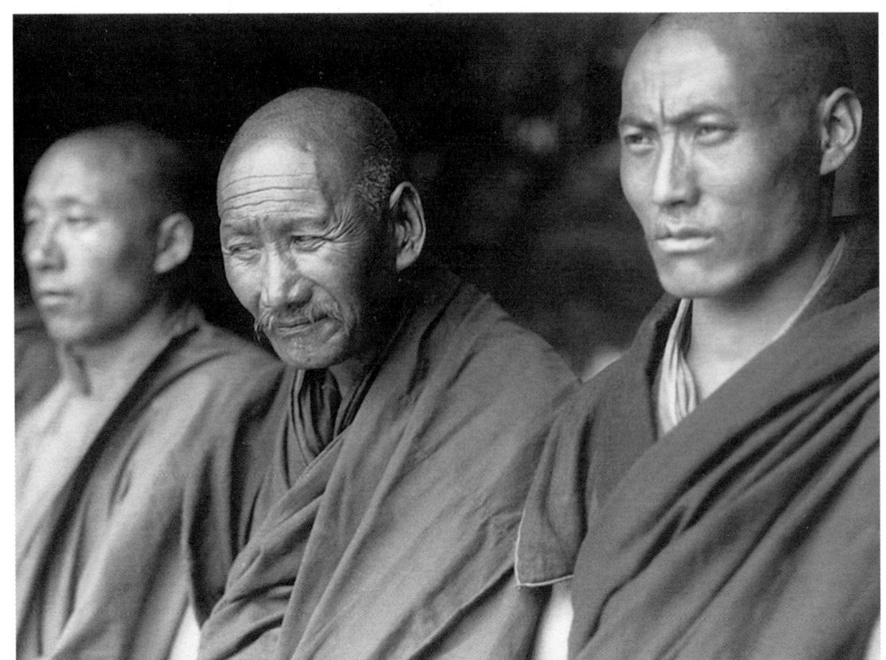

One of the monks, an old man with a gnarled face, shuffled over the courtyard wrapped in his maroon gown, and led Noel to the temple entrance to show him a freshly executed painting, which depicted a speared white man lying below Mount Everest surrounded by guard dogs and a grotesque demon. Was this the pictorial interpretation of the blessing given at Rongbuk?

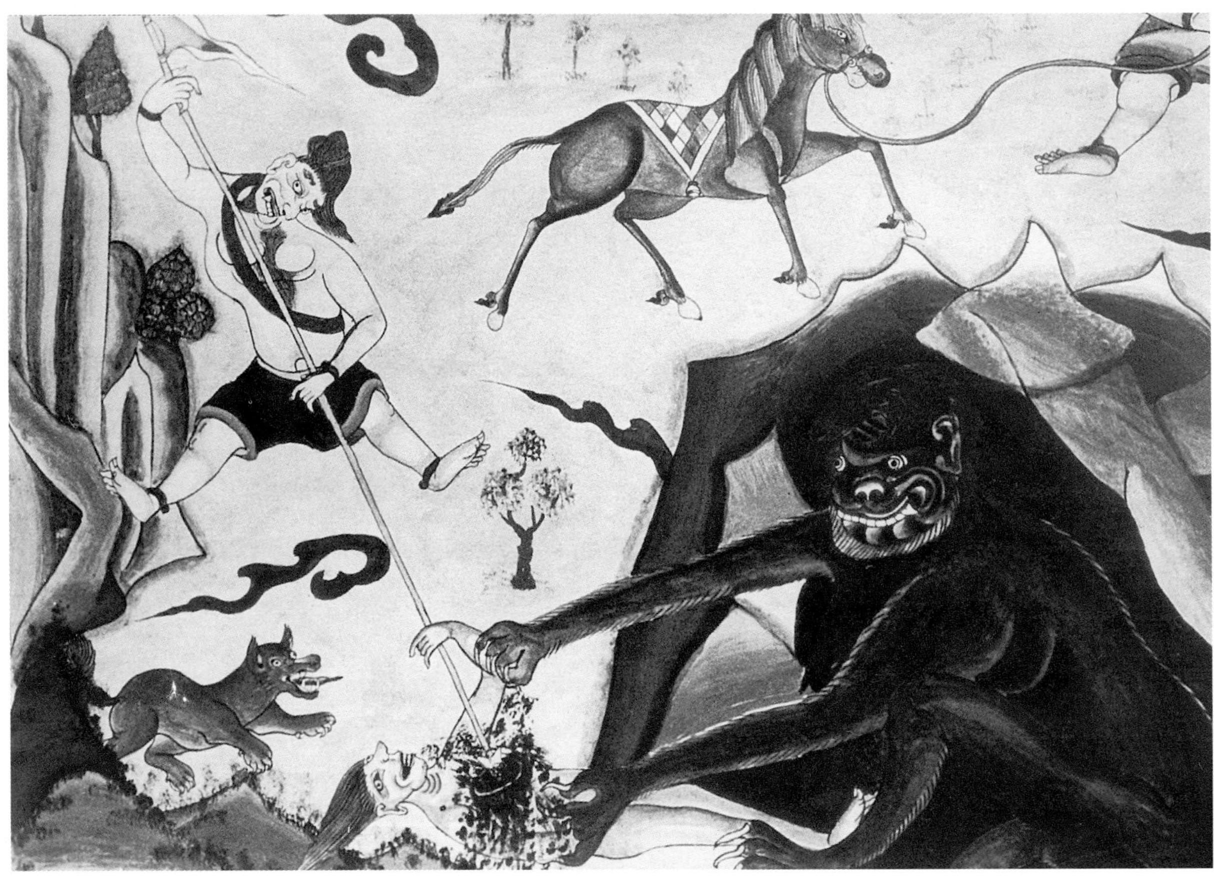

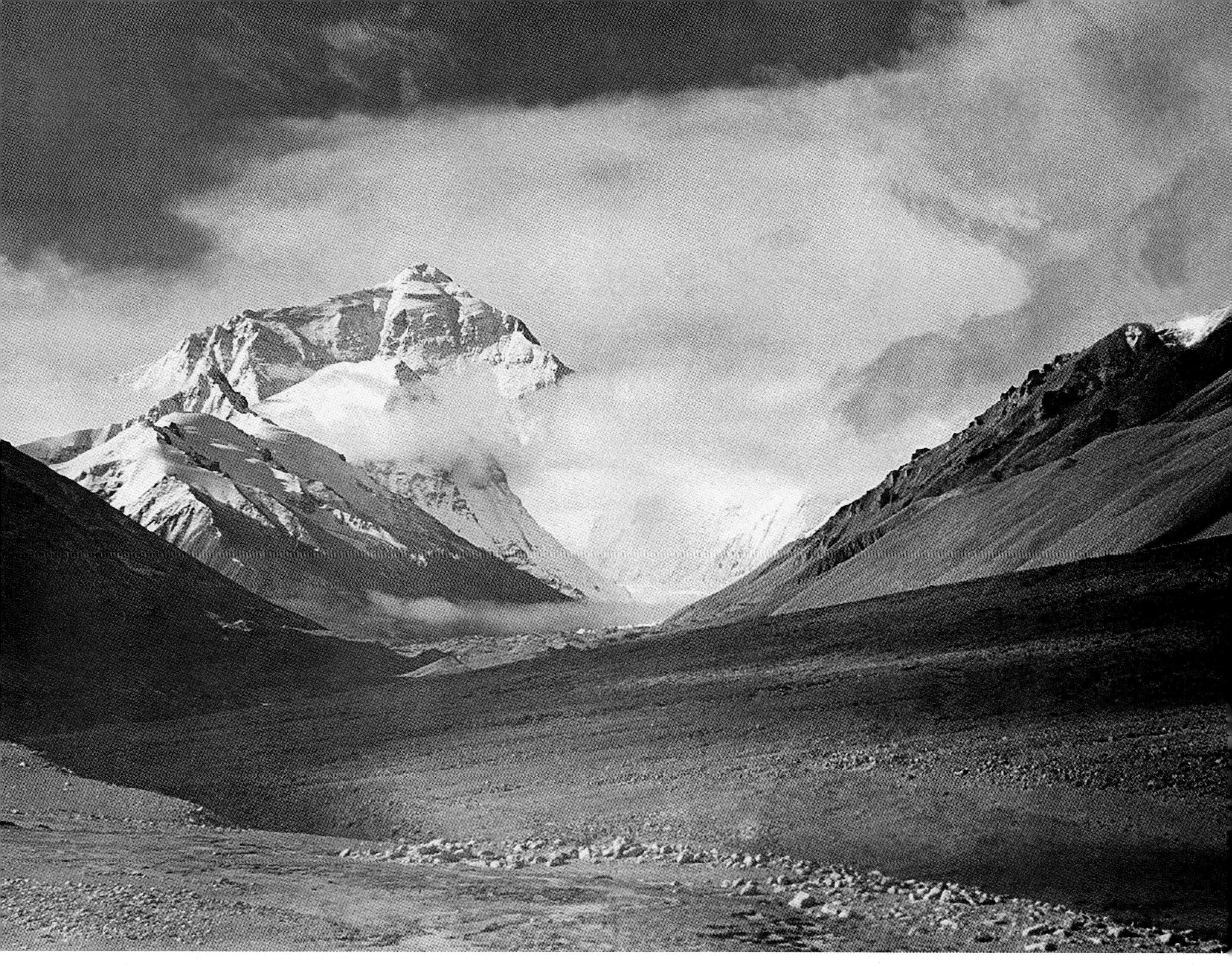

The first view of the great mountain, as they approached Base Camp in late April 1924.

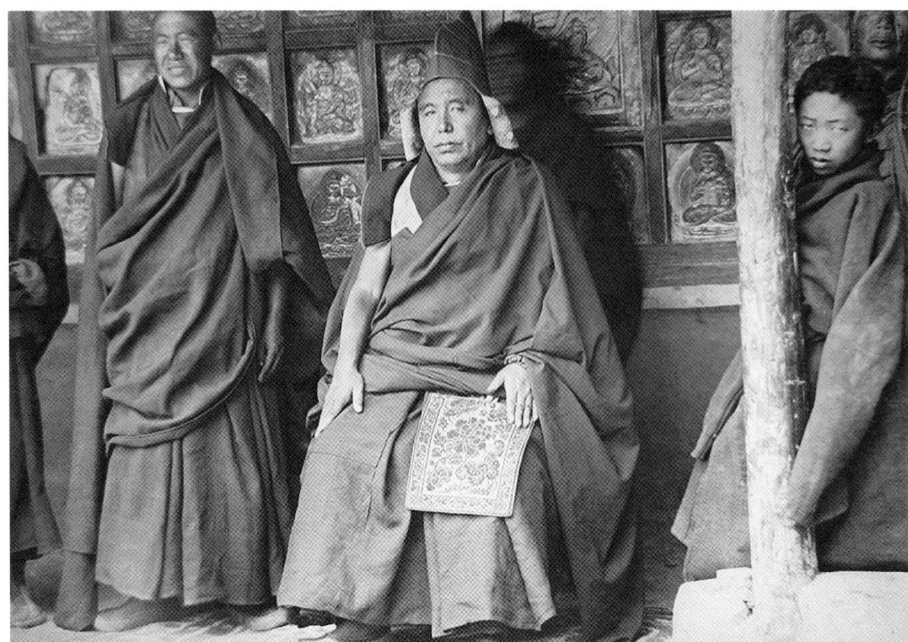

Head lama at Rongbuk. 'Looking closely we saw the face of an elderly man of extraordinary personality. The Mongolian features had a singular cast of thought and beauty.' The silent and motionless figure seemed to look through the European men, and had an almost hypnotic effect on all the expedition members.

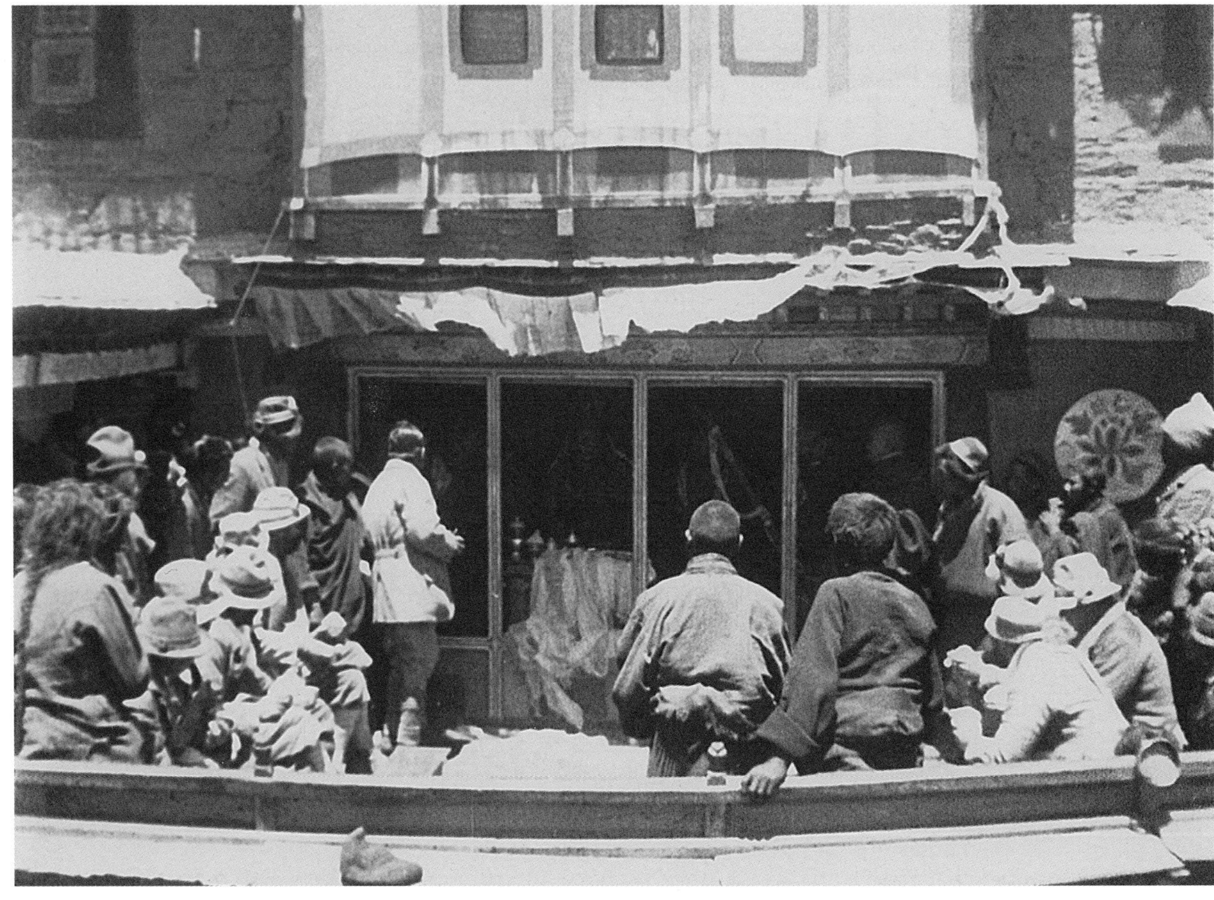

The Blessing at Rongbuk Monastery on 15 May – the head lama can just be seen in the gloomy inner sanctuary. It had taken him and the other monks two days to dress themselves and prepare for the ceremonies.

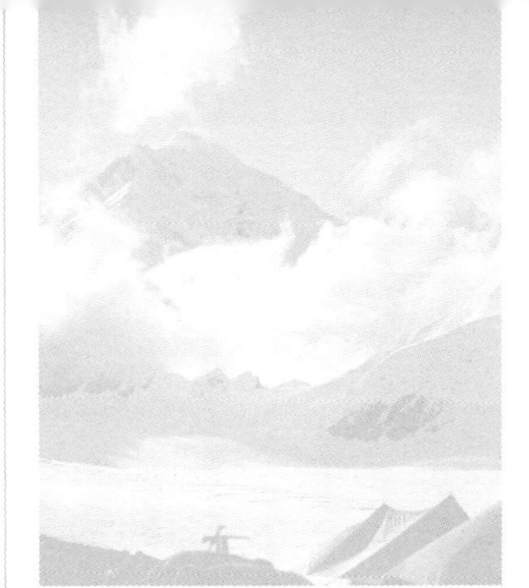

CHAPTER 6

CHOMOLUNGMA – GODDESS MOTHER OF THE WORLD

Everest now lay in sight: from Rongbuk and Base Camp the majestic mountain filled the frame. Bad weather had already delayed progress and the monsoons would arrive any day, so speed was of the essence. The date for the final assault on the mountain was fixed by Norton and the main climbers for 29 May.

A new approach had to be found, avoiding the site of the avalanche of 1922; the memory of the loss of seven porters was ever-present, and it was essential to keep morale high and avoid unnecessary expenditure of energy. In order to reach the North Col they had to negotiate a crevasse. Steps were cut in the 'Chimney', a crack some 60 feet high, and Irvine improvised a rope ladder which made it safe for the laden porters. They were going up in parties with stores for depot-laying, and at one stage four of the porters were marooned after a heavy fall of snow. The risk was that these superstitious sherpas might lose their nerve and hurl themselves down the ice slopes. After four nerve-racking days they were rescued by Norton, Mallory and Somervell.

Noel, watching the drama, prepared his own team of porters, in case it should be necessary to send out more rescue parties. These wretched men needed to rest after their ordeal, so from the reduced porter corps an elite group of fifteen, called the Tigers, was selected to accompany the climbing parties to the high camps. This, together with the delay caused by adverse weather conditions, meant that the plan to attack the mountain in pairs, with or without oxgyen, had to be revised, as the small group of sherpas could not be expected to carry the additional weight of the cylinders to the upper camps. Meanwhile, it fell to Norton, the commander, to marshall the climbers to prepare for an assault. But he was restricted by their physical condition – Beetham had an attack of sciatica and had to be counted out, definitively; Somervell had a touch of sunstroke; Mallory was suffering from 'high altitude' throat – and only Norton, Odell, Irvine and Hazard were fit to continue to the higher camps. One by one the climbers either acclimatized or were smitten with some altitude ailment, and the decision on pairings changed by the minute.

Noel and his porters climbed to 22,000 feet, carrying the cameras, electric batteries for the motor drive and stores of food and blankets – the wait could be long, depending on the physical condition of the lead climbers, and the weather conditions. The topmost point of Everest was three miles away in a straight line, and Noel was ready to photograph any assault on the summit. Eventually he spotted the first pair, Norton and Somervell, at 3,000 yards, a line of figures no larger than dots moving across the snow on the north-east ridge at 25,000 feet. Next day they climbed to 28,000 feet. Norton then struggled on alone, until, only 900 feet from the summit, he could go no further. Apart from the immense altitude they attained without oxygen, they learned that the dry atmosphere (and consequent thirst) is one of the most serious problems on Everest. On the way down Norton developed snow-blindness, another ferocious hazard, as the atmosphere is impregnated with infra-red rays. Despite their supreme struggle, Norton maintained that it would be possible to climb the mountain without any artificial aid, but nevertheless he decided that the next attempt should be with oxygen. Mallory, although bitterly disappointed by all the setbacks, was ready with a bulldog tenacity, and chose Irvine as his climbing companion, with Odell and Hazard in support at the higher camps. They arranged for oxygen cylinders to be carried up.

It was hoped to get two light tents, sleeping-bags and a supply of food and fuel up to 27,000 feet, and a short spell of good weather enabled them to set out with five porters on 6 June for Camp V, at 25,500 feet. Noel photographed them at 26,000 feet, and then received a note from Mallory telling Noel to look out for them at 8 a.m. on 8 June at a certain point on the summit ridge, which he and Noel had previously discussed. There was great optimism in the camps, and the porter who had delivered the note reported that both men were in high spirits and the weather was good. Sadly, it did not remain so. Next day, at daybreak, Noel set up his motion-picture camera, with the long lens trained on the summit pyramid, three miles distant. An hour passed, and there was no sign of the two men. By 10 a.m. cloud and mist obscured the whole summit ridge. From a crag at about 26,000 feet, as the clouds parted, Odell saw them at 12.50 p.m., still on their way up. Concerned that they were three or four hours behind Mallory's schedule, Odell climbed to Camp VI, where he found an assortment of spare clothes and scraps of food, two sleeping-bags and bits of apparatus, but no note. Had the two men left as planned, they would now be on their way down: they would need five or six hours to return to Camp VI before nightfall. Odell left spare provisions and searched a little higher, but by mid-afternoon decided to descend, reasoning that when the two men returned, late, they would be exhausted and would need to rest in the tent at Camp VI, which was incapable of accommodating more than two men. Somewhat refreshed and fortified after a night at Camp IV, where Hazard had prepared hot soup, Odell set out with two porters to return to the higher camps, searching all the time as they climbed. So intense was the cold – the temperature dropped to minus 22 degrees Fahrenheit – that they did not sleep that night, and Odell sent the two porters down the next day as they were suffering from extreme lassitude; again he searched, and again he found Camp VI empty, exactly as he had left it.

Noel and the other climbers were by now all scouring the mountain for any sign of life. He said:

Norton paced backwards and forwards in front of his tent, speaking little, visibly affected, and, I think, already resigned to the worst. Hingston had all his medical aids ready and was prepared to go out at once in answer to a call from the support party up the mountain.

But the signal they saw was not that for which they had hoped – a cross made single-handedly from blankets, which meant that Odell had found no trace of his companions. Hazard was watching and saw the sign of bad news, as did watchers further down the mountain. Norton called a conference and, after much discussion, it was decided that the men could no longer be alive, after such a long period of exposure at high altitude, and that, with the oncoming monsoon and the treacherous weather conditions, Odell and Hazard should abandon their search and descend with their men. Mallory and Irvine had been seen just 600 feet from the summit, closer than anybody had been before. There was much speculation and reasoning. In Norton's opinion it was probably a mountaineering accident which caused their deaths; but if so, why had they been so late? Had the oxygen cylinders been faulty? Did they, in fact, reach the summit and perish on the way down? Did they meet their deaths by being benighted? Further speculation seemed futile, so the dejected group began the weary descent, pressed by the approaching monsoon, troubled by the dreadful uncertainty surrounding the disappearance of Mallory and Irvine, and themselves exhausted by the terrible fight against the forces of nature, which, once again, had won the battle.

To commemorate all those who had died in the quest to conquer the great mountain on the three expeditions, a cairn was built with their names carved upon its rough stones. More, perhaps, than some, Noel was pragmatic about the hazards of the expedition, yet held a mystical belief that his two brave companions had reached the summit. He said:

As you look back over the solitude of the mountain, where these two men remain, there might come to you this thought – if you had lived as they had lived, and died in the heart of nature, would you, yourself, wish for a better resting place than a grave of pure white snow?

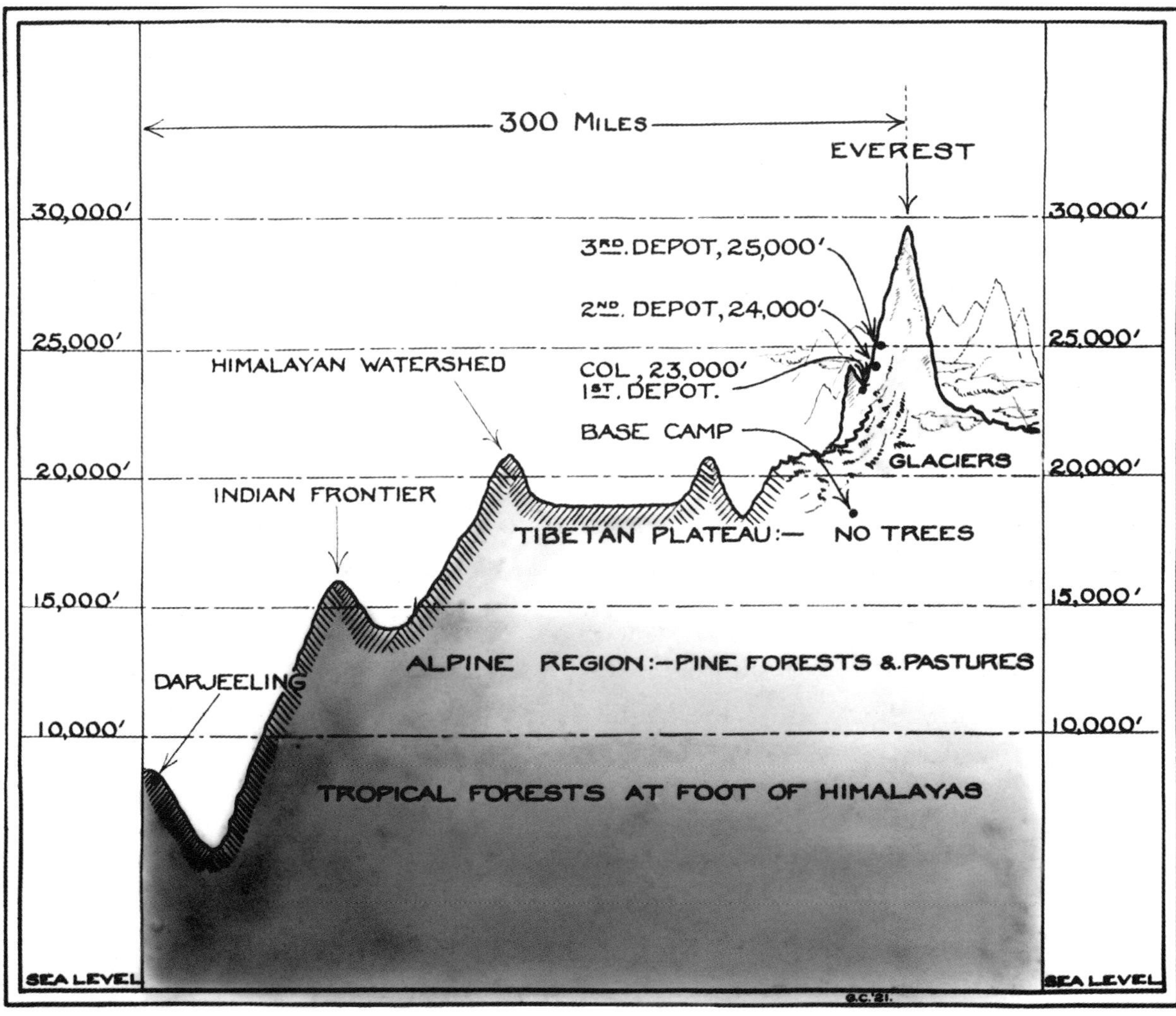

A cross-section of the Himalayas, showing the journey and the heights of the camps.

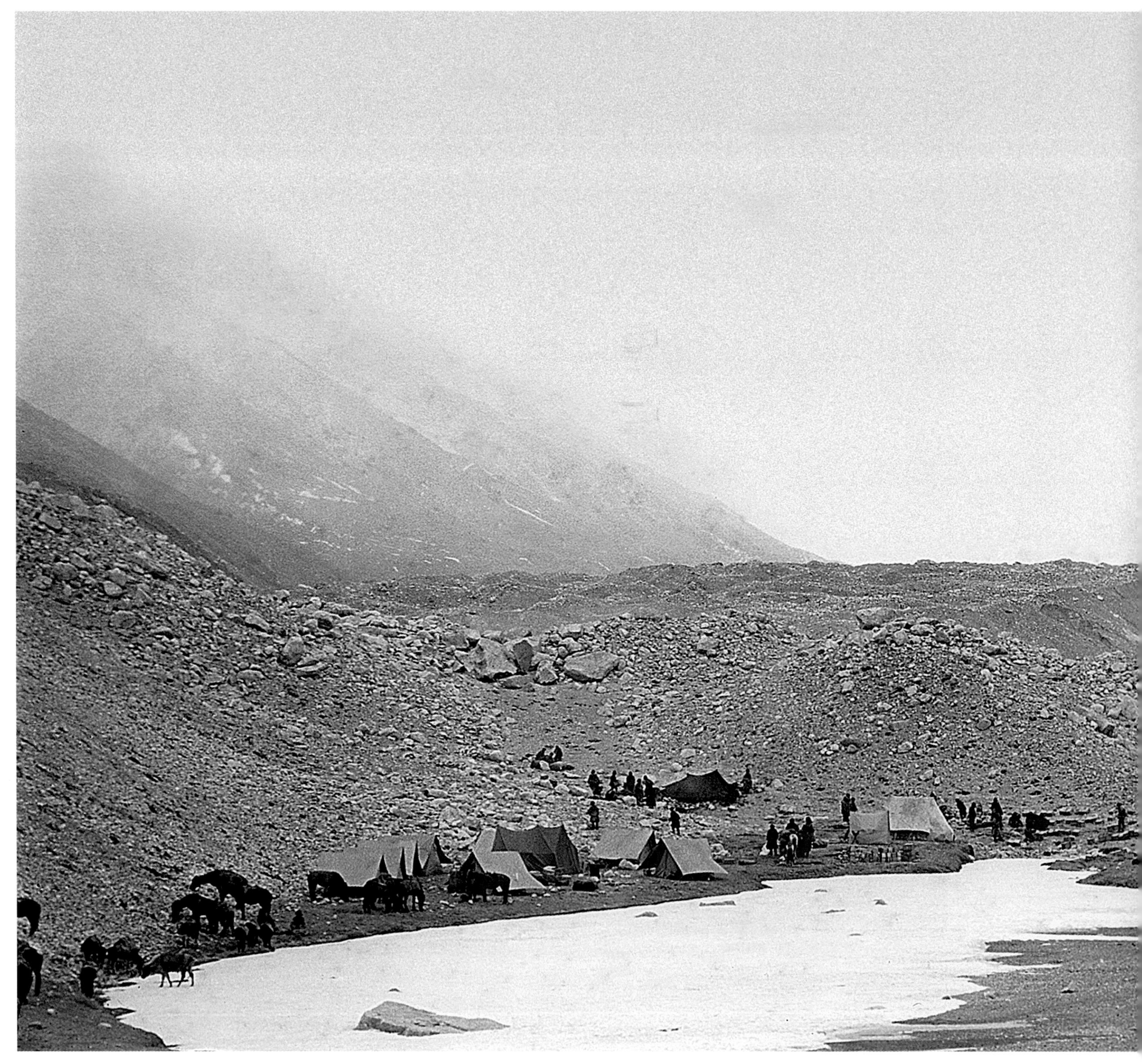

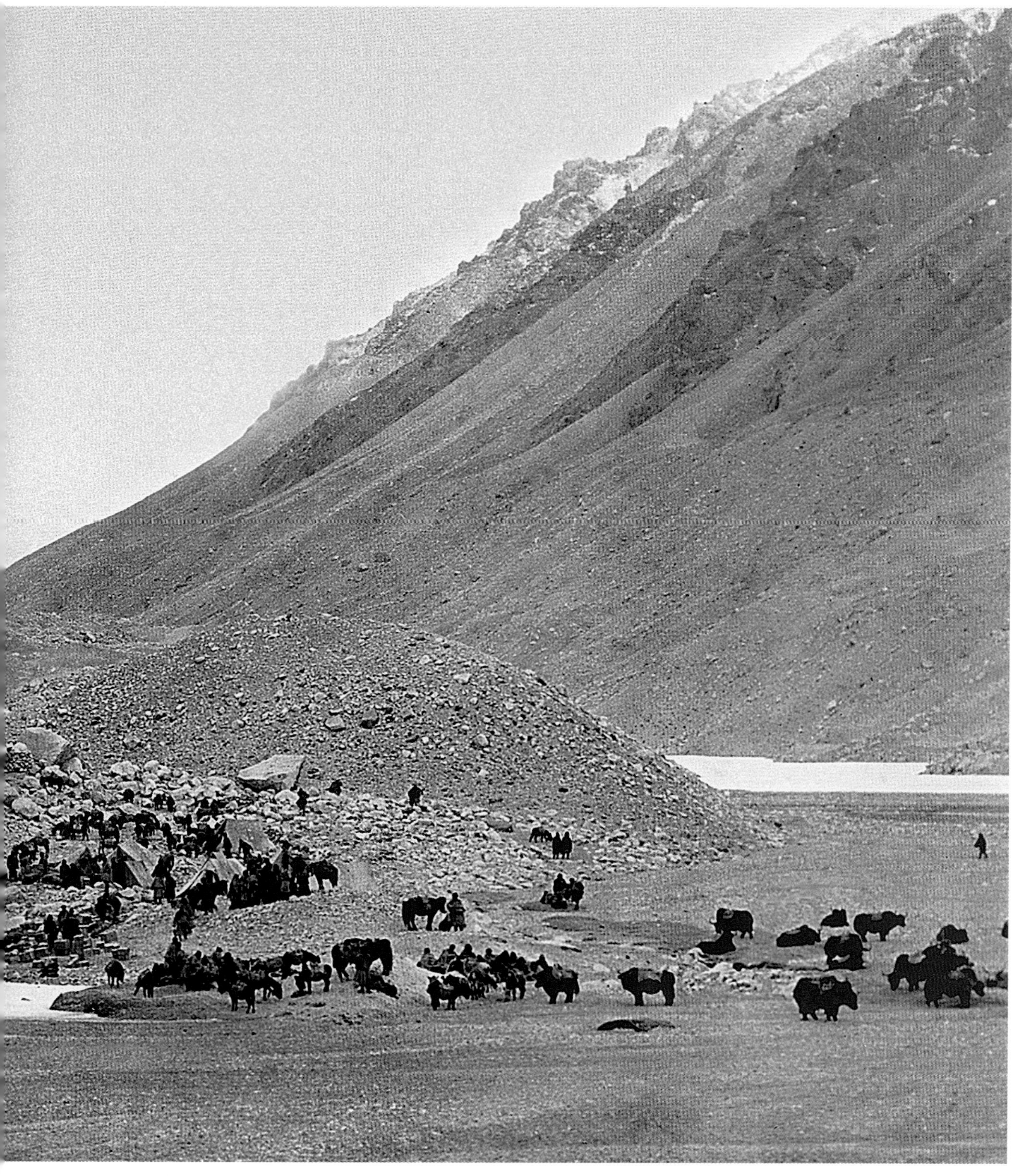

Base Camp, at 16,500 feet. The site had been selected in 1922 and was so favourable that it was again chosen in 1924. It was the intention that General Bruce would be based here, to supervise depot-laying and generally boost morale, but he had been forced to turn back in Phari. His presence was sorely missed, never more so than when atrocious weather forced the expedition back to Base Camp.

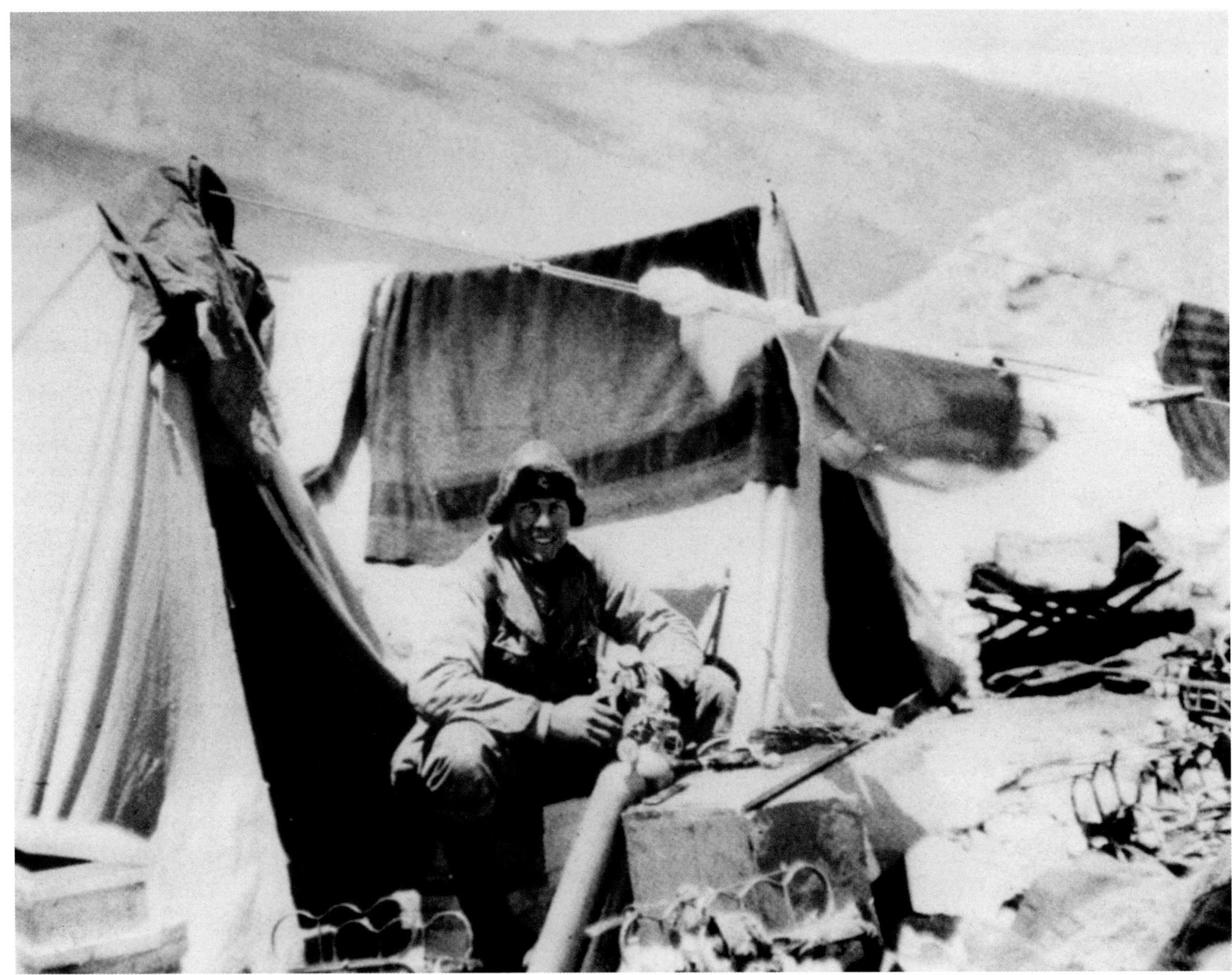

Irvine checking the oxygen cylinders at Base Camp; many were found to be faulty, which may have played a part in the tragedy.

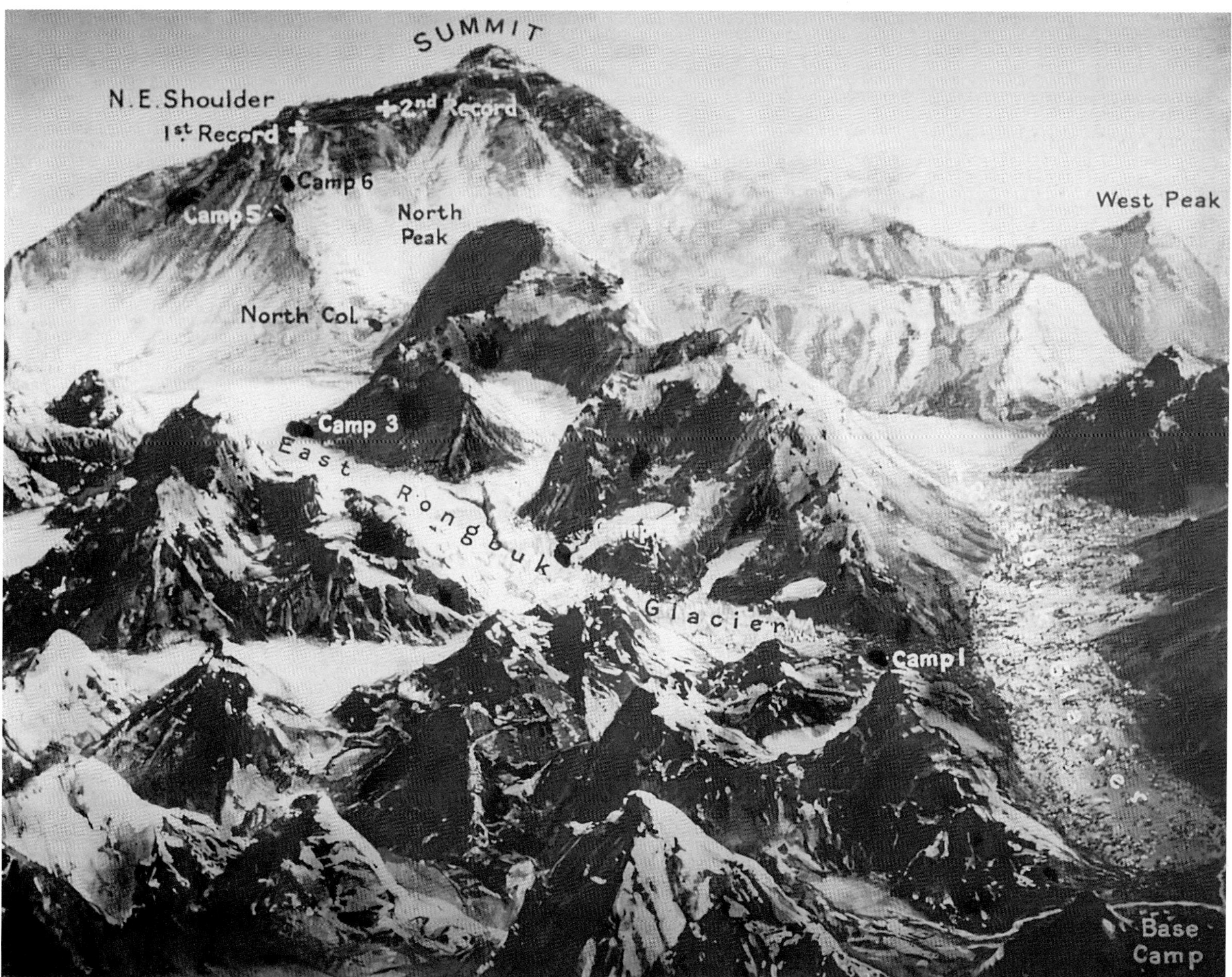

Diagram showing the position of the camps.

Establishing Camp 11. Noel
wrote: 'Unless a man can feel at
home and happy among
mountains, he has no right to
call himself a mountaineer.
Certainly he should never go on
an expedition to the Himalaya.
He should remain where there
are railways and hotels, for
there will be no railway to take
him to the Snowfield Camp
[Camp 111 at 21,300 feet] at
the head of the East Rongbuk
beneath the walls of Everest.'

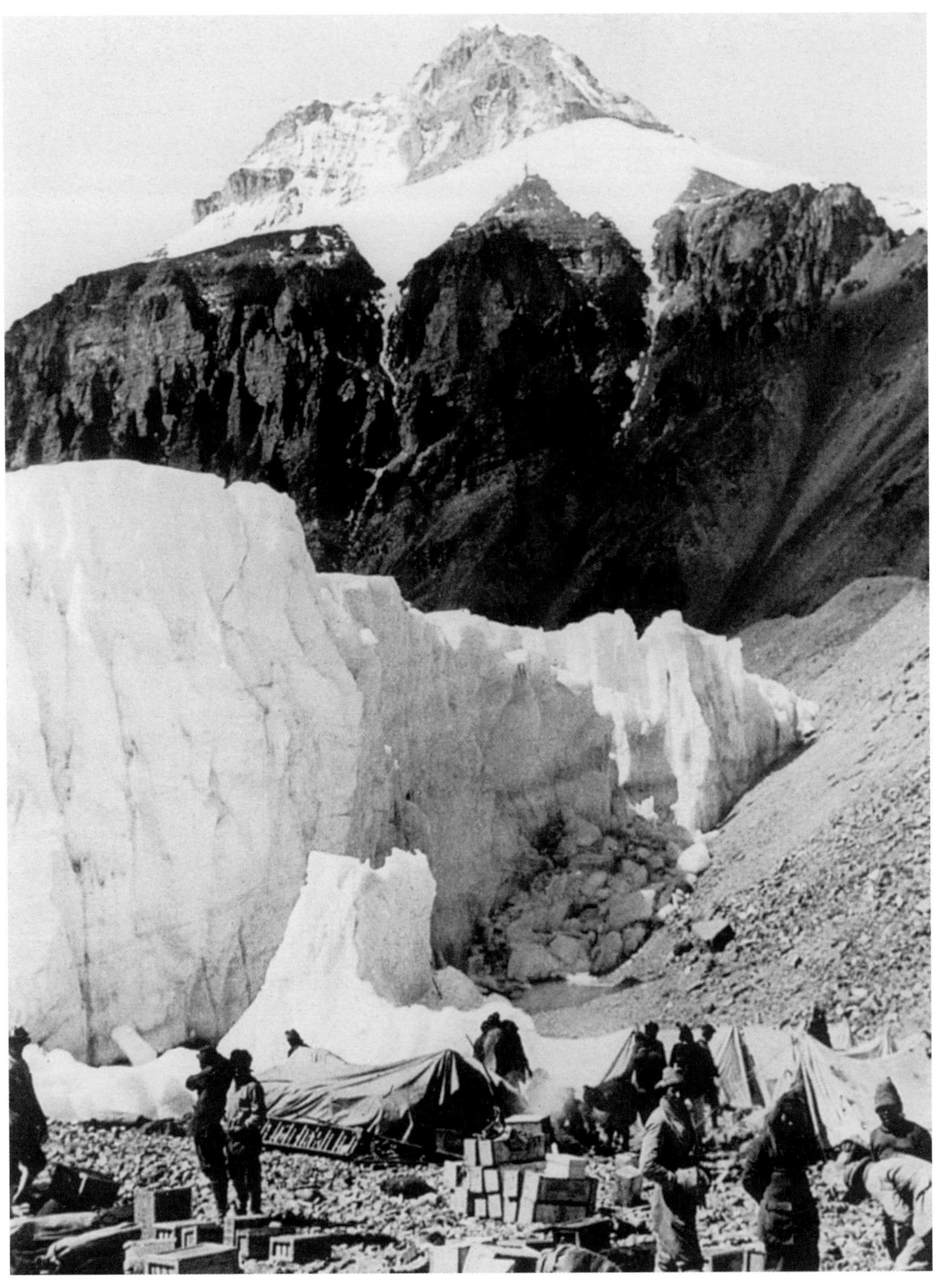

Opposite: A view from Camp III
(Advance Base Camp) at
21,300 feet.

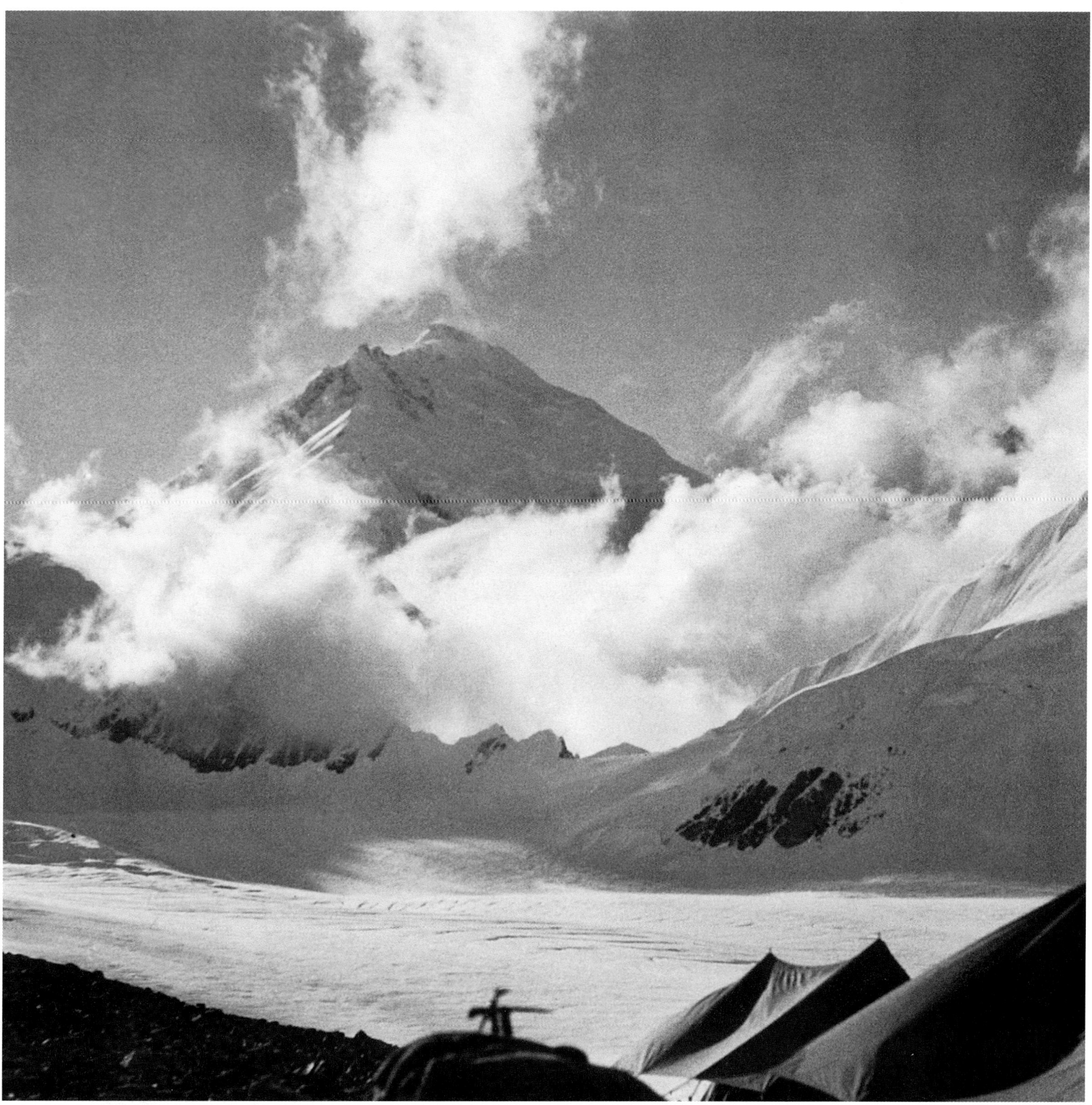

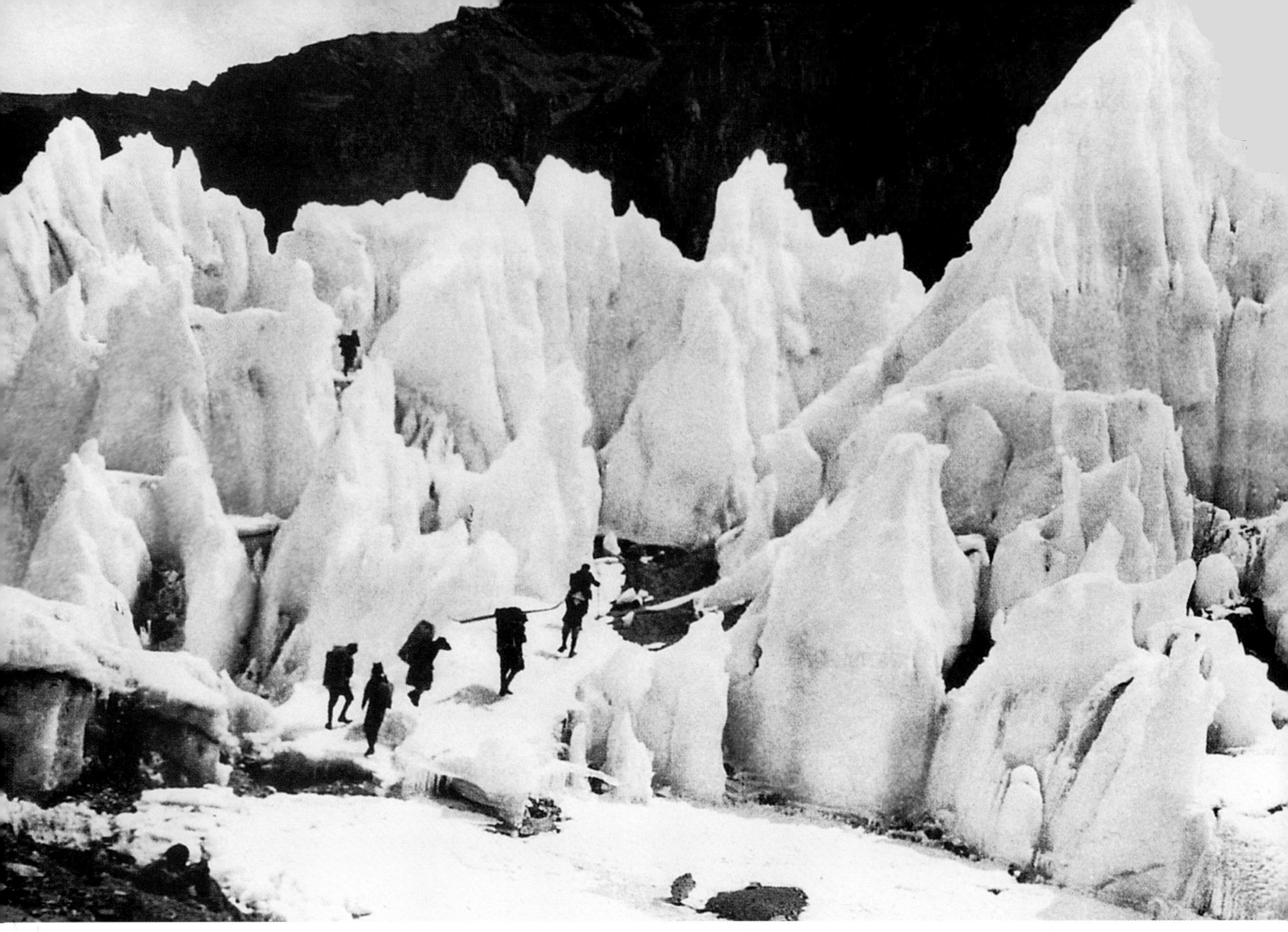

The East Rongbuk Glacier ice corridor and the immense ice pinnacles between Camp III and Camp VI.

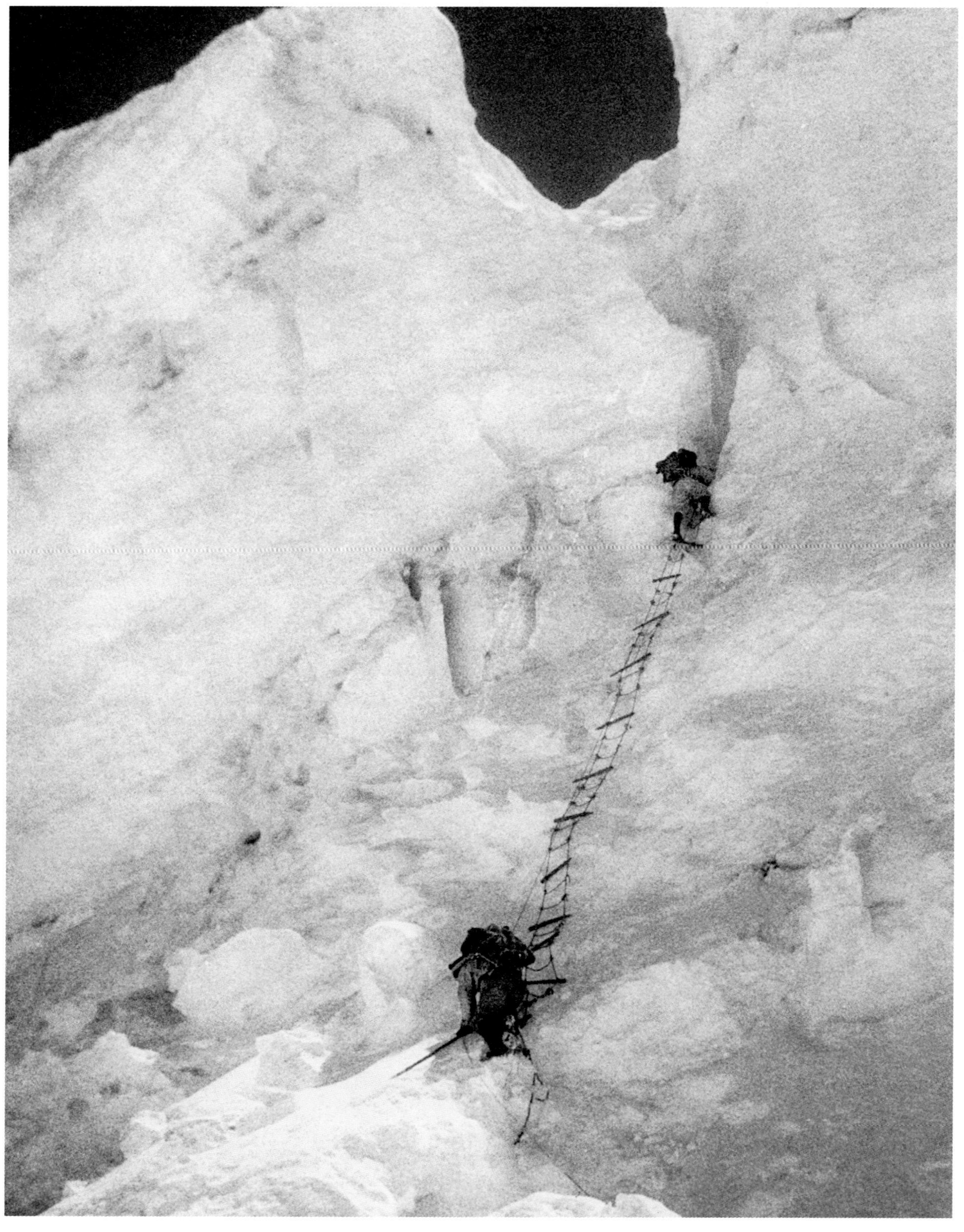

The ice ladder was a new method of climbing the wall, and made it much easier for all the climbers, especially the porters.

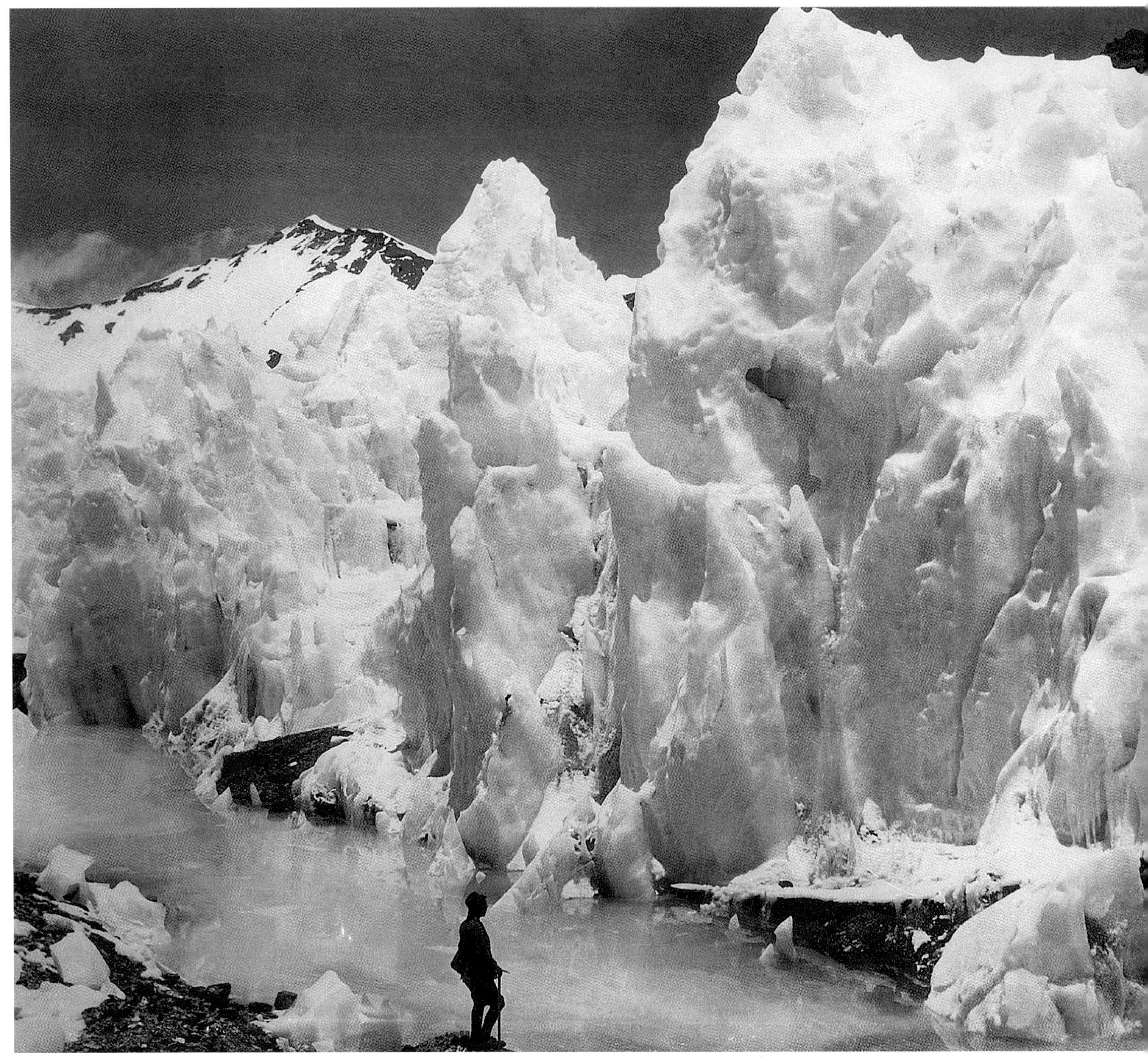

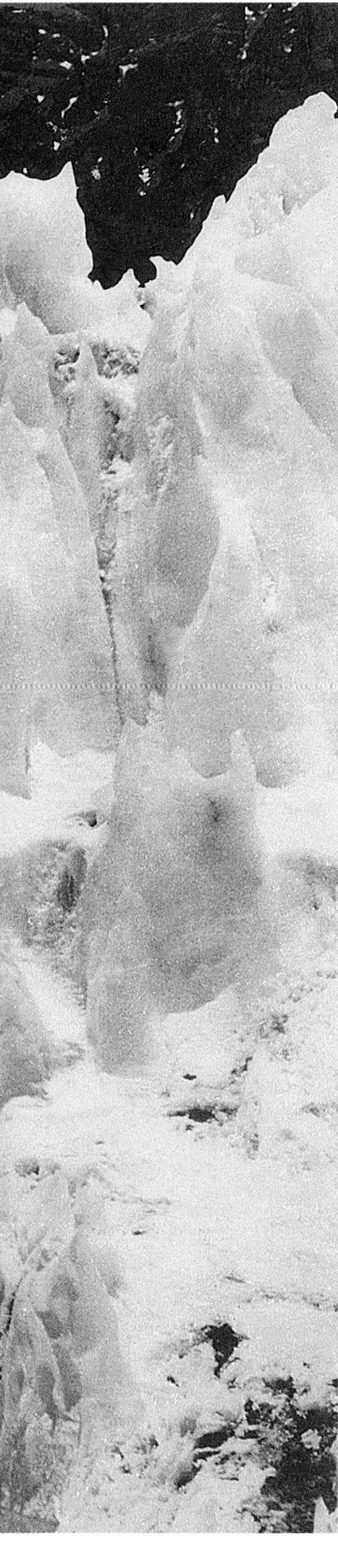

A solitary figure dwarfed by the
huge ice formations.

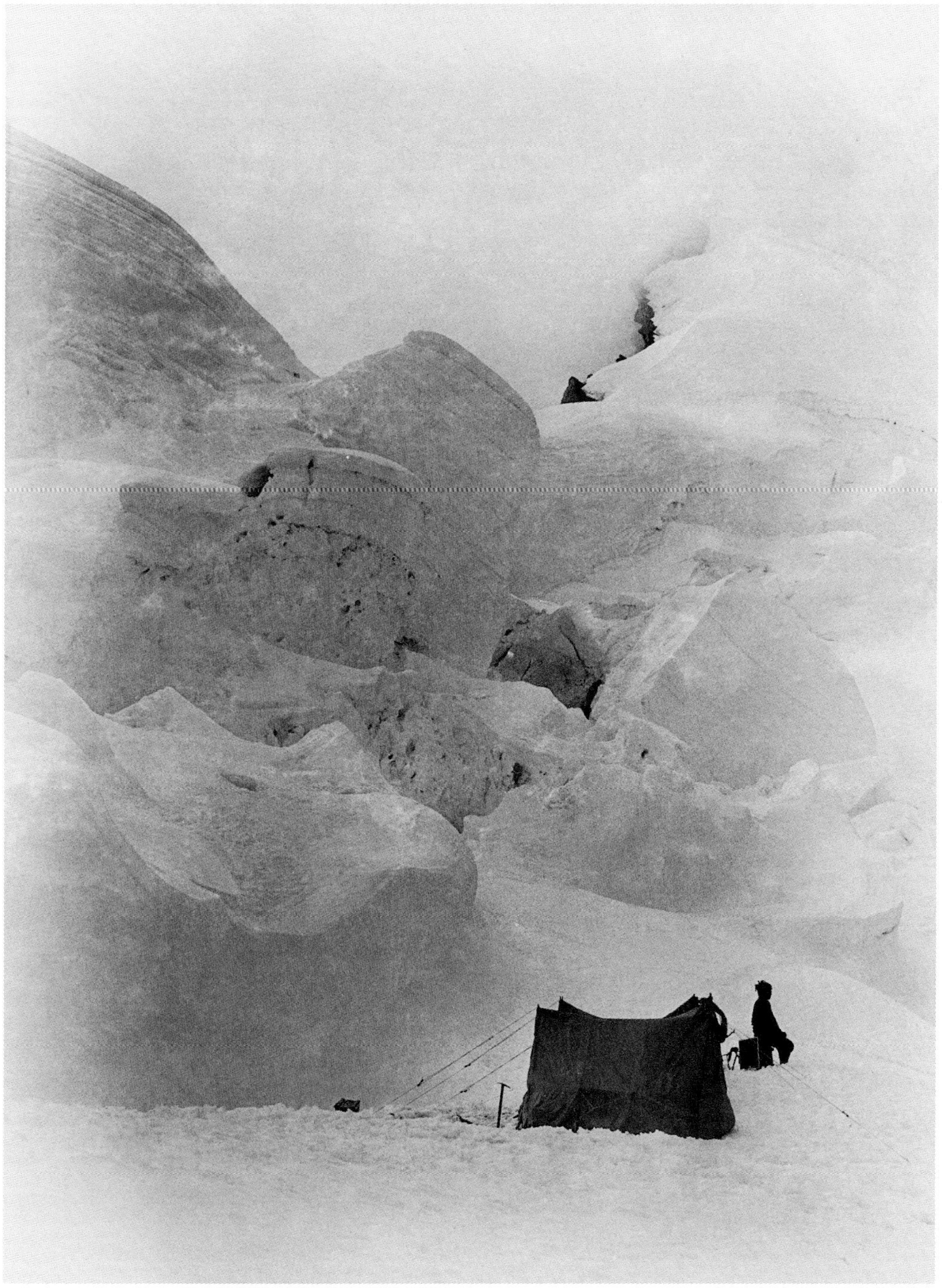

Camp VI, from
which both pairs of
climbers set out.

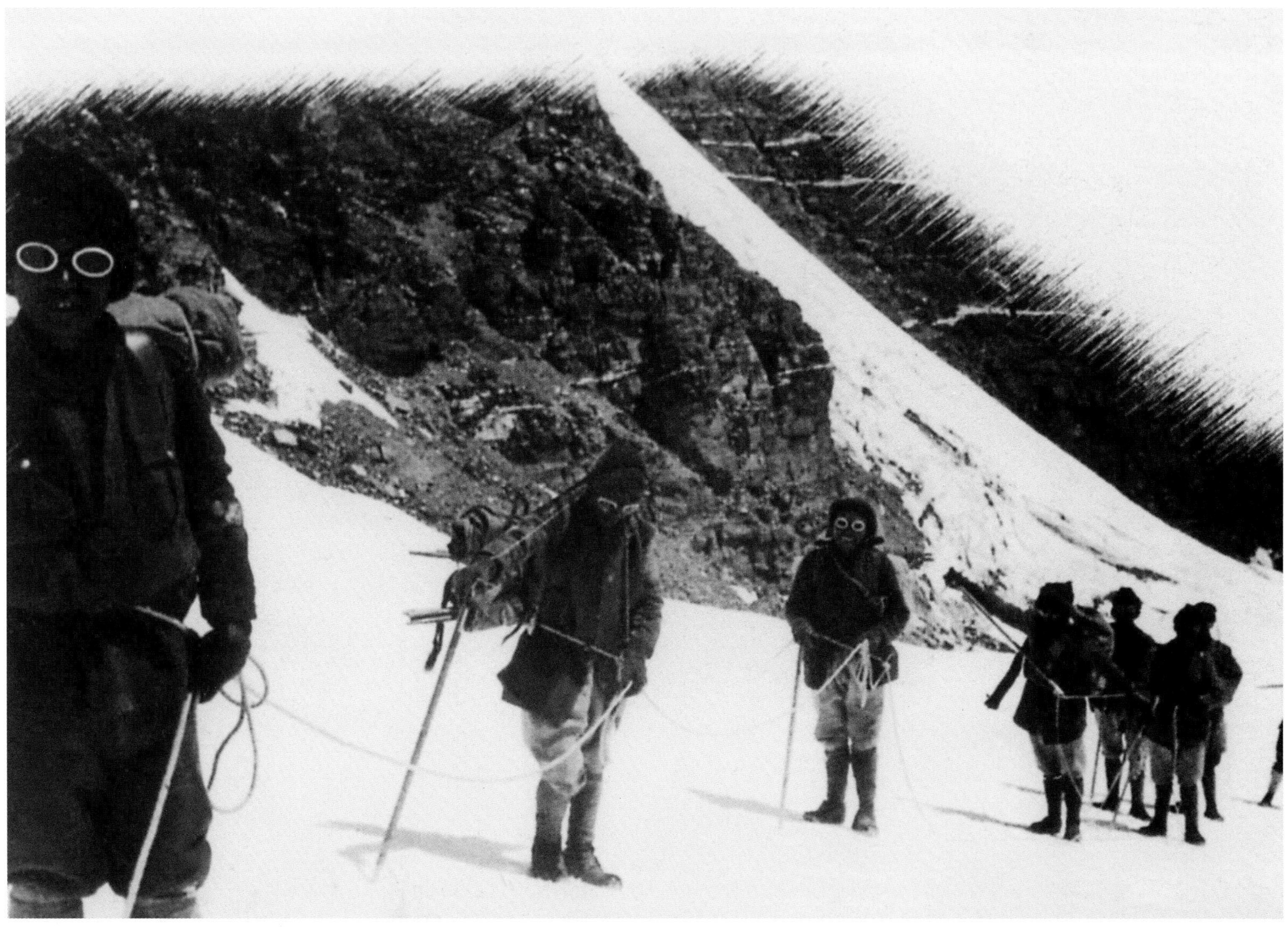

Porters carrying heavy loads. 'When the porters first saw our unsightly and awkward oxygen tanks, they laughed heartily and said, "The air in our country, Sir, is quite good. Why do you bring your bottled air from England?" But later, when, at grips with the mountain, all were at the end of their tether, we used to give the men the gas to revive them. When they tasted it they realised how wonderful it was and how it stilled the heaving of the heart.'

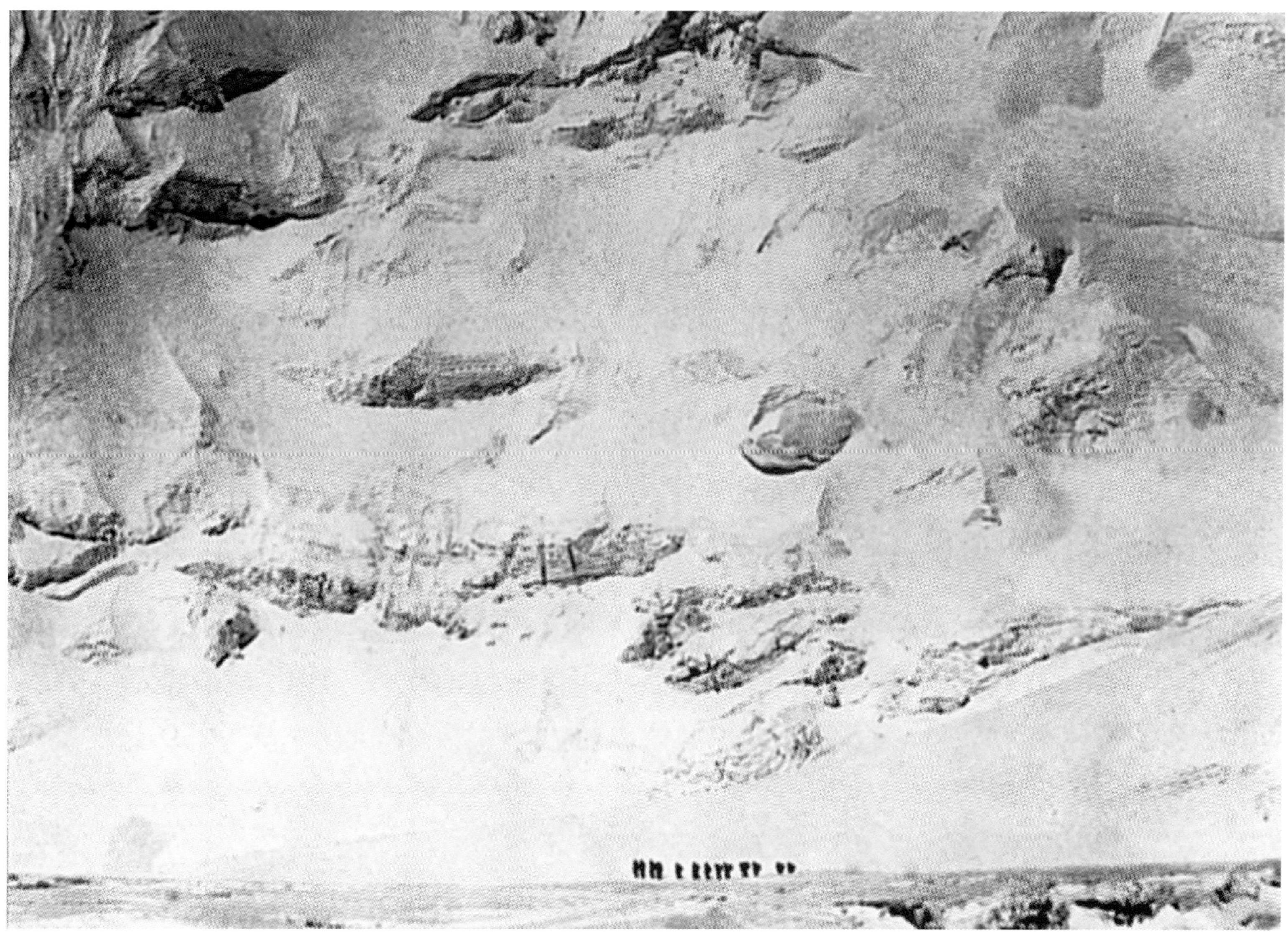

Figures below the North Col, which is a sheer wall of ice 1,000 feet high. It was here that an avalanche killed seven porters in 1922, bringing that attempt to an abrupt and sad end.

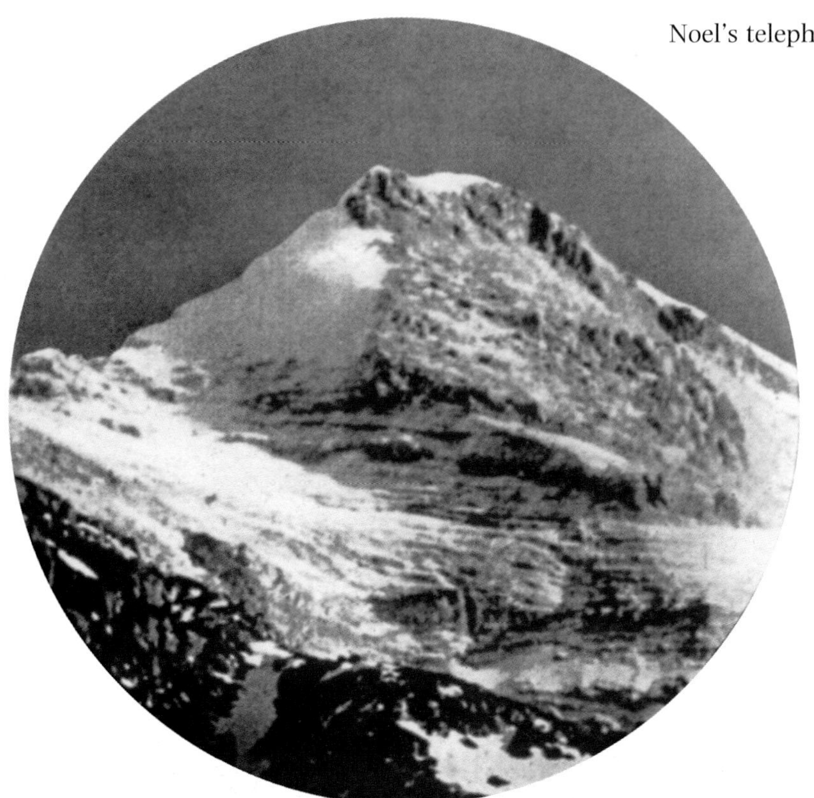

Noel's telephoto view of the summit.

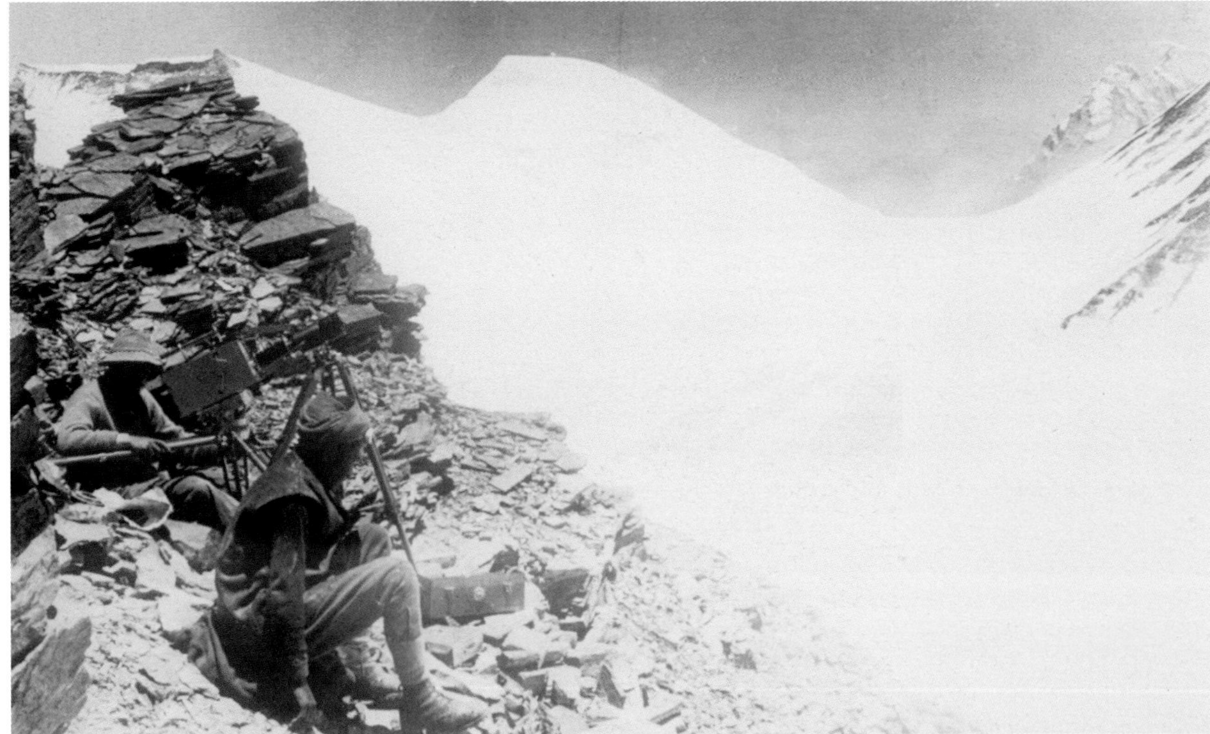

Eagle's Nest, Noel's photographic station.

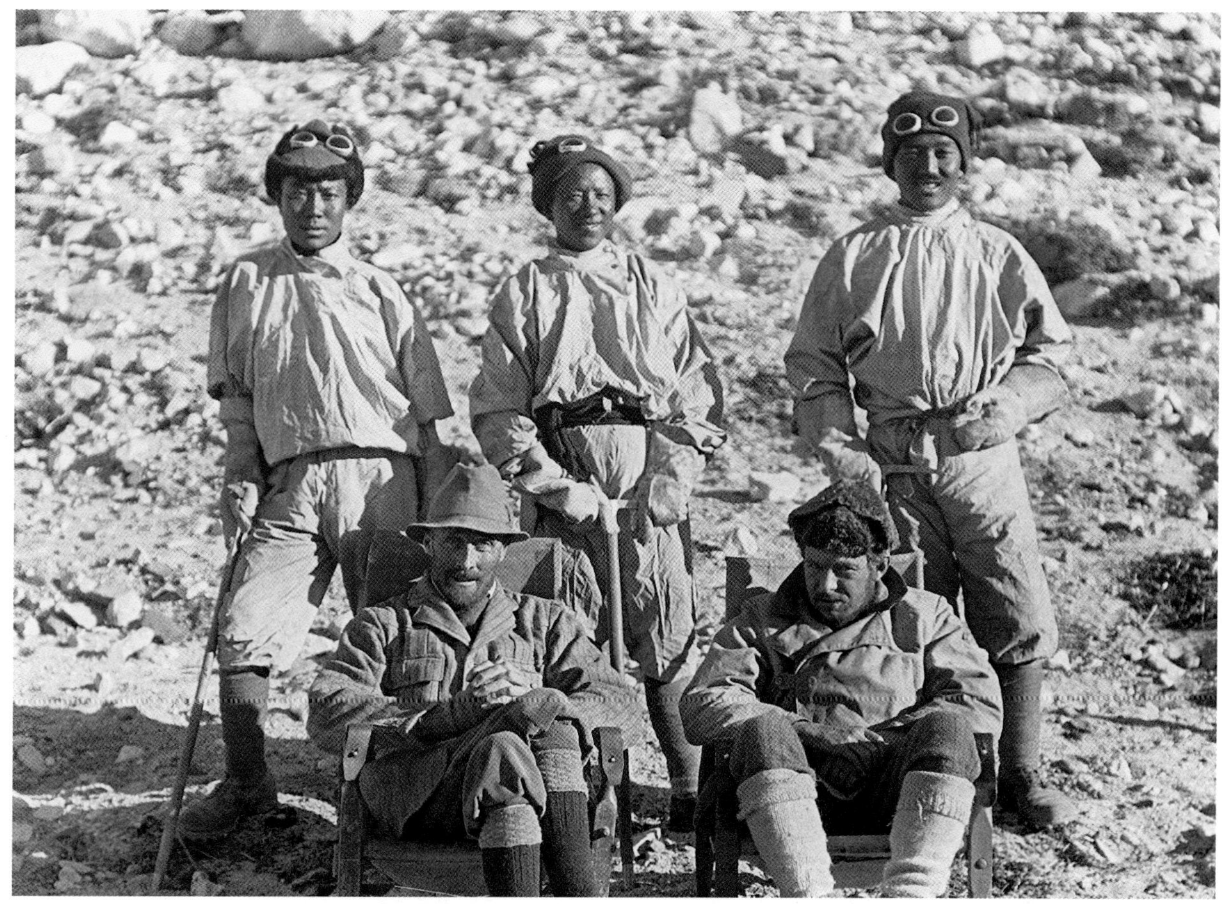

Norton (left) and Somervell with the three porters who assisted in setting up a camp at 27,000 feet. The porters returned down the North Col; next day, in good conditions, Norton and Somervell reached above 28,000 feet without oxygen, but were forced to turn back by complete exhaustion and lack of air to breathe.

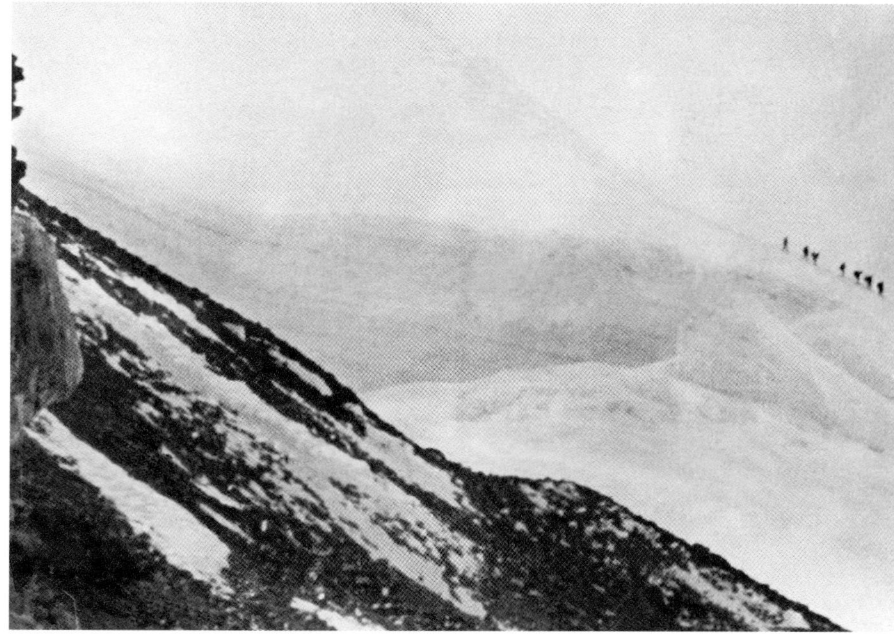

A telephoto view of a party descending.

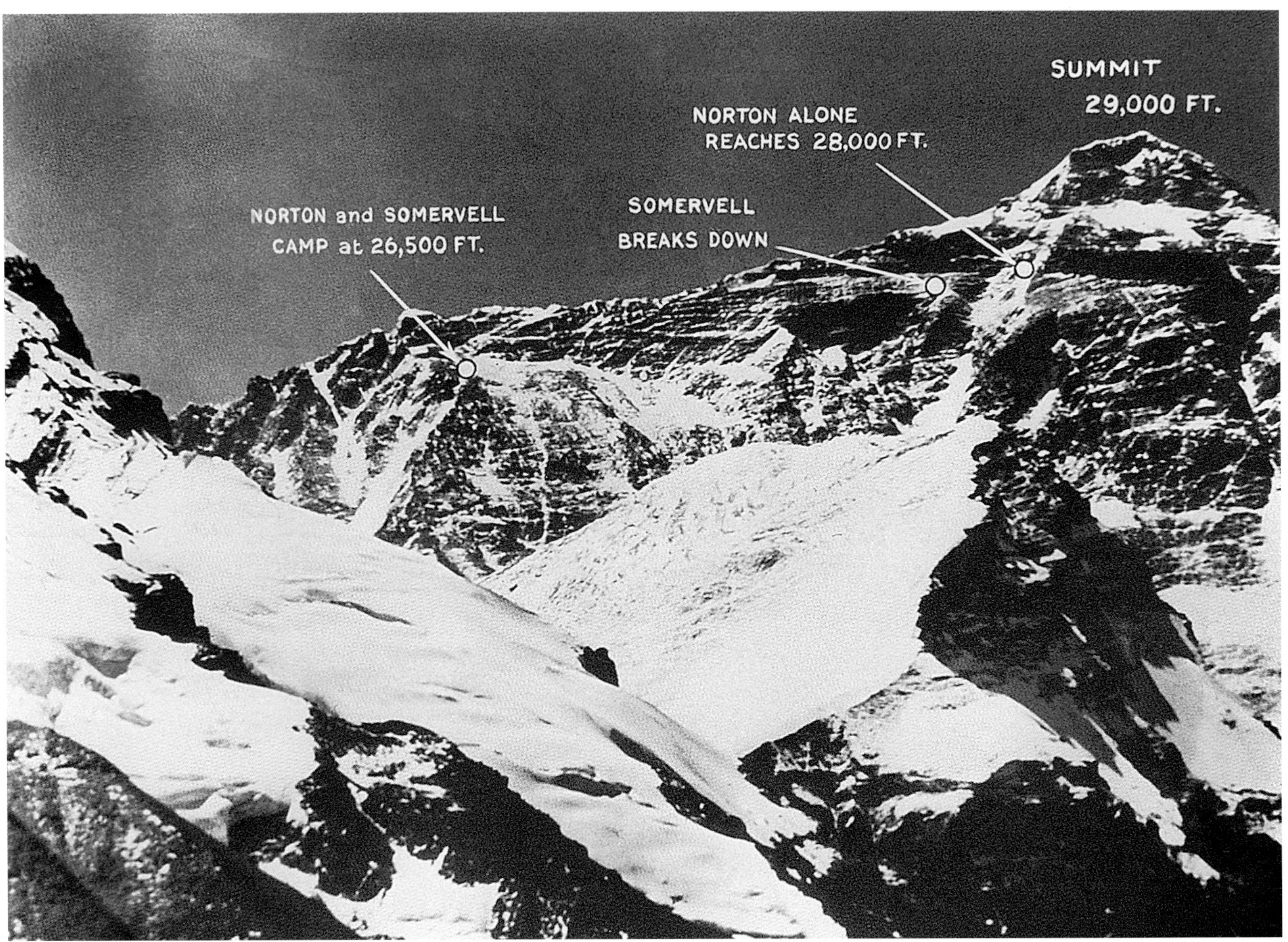

A diagram showing the altitudes reached by Norton and Somervell.

Dear Noel
We'll probably start early to-morrow (8th) in order to have clear weather. It won't be too early to start looking out for us either crossing the rockband under the pyramid or going up skyline at 8.0 p.m.

Yrs ever
G. Mallory

Note from Mallory, stating the time that Noel should look out for them (obviously 8 p.m. should read 8 a.m.).

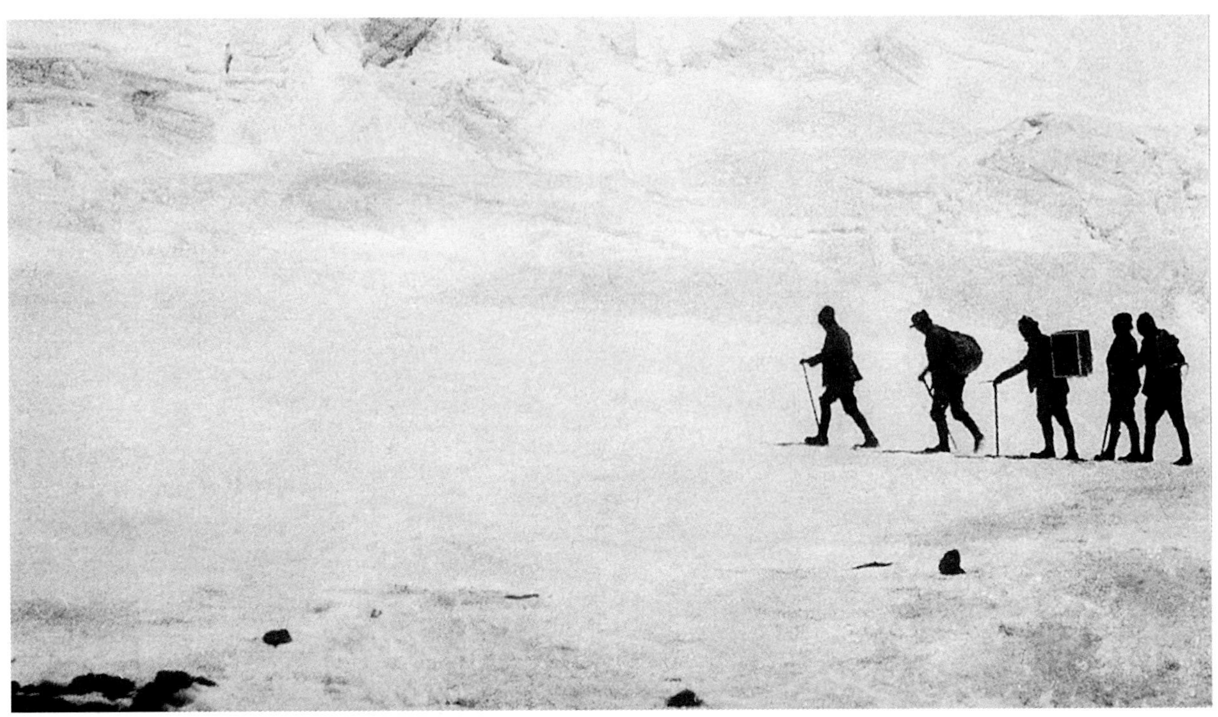

Mallory and Irvine setting out with three porters.

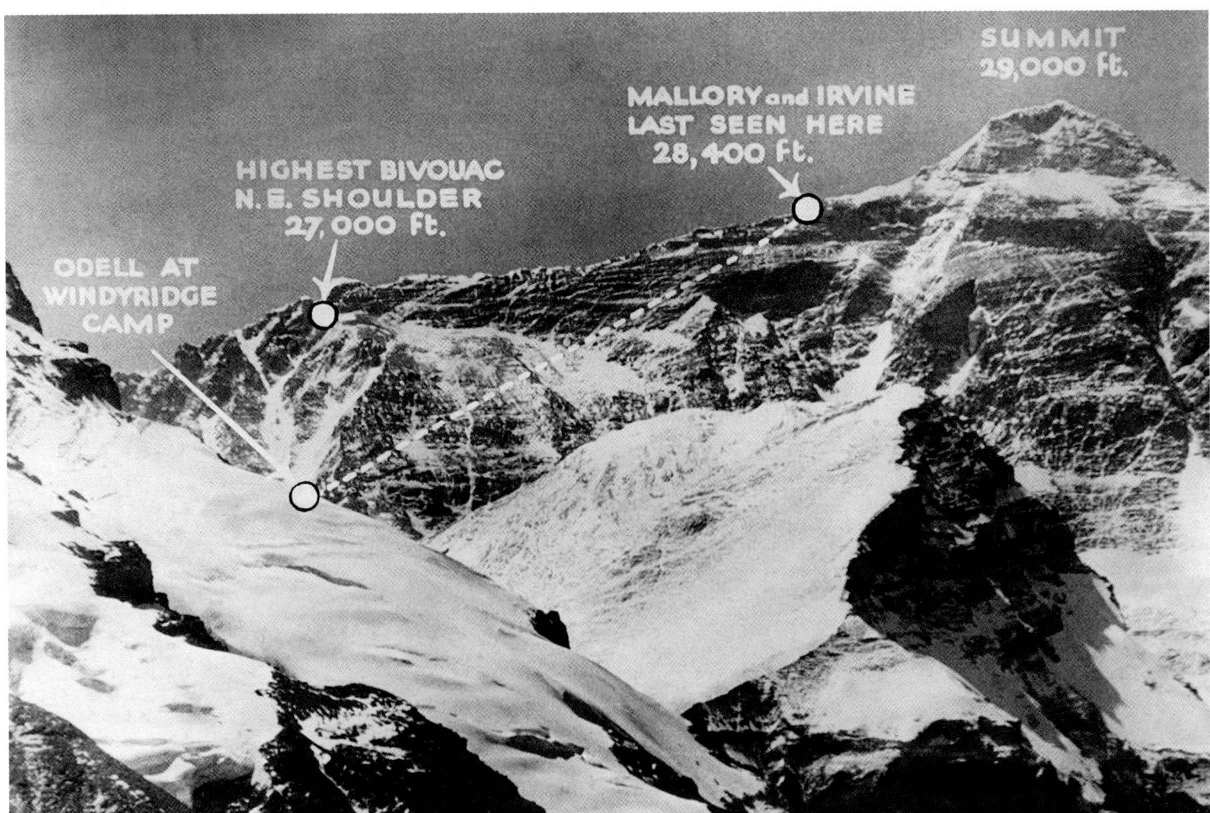

Diagram showing Odell's last sighting of Mallory and Irvine.

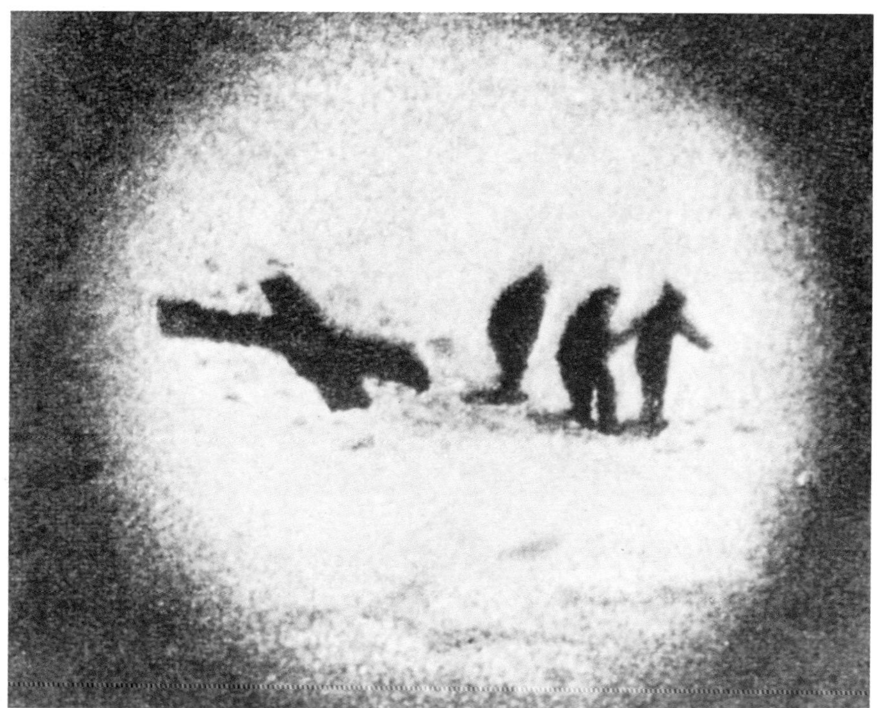

The blankets arranged as a cross, indicating that no trace had been found of Mallory and Irvine.

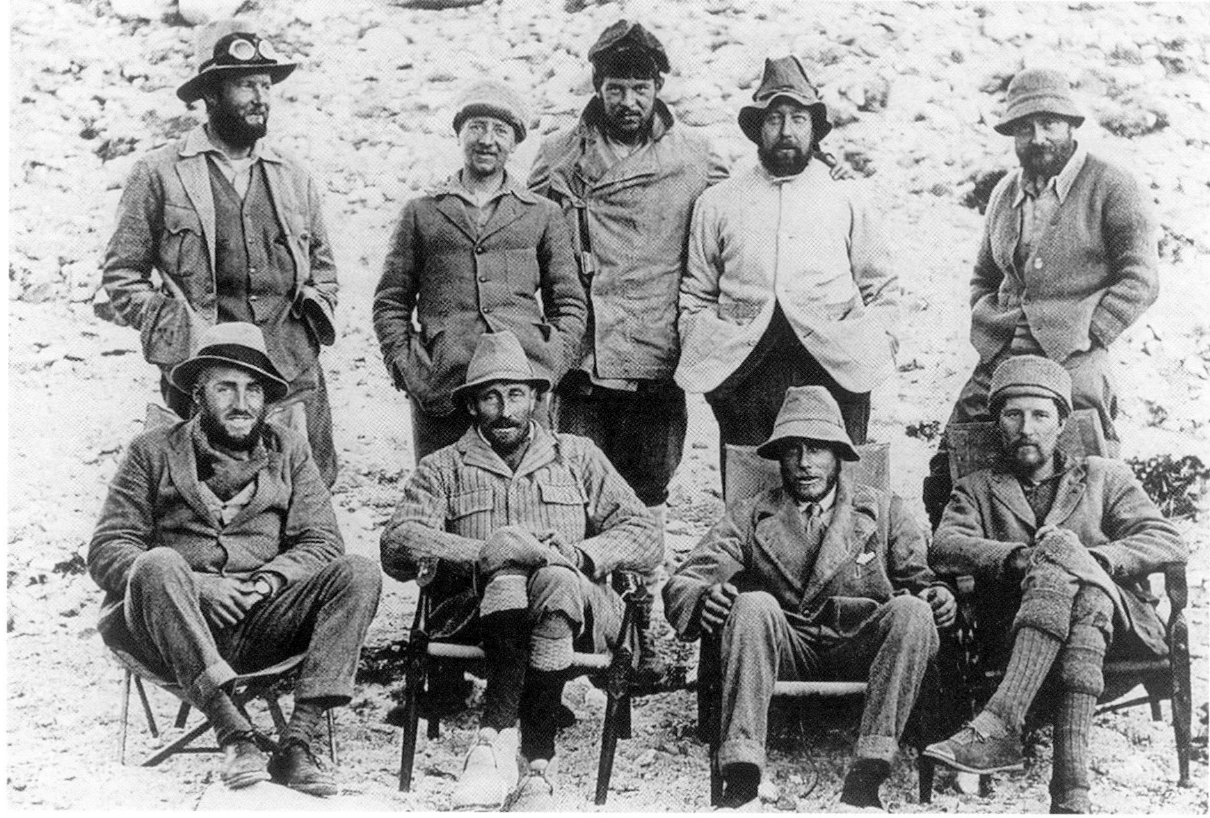

Some of the remaining climbers: Back row, left to right: Hazard, Hingston, Somervell, Beetham, Shebbeare. Front row: G. Bruce, Norton, Noel, Odell.

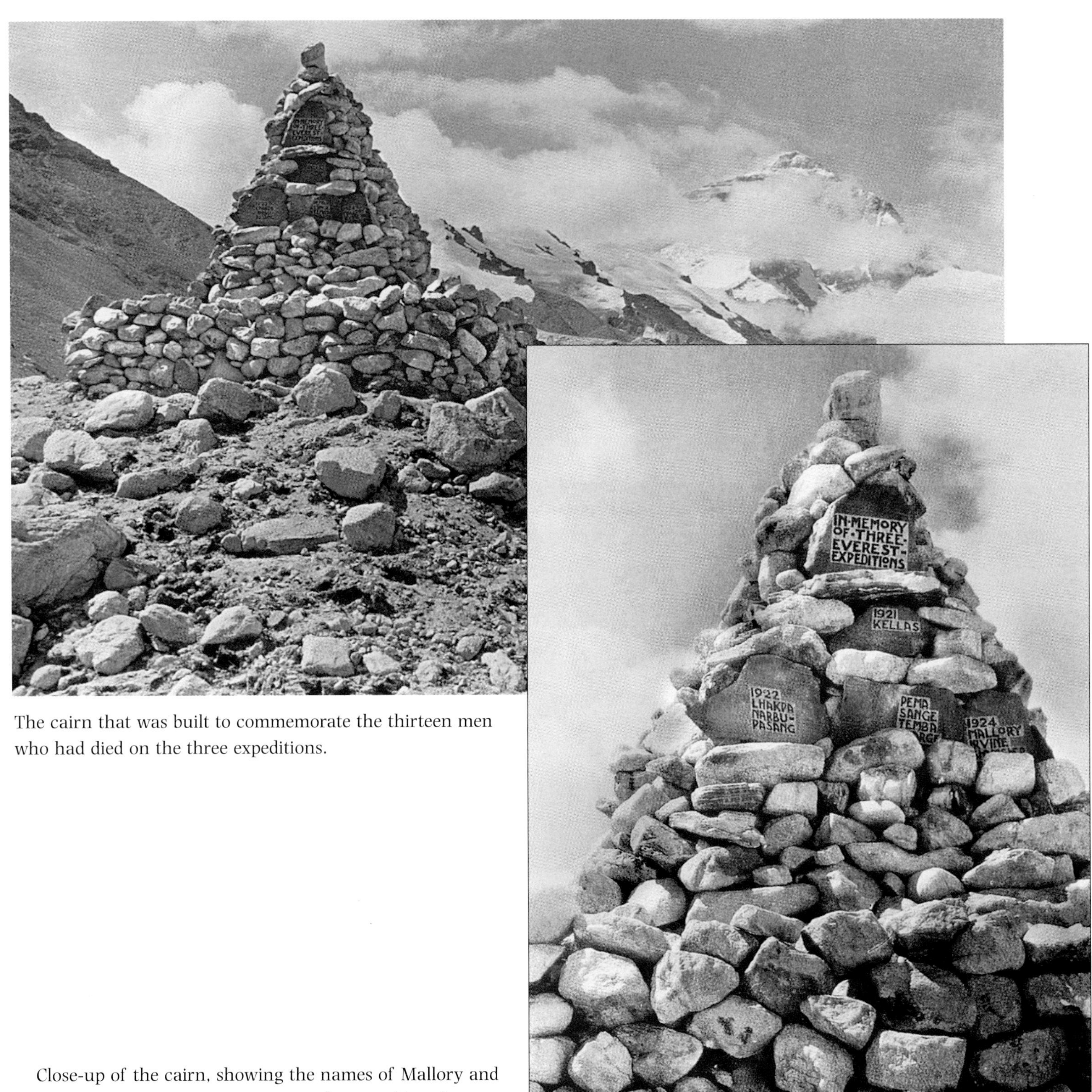

The cairn that was built to commemorate the thirteen men who had died on the three expeditions.

Close-up of the cairn, showing the names of Mallory and Irvine carved on a tablet of stone.

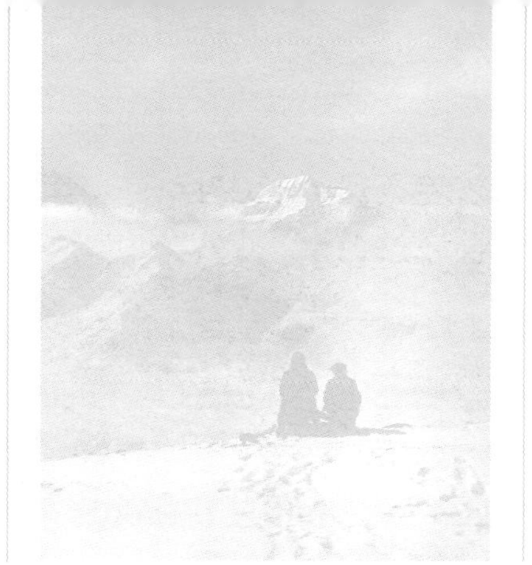

CHAPTER 7

AFTER THE TRAGEDY

The demoralized group of men returned to Darjeeling, thence all to follow their separate paths. News of the tragedy had been sent back to Britain in a brief telegram on 21 June. The intention had been to celebrate the return of the expedition to England on 17 October; instead, the date now assumed a double character, of sorrow for the fallen and of high appreciation for their heroic exploits. The Mount Everest Committee decided that a memorial service should be held in St Paul's Cathedral. It was attended by His Majesty the King, the Prince of Wales, the Duke of York and Prince Arthur of Connaught, members of the 1924 expedition and previous expeditions, members of the Mount Everest Committee, the Royal Geographical Society and the Alpine Club. The address was given by the Bishop of Chester, the Right Reverend Henry Paget, in whose diocese both Mallory and Irvine had lived, and ended with the words:*

* *RGS Journal*, vol. LXIV (6), December 1924.

> Lofty designs must end in like effects,
> Loftily lying,
> Leave them – still loftier than the suspects,
> Living and dying.

For Noel, the disaster on Everest had been a monumental blow; he had twice been on an expedition with Mallory and they had become friends. Noel had found Mallory full of optimism and enthusiasm, ever hopeful that it would be possible to succeed in climbing Mount Everest, and Noel himself had always been one of those keenest to see a man on the summit and be there to tell the story. Now it was the story of the tragedy for which this expedition would be remembered; not only had each member lost friends and loyal porters, but Noel was facing financial disaster. He had staked his money and reputation on the successful outcome of the expedition, which would have enabled him to recoup some return for his fellow company members when the film was shown.

Despite the tragedy, he set about editing the film and continued with plans to begin a lecture tour in London that November. To enhance the atmosphere, and to portray the power of Buddhism, which had much impressed him in Tibet, he arranged for seven lamas to accompany him to England and take part in the lecture tour. This later caused a fuss, as it was claimed that Noel had not obtained permission for these men, as well as one of his most loyal and faithful porters, Lakpa, to leave Tibet. Noel had often been bemused by the influence of religion on the Tibetans. It controls their entire lives: from the moment a child 'tumbles to life' until the vultures swoop down to scavenge the corpse of the dead, every moment of their lives is moulded by the power of the lamas and their faith; and since they believe in reincarnation, life after death is also manipulated by the great gods and goddesses of Buddhism. The Tibetan sees in his every misfortune a relentless fate pursuing him for the sins of his former life. None the less, the presence of the lamas added considerably to the sense of drama and intrigue which surrounded the opening night of the film at the Scala Theatre in London in

November 1924. Noel engaged an orchestra, which included members of the Goossens family, father conducting, Sidonie playing her harp, Leon his oboe. The renowned scene painter Joseph Harker built and painted a set from Noel's photographs and descriptions of Tibetan temples, depicting a monastery courtyard against a background of distant snow-covered peaks. The theatre's technicians devised a system of lights which gradually illuminated the tips of the mountain peaks. The lamas appeared in half-light to perform traditional ceremonies in the courtyard, with the haunting religious music played on long copper horns, drums and cymbals. While the light dimmed, the temple doors swung slowly open. The proscenium curtain fell. The curtains opened again to reveal a screen, and, accompanied by the orchestra, the film – *Epic of Everest* – started to roll.

Among the audience were Prince Henry – later the Duke of Gloucester – and Sir Francis Younghusband. The press notices were exceptionally good: the reviewer of *The Bioscope* (18 December 1924, p. 35) wrote:

> Immeasurably fuller and finer in every respect than the previous Everest film; there have never been screen studies more impressive than the spectacular glimpses of the icy caves and frozen precipices which make Everest's heights like a bizarre giant's palace. Thanks partly to the restrained, yet forcefully expressive sub-titles, partly to the realistic illusion created by those wonderful pictures, one gains a very strong sense of the drama of the climb. With the baffled explorers, one begins to fancy that this dreadful pile of rock, towering demonically behind a veil of mist, is actually a living thing.

In the titles Noel hints at his own discomfort in capturing some of the shots: 'Should you not mind wind or frost of fifty degrees, you may stand on the glacier and watch the evening light beams play over the world around.' He is skilful at bringing out the capricious beauty of this frightening place, with scenes of vapour caressing the mountain, and dark shadows fluttering on the snow beneath the peak. The film perpetuates a tragedy that nobody saw; and it ends by trying to pluck a shred of inspiration from the wreckage of the expedition's hopes.

After touring in the UK and Germany, Noel made seven coast-to-coast tours of North America with the film and still images, which were hugely successful, and he managed to recoup some of his initial financial outlay. He was elected to the Explorers Club of America in 1926. The innovative idea of the postcard sent from Base Camp in the summer and early autumn of 1924 had also been a brilliant advertising tool; at every lecture people approached Noel, proudly clutching the small picture postcard which they had excitedly received from such a distance. With only the newspapers and radio as sources of news, following the progress of the expedition had been a great thrill to many people. Local newspapers covered the story in great detail, with photographs graphically displaying the hardships of the journey, the fascination of the Tibetans and their customs, and the tragic outcome. A set of cigarette cards was issued to commemorate the expedition, and in 1927 Noel published his recollections in *Through Tibet to Everest*.

Sensing, perhaps, that he had been privileged to be one of the last ever to see the great mountain, and with interest in such exploits fading, Noel moved on; but he could never forget. Although time dimmed his recall of detail, never did it diminish his regard for the team members who had given their all, nor his respect for the great mountain, that had taken so much.

'How could it be possible that something more than the physical had opposed us in this battle, where human strength and western science had broken and failed?'

'*Chomolungma* – Goddess Mother of the World'.

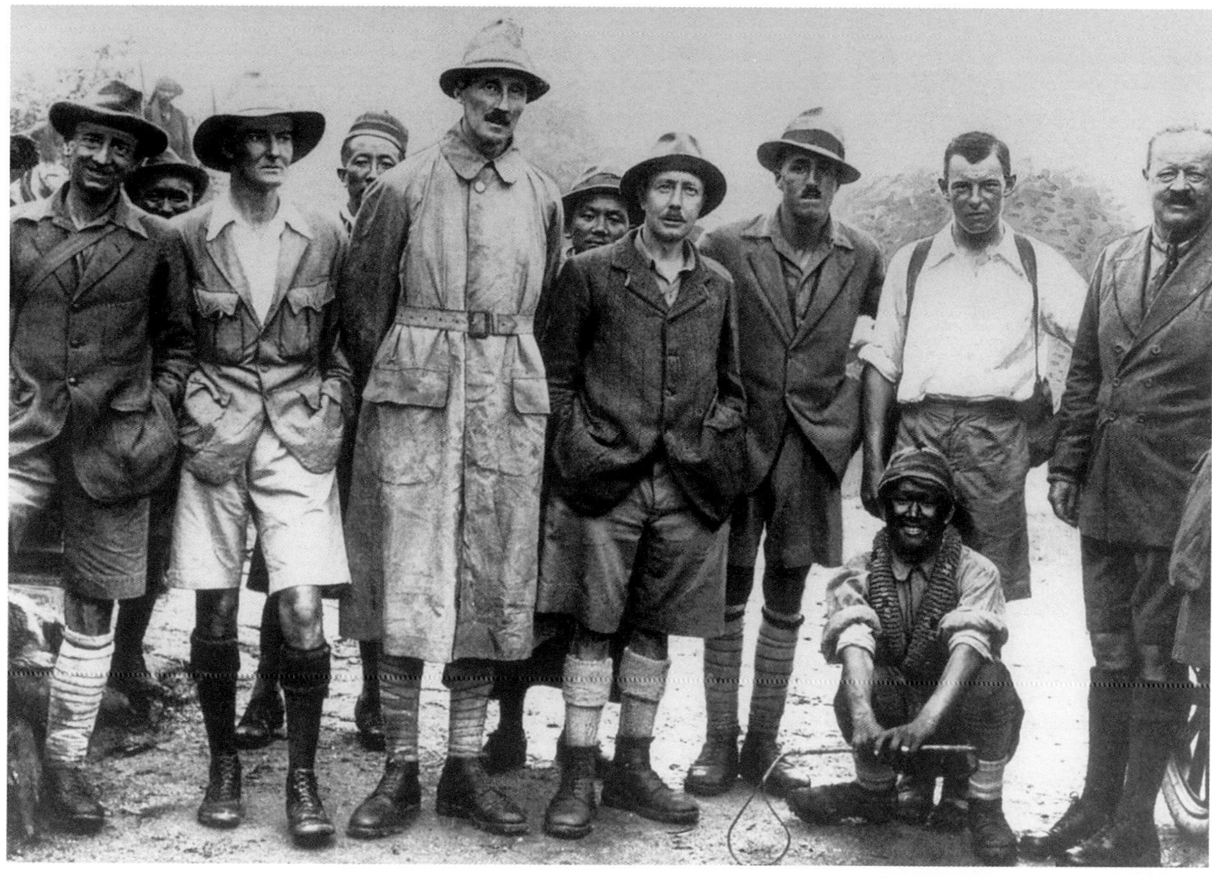

The remaining group arriving back in Darjeeling: From left to right: Hingston, Hazard, Norton, Beetham, G. Bruce, Somervell, General Bruce.

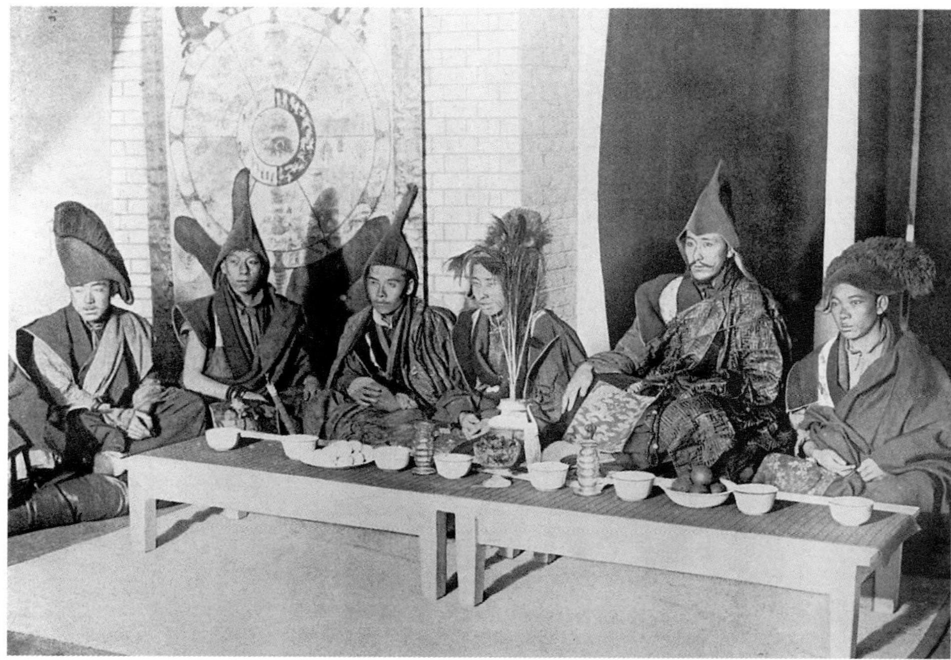

Lamas accompanying the lecture show given by Noel.

MOUNT EVEREST DISASTER.

PIONEER OF THE HIMALAYAS.

Sir F. Younghusband on the Disaster.

MALLORY'S SKILL.

The Man Who Prevented Catastrophe in 1922.

By A "DAILY GRAPHIC" REPORTER.

"Tragic news, the worst you could have brought me," said Sir Francis Younghusband, when I took the tidings to him last night that Leigh Mallory and A. C. Irvine had been killed on the Mount Everest Expedition. Indeed, he was visibly affected.

It was largely due to Sir Francis that the Mount Everest Expedition became possible, for the mountain range flanks the borders of Nepal and Tibet, and both of them were closed countries.

It was General Bruce and Sir Francis Younghusband who persuaded the Indian Government to obtain permission from the Dalai Lama of Tibet for a British expedition to go into the country to explore the approach of the mountain, and if possible to scale it. So, in 1921, a reconnoitring expedition went out.

An Intrepid Climber.

"Leigh Mallory was in that expedition," said Sir Francis, speaking at his home in Westerham, Kent. "He it was who discovered the approaches to the mountain, and the route to the North Col. He participated in the second expedition too, in 1922, and was one of the non-oxygen climbing party who nearly succeeded in getting to the top."

"Mallory was very highly esteemed," continued Sir Francis. "He had great mountaineering capacity, and the vivid qualities he displayed in describing his exploits were of great value—I mean the gift he had for telling others of what he had seen.

"He was very keen to get to the top. It was he who narrowly saved the party from disaster in 1922. On the descent of the mountain, a whole party were swept away by an avalanche, in which seven of the native porters were killed. None of the European climbers suffered any harm, which was largely due to the skill and bravery of Leigh Mallory."

Irvine's Boyish Thrill.

Mr. Mallory was only thirty-six years old. He had been a master at Charterhouse, and had only recently been appointed secretary of the University Extension at Cambridge University. Special leave was granted him to go on the expedition. His father is rector of Birkenhead.

Mr. A. C. Irvine was a youngster of about twenty-two. But he was a very enthusiastic climber, and imbued with the intrepid spirit of youth.

"It is the duty of the Alpine Club to climb as near as it can to Heaven," he exclaimed with boyish thrill just before he sailed. He had had no Himalayan experience. He had just left Merton College, Oxford, and he was one of the Oxford crew in the Boat Race last year.

BRAVE FIGHT IN BLINDING SNOW.

THE tragedy which has overwhelmed the Third Expedition to attempt the conquest of unconquered Everest is told, laconically and poignantly, in a cablegram from Colonel Norton, leader of the gallant little band.

It was despatched (says a "Times" World Copyright message) from Pharijong at 4.50 p.m. on Thursday to the Mount Everest Committee in London. It reads:

"Mallory and Irvine killed on last attempt. Rest of party arrived at base camp all well."

The committee telegraphed to Colonel Norton expressing "deep sympathy with the Expedition in the loss of their two gallant comrades."

LAST ACT OF THE DRAMA.

Details of the disaster are lacking, but what is known both of the frightful hazards of their task and of the proved intrepidity of the Englishmen who essayed it makes it possible to reconstruct some part at least of the last act in the drama of Everest enacted amid the eternal snows.

From the moment the Expedition reached the scene they have had to fight intense cold and violent snowfalls, and twice they were driven to retreat.

The second check was in May, when the party were driven out of their high camp by a 25-hour

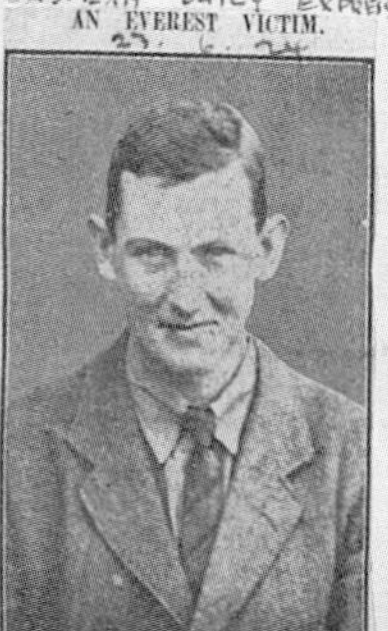

Mr. Mallory.

blizzard and a temperature which for five nights averaged 50 deg. of frost.

Undaunted, the party prepared for their third assault. They must have set off some time early this month for their final daring assault. And then?

The party may have been overtaken in the blinding snow or may have been overwhelmed by avalanche.

"We expect no mercy from Everest," Mallory himself had said after the second check. And to-day's news shows that Everest has given no mercy.

Everest, towering some 29,142 feet into the heavens, remains master.

Mallory and Irvine Killed in the Final Assault on the Summit.

LEADER'S MESSAGE.

Remainder of the Gallant Expedition Returning "All Well."

DISASTER has overtaken the third Mount Everest Expedition in its final assault on the world's highest mountain, two members of the intrepid party being killed.

The two men killed are: Mr. G. Leigh Mallory, at one time a master at Charterhouse School, who was with the Expeditions of 1921 and 1922; and Mr. A. C. Irvine, the Oxford "blue." The rest of the party is safe.

Details of the disaster are lacking. It is known that the Expedition throughout have had to contend with the worst weather ever experienced in the Himalayas, blinding snow and bitterest cold having twice driven them back before the last tragic attempt was made.

WORST SNOW.

Bad luck has dogged the Expedition, but could not damp their high spirits.

First, General Bruce (who led the 1922 assault) was stricken with malaria and had to return to Darjeeling, handing over the command to Colonel Norton.

Next, extreme cold and heavy snow—the worst known—intervened as the mountain's ally, as though to screen from man's touch its virginal summit.

Disaster almost befell the Expedition on the second attempt. One party of native porters was

> ### 'WE EXPECT NO MERCY.'
>
> "THE issue will shortly be decided. The third time we walk up East Rongbuk Glacier will be the last, for better or worse . . . We expect no mercy from Everest."
>
> *[Extract from Mr. Mallory's last dispatch, dated May 26, from Mount Everest.]*

marooned, and was rescued in desperate straits by Col. Norton, Mr. Mallory, and Dr. Somervell.

There is a tragic coincidence in the end of the 1922 Expedition and in that of the Expedition of 1924.

TENSION BROKEN BY DISASTER.

Expectations ran high in 1922 that Everest would be mastered. The final assault was made, and then came silence, while the world awaited news.

The silence was broken by news of disaster, seven coolies being killed in an avalanche. Mallory on that occasion narrowly escaped death.

So to-day. Both in India and in England there was growing confidence that the 1924 Expedition would win through. And after long silence and tense waiting, news of disaster comes to dash the hopes of man's triumph over stubborn Nature.

CANDLELIGHT DESCENT.

When Mallory Broke World's Height Record.

The disaster removes two brilliant and brave climbers.

George Leigh Mallory was the only member of the present Expedition who was with the unsuccessful expeditions of 1921 and 1922. In the latter attempt he broke all records by leading a party, without any artificial aid of oxygen, to a height of 26,800 feet.

The descent from Everest on that occasion was made by candle light.

General Bruce described Mallory's dash as "one of the greatest feats of human endurance in any field of activity."

Absolutely fearless, Mallory had many fine climbs to his credit.

Before joining the First Mount Everest Expedition he was a master at Charterhouse. He was at Winchester, and from there won a scholarship at Magdalene College, Cambridge, where he took his degree. He was 38 and married, with two children.

In the war he served on the Western Front.

OXFORD "BLUE" AND ALPINIST.

Mr. A. C. Irvine, of Shrewsbury and Merton College, Oxford, was another good mountaineer.

Two years ago he rowed for Oxford in the University Boat Race. He was a member of the last two Oxford Expeditions to Spitzbergen.

As skilled an oarsman as he was a climber, he would probably have rowed again for Oxford this year had he not embarked on the greater enterprise of scaling Everest.

This was his first experience with the Expedition.

[Pictures of the expedition and portraits of Mr. Mallory and Mr. Irvine appear on page 16.]

MR. GEORGE LEIGH MALLORY, who has lost his life in the last assault on the mountain.

BIRKENHEAD VICTIMS OF EVEREST.

FATE OF MR. MALLORY AND MR. IRVINE.

FINAL ASSAULT.

EXPEDITION LIKELY TO BE ABANDONED.

Disaster overtook the third Mount Everest Expedition in its final assault on the world's highest mountain when success was in sight. Two members of the intrepid party, both Birkenhead men, were killed.

The news is conveyed in the following message from Col. Norton, the leader of the Expedition, at Phari Dzong:—

"Mallory and Irvine killed on last attempt. Rest of party arrived at Base Camp all well."

A premonition of his fate appears to have been felt by Mr. Mallory. In his last dispatch he wrote:

"The third time we walk up East Rongbuk Glacier will be the last for better or worse. We expect no mercy from Everest."

The deaths are believed to have occurred on June 6, when the party made their fourth attempt to reach the summit (29,000 feet) from a point 23,000 feet high.

The Expedition will now doubtless have to be abandoned.

HIGHER THAN EVER

Disaster When Success Was in Sight.

"The way in which the disaster occurred is entirely unknown as yet," said Sir Francis Younghusband in an interview after the Everest Expedition Committee in London had received the telegram.

"They probably died a fortnight ago—it would take a long time for the news to filter down from Everest to civilized regions.

"The message does not give any information beyond the bare fact of the tragedy."

"I think it is almost certain that the expedition will now have to be abandoned, for this year at least.

"The expedition was within a short distance of the summit—higher, in fact, than it has ever reached hitherto.

"Great difficulties had been experienced in making the ascent. The last despatches informed us that the expedition had been fighting its way at a high altitude through tremendous blizzards which had lasted for weeks.

"The members of the expedition must have been exhausted at the time of Leigh-Mallory's and Irvine's deaths.

"This was the final assault. In this the last endeavour, the expedition had great hopes of reaching the summit. They have gone further than ever before."

WOULD NOT ADMIT DEFEAT.

The death of these two men—George Leigh Mallory, who alone of all those engaged in the present attempt had also taken part in the two previous expeditions, and A. C. Irvine, one of this year's band of recruits—is a tragic ending to the story of the assaults on the mountain that began three years ago.

It is only a few days since Mr. Mallory's own account of the second reverse suffered by the present expedition reached England.

About the middle of last month they had been driven back by the exceptional severity of the weather, "discomfited, but very far from being defeated," from their first attempt to establish the chain of camps necessary for the final effort to reach the summit.

DRIVEN BACK.

After a short stay at the base camp for the rest that was indispensable after their exhausting labours, they returned once more to the charge, only to be driven back again by a blizzard that lasted for 36 hours and a temperature which, for five nights, averaged 50 degs. of frost.

It was this second attempt which Mr. Mallory, at Colonel Norton's request, so graphically described in a despatch published last Monday.

At the time when he was the mainspring of the two fine climbs which the position called for he was suffering, wrote Colonel Norton, from the prevalent high altitude cough, which prevents sleep at night and handicaps the climber.

"Few," added Colonel Norton, "would or could have done what he did."

Three days earlier Mr. Irvine, with Dr. Somervell and Mr. Hazard, had carried out the difficult work of establishing a camp on the old site of Camp IV, afterwards returning to Camp III. It was from Camp IV. that Mallory, Norton, and Somervell rescued the porters who had lost their nerve and stayed behind when Hazard led the other porters down.

He wrote his whole dispatch in the spirit of one who was about to engage in a desperate battle.

"Action," he said, "is only suspended before the more intense action of the climax. The issue will shortly be decided."

> #### THE CATASTROPHE ON EVEREST.
>
> This year, as last year, Everest has waited to the last before striking its blow, and though details are still lacking we may conjecture that the attack was very forcibly pressed to cause so deadly a counter-thrust. Here is all the material of tragedy, made poignant for us by Mallory's last despatch, with its presentation of the mountain as a personal enemy in words now seen to be grim with fate. In truth, however, the tragic issue has developed not out of any real clash of will, but out of the pitting of human courage and determination against the blind forces of nature. It is by virtue of this perpetual battle that man has won his place in creation; yet there are episodes in it which raise the question whether the struggle is worth while. To many it will seem that the tragedy of Everest is a tragedy of heroism wasted. Two splendid lives, of which the younger had barely begun to reveal its promise, have been sacrificed—for what? Only to the end that man might stand on ground untrodden by human foot since the world was made? To such pessimistic questionings the dead men themselves have given the answer. They knew the risks, and thought them well worth while. And because they were men of the type we honour, it is they, not we, who had the right to judge in what way the spirit that was in them should be given expression.

EVEREST

MALLORY & IRVINE KILLED.

DISASTER IN LAST ATTEMPT ON EVEREST SUMMIT.

SURVIVORS' RETREAT

BACK TO BASE CAMP AFTER FAILURE OF CLIMB.

THE Mount Everest Committee have received with profound [sorrow] the following cablegram from Colonel Norton, dispatched [from] Phari Dzong, June 19, at 4.50 p.m.:

Mallory and Irvine killed on last attempt. Rest of [party] arrived at base camp all well.

The Committee have telegraphed to Colonel Norton expressing their deep sympathy with the expedition in the loss of their two gallant comrades, which must have been due to the most unfavourable conditions of weather and snow which have from the first arrival at the scene of operations impeded the climbing this year.

The last message from Colonel Norton, dated May 26, told that the party had been driven out of their high camp for the second time by heavy snow.

It seems probable that they had been able to return to the attack early this month, and that the lamentable accident which has cost the lives of two of the best climbers occurred about June 6.

"Times" World Copyright.

STORY OF A GREAT ADVENTURE.

EVEREST has won again, and has exacted a tragic penalty from those who sought to vanquish it.

Three times in four years an attempt has been made to conquer the great mountain, but on each occasion Nature has proved too strong for man.

The history of the 1924 expedition is

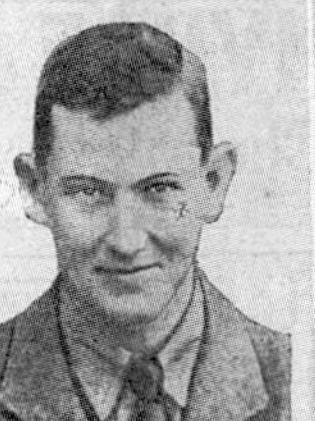

MR. MALLORY.

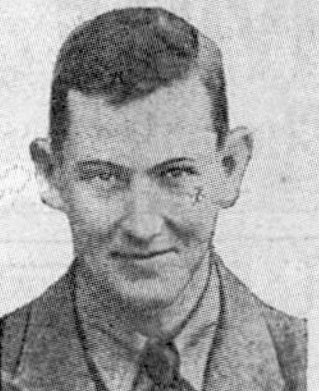

MR. IRVINE.

a lamentable falsification of the hopes with which the party started.

"Three, I take it, is a lucky number," wrote Brigadier-General the Hon. C. G. Bruce, its original commander, when it assembled at Darjeeling.

General Bruce, who also commanded the 1922 expedition, fell ill at Tuna, on the Tibetan plateau, with violent malaria, and had to return to the base. In these circumstances the leadership fell to his second in command, Lieut.-Col. E. F. Norton, one of the three first men to reach the 27,000 feet level in 1922.

The other members of the expedition were as follows:—

Mr. George Leigh-Mallory,[*]
Mr. T. Howard Somervell,[*]
Captain J. B. L. Noel.[*]
Captain Geoffrey Bruce, 6th Gurkhas.[†]
Captain C. J. Morris, 3rd Gurkhas.[*]
Mr. N. E. Odell, Imperial College of Science.[†]
Mr. Bentley Beetham, Cotherstone, Darlington.[†]
Mr. A. C. Irvine, Merton College, Oxford.[†]
Mr. J. V. Hazard, Royal Society's Club.[†]
Major R. W. G. Hingston.
Mr. E. O. Shebbeare, Indian Forest Service.

[*] Signifies member of 1922 expedition.
[†] Signifies member of actual climbing party.

Mount Everest, 29,000ft., the highest measured mountain in the world, has on the frontiers of Nepal and Tibet. It takes its name from Sir George Everest, the first director of the Indian Survey, who conducted a trigonometrical survey of the Himalayas, but until 1921 its white mass had so much as rested in base. It was a mystery, mountain little or nothing was known about it, and it had never been mapped.

The expedition of 1921, which was commanded by Colonel Howard Bury, was really more or less of a reconnoitring affair. It mapped out the only possible route to the summit, and finally succeeded in reaching an [altitude] of 23,000ft.

The 1922 venture might quite probably have succeeded, but for the early coming of the monsoon, which came in the first week of June. On that occasion Captain Geoffrey Bruce and Mr. Finch, using oxygen apparatus, reached the tremendous height of 27,300ft.—over five miles—so that the goal was only 1,700ft. above them when the weather forced the party to abandon the attempt.

The dangers awaiting climbers on Everest were tragically illustrated during the last stage, when an avalanche buried seven porters on the North Col. Three of the party, making the final attempt—Mr. Mallory, Somervell and Mr. Crawford—had exceedingly narrow escapes.

EXPEDITION DIARY.

This year's expedition started from Darjeeling on March 26, forty men and the experience gained in the two previous attempts. Unexpectedly severe weather was experienced on the early stages (Kalimpong-Chumbi) and Phari Dzong (14,400 feet) was reached on April 6.

Two days after General Bruce had taken ill, Lieut.-Colonel Norton went on with the main body, and on May 14 was at Khamba Dzong. The party was still favourable and the expedition was running neck and neck with the progress of two years before. On April 28 Shekar Dzong was reached, and Norton was able to report that "so far with conditions milder and pleasanter than in 1922."

The base camp, on the foot of the Glacier, 10 miles further up, was attained on April 29, two days in advance of the previous expedition's schedule. But here, with the temperature well below freezing point in their tents, the climbing party were face to face with their objective, ten miles away.

The first round opened on May 10, when Mr. Mallory, Captain Noel, Mr. Odell, Mr. Hazard, and Mr. Irvine set out to establish a camp under the North Col.

The party encountered extreme low temperatures than anything experienced in 1922, together with terrible winds, and were forced to retreat. On May 12, and also to report the Lama of Lankca-Nick Shamsherpon, 6th party, died from cerebral hemorrhage.

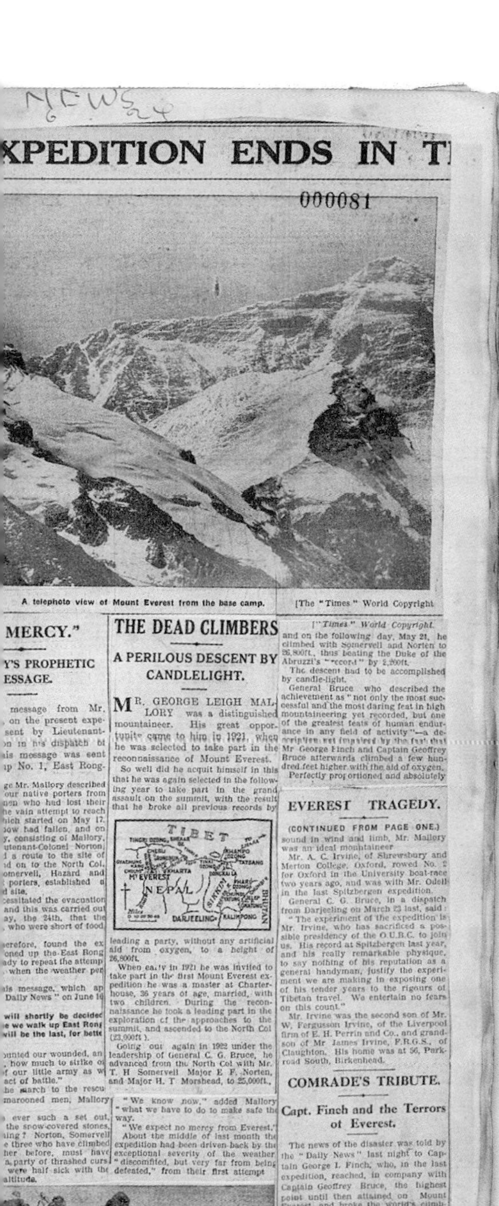

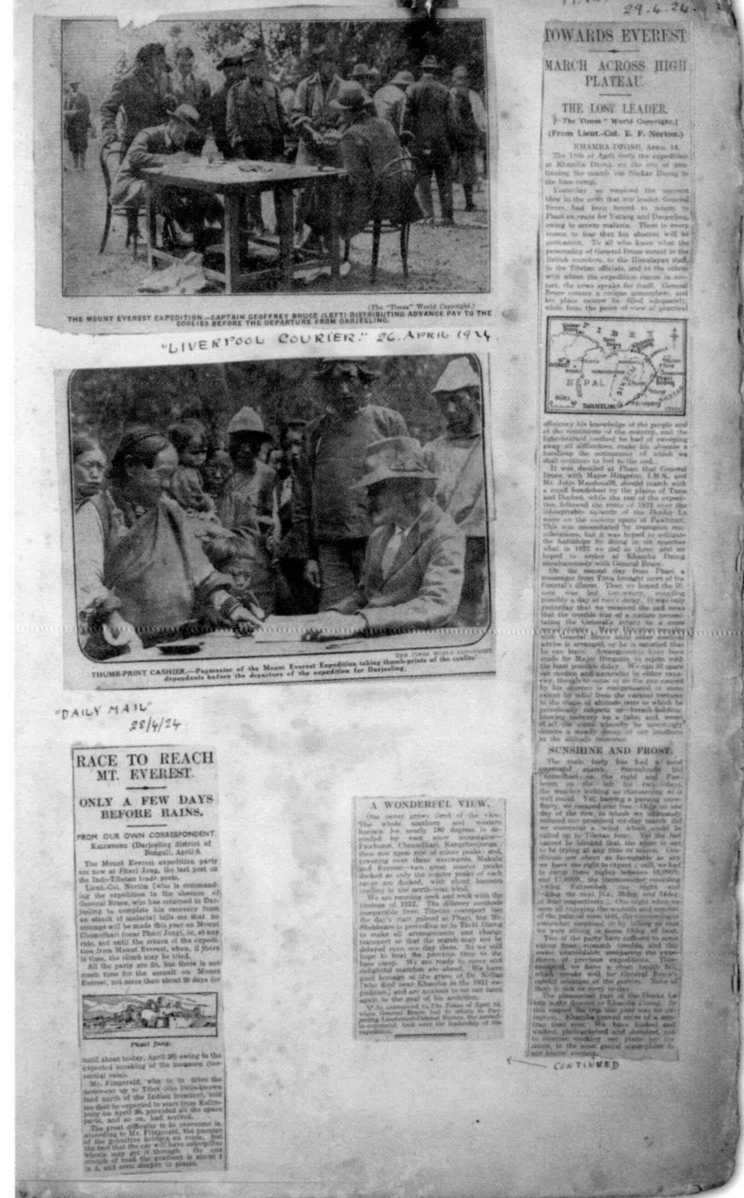

Noel commissioned an agency to collect newspaper articles covering the progress of the expedition in April and May 1924, and there are 200 pages of accounts and photographs. National and local newspapers played a vital role in daily life, as there was no television to spread news, so the written word, cinema and the radio were the only media widely available.

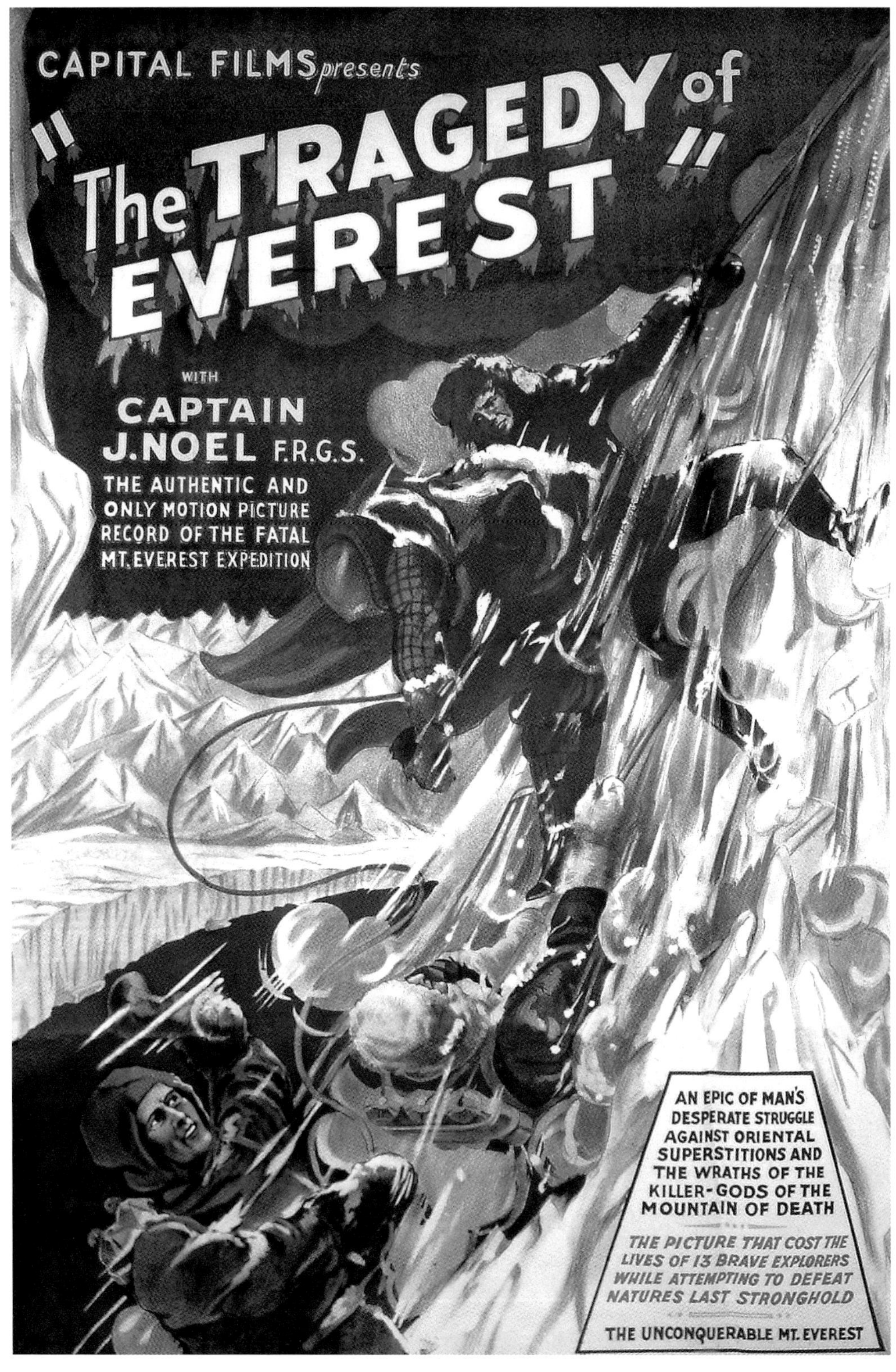

A dramatic poster for Noel's lecture tour in the USA.

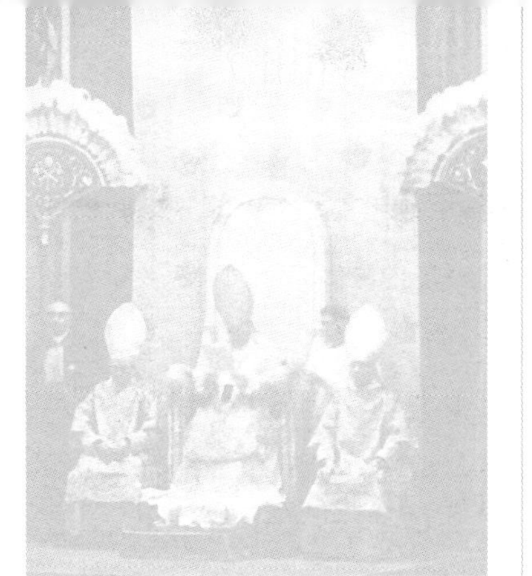

CHAPTER 8

THE LATER YEARS

By the end of the 1920s interest in Everest had waned; Explorers Films, the company Noel had set up to finance the purchase of copyright, had been disbanded. The film and still picture lecture tours had been a great success, and his book had been published on both sides of the Atlantic, and in foreign languages. Nevertheless, the link continued; in 1933 Noel was privileged to attend the canonization ceremony of Saint Bernadette in St Peter's Basilica, Rome. His cousin Augusta Bellingham, Marchioness of Bute, invited him to the ceremony, which was conducted by Pope Pius XI who, before his elevation, had been Cardinal Ratti, an accomplished Alpine mountaineer. Monsignor Ratti had followed the progress of the expeditions, and sent Noel, a Roman Catholic, a limited edition of his book, *Scritti Alpinistici*.* He was permitted to take photographs during the ceremony.

* Acille Ratti (later Pope Pius XI), *Scritti Alpinistici* (privately published); trans. as *Climbs on Alpine Peaks*, Ernest Benn, London, 1923.

At a ceremony at the 1924 Winter Olympics held in Chamonix, medals were awarded to all members of the 1922 expedition. As those on the 1924 expedition were either already on their way to India, or too busy to attend, they were represented by Colonel Strutt, who had been the Deputy Leader in 1922, but was not joining the climb in 1924. Originally there were thirteen medals for the British members, but two more were added for porters. Although the entire expedition was honoured, the official Olympic records list only [General] Bruce's name. It is generally accepted that the decision to award the accolade was a last-minute idea, and there were, in fact, not enough Winter Olympic medals; those brought home by Colonel Strutt are inscribed *VIIIème Olympiade Paris 1924*, which refers to the forthcoming, summer Games.

Meanwhile Noel had purchased two neighbouring properties in Smarden, Kent, and set about their restoration, with help from Nathaniel Lloyd, who readily shared the experience he had gained in restoring his house, Great Dixter, in Sussex. The Second World War brought the project to a complete standstill. During the war Noel worked in Photographic Intelligence, based in Oxford, and, after the success of the predictions for the Normandy landings, sights were set further afield, leading to Noel's main contribution – deducing from aerial photographs the best supply routes from India to the Allied armies in Burma. His creative skill also found an outlet in design: he invented and patented a collapsible boat, although it was not quite ready to go into production by the time the war ended; and he drew plans for a revolutionary design of tent. Sybille, his first wife, had died, and with his second wife he returned to the Kent hall houses, to continue the restoration work.

With the changing political situation in the volatile region of India, Tibet and Nepal, and the memory of the terrible loss of Mallory and Irvine, further expeditions were put aside and interest in the mountain declined. It was to be nearly thirty years before Everest was finally conquered, in 1953, when the photograph of Tenzing Norgay on the summit was shown to the world on the day of the coronation of Queen Elizabeth II. For Noel, it was a great thrill, if a moment tinged with sadness, for he always held the mystical belief that his two comrades had reached the summit on that fateful day in 1924. For a while interest in all expeditions to Everest was keen, and footage from his 1924 film, *Epic of Everest*, was often shown at the cinema and on television screens. He relished every new barrier that was surmounted – sherpas reaching the summit, a successful climb without oxygen, the first woman – and he never looked back on life with too much sentimentality or lost his faith in humanity. He realized and accepted that everything moves on, saying, in fact: 'This world is owned by man. Man has infinite capacity within himself.'

He continued to give lectures, using his hand-tinted slides, and lived in Kent until his death, at the age of ninety-nine, in March 1989, which marked the passing of the last of the Everest pioneers.

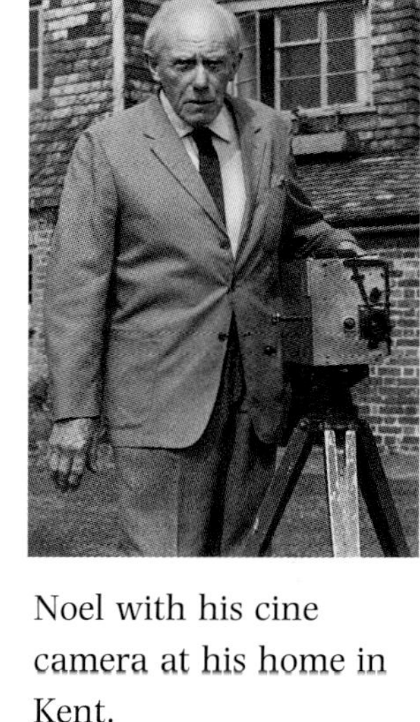

Noel with his cine camera at his home in Kent.

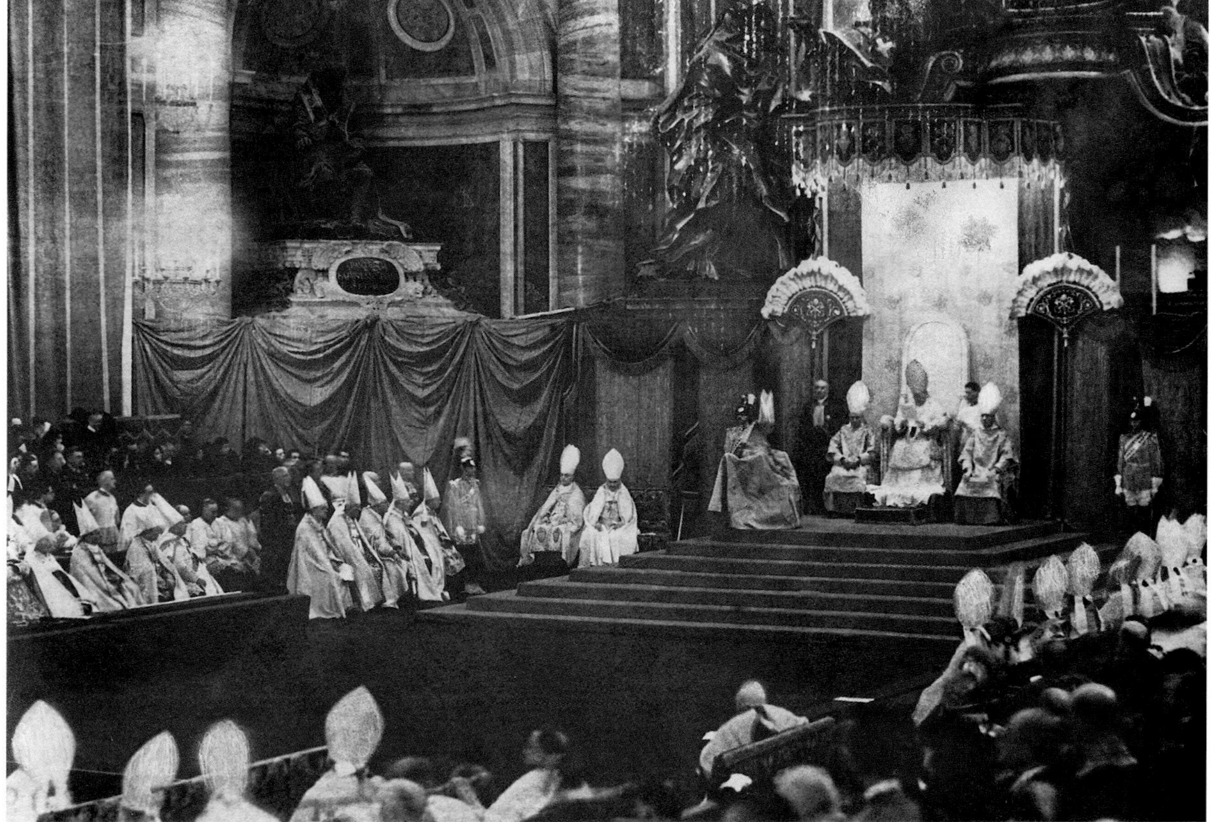

The canonization ceremony of Bernadette of Lourdes, in St Peter's Basilica, Rome, in 1933.

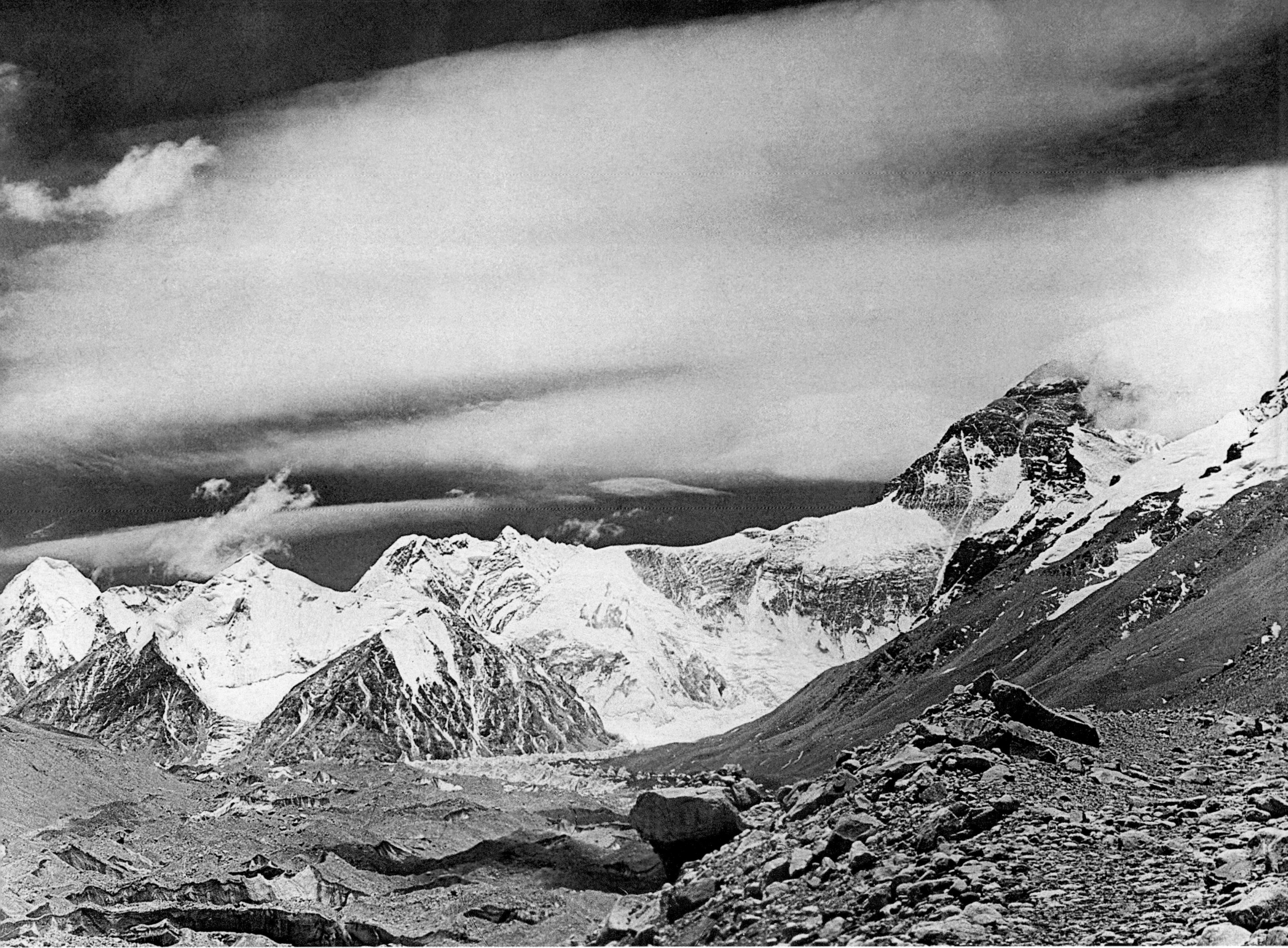

Noel wrote that, in the early twentieth century, little was known of the area, as '. . . The Himalayan passes were walled, barricaded, and guarded by hostile Tibetan soldiery. Beyond the passes the lamas in their fortress monasteries ceaselessly spied the land for foreigners, and captured and tortured any they found. It was hopeless for any white man to attempt to go.' Yet many have accepted the challenge, and some have not returned.

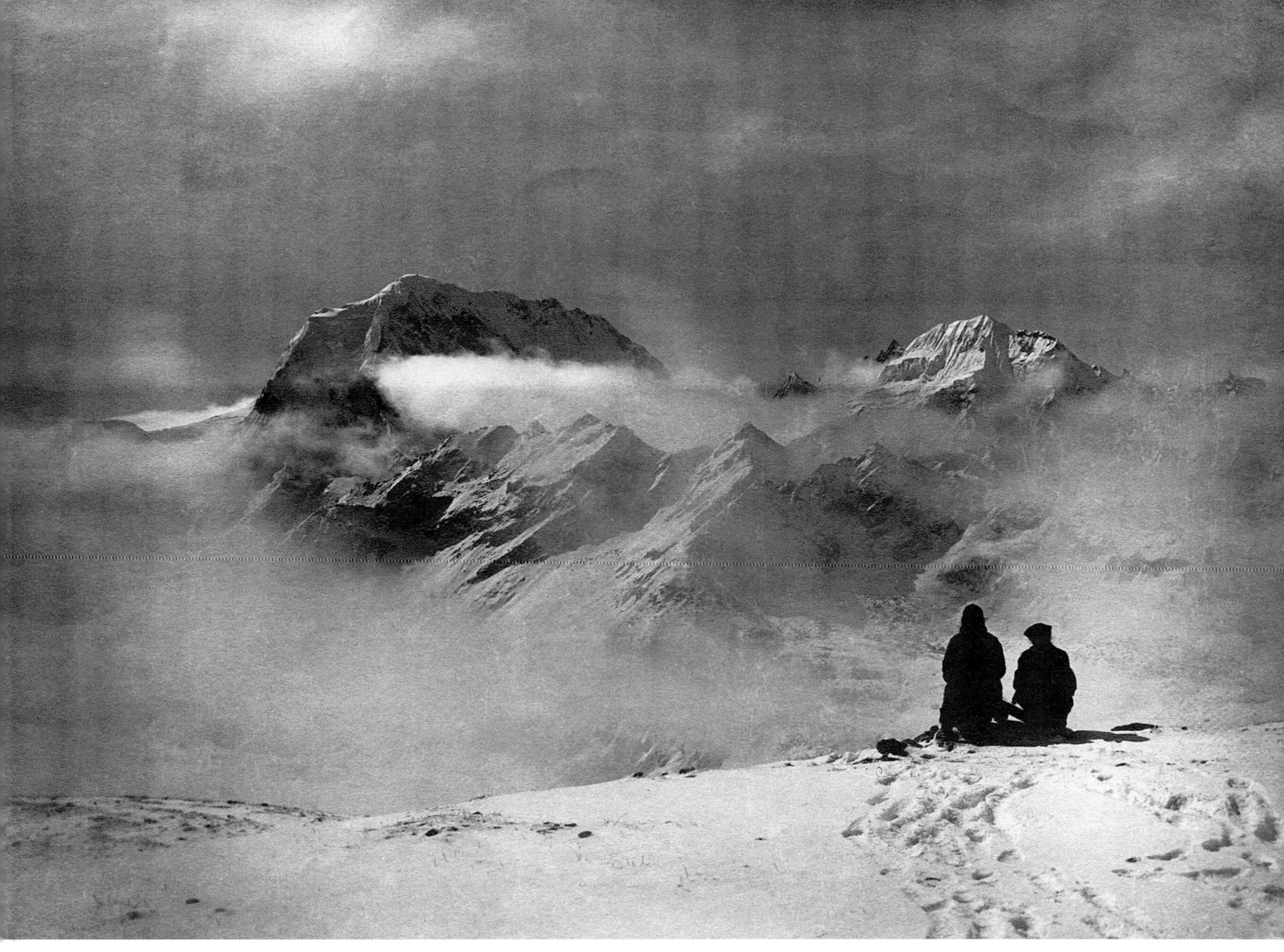

Dawn at 17,000 feet.

FURTHER READING

Bell, Sir Charles, *The People of Tibet*, Oxford University Press, 1928

Blessed, Brian, *The Turquoise Mountain*, Bloomsbury Publishing, 1991

Bond, Lieutenant-Colonel R.C., *The King's Own Light Infantry in the Great War 1914–1918*, vol. III, Percy Lund Humphries and Co, 1929

Breashears, David and Salkeld, Audrey, *The Last Climb: The Legendary Everest Expedition of George Mallory*, National Geographic, 1999

Brownlow, Kevin, *The War, The West, and The Wilderness*, Alfred A. Knopf, 1979

Bruce, Brigadier-General the Hon. C.G., *The Assault on Mount Everest, 1922*, Edward Arnold & Co., 1923

Gillman, Peter, *Everest: Eighty Years of Triumph and Tragedy*, Little, Brown & Company, 2001

Hopkins, Peter, *Trespassers on the Roof of the World*, Murray, 1982

——, *On Secret Service East of Constantinople*, Murray, 1994

Hunt, John, *The Ascent of Everest*, Hodder & Stoughton, 1953

Johnson, D.R., *A Record of Virtuosity – a Selective Annotated Bibliography of US, British and Canadian Government Manuals, Manufactures, Pamphlets and Books on the Art of Pistol Shooting from 1835–1965*, Privately published

Noel, Captain J.B.L., *The Story of Everest*, Litte Brown, 1927; as *Through Tibet to Everest*, Edward Arnold, 1927; repr. Hodder & Stoughton, 1989

Noel, Sybille, *The Magic Bird of Chomo-Lung-Ma*, Doubleday, Doran & Co., 1931

Norton, Lieutenant-Colonel E.F., *The Fight for Everest: 1924*, Edward Arnold & Co., 1925

Royal Geographical Society, *Everest: Summit of Achievement*, Bloomsbury, 2003

Waterfall, Arnold, *The Postal Service of Tibet*, Christies-Robson Lowe, 1981

Winans, Walter, *The Art of Revolver Shooting*, Knickerbocker Press, 1901